ON THE FIRELINE

FIELDWORK ENCOUNTERS AND DISCOVERIES

A Series Edited by Robert Emerson and Jack Katz

ON THE
Fireline

Living and Dying with Wildland Firefighters

MATTHEW DESMOND

THE UNIVERSITY OF CHICAGO PRESS
Chicago and London

Matthew Desmond is a doctoral student in the Department of Sociology at the University of Wisconsin–Madison.

The University of Chicago Press, Chicago 60637
The University of Chicago Press, Ltd., London
© 2007 by The University of Chicago
All rights reserved. Published 2007
Printed in the United States of America

16 15 14 13 12 11 10 09 08 07   1 2 3 4 5

ISBN-13: 978-0-226-14408-5   (cloth)
ISBN-10: 0-226-14408-9   (cloth)

Portions of this book were previously published in *Ethnography* 7(4): 387–421, and are reprinted by permission of Sage Publications Ltd.

Library of Congress Cataloging-in-Publication Data

Desmond, Matthew.
    On the fireline : living and dying with wildland firefighters / Matthew Desmond.
        p. cm.
    Includes bibliographical references and index.
    ISBN-13: 978-0-226-14408-5 (cloth : alk. paper)
    ISBN-10: 0-226-14408-9 (cloth : alk. paper) 1. Wildfire fighters—West (U.S.)—
Biography. 2. Wildfires—Prevention and control. 3. Hazardous occupations.
4. Risk-taking (Psychology) I. Title.
SD421.24 .D47 2007
363.37092'273—dc22

                                                                    2007010878

To my parents,

NICK AND SHAVON,

for everything

"It wasn't unusual to get called out at six o'clock, head back, drive all night to an incident, get there, get breakfast, get briefed, and go out on the line."

REX THURMAN

Contents

Introduction

I began fighting fire because someone asked me to. In the winter of 1998 I'd come home from my first semester at college to my parents' ranch-style house, nested in the country between the Navajo reservation and a small Arizona town. On a mild December day, as I was relaxing at home, Owen Mills drove his rusted Chevy across the lawn to deliver a cord of freshly cut pine. Owen, a middle-aged man from my father's church who usually spoke with a smile beneath his orange mustache, was then head supervisor of the U.S. Forest Service's Elk River Firecrew. In his soft-spoken way, he asked if I wanted to fight wildfire that summer. I piled a few more logs on the stack and said yes. That was it. He helped me finish the woodpile before shaking my hand and driving away.

So in May 1999, one day after the spring semester ended, I found myself at Elk River, wide-eyed and ready to learn about fire behavior, weather, frontal assaults, backburning, and the Ten Standard Fire Orders and Eighteen Situations That Shout "Watch Out!" I received training on how to load a helicopter, how to duck and cover to dodge slurry drops, and how to wield a chain saw. But most important, I learned how to dig. The veterans taught me that no job was more important than *digging line,* that primitive craft of creating a yard-wide trail of mineral soil between a moving fire and unburned fuel. I practiced digging with different hand tools and different techniques, and I dug line on my first fires. When the summer ended, I walked away with a few blisters on my hands, a few cuts in my boots, and a deep longing for the next fire season. I returned to Elk River for four seasons. During 2003, which would be my last, I carried a tape recorder and a notepad. I was simultaneously firefighter and ethnographer.

As a member of the firecrew, from early May until late August I worked, ate, slept, traveled, socialized, and fought fire with fourteen other men stationed in the woodlands of northern Arizona. Every day I carried a small notebook in the side pocket of my dark green Nomex fire pants and recorded observations, conversations, and events every chance I got. In addition, I conducted in-depth interviews lasting from forty-five minutes to three hours with all fourteen of my fellow crewmembers and several U.S. Forest Service supervisors. Most of the interviews took place after work in the firefighters' quarters, though some were carried out on the clock in offices, under shade trees, or on tailgates. I also collected documents such as training materials, fatality reports, press releases, guidebooks, and anything else I could get my hands on that would shed light on the inner workings of the Forest Service. I promised all my crewmembers confidentiality, and any names of people or places that would break that promise have been camouflaged by pseudonyms.[1]

During my last season at Elk River thirty wildland firefighters died across the United States—the most since 1994, when the body count reached thirty-six because of the deadly South Canyon fire, which alone claimed fourteen lives.[2] From twelve to twenty-two wildland firefighters die every year. Since 1910, the year the Great Fires of Idaho and Montana killed seventy-two, over nine hundred wildland firefighters have died fighting fire. Most of them burned to death.[3] And burning on a mountainside is a hellish death. When firefighters die in a forest fire, they burn from the inside out. The fire prepares its prey before it arrives by emitting a radiant heat that cooks the air. Trapped firefighters hysterically inhale the on-fire oxygen, which melts their lungs before the ravaging crematorium consumes their bodies. Imagine moving closer and closer to a whistling kettle, through its steam, until finally your lips wrap themselves around the spout and you suck in with deep and frequent breaths.

On all fires, no matter their size, wildland firefighters must carry a fire shelter—a single-person tent made of paper-thin aluminized material neatly folded into a four-by-eight-inch package—belt-strapped at the base of the spine. During a fire entrapment, and only as a last resort, they pop their shelters and deploy by lying face down on previously cleared ground with their hands and feet anchoring the rectangular shelter and their faces pressed against the dirt as the world ignites around them. But seasoned firefighters know that deploying a shelter doesn't buy much, for though shelters can deflect some heat, they can't hold back the white-hot air.[4] The shelter affords trapped firefighters only two advantages: it serves as a makeshift temple where they can pray for a salvation that does not resemble the hell consuming them, and it makes it easier to identify their bodies. In the words of Rex Thurman, head supervisor of the Elk River Firecrew, "The only thing your shake and bake will do is allow you to have an open casket funeral."

Rick Lupe's funeral was no open casket affair. A strong gust wrenched his shelter from his hands seconds before the fire overwhelmed him, exposing his body to the thousand-acre inferno on Sawtooth Mountain that swallowed him up on May 14, 2003. After the burnover, Lupe crawled out of the charred ravine, smoking and smelling of burned hair and flesh, and stumbled toward his crew. The fire had seared over a third of his body to the third degree. His legs and arms absorbed the brunt of the attack. In some places the flames dissolved skin and muscle, leaving only apyrous bone. A helicopter transported Lupe to the nearest hospital, where he soon slipped into a coma. He held on until June 19, long after firecrews had extinguished the fire at Sawtooth. He was forty-three.

The day Rick Lupe died, a light breeze floated through the pines on a calm, cloudless afternoon at the Elk River Fire Station. At 5:15 Kris, Diego, and I were taking advantage of the fine weather by sitting on lawn chairs outside our quarters and bullshitting, as was the normal custom following a rare 5:00 whistle. I was greasing my boots with an old cotton sock and nursing a glass of Glenfiddich. Kris was comparing my glass of scotch with his can of Keystone Light and making sure to call me "sophisticated" for my liquor selection, meaning rich and prissy, not cultured and polished. We were teasing and talking about everything and nothing at all. Then Peter Ferguson interrupted our lazy chatter. The plump and ruddy engine operator strolled up to us, bare-chested, and announced the bad news.

"Uh, you know that Rick Lupe?" Peter asked.

"Yeah," Kris replied, looking up.

"Well, he died today."

Everyone paused and looked away, though only for a second.

"Well," Peter added, turning away, "he lasted about a month."

Peter left us and began fidgeting with the exhaust pipe of his Harley. Kris went back to drinking his beer. Diego released a loud belch and struck up conversation with Kris again. Lupe's death didn't seem to bother or perplex them in the least. But it disturbed me deeply. I felt close to Lupe—connected, familiar, fraternal—and hence threatened, for Lupe was no newcomer to fire. He had battled hundreds of blazes during his twenty-plus years as a wildland firefighter. Lupe had been supervisor of an elite firefighting unit, the Fort Apache Hotshots, and was deeply familiar with wildfire. For years, during the hot months he had guided a twenty-person crew into the most perilous and inaccessible wildfires of North America. Many even called him a hero because his crew had saved two small towns from the monstrous Rodeo-Chediski fire of 2002, which destroyed half a million acres. My crewmembers knew Lupe. Peter had fought fire with him; Diego knew of him; and Kris's father, also a wildland firefighter, had walked many firelines with him. Yet the news of his death did not cause them the slightest pause, and their indifferent nonreaction, their mere shrug of the shoulders, turned my stomach almost as much as Lupe's death itself.

That moment served as the impetus for this book because it forced me to puzzle over something I had never before found puzzling: how firefighters understand risk and death. Through many reflexive double-takes, I attempted to treat the familiar universe of wildland firefighting as a context to be questioned and denaturalized, to convert my home into an alien land in an effort to carry out what Pierre Bourdieu calls "an epistemological break" with my own uncritical understanding of firefighting and its occupational hazards.[5] This book is the result. As an intimate inquiry into the world of wildland firefighters, it analyzes their lives during all stages of the day, on and off the clock, in an effort to reconstruct the practical logic (crafted in part by the organizational logic of the Forest Service) with which firefighters make sense of danger, safety, and death.

In an occupation like firefighting, the death of a friend, coworker, or fellow firefighter is something one must deal with sooner or later, and it didn't take me long to realize why Peter, Kris, Diego, and the rest of my crewmembers dealt with Rick Lupe's death with such ostensible lack of interest. My crewmembers did not pose any new questions at the time of Lupe's death because the only questions that mattered to them had already been asked (and answered) a few days after he was burned: What did he do wrong? What should he have done differently? These questions, though they can take many forms, are but one question—the question of fault—and it haunts all who demand to know why wildland firefighters get caught up in deadly situations.

Fascinated by the question of fault, Norman Maclean pursued it into his eighties. The author of *Young Men and Fire* indefatigably retraced the steps of twelve smokejumpers who died in the Mann Gulch fire of 1949. The itch, it seems, was genetic, for seven years later his son, John Maclean, attempted to uncover what went wrong for the fourteen firefighters who died in Colorado's South Canyon fire of 1994.[6] Sociologists, psychologists, and organizational theorists also have tried to understand why firefighting crews break down.[7] But the question of fault has been pursued with the deepest devotion by those most invested in the answer: agents of the U.S. Forest Service. Immediately after any burnover, an interagency and interstate investigative team descends on the burn scene with cameras, notebooks, tape recorders, and authority from the highest offices and soon emerges with a lengthy document, definitively titled a "Factual Report," that itemizes the causes that led to the firefighters' demise.

This book has little to do with the question of fault, and it is not obsessed with the circumstances that may have led to Lupe's burnover. After all, why should his death shock us? Rick Lupe stood in the heart of an inferno consuming hundreds of trees standing over sixty feet tall, like incandescent matchsticks, sending out a heat so intense it could melt a dump truck. His death was not anomalous; about seventy firefighters a year find themselves in similar situations, that is, fire entrapments.[8] What is perhaps most surprising about those who continue to pursue the question of fault is how surprised they are over the deaths of firefighters. When a firefighter dies, when death fulfills its threat, they grow zealously inquisitive and raise the question anew.

Far from answering the question of fault, this book *questions* the question of fault. It examines the taken-for-granted assumptions that allow us to pose such a question in the first place. This leads us back to a more fundamental question: Why was Lupe there to begin with? What motivates firefighters to deploy their bodies on the seam between the edge of life and a fiery death? Why do they risk? Why do they seek out such a dangerous occupation when safer ways of earning a living are available? Why did I? Moreover, how do firefighters become acclimated to the dangers of their profession? How are they socialized to risk by the Forest Service—an organization known for its ability to successfully "[inject] its own outlooks into its men"?[9] And what can they teach us about how high-risk organizations motivate workers to undertake life-threatening tasks?

: :

There are several social-scientific theories of risk taking, including various sociological explanations, economic models, and psychological accounts.[10] However, one theory in particular deserves special scrutiny here because it has avoided scrutiny for many years. In fact it is so widely accepted and entrenched in our commonsense conceptions of risk taking that I hesitate to call it a theory and not an axiom. This idea above suspicion, captured in the locution "to risk is to be a man," was first articulated (at least in so many words) by sociologist Erving Goffman almost forty years ago. (Those who are not so concerned with this book's theoretical interventions can skip the rest of this introduction and begin reading about the Elk River Firecrew in the next chapter. Those who are interested in such things should continue reading. Both kinds of readers, unless they are already familiar with the language of wildland firefighting, might benefit from the glossary at the end of the book.)

In his famous essay "Where the Action Is," Goffman sought to uncover individual motivations for risky behavior, or "action," which he defined as those "activities that are consequential, problematic, and undertaken for what is felt to be their own sake."[11] Throughout the essay he played with this last part of the definition and at first seemed to subsume the motivation for action under its description. However, the mantra "action for action's sake" was only a rhetorical trope for Goffman; his real argument rested on the intimate relation between action and *character*. "The voluntary taking of serious chances," he remarked, "is a means for *the maintenance and acquisition of character;* it is an end in itself only in relation to other kinds of purpose."[12] Thus one risks to gain social recognition, and he must risk again and again lest this recognition expire.

If this is the case, Goffman argued, it is because society, at its most basic level, is made up of two very different types of people: those who are willing to make a "commitment" and those who refuse.[13] Paradoxically, the thrill seeker's motivation for action rests on passive observers' greeting that very action with awe and attributing to the thrill seeker such qualities as "courage," "guts," or "heroism." Goffman's universe is populated with sacred daredevils on the one hand and profane bores on the other: "Looking for where the action is, one arrives at a romantic division of the world. On one side are the safe and silent places, the home, the well-regulated role in business, in industry, and the professions; on the other are all those activities that generate expression, requiring the individual to lay himself on the line and place himself in jeopardy during a passing moment. It is from this contrast that we fashion nearly all our commercial fantasies. It is from this contrast that delinquents, hustlers, and sportsmen draw their self-respect."[14]

Above I referred to the risk taker with the pronoun "he," and I did so because the risky activities that commanded Goffman's attention were male-dominated games (e.g., gambling, bullfighting, street hustling). By "risk" Goffman meant "men's risk," and by "character" he meant "masculinity." And if one strips his argument to its core, it comes down to the idea that the pursuit of masculinity is the driving motivation behind risky behavior.[15] This cornerstone idea supports most sociological conceptions of risk taking. In *Masculine Domination,* for example, Pierre Bourdieu writes, "It is [masculinity's] vulnerability which paradoxically leads to sometimes frantic investment in all the masculine games of violence, such as sports in modern societies, and most especially those which most tend to produce the visible signs of masculinity, and to manifest and also test what are called manly virtues, such as combat sports."[16] And a prominent sociologist of masculinity notes, "We test ourselves, perform heroic feats, take enormous risks, all because we want other men to grant us our manhood."[17] If masculinity, then, is an impossible and fragile social construction that teeters precariously on its rejection of femininity, the drama of manhood must be performed ardently, publicly, and without end, and one way this is accomplished is through activity that threatens male bodies. Ever since Goffman argued that "men must be prepared to put up their lives to save their faces," social scientists have believed that men take dangerous risks in order to acquire masculine recognition.[18]

Following this logic, most researchers investigating arenas of professional risk taking have suggested that the hallmarks of a good firefighter, police officer, or soldier are hypermasculine traits such as courage, aggressiveness, and toughness.[19] Most researchers conceive of soldiers, for example, as driven by courage, willpower, and confidence, qualities that "inspire men to hold their ground when every instinct calls upon them to run away." The successful soldier is the unrealistic one, the actor who sees himself as bigger, stronger, and more aggressive than his enemy (psychologists would say that the wartime fighter is filled with "positive illusions").[20] Police officers are thought to have similar traits. Functioning under what one sociologist calls the "machismo syndrome," they are believed to live for the "life-threatening intervention at a crime scene": they long for the rare thrill of the chase, the fight, the arrest. Although many officers are filled with anxiety when coming on duty because "uncertainty structures police work," as another sociologist puts it, they compensate by making a virtue of necessity, lauding the ambiguous and risky nature of their job as a primary attractant.[21] The same goes, many others claim, for firefighters. The firehouse is believed to be a refuge for the most courageous of citizens. (It is no coincidence that the New York City firefighters are called "the Bravest.") "In traditional fire departments," one researcher notes, "physical size, strength, and prowess are highly valued; courage, toughness, and aggressiveness have become the hallmarks of a good fire-fighter."[22]

The story does not change when we review the literature on dangerous jobs in the industrial sector. One analyst finds that although high-steel ironworkers feel fear when "running the iron," they must suppress this fear to earn the trust of their fellow workers. The most respected iron-worker displays the most bravado, takes the most risks, and volunteers for the most dangerous jobs; by contrast, the least respected worker, the one considered the least trustworthy, is cautious, avoids risks, and steers clear of the most dangerous tasks.[23] Likewise, underground miners, a number of analysts claim, manage their fears by forming a masculine "occupa-tional subculture of danger."[24] And several scholars have suggested that men working in especially dangerous occupations often ignore safety procedures and refuse to don protective gear not only to meet produc-tion pressures, but also to avoid violating a masculine ethos by showing weakness.[25]

Risk takers thus conceived, in times of war or times of work, fully rec-ognize the dangers they face and charge toward them. Some fear the dan-ger and wear a mask of courage, while others crave the sensation of the dropped stomach, the stolen breath, or the quickened and quaking heart-beat. But in all cases, to the ones who cross the line first, who push their limits furthest, who step most defiantly into the shadow of some Goliath, goes the glory, the honor, or in Goffman's word, "the character."

But this is not how things work at the Elk River Fire Station. In fact, the opposite is true. Over the course of my fieldwork, I discovered that firefighters prize competence and control above all other attributes and (contrary to most accounts) view masculine aggression and courage as negative qualities. The distinctive mark of a good firefighter is his ability to know—not to test—his limits and to master his destiny on the fireline. The quest for masculinity and the pursuit of an adrenaline high matter very little to wildland firefighters. They do not resemble danger-lusting heroes who laugh in the face of death, as they are commonly depicted by journalists, movie directors, and social scientists alike. Far from un-derstanding risk as an avenue to a euphoric "adrenaline rush" or a route to acquiring masculine character, firefighters view risk as something that can be tamed, safety as something they are personally responsible for, and death as completely avoidable through competence.

Why did sociological theories of risk taking prove insufficient at Elk River? Because current theories are afflicted with an assumption that causes those who come under its spell to overlook crucial contexts. That assumption is that it is legitimate to conceptualize risk taking in a vacuum, divorced from the specific environment and circumstances where it takes place. Grouping all risk takers into a single class, analysts proceed to assign a master logic, a grand narrative, to explain all types of risky behavior. For Goffman, looters, gamblers, hustlers, downhill skiers, motocross racers, police officers, and soldiers (the list could go on) are all the same creature ("chance takers"), driven by the same impulse (the pursuit of "character"). By disregarding the social complexities that surround, influence, and define different varieties of risk taking, most theories treat professional risk taking, the duties of the SWAT team officer, as something that can be explained by the same mechanism as any other type of risk taking, say, the deadly gamble of Russian roulette. Their free-floating analyses, however, come with several conceptual shortcomings. Current theories of risk taking fail to scrutinize the intimate connections between class relations and professional risk taking; ignore the powerful influence of organizations; and assume that individuals who engage in behavior defined as risky do so through rational calculation and share the same understanding of "risk" as the analyst who studies that behavior. In what follows, I take up these three criticisms in turn.

Because the distribution of professional risk takers reflects the established social order, to study risk is to study power and inequality. Many sociologists and psychologists of risk have failed to realize this. By reducing risk taking to escapism or recreation, they treat chancy behavior as completely voluntary and ignore social structures. The sacrifices that professional risk takers endure are borne primarily by a narrow segment of society—mainly working-class men—not simply by "brave," "heroic," "thrill-lusting," "action-seeking" individuals from all walks of life. The men who fill the ranks of America's million-and-a-half-person fighting force (only 12 percent of military positions are staffed by women) are the sons of steelworkers, railroaders, and teamsters; men of color are overrepresented in subordinate military positions, and the educated and the rich are strikingly absent from the army's ranks. The same is true in the world of wildland firefighting, a working-class world in which approximately 80 percent of firefighting positions are filled by men.[26] Working-class men staff most of the positions within high-risk organizations while their well-to-do counterparts watch from a safe distance. Certain bodies, deemed precious, are protected, while others, deemed expendable, protect. Yet despite the inherent working-class composition of dangerous occupations, current approaches to risk taking fail to account for how individuals' classed lifestyles and backgrounds influence their decision to sign up for jobs that could kill them or how individuals' social positions, personal histories, and specific paths through life predispose them to the rigors of risky work.[27]

Besides ignoring social positioning, current approaches to risk taking pay scant attention to how organizations influence professional risk takers' perceptions of risk.[28] The firefighter and the football player are seen as men desperately striving to uphold masculine identity through risk and violence, yet very little notice is given to how the firehouse or the locker room shapes their conceptions of risk. Many sociologists and psychologists begin their investigations of risk by focusing on individual characteristics and decision-making processes and neglect the power of organizations altogether. But a rigorous analysis of occupational risk taking cannot begin or end with an analysis of the risking agent. As Mary Douglas points out, "If it is conceded that institutions play any role, then it would follow that much of the inquiry about risk perception has been applied to the wrong units, to individuals instead of institutions."[29] Accordingly, analysts must investigate how institutions make people deployable by concentrating on the ways they train, educate, motivate, and discipline workers to ensure that they will place their lives on the line when "duty calls."

The two criticisms presented above deal with the negative consequences that result when theories of risk taking ignore important contexts. My third criticism deals with something more fundamental—the theory of action used to explain risk taking—and accordingly requires elaboration.

Firefighting—marching, digging, chopping, crawling, and running among torching trees and smoldering ash—is a corporeal activity, and in the swelter of infernos firefighters' bodies react to the dangers they face. *How far should I go down the canyon wall? How much heat can I take? Is this dangerous, or am I scared? Is that oak burned straight through? Is that smoke or steam? Should I keep digging, or should I fall back?* On the fireline thousands of questions like these must be asked and answered with such celerity that they exist in cognitive form only fleetingly, if at all. Decisions of risk are made at the bodily level and cannot be fully translated into articulate verbal accounts. The visceral experience of risk taking transcends linguistic expression: it is unutterable, ephemeral, known only *deep down.*

Yet the intuitive logic of risk—characteristically blurry and grasped only in the whirl of action—has been disfigured beyond recognition. Or better, it has been made *too recognizable.* Rational-choice theorists and economists—who, more than any other breed of social scientist, have paid attention to questions of risk preferences and risk taking[30]—tend to assume that risk is unvarying, precise, and self-evident enough to be formalized in a sanitary equation that multiplies the probability of the bad event by the severity of the harm: $r = Pr[E]he$. But rational-choice theorists and economists are not the only ones who use this mechanical way of thinking when trying to make sense of risk taking. Many sociologists, including social psychologists who would never self-identify as rationalists, reason in a similar fashion, claiming that risk takers decide to dive off a cliff or storm into battle—actions treated as indistinguishable, though different in every way aside from the threat of injury—only after carefully weighing the bonus of the rush against the possibility of harm.[31] Even Goffman confines risk to a cost-benefit calculation: "We can begin to see that action need not be perceived, in the first instance, as an expression of impulsiveness or irrationality, even where risk without apparent prize results. Loss, to be sure, is chanced through action; but a real gain of character can occur. It is in these terms that action can be seen as a calculated risk."[32] Goffman is correct to assert that the risk taker is more than a rash brute; but the alternative he provides—a cold calculator—is equally flawed, for at least two reasons.

First, Goffman's alternative can account for only individual feats, not collective ones. Theories that understand risky behavior as the result of a calculation take as their fundamental unit of analysis the rational individual. This makes it impossible to explain collective forms of dangerous behavior, such as warfare or firefighting, without treating collectives as anything but a bunch of rational decision makers (motivated only by individual choices) who happen to be in the same place performing the same dangerous act. Although some (e.g., social engineers, military strategists) have found this approach useful, accepting it means ignoring all that makes collective risk collective, including leadership, solidarity, and communication. It also means not recognizing that the definition of "risk" and the decision to risk are often made at the institutional, not the individual, level.[33]

Second, theorists who assume that daredevils engage in intense thought during the same moment that they engage in intense action inject scholastic thought categories into the heads of nonscholastic actors. Guilty of what Bourdieu calls the "scholastic fallacy," they assume that people in action are at the same time people in contemplation and view an acting actor as "a sort of a monster with the head of the thinker thinking his practice in reflexive and logical fashion mounted on the body of a man of

12 action engaged in action."[34] Yet firefighting (or any risky engagement, for that matter) cannot be sufficiently analyzed through tidy rational equations, which only suffocate bodily ways of knowing exhibited in the fast-paced commotion of action. Lighting a patch of shin-high plain grass with a drip torch, digging a scratch line with a combi to cut off an advancing head of fire, felling a towering conifer smoldering at its top: these are all practices of wildland firefighting that require corporeal knowledge, gained through experience—through history—not simply mental acuity acquired through rational calculation.

The logic of the risk taker cannot be assumed to conform to abstract models of rationalism. The logic of the risk taker is not a given but a question. It is a curious something that must be reconstructed, and reconstructed in a fashion that takes into account the risk taker's background as well as his organization.

: :

Accordingly, this book reconstructs the practical logic of firefighting specifically by focusing on how firefighters' dispositions and skills acquired from their rural, masculine, and working-class upbringings connect with the organizational common sense of the U.S. Forest Service to form a *wildland firefighting habitus*. What is a habitus, and in particular a wildland firefighting habitus? A habitus is the presence of social and organizational structures in individuals' bodies in the form of durable and generative dispositions that guide their thoughts and behaviors. As embodied history, as internalized and forgotten socialization, one's habitus is the source of one's practical sense.[35]

We can further distinguish between a *general* and a *specific* habitus. As Bourdieu points out in *Pascalian Meditations,* a general habitus is a system of dispositions and ways of thinking about and acting in the world that is constituted early in life, whereas a specific habitus is acquired later through education, training, and discipline within particular organizations.[36] Thus a judge comes to develop a juridical habitus, molded by the structures of the legal system, which projects authority and confidence from the bench; a professor acquires an academic habitus, conditioned by practices of the university, which allows her to lecture, instruct, research, write, and criticize with ease and command; and through years of seminary training and religious practice, a Catholic priest develops a pastoral habitus, which allows him to perform the rituals of the Mass seamlessly. A wildland firefighter also possesses a specific habitus, one that guides his understanding of risk, safety, and death and his responses to the mercurial, powerful, and at times overwhelming force of wildfire. If some individuals take to certain professions better than others—if they seem to be "naturals" at soldiering or are "born to be police officers"—it is because they bring to the organization a general habitus that transforms into a specific habitus with little friction, whereas others possess a general habitus that is at odds with the fundamental structures and practices of the organization. By examining how one's most deep-seated dispositions transform into a specific habitus, by investigating how organizations tap into, build on, and condition these dispositions when producing firefighters, soldiers, or police officers, we can gain insight into how the social order reproduces itself through individuals with such "mysterious efficacy."[37]

As a result of my in-depth, participatory investigation, one that employed a *dispositional theory of action,* I discovered that the practical logic the firefighters of Elk River use to make sense of the risks incurred on the fireline, the logic of their specific habitus, differs greatly from the abstract context-independent logic that theorists tend to posit. In what follows I explain—in ways that Goffman's theory could not—why my crewmembers decided to become firefighters, how they understood risk, the nature of their relationships, and why they charged toward the flames when the alarm sounded.

My arguments unfold across eight chapters, separated into three parts, that follow the developmental life cycle of firefighters: from early childhood, adolescence, and initiatory training courses to days and nights at the fire station and on the front lines of chaotic wildfires, and, finally, to firefighters' fiery deaths. The first two chapters, grouped as part 1, describe the crew's makeup and investigate the social trajectories that led crewmembers into its ranks. They recount firefighters' class backgrounds and life histories in order to piece together all the key factors and events that contributed to their decision to forgo safer ways to earn a paycheck in favor of a life of chasing smoke. Chapter 1 examines how my crewmembers initially decided to become firefighters and how a rural working-class upbringing predisposed them to the universe of wildland firefighting by equipping them with certain competences and attitudes. Chapter 2 investigates why firefighters return season after season and explains why my crewmembers adore Elk River even more than the thrill and fascination of firefighting itself: the fire station serves as a haven for maintaining and reproducing their country-masculine dispositions.

The four chapters that make up part 2 pay special attention to the interface between the preformed dispositions and skills discussed in part 1 and the organizational common sense of the U.S. Forest Service. Flowing from "informal" mechanisms of socialization to more "formal" ones, they investigate how firefighters are educated, trained, and disciplined by their supporting organization. Chapter 3 explores the brotherly bonds forged between firefighters at Elk River by focusing on the sometimes unbrotherly practices of repartee and aggressive teasing; it also highlights how crewmembers discipline one another and how they espouse and act on key principles of the Forest Service through ostensibly innocent everyday practices. Chapter 4 explains how firefighters are introduced to the common sense of the Forest Service through its symbolic struggles against environmental groups over the right to manage the forest and against structural firefighters over the title "real firefighter." By participating in these struggles, crewmembers begin to see the world through the eyes of the Forest Service and soon come to identify with their host organization. Chapter 5 analyzes how the Forest Service trains firefighters and how this training is—and is not—employed on the fireline. Chapter 6 explores how the Forest Service cultivates within firefighters a specific professional disposition toward risk taking, what I call *the illusio of self-determinancy,* a collective belief that the uncontrollable force of wildfire is completely within firefighters' control and therefore devoid of danger.

It would be easy for firefighters to maintain that their job is devoid of danger if every fire were fought effectively and no one were ever hurt, but what happens when things go wrong? Part 3 explores the two events that test a firefighter's illusio of self-determinacy more than any others: a wildfire that rages out of control and the death of a fellow firefighter. Chapter 7 tells the story of the Beaver Creek fire, a blaze where my crewmembers and I had to drop our tools and run for our lives. And chapter 8 returns to the funeral of Rick Lupe and documents the process through which the Forest Service manages death. A conclusion follows, in which I discuss the theoretical, methodological, and practical implications of this book. An appendix on fieldwork brings up the rear.

The reality of death and flesh-and-blood sacrifice hangs as the silent backdrop to all arenas of professional risk taking. Behind the jovial rancor of the firehouse meal or the polished uniform of the Marine lurk the freeze-frame memories of charred bodies, gut shots, and fallen friends. Why, then, do these individuals place themselves in harm's way, and how do their host organizations make sure they stay there? Why do individuals deploy themselves, and how do high-risk organizations make workers deployable? At Elk River I found answers to these questions, answers that differ greatly from the limited theories of risk taking previously advanced by social scientists. Contrary to the general belief, motivations for risk taking are not adequately satisfied by one-word clichés such as "heroism," "adrenaline," "masculinity," "adventure," or "character." Rather, they are buried deep beneath the surface.

We must keep digging.

PART ONE

History and Place

1

Country Masculinity

"It just *builds up* in you," he says.

"What? What do you mean?" I ask, squinting.

"Just being in the forest, it's, it's—" Nicholas Masayesva pauses and rubs his thin black mustache in a contemplative rhythm. He starts again. "It's just being Hopi, it's being close to nature. The *joy* of it. It's hard work, and we all have to have money now. And most of it is not much money, but the joy of being here. Working with your comrades. But it's not for everybody, fighting fire. You have to learn to like it, to love it. And I guess that I'm one of those guys who like it, or love it. So I guess it just builds up in you or something. . . . I guess it's hard to explain how you really feel about something like that."

Nicholas is a spiritual man. The forty-year-old Hopi prays at dawn and regularly travels back to the Second Mesa Reservation to participate in dances and ceremonies. He inherits his beliefs and practices from his father, who taught him Hopi folklore, medicine, and language. He also inherits the tradition of fighting fire.

"My dad was a firefighter. My dad and his dad," Nicholas tells me with a tincture of pride in his voice. "And my great-grandfather, he was one too. My uncles . . . I guess their blood was in me."

Nicholas began fighting fire at age eighteen to prove to his parents that he could do something more than get drunk and high. He quit high school three months before graduation and started working odd jobs on the Hopi reservation before selling drugs. When he decided to clean up his act, he applied for a job through the "all-Indian" job corps center called Kicking Horse, located in Montana. Nicholas requested a position in forestry and was hired onto a helitack squad.

Wildland firefighting did not seem so strange and alien to Nicholas, since his father, grandfather, and great-grandfather had all chased smoke. It came naturally to him. It was in his blood. Since that day he joined the helitack crew, he has returned season after season for twenty-two years.

What kinds of people find their way to firefighting units? What do they have in common? Where do they come from, and what do they bring with them? Are they young, as Nicholas was? Are they the sons of sons of sons of firefighters, like him? This chapter describes the circumstances that led my crewmembers to wildland firefighting, and more important, it focuses on the dispositions and skills they brought with them.

Family Traditions and Hometown Connections

Besides Nicholas, three other crewmembers at Elk River are following in their fathers' footsteps. Bryan and Kris's father has fought wildfire for thirty-three years. Aside from a pair of biological parents (one black and one white), an addiction to chewing tobacco, and a passion for firefighting, these brothers have little in common. Bryan Keeton, twenty-two, attends Northern Arizona University in the off-season and majors in forestry. He has already secured a permanent position with the Forest Service and will most likely fight fire for the rest of his healthy life. A large black tattoo of flames covers his left shoulder, signaling his devotion to the profession. As a child, Bryan emulated his father and played with toy chain saws and hatchets; in fact, his parents prize a photograph of four-year-old Bryan proudly wielding a plastic chain saw as his father uses a real one. When other kids pretended to be superheroes or cowboys, Bryan dreamed of being a firefighter. Kris Keeton, nineteen, attends the University of Arizona and fills his schedule with history courses. Previously he filled it with physics and optics courses. Before a medical examiner at West Point rescinded his successful application on account of poor eyesight, Kris was driven and determined, but now he is fairly noncommittal about his future. Whereas Bryan wears plaid button-down shirts, tucked in, and flip-flops, Kris tries to look as disheveled as possible in old mesh caps, torn jeans, stained T-shirts riddled with holes, and scuffed boots. Bryan can bench-press over three hundred pounds; Kris can speed-read a book on World War II in a day. It could be said that Bryan takes after his father the firefighter, while Kris takes after his mother, a dean of mathematics and science at a community college. The two brothers respect one another, and if one were against the ropes, the other would be the first to bound into the ring, fists clenched. But most of the time Bryan and Kris wear on each other's nerves and try to keep their distance.

The Keeton brothers grew up with fire. As Kris put it, "We've been around fire for *years*. . . . My father told me stories about having to lead crews on ridgetops at night where you would have to crawl. He told me stories about having to lead crews, you know, to get to a safety zone, having to walk through a little bit that was on fire."

Peter Ferguson's father also fights fire; his mother is a stay-at-home mom. When he was a child, Peter would run to greet his father at the door and eagerly ask, "Hey, hey, did you have any fires today?" Like Bryan, Peter was enthralled with fire from an early age, and when his father asked if he wanted to work for the Forest Service, a few months before his high school graduation in 1994, Peter said yes. He quickly moved up the organizational ladder, advancing from engine crewmember to assistant engine operator, until he quit in 1997 because his girlfriend did not approve. Much to Peter's chagrin, the relationship ended only weeks after he resigned from the Forest Service. He took a job as a plumber in Phoenix. But then the forest lured him back: in 2001 he returned to Elk River. Peter is currently an engine foreman, a low-level supervisory position that comes with a handful of crewmembers and a large fire engine to drive.

Peter likes beer, gambling, women, country music, Copenhagen chewing tobacco, the rodeo, hunting, a good joke, and the brand-new Harley Sportster bought for him by his new girlfriend, who does approve of his job. Peter describes himself as "a plain ol' white guy," but he is anything but plain. At twenty-seven years old, twice tattooed with yellow-and-orange flames garnishing each arm, he grimaces at the thought of growing older, and Peter's active pursuit of youth makes him one of the most popular men on the crew. After dark, his room at crew quarters regularly erupts with Johnny Cash on full stereo, sporadically drowned out by anguished curses or roars of joyous laughter depending on how the poker cards fall. Sometimes I lie awake contemplating whether to tell Peter and his party to shut up (his room is next to mine), but most of the time I join in. I find it hard to resist Peter's warm company, generous spirit, foul mouth, and fridge well stocked with Keystone Light.

As children, Nicholas, Bryan, Kris, and Peter became familiar with the smell of smoke wafting from their fathers' clothes. As teenagers, they knew the terminology, commands, and regulations of firefighting, and as eighteen-year-olds, these Forest Service brats all joined wildland firefighting crews as if by reflex.[1]

As for the first-generation firefighters, most come from working-class families with personal ties to the Forest Service. Seamus "Tank" McNamee, the rookie, is a gregarious and relaxed twenty-year-old. He does not recall when, how, or why he earned the nickname Tank, which suits his short and skinny body about as well as "Killer" would suit a French poodle, but somehow it stuck. It would make more sense if the name applied to Seamus's father—a tight-lipped motorcycle-riding giant of a man whose tall figure and broad shoulders require him to stoop and shuffle sideways through most doorframes—but it belongs to Seamus, and just about everyone who knows Seamus knows him only as Tank. Even his mother calls him Tank.

Tank's mother is a bank teller, and his father is a conductor for the Santa

Fe Railroad. Although Tank does not come from a firefighting lineage, he has been best friends with Kris Keeton since grade school and knows his father well. Growing up, Tank knew many wildland firefighters, and after his first year at the University of Arizona, where he is desperately trying to get accepted into the well-respected School of Architecture, he applied for a firefighting position. He was unsuccessful but landed a job working at a Forest Service slurry tanker base, filling the bellies of old World War II planes that are now used for more constructive purposes: they drop thousands of gallons of an extinguishing chemical on wildfires by diving down among the flames and kissing the treetops as they release a red cloud into the black smoke. Tank grew dissatisfied with that position, however. The following summer he tapped into the long-standing network made up of Mr. Keeton and other Forest Service officials he knew, as well as new connections he had established at the tanker base, and managed to secure a coveted position on the Elk River Firecrew.

J.J. López's father is also a conductor for the Santa Fe Railroad. He operates mile-long trains delivering anything from cattle to coal from Arizona to New Mexico to Utah to California. His mother is a stay-at-home mom. In the off-season, J.J., twenty, attends a community college in the Phoenix area and focuses on criminal justice. Born and raised in Atwater (population 9,000), a town fifty miles south of Elk River, he took second in state two years in a row in wrestling and, surprisingly, lettered three years in football as the team's starting running back, though he stands just six inches over five feet.

Most of the other men on the crew drive pickup trucks, but not J.J. He cruises to work in a brand-new silver Ford Mustang GT, which swaggers just the way he does. He is the first one to offer a verbal jab if your fly is unzipped or if you are a few minutes late for work, and his wit is matched only by his verbal cruelty. Through his community college courses, this joker of the highest degree aspires to work one day in a very serious job—as a SWAT team officer.

Though J.J.'s father does not make a living chasing smoke, he did fight fires when he was in his early twenties, and his family knows several high-ranking Forest Service officers. In the same vein, although Donald Montoya's father is not a firefighter but a mechanic at the local power plant, his two older brothers fight wildfires in a neighboring forest. His brothers introduced him to the world of wildfire and helped him secure a position on the Elk River crew.

Not all my crewmembers come from what are traditionally known as working-class families. George Canton's father is a radiologist, and Steve

Grove's father is a school superintendent.[2] Like Tank, J.J., and Donald, Steve found his way to the Forest Service through hometown connections. In fact Owen Mills, the same man who invited me to fight fire, recruited Steve to Elk River after Mills's son, Steve's best friend, suggested he apply. And like Tank, J.J., George, Kris, and Bryan, Steve is from Atwater. Through small-town social connections, most crewmembers were recruited to the Forest Service informally over dinner conversations or chance meetings at the local supermarket. In this way these crewmembers do not differ from most blue-collar workers (or professional, technical, or managerial workers, for that matter) who predominantly use personal contacts to find and land jobs.[3] However, a handful of crewmembers found out about potential positions in wildland firefighting through personal contacts but applied for these positions when Rex Thurman formally recruited them during their senior year at Atwater High School. Diego Alvarado was one such crewmember.

Diego is a twenty-year-old self-described Chicano who spends his free time fixing up old cars. His father, a high-spirited man with thick, wavy gray-and-black hair and a burly cowboy-style mustache that trails below his chin, is a letter carrier for the Post Office. His mother, a short middle-aged woman who wears round wire-framed glasses and two necklaces with three *medallas* displaying the Lady of Guadalupe and two saints, is a teacher's aide at an elementary school. In the off-season, Diego works as

a cook at La Hacienda, his family's Mexican restaurant in Atwater. Good-humored and sharply intelligent, Diego, I believe, would have excelled in college (majoring, he tells me, in archaeology) could his family have afforded it. But instead of being recruited to college, he was recruited to the Forest Service.

"When I went to high school," Diego recalls, "they had us fill out this form that tells you what to do with college and scholarships. Well, I just filled out that I was interested in forestry and outdoors work, and one day I got a call from Mrs. Ingersol [the guidance counselor], that there was a man looking for recruits for firefighting. And *lo and behold* it was Rex Thurman at the high school!"

Diego laughs to himself and continues. "Thurman was sittin' there. He didn't have a beard. He was clean-shaven. And he had, uh, J.J., George, me, and that was it, just us four. . . . From what Mrs. Ingersol was telling me, as long as I'm working in the Forest Service they'll pay for college. I said, shit, that's a good deal. . . . And I knew Thomas Hernandez [a retired supervisor from Elk River]. Yeah, his wife was my teacher, and I've known her forever. And I just met Thomas a couple years beforehand. I met him out here. So, Mrs. Hernandez was telling me that Thomas could help me out getting a job. . . . Fuck, the next thing you know I fuckin' get a call, a letter in the mail saying I should buy three-hundred-dollar boots and all this shit. And 'engine crew.' I said, shit, engine crew will be nice and easy. . . . It wasn't as easy as I thought."

In the urban fire sector, especially in East Coast cities such as New York and Boston, many firefighting genealogies can be traced back to the 1800s.[4] In a similar way, most of my crewmembers knew firefighting long before they entered its ranks. Their fathers and friends had dug line before them, and because they were embedded in networks of firefighters, they did not find the profession alien. Most crewmembers were recruited either informally through interpersonal network ties or formally through high school presentations by Thurman. Vince Yazzie, however, found his way to firefighting through more peculiar circumstances. He was punished into it.

Good-natured and shy, Vince is a twenty-five-year-old father of three who was raised in a small Arizona town (there were twelve in his graduating class) near the Grand Canyon. When Vince was two, cancer took his biological father's life, so Vince was raised by his stepfather, who did not care much for bringing up children. By Vince's account, his stepfather was an alcoholic and "a jerk" who was short with his tongue and quick to anger. Growing up, Vince was close to his mother, who worked as a janitor at a laundromat. Unlike his fellow crewmembers, whose parents often took them hunting, camping, and fishing, Vince had to introduce himself to the workings of the wild. Because his shyness kept him from making many friends in school, and because his mother worked long hours at the laundromat to support Vince and his stepfather's drinking habit, Vince spent much of his childhood playing by himself.

On one such occasion, at the tender age of ten, Vince began playing with a box of matches behind his house. He ignited a small leaf, but the flames quickly spread, and soon Vince found himself running away from a fast-growing fire that threatened his house. Firecrews arrived and corralled the blaze, but not until it had claimed half an acre of forestland. Vince confessed that he had started the fire; so to teach him a lesson the fire supervisor made him a junior firefighter for a day. Vince had to hold the chain saw to feel how heavy it was; he had to help the firefighters fill the engine tanks with water; and he had to sharpen and replace tools. But Vince did not find this punishment all that punishing—he found it fascinating. After this brief apprenticeship, he began reading books on wildland firefighters, and his mother encouraged him to pursue the profession because "there was money in it." Eight years later Vince earned a spot on a Park Service wildfire crew stationed at the North Rim of the Grand Canyon.

Vince reflected, "My first year was a little bit about the money, and then, aft— , well, not even after the first year, more like the first couple months, it was about the money. Then, after that, it wasn't about the money any more."

"What was it about?" I asked.

"It was 'bout the fire!"

Backcountry Boys

Of the fourteen other male crewmembers at Elk River, most are young, in their late teens and early twenties, although Nicholas recently turned forty and Allen Honawa is fifty-five. Nicholas and Allen each have over twenty years of experience. For the rest of the crew, however, the modal number of seasons is three. Tank is the only rookie. Kris and Scott Saufkie (twenty-three) are in their second season, and George, J.J., Diego, and Donald are beginning their third. For Bryan, Paul Fineman (twenty-one), and me (twenty-three), this season marks our fourth at Elk River, and Steve, Vince, and Peter have been fighting wildfire for seven summers. All the men are single except Vince (married with three children) and Allen (married with two children). Nicholas and Steve are fathers as well and have long-term girlfriends who occasionally visit Elk River and cook dinner for the entire crew.[5]

Four men are Native Americans: Allen, Nicholas, and Scott are Hopi; Vince is Navajo. J.J., Diego, Tank (whose father is Irish), and Donald (who describes himself as "a true melting pot") are Hispanic. The Keeton brothers are biracial, and Peter, George, Paul, Steve, and I are white. Crewmembers vary in racial composition, age, religion, interests, and what they do after the season ends. But all are bound together by their rural upbringing.[6] In fact, every wildland firefighter I have ever met comes from rural America. Norman Maclean, while writing about smokejumpers, encountered the same trend: "So basically they had to be young, tough, and in one way or another from the back country."[7]

Raised in small towns with populations under 10,000, most of my crewmembers have known each other since kindergarten, played on the football team together, and are familiar with each other's families. Allen, Nicholas, and Scott were raised on the Hopi reservation. Most are not proud of their hometown per se; rather, they take pride in being from a small town in general, as opposed to a big city. My crewmembers are country boys, and the culture of the country—that "small town way of life" thought to be distinctly different from urban modes of existence—greatly influences how they perceive themselves and what "being a man" means.[8]

Many of my crewmembers are deeply familiar with the woods they protect. They know where the best fishing spots are and where to find wild turkey at the right season. They know the different types of vegetation, where to gather the best firewood for winter, and the hundreds of miles of dirt roads, mapped and uncharted, running like tributaries through millions of acres of the Wannokee Forest, the site of Elk River. This knowledge is important to them. It provides a sense of place, comfort, and ownership, and it lets them know where they belong.

"I've always liked being in the woods," Diego reflects. "I would come here since I was little, camping, hunting, fishing. I've been here forever." Most of the men at Elk River feel the same way. Their family albums are filled with photos of small boys hoisting stringers of fish or dressed in Mossy Oak camouflage, smiling for the camera next to a freshly killed buck. Many have been going hunting with their fathers for as long as they can remember, and they are possessed by the sport. They find great satisfaction in downing a thousand-pound bull elk with a four-hundred-yard shot or striking an antelope straight through the heart with a razor-tipped arrow launched from seventy yards away. Since permits to hunt deer, elk, and antelope (among other game) in Arizona are issued through a weighted lottery system called "the draw," many crewmembers apply for big-game tags in mid-May and wait impatiently until the results are posted a few months later.

In 2003 the draw results were released on the morning of July 16—and at Elk River nothing else mattered. Professional duties were suspended until crewmembers could get their results. Some gathered around the dirty and outdated computer, mounted on a small desk in the corner of the conference room, and tried to access the results through the Arizona Game and Fish Web site; others repeatedly dialed and redialed Game and Fish's toll-free number, which returned one busy signal after another (since hundreds of eager hunters around the state were dialing the same number). Finally, after about an hour of pushing the redial button and refreshing the Game and Fish Web page, the results were posted on the Web site and everyone knew where he stood.

Steve drew a coveted bull elk tag. Both Scott and Donald pulled cow elk tags, which, though they were no trophy hunts, were better than nothing. Most crewmembers came up empty-handed and loudly aired their disappointment. Curses were yelled; walls were punched; doors were kicked; lunchboxes were thrown.

"Son of a bitch!" J.J. yelled after learning he was not drawn for any of the three hunts he had applied for. Angrily, he pushed himself away from the computer monitor and continued, "That's, *errr* {sigh}, that's like the *worst* thing you can hear in your *life*: not drawn, not drawn, not drawn."

"Whatsa matter there, López?" Steve consoled with false sympathy. "No luck this year?"

"Screw you, Steve! Fuckin' fairy-ass fuck."

Steve burst into gloating laughter and stuck out his tongue in J.J.'s direction. "It's okay López, maybe I'll let you come with me this year. You could be the camp cook."

"Shee-it, shut up, bitch," J.J. replied with a grin. Then his smile dropped, and he vented, to no one in particular, "Damn, I'm pissed—*errr*. And I'm gonna stay pissed all day!"

Unlike J.J., Donald was in high spirits for the rest of the day. He would be hunting the snowy fields that winter while his best friend and roommate stayed home. Donald Montoya yearns for each hunting season. The short and stocky twenty-two-year-old has been hunting all his life. All of Donald's recreation revolves around the outdoors, explaining why he loves working and living at Elk River: "I came up here, and I love it. I love the woods. I've been growing up in the forest my whole life. Fighting fires is fun. The work is great. I love the work. I mean, how much better can you get than being in the woods? . . . I love being outdoors. I can't be stuck in a house putting pipes in all day like I was before. I just can't do that. I *have* to be outdoors."

To my crewmembers, the fact that they can earn a paycheck while "playing in the woods" seems like a too-beautiful con. This is why most of them pick up odd jobs in the off-season that allow them to work outside, like construction work or furring, and why most fantasize about securing a full-time position with the Forest Service.[9] As self-described "outdoor people," my crewmembers fervently reject any type of indoor work, regularly symbolized by the dull, predictable, sanitary desk. "I guess I've always been an outdoors person," remarks Nicholas. "You know, I've never been like an indoor type of guy, a desk or something." Making a living indoors, under the hum of fluorescent lights, in front of the bluish glow of computer monitors, is thought to be a terrible way to live. Although they would enjoy a larger salary, they view the cubicle, computer, and necktie that accompany white-collar professions as too large a sacrifice. The desk represents the world of paperwork, sycophants, and middle-class managerial masculinity. The forest represents freedom, wilderness, and working-class masculinity.[10]

The rejection of indoor work, the denial of the desk, reinforces a major distinction in the minds of the men of Elk River. This distinction between "outdoor" and "indoor" people, between "the country" and "the city," functions as their primary symbolic binary. (And as we will see in later chapters, this distinction is of fundamental importance when comprehending not only how firefighters understand themselves but also the reasons they trust and come to identify with the Forest Service.) It is the "fundamental principle of division," as Claude Lévi-Strauss would call it, since, more than any other antipodal cultural pairing (e.g., man/woman, white/black, rich/poor), it reinforces a foundational boundary separating known from unknown, familiar from foreign, and pure from polluted.[11] To paraphrase Bourdieu, the *social structures* of regional divisions (between city and country) are transferred into *mental structures* of symbolic divisions giving meaning and identity to the firefighters at Elk River.

All social groups, in all places, over all time periods, resemble each other in that they all practice (or have practiced) the perseverative human propensity to create and recreate differences. People divide people. They commit great amounts of energy to defining precisely who are "we" and who are "they." And many social theorists have suggested that uncovering the symbolic antinomies at the bottom of groups' divisive cultural codes is an essential exercise, one that holds the potential to reveal how people structure their lives, the mechanisms of social reproduction, and processes of discrimination and identity formation.[12]

The division between the country and the city is not created at Elk River; it is reproduced and reinforced there. Crewmembers bring this polarized scheme to the fire station. As we saw, most of my crewmembers come from working-class rural America, and they bring with them specific masculine dispositions structured by their working-class and country backgrounds. In other words, they come to Elk River with a *country-masculine habitus*. The country-masculine habitus guides the firefighters' thoughts, tastes, and practices. It serves as their fundamental sense of self, guides how they understand the world around them, influences how they codify sameness and difference, and determines who does and does not belong at Elk River.

Middle America

Every morning, Clarence Kraus steps onto the weathered wooden porch of a one-person cabin before climbing hundreds of aluminum steps to reach a birdcage called the Paquesi Perch Lookout Tower, 160 feet above the ground. For at least eight hours a day, he sits in an eight-by-eight-foot box with windows covering every wall and surveys the horizons of the Wannokee Forest for the slightest smoke. He is sixty, white, a grandfather, a disciple of Edward Abbey (who also was a lookout), a retired high school science teacher, and a Wal-Mart greeter in the off-season. He moved to Arizona from North Carolina three years ago. He loves his job.

Clarence spends most of his time in solitude reading, reflecting on his life, and studying the mapping devices used to pinpoint the coordinates of smoke. He sometimes goes for days without seeing another human being, but when he does get a chance to talk to someone, the reflections and stories bottled up from days of being alone gush out all at once. When Clarence catches your ear, he holds on to it for as long as possible, since he doesn't know when the next one will come his way.

Sometimes some of the Elk River crew climb the steps of Paquesi Perch to listen to Clarence chatter, since he usually has something funny and interesting to say. On one such day, I squeeze into Paquesi Perch with five of my crewmembers.

"Hidee-ho!" Clarence welcomes us with a warm smile. The brim of his dark blue hat rests on a large pair of dark sunglasses. Seated on a bar stool in the corner of the lookout box, Clarence swivels his head from us to the treetops and back again.

"Ah yes, it's good to be up here, boys," Clarence remarks, almost to himself. "Sittin' here starin' at a little piece of heaven. You *betcha.*"

The view is breathtaking. The world is rows of ponderosas sprinkled with oaks, conifers, and blue firs, gray and white bluffs, dirt roads, and cautiously stepping elk under an aqua sky. It looks old to me, undefiled. The only sign of modern life is a long row of metal telephone poles, looming intrusively above the treeline.

My crewmembers and I stare quietly out the windows at the thousands upon thousands of acres below us and wait for our host to start talking. We don't have long to wait.

"You know, I was talkin' to someone here the other day about that new development down there, where that millionaire, Hutchinson or whatever his name is, is buildin' them fuckin' luxury vacation cabins, and supposedly he is gonna buy more land across the road and build there too. They say he's gonna dig two lakes on his property and gonna stock 'em with fish—"

"He *is,*" Steve interrupts. "We drove the engine back there the other day and saw them digging two big old holes behind where I guess the cabins are gonna go. And I mean *big* old holes." Steve stretches out his arms to demonstrate.

"And there were two big piles of gravel right there too," Scott adds quietly.

Clarence reddens, and his voice grows sharper. "You know, that's a damn shame. You know what's gonna happen don'tcha? Pretty soon we're gonna be pavin' these damn roads and all sorts of fuckin' people are gonna be comin' in from Phoenix and from Tucson and wherever. They're gonna be driving their little Buicks up here. Shit, the Buick crowd is gonna replace the pickup crowd if Hutchinson has them roads paved."

"What's the difference between the Buick crowd and the pickup crowd?" I ask.

"The pickup crowd is guys like us, people that aren't afraid to eat beans out of a can."

I wait for more, but Clarence only gives me a "you know what I mean" look before turning to glance at the trees below.

A few seconds pass before Clarence turns back to the crew and asks, "Do you know that the public has no idea about this? This is a whole 'nother world out here. You're good people, you know, people that keep America runnin', who the military draws from. You are middle America right here!"[13]

Clarence pauses, and a smirk lifts his cheeks. "And I'll tell ya somthin' else boys, I'll tell ya somthin' else. Goddamn, every swingin' dick in here is gonna pay my Social Security!"

Paquesi Perch explodes with laughter.

After a half-hour more of Clarence's telling us about his being a science teacher, the evils of big government, the weather, and his plans to be buried in an unmarked grave somewhere on public land, just like Edward Abbey, we tip our hats, climb slowly down the steps of Paquesi Perch, and drive back to the station.

If it were up to Clarence, weekend campers entering Wannokee Forest would be greeted with signs reading, "Posted: All those who drive Buicks are advised to keep out!" Clarence would not allow Hutchinson to manipulate the forest; he would keep things pure, primitive, and protected to ensure that his "little piece of heaven" remains heavenly. But what upsets Clarence is not the clear-cutting and fence building that Hutchinson is ordering. Clarence is troubled not so much by the environmental damage caused by the new development or even the construction of made-to-order oversized cabins per se. He is worried not about the importing of nonnative trout to fill Hutchinson's fake lakes but about the importing of noncountry people to fill his luxury resort. What brings a flush to Clarence's cheeks and makes him grind his teeth is the thought that city people might overrun the forest.

My crewmembers often divide the world along similar lines. On a sunny day near the end of June, after looking for signs of new growth and erosion in a patch of land where a fire tore through a few years back, Kris, J.J., Donald, and I climb into a Ford F-150 extended cab and start back for the station. J.J. steers the truck down a dirt road overlooking a rocky and rugged escarpment. We take in the ponderosa-lined plateau country that spreads out hundreds of feet below us and listen to country music on the radio.

"Look at this shit," J.J. says.

The comment makes us shift our eyes back to the road, where we observe a beige Lexus coupe speeding toward us, its undercarriage and tires caked with reddish and brown dirt from the roads. All four of us lazily wave as the Lexus passes. Our gesture is not returned.

"Lexus. Nice car," Donald observes.

"I had this college roommate. His dad drove a car like that," Kris adds. "He was a rich kid, spoiled ass."

Kris begins to chuckle and, after spitting a line of tobacco into an empty water bottle, continues. "One time, me and my roommate got to talkin' about campin' and stuff. He told me his dad owned some land up by Prescott and that he'd been campin' lots of times. So he thinks he knows a lot about being in the woods. Told me he had a sleeping bag."

"Shee-it," J.J. observes, beginning to giggle. Donald and I are smiling too.

"Yeah, shit, this fool goes up to Prescott a few times and stays in his daddy's cabin and calls that shit campin'; thinks he knows something about out here. I said, 'Man, you don't know *shit* about the woods.' I said, 'Let me take your ass campin'. I'll show you what campin' is!'"

We all laugh and shake our heads. Then Donald tries to one-up Kris's story.

"No, I met this *tr-ue* city boy at my cousin's wedding a while ago," Donald recalls, leaning forward in his seat. "The wedding was back in Show Low, and I was hanging around at the reception and met this guy. Big guy, kinda fat. He had dark sunglasses on, thought he was all badass. He said he was from Phoenix, so I started asking him if he saw any elk on his drive up.

"'See any elk?' I said," Donald recalls, recreating the conversation.

"'Yep,' he says, 'saw a lot of them.'

"'Well, you better be careful,' I said.

"'Nahhhh,' he's all, 'they wouldn't hurt my truck.'

"So I asked him what kinda truck he had, and you know what he said?"

We wait in silence for the answer. Donald, beaming, withholds the punch line for a handful of seconds before it slips through his lips: "A Cadillac Escalade!"

We all burst into loud laughter.

"Cadillac Escalade," Kris repeats in a mocking tone. "Man, an elk will fuck up an Escalade. I hope he hit an elk on his way home. Then, he would see how his Escalade holds up!"

"I know," Donald, still giggling, agrees. "Yeah, yeah, I was like, '*you* are a major dumb ass!'"

A Cadillac Escalade, to the country boys at Elk River, is, of course, not a truck, let alone a truck that could successfully withstand barreling into a five-hundred-pound animal. Donald's acquaintance revealed his city-boy stripes on two accounts: he believed he drove a heavy-duty truck and he thought, ridiculously, that hitting an elk was no big deal. We knew better, and we laughed at the utter foolishness and arrogance of this city boy par excellence.[14]

Several days later I asked Kris, "So, what exactly *is* a city boy?" as he tipped back a can of Keystone Light in my room in crew quarters. I was having my usual glass of scotch.

Kris smiled, leaned back in a chair, and answered, "There's nothing wrong with being a city boy. Like *you,* there's nothing wrong with being in the city. You're a pretty boy, you can't help it. You get hit on by guys all the time, you just like that. You like the attention. *That's* what a city boy is. They just love the attention of being hit on by other guys, I mean, regardless if they are homosexual or not, you know, I know most of them aren't, but they just like the attention, and that's a city boy."

Kris was "snapping on me," as he liked to say; he was joking around. But his tease stung nonetheless, and I hid my pricked pride under a laugh. It stung not only because I self-identify as a country boy but also because I had begun to sense that my country masculinity was quickly becoming diluted in the cosmopolitan academy. When I entered college at Arizona State University as an undergraduate, I quickly discovered that many of my male peers surrounded themselves with artifacts of wealth like new sports cars, expensive clothes, and VIP passes to the hippest clubs. They had been to foreign countries, met famous people, and ate fancy foods. Their parents lived in some exclusive neighborhood, down the street from some exclusive celebrity, and were invited to exclusive events to rub elbows with exclusive politicians. My parents went out to eat at Denny's and drove a used van because that's what they could afford. I reacted to my well-to-do peers, with the help of my roommate and best friend John, by sissifying and citifying them. John and I erected a country-masculine sanctuary in our dorm room, equipped with canned pork and beans, a pyramid of Bud Light cans, cowboys hats, and fishing poles. We made sure to let our dormitory neighbors know when we were going hunting or fishing; we romped around the city in our muddy, beat-up old trucks; and we attended classes clad in faded Wranglers or Levis displaying a ring of chewing tobacco in the left back pocket. We preferred camping trips to Friday night clubbing, two-buck domestics to seven-dollar mixers, and the Oak Ridge Boys to the latest Top Ten artist. And of course, each summer John and I returned to Elk River to fight fire. By rejecting what we could never become and reveling in what we already were, we hoped to show our peers in the big city that we were there, but we sure as hell didn't belong.

But lately, since enrolling in graduate school, I had been feeling that I belonged more and more in the city—or, at least that I should *want* to belong there. The city, the center of intellectual and artistic life, the manifestation of modernization and "progress," seemed to be where those "three faces of God"—Art, Knowledge, and Love—went to live.[15] And with the academic adoration of the city, it seemed, came contempt for the country. My first year in graduate school left me with the impression that some academics and graduate students were quick to poke fun at small-town folk, that they enjoyed stereotyping their thinking as conservative, religious, and parochial. Graduate school had left me with the impression that to be a sociologist was to be enthralled with urban life and to find country lifestyles and country people curious at best, downright backward at worst.[16]

Where, then, did I belong? Were the hands of the university molding me into a city boy? I didn't chew tobacco anymore, and I didn't eat red meat. When I turned down a Keystone Light that Craig Neilson, a forty-five-year-old firefighter, offered me, he was offended and jeered, "What's a matter, boy? You got rich blood now?" And some of my crewmembers told me I talked in "school talk." Paul even referred to me as "the genius," a sort of backhanded compliment. Comments like these produced in me a feeling of disconnection. I felt fractured, in between the city and the country, in both worlds but belonging wholly to neither. My old nature belonged to the country, but I was cultivating a new nature in the confines of the city.[17] I knew I had lost some of my countryness, but, in my mind at least, I was no city boy. The ideal-typical city boy is a fickle, materialistic, hip, stuck-up, manicured and waxed, overeducated, rich, sweater-wearing, vain, urban-dwelling "metrosexual" weak-willed sissy who doesn't know the first thing about the outdoors. I certainly didn't want to be identified as one, and perhaps Kris picked up on my feelings, because he began to backpedal.

"Naaahhhh," Kris said with a grin. "Matt's not a city boy; he has his country roots *somewhere* in there. *What issss* a city boy?"

He paused to contemplate, kneading his unkempt goatee. After a few seconds, he shrugged and settled on an obvious definition: "A city boy is, when I think of a city boy, I think of them as, they are in the city. . . . And all the influences they see are from the city, the concrete jungle. And to me it's someone who doesn't like to sit there and drink beer and chew Copenhagen. I don't know, just different than a country boy."

When Kris observed that my roots remain country, no matter where my branches stretch, I happily agreed and assured myself that I still remained a member (in fair standing) of "the pickup crowd." Being country mattered to me just as much as it mattered to my crewmembers.

By dividing the world into country boys and city boys, pickup drivers and Buick drivers, my crewmembers align themselves with a group of like-minded folks, folks like their parents, like their best friends, who share many of their values, priorities, tastes, and morals.[18] It would be a crude mistake to reduce the citified Buick drivers to representatives of the upper middle class. When Clarence sneers at Hutchinson and when Kris effeminizes city boys, they criticize a specific *style of life* that in their eyes differs dramatically from their own, not simply a specific "class" in the orthodox Marxian sense. Members of the pickup crowd are part of the working class, but they also belong to a specific "status group," in the Weberian sense, since they regulate themselves through certain ways of interacting, dressing, consuming, speaking, and eating that set them apart from other members of the working class, specifically those in metropolitan areas.[19] Through the reproduction of a certain lifestyle, the country boy who drives a pickup, chews tobacco, listens to Johnny Cash, hunts, fishes, drinks cheap beer, and lives in the forest during the summer fighting wildfire erects boundaries between himself and city boys.

Crewmembers come to Elk River from similar positions in the social landscape and with a similar vision and division of the world constituted by that social landscape. They come knowing, implicitly or explicitly, that the kind of men who fight wildfire are the kind of men their fathers are, the kind they are, or at least the kind of men they want to be. They belong at Elk River and feel at home here because they concur, mind, body, and soul, with a firmly established corporate sense regarding the beliefs and practices that make up a country-masculine lifestyle.[20] Out here no one considers hunting barbaric. It's simply what men do in the winter. Out here one would not think to criticize the owner of an oversized truck for its poor fuel economy. You need such a truck to get around these parts. Because they know such things in advance, because they come to Elk River with preformed country-masculine dispositions, crewmembers gravitate to the world of wildland firefighting not only for the money or the adventure, but also (and more important) for the esprit de corps that comes with a collective lifestyle. I will take up this point again in the next chapter.

Although "the city" functions as a foreign place in the minds of my crewmembers, it is not a homogeneous entity. Many types of men live in metropolitan areas, and certainly not all of them fit the mold of "city boy" as defined by my crewmembers. Who is the city boy? Is he the president of a major corporation, a university professor, a bank teller, or a homeless man? I believe Clarence's loathed Buick can be found parked in the driveway of a nice *suburban* home. The suburbanite drives his shiny new car into the forest, leaving his three-car garage and well-trimmed lawn behind for a weekend in "the great outdoors." He looks forward to a comfortable stay in Hutchinson's cabins. But the "wimpy suburbanite" is not the only city boy referenced by my crewmembers. The hard and violent *inner-city* dweller also lurks in their representations of the city. If the suburbs are weak, wealthy, and vain, then the inner city is dirty, dangerous, and poor.

Donald explains, "In a small town you get to know your neighbors. You don't have ambulances and police cars driving by every night. You don't have those problems. . . . But in a big city, you don't know who [your kids are] hanging out with at school. You never meet their families because there is so many kids there. And they actually have a chance to do something like play sports or whatever. They come home after school. They don't have to take a public bus or anything. . . . There's just so many people. You go to the mall and you'll be walking around. There's gangsters walking by you, and they're just looking for someone to mug or whatever they're going to do. They might even get in a gang fight and you get caught in the middle of it. So, you gotta watch your back really bad there."

George agrees with Donald. "I would rather be in a place that I wouldn't have to worry about watching my kids all the time, where I feel safe letting them go to a friend's house, you know, walking there. I like a carefree life, not having to worry about a whole bunch of stuff that's gonna happen."

Donald and George believe the inner city is a breeding ground for gangs and drugs. Both men grew up in small towns and want to raise their families in small towns to avoid metropolitan vice. What do Donald and George's criminals look like? Are they black, white, or Hispanic? All three racial groups have powerful and distinct gangs in the Phoenix metropolitan area. Though it is clear that a fear of crime abounds in their construction of the city, none of my crewmembers used racial stereotypes when describing their fears. Further, both my white and nonwhite crewmembers viewed the inner city as a site of violence and vice.[21]

Thus the symbolic construction of the country gravitates between two equally rejected conceptions of the city. The inner city is associated with crime, danger, and vice, the suburbs with money, fashion, and manners. The inner city is too dangerous, the suburbs, too safe. The country resembles the inner city in that it is gritty and the weak-willed cannot survive, but unlike the inner city it is a place of security and wholesomeness. In its security it resembles the suburbs, but unlike the suburbs the country is rough. This safety cannot be bought; it must be earned.

Women Firefighters

If my crewmembers expel city boys from the ranks of those who belong at Elk River, how do they feel about women firefighters? Countless articles and books on the subject of women working in male-dominated work sites contend that male workers often think of their female counterparts with an erotic imagination; and crewmembers sometimes frame women firefighters in these terms.

On a sunny afternoon in the middle of June, I swept an area of a newly extinguished fire looking for hotspots with a handful of crewmembers from Elk River and from Jameson, a neighboring station named after the small town where it was located. It was slow and tedious work, and we passed the time chatting with firefighters from other districts. We approached an older man and woman dressed in fire gear—green Nomex pants, long-sleeved yellow flame-resistant shirts, and yellow hard hats—and learned that they were from Oregon, dispatched to this fire through a private contract with the Forest Service. Jeb was a soft-spoken gray-bearded white man in his fifties, and Carla was a tall white woman in her forties with long brown hair, who sported a silver ring and matching bracelet carved with flames on one hand and a wedding band on the other.

The conversation ebbed and flowed around the topic of fire. *What fires have you been on? Oh, you were at the Treefork fire? So were we. What kind of pump do you have on that engine? Well, we do things a bit differently here.* We tried to nourish the conversation until the silences grew longer, but we soon found ourselves quietly standing around kicking the ash with our boots.

"Well, what do ya'll say we head over to the west side and grid there a bit?" Peter suggested, breaking the silence.

Just as we got beyond earshot of Jeb and Carla, Malcolm, a firefighter from Jameson who enjoyed being vulgar for the sake of vulgarity, turned to me and smiled. He placed his arm firmly on my shoulder and whispered, "Man, I'd do her doggy style and stick it in her butt. Use my fingers like a gun!"

Demonstrating his fantasy technique, he extended his pointer finger and thumb so they formed an L and continued, "This finger would be on her clit. She probably has a clit three inches long!"

Malcolm giggled impishly, stuck out his tongue, and slung his arm around my neck. Although I had heard this kind of talk before, his comment struck me as especially pornographic.

"Gawd, Mal!" I said, almost embarrassed.

"Gawd nothing," he replied, mockingly. "I just hope to Gawd's sake you don't put that in your fuckin' book!"

Some weeks later I joined one of my crewmembers in his room for late-night drinks. He swung his dirty socks up onto a coffee table and took a hearty swig of beer. He spit tobacco juice into an empty beer can as we chatted.

After a few rounds of beer I asked, "So, what's your opinion on women firefighters?"

"I have no problem with them at all," he answered matter-of-factly. "There's some very, very good women firefighters. There's not as many of them that do it, but, not because they're women, but just because they're *built* physically different than men."

Then he lowered his voice to a caveman grumble. "Men are big, grrr, hairy fucking, grrr. GRRRR. They got big balls! You know? Fucking gross, stinky fuckers, hairy-back bastards!

"And you got women," he raised his voice to a high-pitched squeak. "'Ewww.' Son of a bitch! What the fuck's gross about that? God, they got a *pussy* and *eeerrrrrr*! That's the *only* thing will *really* excite a man. In fact, the only thing that excites me more than fuckin' fire is pussy. That's the honest to God truth!"

In the same breath, this crewmember validated female firefighters yet exaggerated their physical differences; he observed that he has worked beside "very good" female firefighters but joked about "pussy" as being women's ultimate feature and men's ultimate attraction.

The power of the prurient joke is in what it erases. In the case of female firefighters, it erases their skills, work ethic, experience, and knowledge, since women are framed in exploitative discourse to serve but one function.

Sociologists who have investigated the experiences of women in male-dominated work spaces have found that firefighters, police officers, and military cadets (to name a few) regularly inflate gender differences and practice sexist discourse.[22] And if this happens, it is perhaps because when the female body is the one doing the rescuing, the fighting, the dying—in short, the risking—orthodox binaries that label certain work "manly" and other work "feminine" come under attack, and therefore so do fundamental orthodox binaries separating men from women. Accordingly, women are often excluded from these spaces through verbal harassment and institutionally sanctioned handicapping (e.g., promoting a man instead of a woman, though the man is less qualified).[23] However, when such "soft violence" fails, many times overt violence takes over, though this never occurred at Elk River. In 1985, for example, a team of London firefighters were fired after they exposed themselves to a twenty-three-year-old female recruit after strapping her to a ladder and drenching her with urine that they had been collecting in a bucket for days.[24] They called it an "initiation." In a survey of five hundred female firefighters carried out by Women in the Fire Service Incorporated, 88 percent of respondents reported experiencing some form of sexual harassment on the job, and half claimed they had experienced "unwanted physical contact" from their male crewmembers. Women in the armed forces often suffer violent forms of harassment as well.[25] It might be said, then, that high-risk organizations are doubly dangerous for women, for when women partake in the bold act of fighting for a spot in these male-dominated organizations, they are confronted with great risks that their male counterparts do not face—risks that occur not on the battlefield but in the bunkhouse, not on the fireline but in the barracks.

While it is undoubtedly true that many of the men at Elk River often offered brusque and boorish remarks and jokes about women—encouraged not only by the masculine makeup of the youthful crew but also by the sheer isolation of the Elk River Fire Station[26]—this does not mean they desired to cordon off Elk River from women or that they thought that women en masse were incapable of becoming good firefighters. When the crewmember quoted above claimed that he had "no problem" with female firefighters during one moment and kidded about pussy the next, he did not contradict himself; rather, he voiced two quite different positions on women firefighters that he viewed as noncontradictory. As Kris put it to me once, "Just because it's a sexist environment doesn't mean that the guys don't think women can do it."

Most of my crewmembers believed that if a woman could hold her ground on the fireline, if she could hike and crawl and eat smoke just as well as the next guy, then she was welcome. "I have no problem with women firefighters in general," Kris claimed. "I have no problem with male firefighters in general. Regardless of gender, it rests only on their ability to perform. . . . You're only as strong as your weakest link, and that's where that comes into play. There are women that can kick my ass." This sort of view was not held exclusively by younger firefighters. Consider Nicholas's comments: "I think [women] have a place, you know. If they want to do this, it's more power to them. . . . I don't have nothing against women fighting fire, if they can hold their own, you know, and if they want to be one, let them."

Crewmembers often acted on such ideals by treating certain women firefighters with great respect. For example, Gloria Mata, an experienced female firefighter from a nearby district, was well liked and respected by my crewmembers. Gloria was in her late twenties, the wife of a senior firefighter named Arturo (who used to work at Elk River and was also respected by my crewmembers), and a firefighter with over a decade of experience on the fireline. I never heard my crewmembers crack a dirty joke about Gloria or question her aptitude; on the contrary, many of them readily admitted that her firefighting abilities were far superior to their own. Donald, one of the strongest and healthiest men at Elk River, once confessed to me, "I've seen girls do a hell of a job, stay in there longer than I have. Gloria was one of them, Arturo's wife. I stepped out to get fresh air and she kept going, when I was with the Hotshots. That was impressive. I mean, there's less women in the firefighting organization, but some of them can probably hack it better than men can, or just as well."

My crewmembers were not the only ones who bestowed a high level of respect on Gloria; Thurman also valued her competence and experience. When overseeing fires, he often placed her in positions of leadership, and my crewmembers followed her instructions without question. Once he asked her to command a two-person "nightshift crew," a crew that would spend all night alone on the fireline. Gloria readily accepted. Actions like these led my crewmembers to view Gloria as "cut out" for the job.

Although all my crewmembers looked up to Gloria, some saw her as anomalous, more the exception than the rule among women firefighters. Consider, for instance, J.J.'s comments: "You have a guy like Bryan that can do enormous amounts of stuff because he's a big guy, but we also have Gloria, who pulled her weight all those seasons with the Hotshots. . . . Gloria's a badass, and I think it's cool that girls can do that shit. It's awesome. But not too many girls can, very few." Some crewmembers, then, viewed "badass" women firefighters like Gloria as token exceptions, and if so, then we should keep in mind that such exceptions in no way work against stereotypes—in fact, they often have the opposite effect.

Gloria was not the only woman firefighter my crewmembers respected, and Carla was not the only woman firefighter they disrespected. In general, women firefighters, like their male counterparts, are treated differently depending on how well they interact with fellow crewmembers and, above all, how well they perform on the line. This is not to say that the playing field is level by any stretch. Only women firefighters could be (explicitly) viewed or joked about as potential sexual partners. Moreover, women, it seemed to me, had to work harder than their male counterparts to earn respect. Nevertheless, my crewmembers gave women firefighters credit where credit was due. Perhaps Kris put it best when he told me, "You know, women firefighters, it's not their traditional spot. They're gonna have a lot of trouble getting into it, and they're gonna have a lot of trouble once they're in it. But if they—well, it's not even 'if they'—if it's gonna be done, it's gonna *be done*." In other words, my crewmembers judged many women firefighters by the same yardstick they used to measure male firefighters: firefighting ability and country competence.

Country Competence

George is from Atwater and in his third season at Elk River. A large cross, tattooed in blue with magnificent detail, draped with a banner that reads (a bit ironically), "Only the Strong Survive," covers George's sun-spotted white left shoulder; on his right shoulder "GEORGE" is tattooed in large letters, encased in a jagged border and surrounded by green and blue stars; and in the center of his back, directly between his shoulder blades, is a hand-sized Maltese cross, filled in by the Stars and Stripes and surrounded by orange and yellow flames that reach up to the bottom of his neck.[27] A bit of a daydreamer, George earned the nickname "Space Case" from his crewmembers, "S.C." for short. George turned twenty-one in June, and the crew made sure to migrate to Atwater to give him a bibulous welcome into the ranks of legal drinkers. He stumbled out of the bar grinning from ear to ear—but then George always seems to have a smile on his face.

On a hot Friday afternoon George drove the chase truck, an F-150 painted in Forest Service green, down a dirt road congested with weekend campers eager to secure the best spots. I watched from the passenger seat as cars zoomed past at dangerous speeds. As we rounded a corner, a teal two-door hatchback, whose driver had let the car drift too far toward the outside of the road, jerked back onto the right side and sped past.

"Fuckin' valley rats," George grumbled as he guided the truck slowly along.

A "valley rat" is a city boy. "Valley" is a reference to Phoenix, the metropolis of Arizona, where over a million people find refuge in a low desert valley. "Rat," however, is another matter.

"So, why do you call them 'rats,' George? What's a valley rat?" I asked.

He glanced at me from behind the steering wheel with a puzzled look. George often looked puzzled. He turned his eyes back to the road and contemplated his answer. Staring at his freckled face shaded beneath a faded blue baseball cap, I waited as George meditated on his phrase by repeating quietly, "Valley rat? Val-ley rat? What would I say is a valley rat?"

He settled on an answer: "Someone who's not been around, around here. I would say a valley rat is someone who has been in a big city for most of their life. They don't really, they, they have *an idea* of what happens in small towns, but they don't *really* know how things work."

"So, George, would it be an insult if I called you a valley rat or a city boy?" I asked, smiling.

He returned my smile, looked at me out of the corner of his eye, and replied, "It wouldn't be an insult. I'd just think you didn't know what the hell you're talking about."

Valley rats could not distinguish poison oak from wild sumac. They are ignorant of all things wild. The men at Elk River, by contrast, see themselves as possessing a specific body of knowledge—a country competence, a woodsy *techne*—that makes them country boys and the lack of which makes other men city boys.

Country masculinity is practiced and displayed primarily through country competence. At Elk River, crewmembers' practical knowledge of the woods, their embodied outdoorsmanship—the way a hand grips an ax, the way a foot mounts a trail—is directly bound up with their core sense of self, their masculinity and identity, for that which is "'learned by body' is not something that one has, like knowledge that can be brandished, but something that one is."[28] This means that an attack on one's outdoorsmanship translates into a direct attack on one's masculinity. This is why Bryan did not take it lightly when he heard that George thought he could run a chain saw better than him.

It happened on a lazy Wednesday morning. Most of the crew had gathered in the shop, carefully avoiding the gaze of the supervisors. Crewmembers spread out through the large warehouselike room lined with tools, a freestanding drill, a long wooden countertop, and a cherry picker used to pull engine blocks. Conversation was slow. Donald fidgeted with a metal rod on an anvil, and most of us milled around and watched him, since there was nothing else to watch. George propped himself against the concrete wall and drifted off to sleep, but his nap did not last long, because minutes later Bryan stomped into the shop, marched straight up to George, stopping inches from his face, and in a confrontational voice barked, "You think you can run a saw better than me?"

Everyone in the shop turned to watch. Bryan's loud voice signaled the beginning of an altercation both in tone and in subject. He was talking about a chain saw, a crucial tool used in wildland firefighting. Because of its mass, violence, and ability to harm, only the strongest, most skilled, and most experienced firefighters wield a saw. Thus, sawyering skills signal much more than the ability to drop a full-grown oak; they represent a skilled firefighter—more, a competent and mature country man. Bryan had advanced a serious response to a serious challenge supposedly advanced by George.

George blinked. He blinked again. He stared silently up at the large man in front of him. George was at once confused, startled awake, and a bit scared. He slowly peeled his body away from the wall and stuttered, "Wh-what?"

Immediately Bryan snapped back, "Someone told me you were saying you could run a saw better than me. Is that true, *George*?"

Bryan's shoulders rolled to the front, his arms ready at his sides; balanced over his legs, he pushed his torso toward George. Bryan was not kidding around. A casual observer taking in the scene from a distance might have guessed that George had made an uncouth remark about Bryan's sister. But the remark in question was about a chain saw.

"Uh, uh, no. No. I never said anything like that," George denied.

The room remained silent. Crewmembers stared at the immobile Bryan to see if he was satisfied by George's refutation.

"Are you *sure* George? 'Cause somebody told me that you said that." Bryan wanted to hear George deny it again.

"Yeah. I mean, I don't know who told you that, but I didn't say nothin' about that."

"Well, *do* you think you can run a saw better than me, George?"

George thought about the question before answering. "No. Not *better*."

"Are you sure?"

"Yeah."

After a few seconds Bryan turned away and marched stone-faced out of the shop. "That's what I thought, *George*."

A week later the crew responded to a one-acre fire called the Alligator Juniper fire. I was assigned the task of spotting the sawyer. Bryan made sure to grab the chain saw first. I hoisted an army green bag full of chain-saw equipment such as hatchets and wedges onto my back, and we went to work. We policed the fire in search of trees with the potential to topple and came upon a medium-sized (B-class) pine seared most of the way up, which, we thought, needed to be dropped.

Bryan stood in the ashes and began to cut into the trunk while I looked on to make sure the tree was stable and would fall in the direction we

wanted. He maneuvered the saw in and out of the trunk by making two
front slices to form a pie cut a quarter of the way into the wood followed
by a perfectly straight back cut. Wood chips flew out from behind the saw
in a light brown cloud to the familiar high-pitched whine of the chain ferociously whipping around the bar. When the pie cut began to close in on
itself and the tree started to bend, Bryan pulled the saw out and stepped
back, staring up at the falling trunk. The pie cut narrowed, and the tree
tipped to the slow cracking of breaking wood. It hit the blistered ground
with a *slam* and stirred up a cloud of ash. The cut was picture perfect, and
Bryan knew it. He shut off the saw with a flick of his thumb and, turning
to me, bragged, "And George thought he could run a saw better than me.
I said, 'George, I've been running a saw since I was thirteen!'"

Just as working-class men tend to judge the measure of a man through
a value system that prizes attainable attributes (breadwinning, a hard work
ethic, integrity) over ones perceived as unattainable (wealth, education, a
powerful career),[29] county boys define masculinity through standards of
country competence. The men at Elk River value their "human capital,"
country competence, over economic capital and city competence. This is
why, although Hutchinson might *own* some land, Clarence and my crewmembers *know* the land, and as such they believe they have more rights
to the Wannokee Forest than some millionaire developer. They, country
boys, belong at Elk River, and they feel it belongs to them.

Knowledge of the country is a practical and specific type of knowledge.
If one can gut an elk, string a catfish line, reload .45 bullets, fell a juniper
with a twelve-pound chain saw, or throw a rig into four-low and climb
a rocky hill, then one exhibits country competence. This knowledge not
only binds crewmembers together (as Kris observes, "I'm not concerned
with the similarities between their backgrounds, you know, where they're
from, or their race or their ethnicity. I'm looking at the similarities of,
like, their knowledge that pertains to the forest. I'm looking at their similarities for the love for the forest or why they are even out here."), it also
allows them to adapt to the rigors of wildland firefighting as well as to the
organizational common sense of the U.S. Forest Service with quickness
and aptness, as I demonstrate in ensuing chapters.

Vince's Meager Seven Years of Experience

Although he was raised in a small town, Vince was not brought up the
same way many of his crewmembers were. Vince did not grow up with
family camping trips or weekend woodland outings. Whereas most crew-

members at Elk River were raised by their biological fathers, who introduced them to the outdoors very young, Vince had a stepfather who taught him much about the receiving end of a leather strap and little about the delicate movement of a home-tied fly lure atop a still lake or the rash actions of deer in the rut. Thus he did not acquire much country competence growing up, competence that would have helped him adjust to the tasks of wildland firefighting.

Moreover, Vince was not socialized into a masculine sporting culture as were many of his crewmembers. Apart from one season on the junior varsity basketball team his sophomore year, Vince did not play sports. Whereas many of his crewmembers spent considerable time in homosocial male environments, Vince's first significant experience of this kind came when he joined the Forest Service. Accordingly, he was not accustomed to masculine styles of communication and joking (more on this in chapter 3). He did not enter the Forest Service with years of experience working beside other men in a collective setting, nor was he used to taking curt orders from a masculine boss.

Vince *grew up* in the country, but he was not *brought up* in a country-masculine way; he was *from* the country but not *of* the country.[30] As a result, he had a much harder time acclimating to the demands of firefighting than did his fellow crewmembers. Although the summer of 2003 marked Vince's seventh season as a wildland firefighter, he did not hold a position of authority like other crewmembers with comparable years of experience, such as Peter or Steve; in fact, many crewmembers with less experience outranked him. While Vince was still a bottom-level seasonal crewmember, by his fourth season Bryan was assistant foreman and a permanent Forest Service employee. Paul had also acquired a permanent position by his fourth season. If Vince did not hold a position of authority in line with his years of firefighting it was because he did not assert himself as a confident leader or demonstrate significant firefighting competence.[31]

This became clear through dozens of everyday practices on and off the fireline, practices that, taken together, separated Vince from other crewmembers, stripping him of firefighting (and masculine) capital. For example, during fires Vince never grabbed a Pulaski, the lead tool (nor was he ever handed one); thus, when digging line, he never directed his crewmembers but always followed someone else. Although the most experienced firefighters carry radios during a fire, I never saw Vince carrying one. When we were assigned to sharpen tools, Vince usually sanded the handles, a task my crewmembers understood as easier and less important than taking a file to metal and grinding the edge of a combi or the blade of a Pulaski. Although he was certified to do so, Vince rarely drove the chase truck, and on the rare occasions when he did, he was overly grateful for a turn behind the wheel. Vince never volunteered to accompany the Hotshots on a fourteen-day detail.

All wildland firefighters must buy their own boots: all leather, at least eight inches high, without steel toes (which heat up too much), and with Vibram soles. Vince wore a pair of $180 fire boots (Georgias), which would give out after one season, whereas Bryan, Paul, and other crewmembers with several seasons of experience wore boots that set them back several hundred dollars but would last many seasons (such as Whites). This was important, for a firefighter's brand of boot, and its price, communicated his commitment to the occupation—the more expensive the boot, the more "genuine" the firefighter. Peter even went so far as to buy his own fire pants (beige cargo pants with ankle straps), which distinguished him from other crewmembers who wore the dark green Nomex pants issued by the Forest Service. Of course, most of Vince's money went to support his wife and three children; he could not afford to spend a quarter of a month's salary on a pair of boots.

In short, Vince did not take to the formal and informal requirements of the job with the same confidence and competence as other crewmembers. One seemingly trivial event effectively illustrates this point.

After a morning of patrolling the forest, Allen pulled Engine Seven-One into the Rompart Lake Store's parking lot, in the middle of Wanno-kee, because he wanted to buy a package of sunflower seeds. Allen Honawa was the supervisor of the Elk River crew when Thurman was not around. A fifty-five-year-old Hopi with thick black hair and a thin mustache, both peppered with gray, he had faded blue tattoos on each forearm, snakes coiling around swords, that he gave himself as a teenager. He drove a rusted and scratched blue-and-gray Chevy truck that rolled off the assembly line in the 1970s, whipped many crewmembers half his age on the running trail every morning, and spent his days off tightening leaky pipes, mending cracked tiles, or fixing some other household emergency around his home in Atwater. Allen had fought fires for over twenty years, but 2003 was his first year as a permanent worker, after previous seasons as a temporary hire. He drove an engine, a position of authority, but would be laid off at the end of each fire season and collected unemployment until the hot months rolled around and the fires picked up again. Last year, however, the supervisor of Elk River transferred districts, and Thurman asked Allen if he wanted the permanent position. At first Allen was hesitant because he enjoyed the extended months of unemployment, but being fifty-five and without benefits or a retirement package worried him, so he accepted Thurman's offer. Allen and Thurman embodied very different leadership styles: whereas Thurman made quick, authoritative decisions, Allen liked to take his time and ask crewmembers' opinions. And Allen was soft-spoken whereas Thurman had a tuba for a voice. Accordingly my crewmembers liked Allen but did not respect him the way they respected Thurman; but then again, they didn't extend anyone else that level of respect.

George parked the chase truck beside the engine, and we joined Allen, Vince, Donald, and Tank in the store. We all bought snacks, at a 10 percent "firefighters' discount," then headed back to the trucks and set off patrolling again. Vince and Tank rode in the engine with Allen while I rode in the chase truck with George and Donald. As Allen turned the engine down a familiar dirt road, George followed close behind. The forest was hot and dry, and the engine was kicking up a steady cloud of dust that covered the windshield of the chase truck, severely obstructing our vision. George didn't seem to mind. He unwrapped an ice-cream sandwich with both hands while steering with his knees. Suddenly the dust cloud cleared and the engine appeared before us—stopped dead in its tracks.

"Watch out!" Donald yelled from the backseat.

George dropped his ice cream on the floor, grabbed the wheel with both hands, and jerked the truck to the left, missing the stalled engine by inches. He stomped on the brakes, and the truck skidded to a halt in front of the rig. If a vehicle had been coming the other way, we would have rammed it head on. Aware of our luck, George, Donald, and I silently exchanged nervous grins.

"Holy shit!" Donald giggled. "That was fucking *close!*"

The three of us bounded out of the chase truck to investigate.

"What happened, Allen?" George yelled as we approached the engine.

"I don't know," Allen hollered back, jumping down from the driver's seat, "I couldn't steer!"

"Look at that," Donald observed, pointing to the front passenger-side wheel, which was protruding two feet from its wheel bay.

Donald dived under the engine to diagnose the problem. After a few seconds, he shimmied out and said, "The tie-rod came off. It's no big deal."

He stood up, wiped the dust off his green Nomex pants and the back of his T-shirt, and continued, "We just need to find the castle nut that's sprung off so we know what size cotter pin fits in it."

After a few minutes of searching the road, Tank found the castle nut and handed it to Donald.

"See?" Donald explained, looking at Allen and pointing to the break. "We could run back to the station and just get another cotter pin that fits this one."

"Uh, okay," Allen agreed. As George, Donald, and I rushed back to the chase truck, Allen added cheerfully, "Hurry back! I want to get home on time tonight. We're having steaks, *uh-huh!*"

Once we reached Elk River Station, Donald jumped out of the truck, ran into the auto shop and picked up a few cotter pins, then we headed back to fix the engine. When we met Allen, Donald slipped underneath the engine again. With a little help from George and me, he had the wheel back in place in minutes. Allen drove the engine back to the station with a heavy foot, so as not to let his steak get cold.

My crewmembers handled this incident with efficiency and speed. Their knowledge of how to fix the broken engine was not acquired through any training the Forest Service offered; they obtained it some time before coming to Elk River. Donald and George knew what a cotter pin was—they knew how it worked and how it secured a castle nut—but I did not. I had no idea what a cotter pin looked like until Donald showed me. I did not know how to diagnose, let alone fix, Allen's busted engine, but my crewmembers attended to the problem masterfully. Accordingly, I began to wonder how many of my crewmembers could have done what Donald did. More specifically, I wanted to know how many of my crewmembers knew what a cotter pin was.

So the following day I tried to satisfy my curiosity by asking each crewmember if he knew what a cotter pin was and how he learned. Paul had known since he was seven years old, because he used to help his father work on trucks. J.J. learned about cotter pins in tenth-grade auto shop, as did Tank. When I asked Peter what a cotter pin was, he drew a diagram on the wall of the tool cache and told me he learned when he was about thirteen, through helping his father and brothers. Allen and Nicholas knew what a cotter pin was, though both of them learned so long ago that they couldn't recall exactly how they knew. Diego told me he learned when he was about fourteen.

"Hey, do you know what a cotter pin is?" I asked, as Diego sharpened a combi in the tool cache.

"Yeah, it's like a metal bobby pin that slips through a nut—they call it a castle nut—like this," Diego answered, demonstrating with his fingers.

"The cotter pin goes through these slits in the castle nut so the nut don't turn."

"Huh. So who taught you?"

"Family—uncles, cousins, dads," Diego answered, playing "informant" with curiosity and smiling at the awkwardness of disinterring buried information of interest only to some cockamamie ethnographer.[32]

"So did you find out any of this through books?"

"No, all through experience."

Vince, however, lacked such experience. Besides me, he was the only crewmember who did not know what a cotter pin was or how it worked. He did not know that the tie-rod had slipped off, and he certainly couldn't have recognized the problem and solved it as Donald did. Nor could I, for that matter.

My crewmembers thought my questions about cotter pins were silly. To most of them this was old knowledge, commonsense know-how acquired sometime during their childhood or adolescence. I felt that asking crewmembers about the design and function of cotter pins was like asking students about the nature of pencils. Everybody seemed to know about cotter pins, except Vince. Vince did not have a father who spent Sunday afternoons with him under the hood of a truck, and he did not learn about cotter pins in auto shop.[33] What was obvious to my crewmembers was news to Vince.

Of course, one does not need to know the secrets of cotter pins to be an effective firefighter, but this bit of knowledge is a simple example of how crewmembers draw on their histories, their country competence, while performing everyday practices of wildland firefighting. It illustrates a time when my crewmembers possessed knowledge that Vince lacked— knowledge of something simple, yet something of dire importance the afternoon the tie-rod slipped loose. But something more fundamental is at stake here. Vince did not simply lack knowledge of cotter pins; he lacked the confidence that he could actually fix the broken engine with his own hands. When crewmembers snapped the tie-rod back in place, they displayed their "working knowledge," the practical and variegated expertise of the crackerjack craftsman that urged them not to phone for help when something went awry, but to roll up their sleeves and dive right in.[34] Beneath their knowledge of the cotter pin was a disposition to confront the problem, to tinker, to put it all back together, a disposition conditioned by their rural, working-class masculine upbringings.

Do you know how to tie a slipknot? Do you know the difference between four-low and four-high? Can you drive an ATV? Can you weld? Do you know what poison ivy looks like? Do you know how to pick up a snake? Can you hike fast without wasting your energy? Have you ever slept in the woods without a tent? Do you know what a cotter pin is? Most of my crewmembers could answer yes to more questions like these than Vince could; that is, whereas most of them came to Elk River with a refined and well-developed set of country-masculine skills, Vince had fewer resources to draw on. Most crewmembers adapted to the everyday practices of wildland firefighting—from digging line to repairing vehicles—more easily than he did. Thus, although it seems strange that Vince was not well adjusted to the world of wildland firefighting after seven years' experience, we might now say that he had *only* seven years' experience, whereas other crewmembers, regardless of the number of summers they had been employed by the Forest Service, had lifetimes'.

The Sanctuary of the Forest

2

The profession of wildland firefighting requires seasonal workers to abandon whatever jobs they held in the colder months for one that pays roughly ten dollars an hour (give or take) and that obliges most of them to live in a forest encampment, largely isolated from family and friends, in surroundings that can at best be described as less than glamorous. It is a consuming, demanding, and "greedy institution"[1] that often erases conventional divisions between work and play, office and home, family and coworkers and demands that firefighters make themselves radically available. As Thurman regularly warns, "If you go available, you're available. Period. No excuses." Sometimes crewmembers do not come in contact with people besides other members of the firecrew and occasional campers for weeks at a time. Summer days are monopolized by the priority of fire, and when a blaze busts, firefighters rush to the scene armed only with hand tools, flame-resistant clothing, hard hats, and fire shelters ("shake and bakes") to dig line in front of a lethal combustive force that thrives on destruction. Those who choose to square off with "the Black Ghost" must regularly work fourteen hours (or more) on end, crawling through ash and dirt, hiking over steep terrain carrying twenty pounds of gear, swinging axes and shovels, sometimes miles from the nearest paved road, let alone the nearest hospital.

What compels people to accept the burdens of firefighting?

56

Why do they choose to take part in such a demanding and dangerous enterprise? In this chapter I demonstrate that the answers are to be found in the least likely place (least likely, that is, according to current theories of risk taking): *downtime*. Many sociologists have suggested that risk takers understand downtime as meaningless and dull.[2] I argue that at Elk River periods of waiting are saturated with meaning. Far from being "killed time" or "wasted time," downtime is *primetime*.[3]

I do not mean firefighters do not ache for fire. They do. Some pray for fire. Some, driven by overpowering pyromania, start fires at night so they can fight them in the morning. Nor, for that matter, do I mean that firefighters do not appreciate the relatively large paychecks they often collect over the course of the summer (not because their wages are impressive but because they work incredibly long hours). The love of adventure and the need for financial sustenance are part of the reason my crewmembers flock to the world of firefighting. But they are not the most important enticements. Elk River offers them something else, something more alluring than rushes or riches—something having to do with their country-masculine habitus.

Pyromaniacal Passion

Most of the firefighters at Elk River are temporary workers who spend their time very differently in the off-season. Five of them go to college full time: J.J. attends a community college in the Phoenix area; Kris and Tank are both in their second year at the University of Arizona; and Bryan and Scott attend Northern Arizona University. Others pick up odd jobs here and there in the winter. Last year George worked for a construction company, as did Nicholas. Donald is a furrier who collects coyote and bobcat pelts all winter to make a living. Paul helps out on his family's farm and sometimes tags along with his father on cross-country trips in his Big Rig. Diego cooks at his family's restaurant and takes night classes at the local community college in Atwater. Vince prefers to lie low during the winter, collecting unemployment checks and spending time with his children until the next fire season rolls around. Only the engine operators, Allen, Peter, and Steve, work all year. Each is responsible for a fire engine and the crewmembers who staff it. In the winter they perform other duties in the forest such as thinning trees and repairing trails. Even though my crewmembers spend most of the year doing other things, they see themselves primarily as firefighters and secondarily as students, construction workers, or furriers.

"When you're in the off-season, like say last year when you worked at La Hacienda, and someone would say 'What do you do,' what would you say?" I ask Diego.

"I'm a firefighter," he answers. "I never said I'm a cook at La Hacienda. First I'd say, 'I'm a firefighter,' and *then* I'd say, 'But I'm not working there. For six months out of the year, I'm a cook.'"

"So firefighting becomes your main identity?"

"Yeah. Who wants to be known as a cook, unless you're fuckin' Emeril Lagasse or something?"

The summer is when Diego trades in his spatula and apron for a Pulaski and a pair of fire boots to serve, for a few months, in a capacity that defines his occupational identity for the rest of the year.[4]

To the wildland firefighter, there are not four seasons. There are but two: fire-season and off-season, summer and winter, sacred and profane. The fire season begins in mid-April and, depending on weather conditions, usually closes around the end of September. The rest of the year is "winter"—meaningless, dull, and cold. Summer is exciting and eagerly anticipated; it gives life. The winter is a pause, a delay, a queue; summer imparts meaning, color, and action.[5]

George eagerly anticipates each fire season. As he drives an F-150 down a quiet dirt road on a seventy-five-degree day, I adjust myself in the passenger's seat and causally ask, "So George, what do you do in the off-season?"

"Oh, nothing really big," he replies, shaking his head. "I'm always just anxious for fire season to come back again to do what I like to do."

"Tell me what you like most about the job."

"The adrenaline rush is a big thing. I like the rush it gives me. Um, I like actually knowing how fires work. You know, it's fascinating to me just being able to know what a fire's gonna do, how it's gonna burn. . . . I like being out in the woods and getting to know, being in a tight group with the people you work with. It's a good environment and I like being in it. Um, it's fun, and once you have a taste of it you *always* come back. . . . It's very addicting—it *is*. For some people, once they see it, they either love it or they hate it. The people that I've fought fire with, they've always came back. . . . I think it's once you get a taste of it, it's kinda like a tattoo: once you get one, you gotta go back for another. There's something about it."

I smile, knowing that George has a few tattoos and is planning another, and I ask, "So explain to me why, um, why fire's so addicting then. What's so *special* about it?"

George pauses, and a shy smile forms. He turns away and stares out the truck window. After shooting a quick line of Copenhagen juice into a plastic water bottle, he replies, "Fire kinda has—"

He pauses again and extends his right hand pleadingly, palm up, as he tries to express something so familiar it is ineffable. He finishes his thought, "—its own *personality,* you could say. I mean, it's a breathin' thing. It's somethin' that, it kinda . . . I'm trying to think of the word . . . It kinda gives you self-confidence to know that you can control something so wild, I guess is a way to say it. Um, especially when you get on big fires—to know that something that big, and that furious, there's, it kinda makes you feel good that you can stop something that's so big and something that will tear anything that gets in its path."

To George the summer brings the rush of firefighting, the camaraderie of crewmembers, and the serenity of the forest. But it also brings a chance to interact with that mercurial and vivacious creature. George has seen fire snake quietly beneath a dry patch of duff and pine needles, leaving only a faint trace of smoke, and he has seen it ascend from the ground to the tops of trees with the speed of a panther; he has watched flames twist themselves into a blazing tornado called a fire whirl and dance through groves of saplings; he has set eyes on the pulsing orange-and-yellow glow of a coal-crusted earth against a pitch black night. And George continues to be enthralled with every vision of fire. He loves being close to fire not only because of the adventure, but also because he is infatuated with the lick of the flames and the taste of the smoke.

Many of my crewmembers develop a deep, almost spiritual, fascination with fire. To them fire is mysterious, powerful, and beautiful; more than an element, more than a combustion of substances, it is a form of life, and a romantic one at that.[6] Many firefighters love fire deeply. They develop an attraction to fire, a pyromaniacal passion that goes well beyond battling it. In this respect they resemble soldiers, who often experience a similar sensation when marveling at utter destruction. Compare, for example, the following words written by Vietnam veteran Tim O'Brien: "For all its horror, you can't help but gape at the awful majesty of combat. You stare out at tracer rounds unwinding through the dark like brilliant red ribbons. You crouch in ambush as a cool, impassive moon rises over the nighttime paddies. You admire the fluid symmetries of troops on the move, the harmonies of sound and shape and proportion, the great sheets of metal-fire streaming down from a gunship, the illumination of rounds, the white phosphorous, the purply orange glow of napalm, the rocket's red glare.

It's not pretty, exactly. It's astonishing. It fills the eye. It commands you. You hate it, yes, but your eyes do not."[7]

Fire engenders life and death. It gives firefighters purpose, identity, and paychecks, and it has the power to take it all away. Images of fire surround my crewmembers in their quarters and vehicles and on their clothes and bodies. An enormous sticker of a wickedly smiling flame covers nearly half the back window of George's teal Honda Accord. The seatcovers in Diego's red GT bear elongated red and yellow flames. Peter, Bryan, George, and Paul all flaunt tattoos of flames. These symbolic artifacts not only signify a connection between the occupation of firefighting and masculine identity, they also allude to a special relationship with fire itself. Many firefighters are drawn to the creature of fire just as much as to the fight. After all, they adorn themselves with flames, not hoses.

Sometimes firefighters ache for fire so much that they set ablaze the forest they are in the business of protecting. One firefighter from another crew disclosed to me that he had committed arson in the past. He confessed without my prompting, as if he had been waiting years to tell someone and my promise of confidentiality provided a safe opportunity. We were rolling fire hoses that had been washed and dried and strapping them with large strips of black rubber sliced from inner tubes. The hot day slouched slowly on, as had the day before and the day

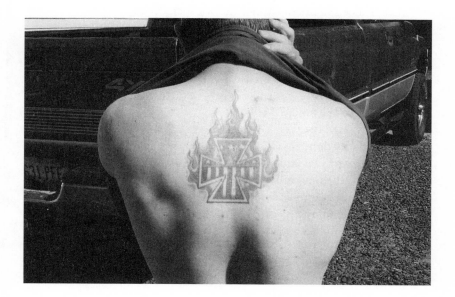

before that. I stationed myself with him at a hose roller, isolated from the rest of the group.

We worked silently and efficiently before he said, "Slow day, huh?"

"Yeah," I answered, keeping my eyes on the task. My arm spun a wide circle as I cranked the rolling lever. He held the advancing hose to make sure it did not tangle.

"I wish we had a fire." His eyes left the hose and searched the horizon, looking, perhaps, for a specter of smoke dancing upward from the trees below.

"Yeah, me too. Seems like we haven't had one in forever."

"Not since the Greer fire for us, and that was just a little one, you know."

"Yup," I mumbled. We yanked the hose off the roller, stretched an inner tube tie around it, and threw it on the pile.

He reached for another hose and asked, "Have you ever wanted to *start* a fire?"

"Sure, maybe fly a plane over and drop some fusees out," I joked.

"I did," he said quietly.

"Did what?"

"I started a fire once."

"*You what*?" I said, lowering my voice and turning to him. Our eyes met, and I sensed that he regretted telling me.

"Yeah, I started a fire one time," he whispered.

"*Why?*" I stood bug-eyed with my arms limp at my sides.

He looked away with pursed lips for a passing moment, as if recalling the event. "Because I, well, I . . . I didn't need the money. I *wanted* the *fire*." The word fire lingered on his tongue. A smile came to his face, and his eyes widened.

"You wanted the fire?"

"Yeah. I wanted the *fire*."

"How did you do it?"

"Just after work, I got some stuff and a lighter." His voice turned from the mystical to the practical, and he resumed working. I was disenchanting his special moment by asking for the boring details.

"How big did it get?"

"A half acre. Well, not even a half acre."

"And how did—"

"Hey Matt!" Vince yelled from the other side of the hose rack. "You got any rubbers over there?"

I looked at Vince, grabbed a handful of inner tube ties, and waved them in the air. He began walking toward us.

"Don't tell anybody, okay?" he asked quickly in a nervous whisper.

I nodded silently, looking him in the eye. We never spoke of it again.

This firefighter risked incarceration to be on one more fire. He craved the smell of burning sap, the sound of wood fracturing under enormous heat and pressure, and the sight of swelling folds of hot air, ash, and thick bubbling smoke. He so much desired to see the flames just once more before the season ended that he became an arsonist at midnight to be a firefighter at dawn. Economic incentives did not move him, nor was it thrill lust. No, he wanted the fire.

The line between firefighter and arsonist is a fine one. "Firefighter arson" afflicts both wildland and structural firefighting organizations. In 2005 a veteran U.S. Forest Service firefighter, who commanded crews not only during the monstrous Rodeo-Chediski fire but also at New York City's "Ground Zero" and who was stationed in a forest neighboring Wannokee, was arrested for starting wildfires in his district. In 2004 a wildland firefighter pled guilty to lighting three fires in the Los Padres National Forest in California, fires that burned over seven hundred acres and cost more than $2 million to extinguish. And as I discuss later, the man responsible for igniting the Rodeo fire of 2002 was a wildland firefighter stationed on the White Mountain Apache Reservation. Firefighter arson is a significant enough problem in structural firefighting units that government agencies such as the FBI and the U.S. Fire Administration (under the auspices of FEMA) have released research reports detailing the motives, methods, and characteristics of firefighters turned arsonists.[8]

Many of my crewmembers recall being fascinated with fire and having arsonist tendencies since childhood. As boys, they enjoyed playing with matches and magnifying glasses, and Vince was not the only crewmember who had set his backyard on fire.

Over a beer in my room in crew quarters, Bryan remembered, "Oh, I played with matches and stuff. And I remember lighting the backyard on fire."

"You lit your backyard on fire?"

"Yeah, it was pretty funny. It was when we lived near the Twin Lakes Ranger Station. I was just out in the backyard, lighting matches and throwing them, you know, and pretty soon a little patch of pine needles and grass started to catch on fire." Bryan paused and chuckled to himself. "But it only spread a little bit. Kris and I put it out before my dad found out. But, yeah, I've always played with matches and stuff like that. You know, fire fascinates me."

On another occasion Bryan told me, "If you can't get a job starting fires, you might as well get a job putting them out."[9]

In the same vein, Peter claimed that firefighters, at base level, are nothing more than "pyromaniacs with their emotions under control": "But I do like seeing the fire. . . . I do like fire itself. It's amazing, just seeing it. I like to see it. It's amazing how something can go from nothing to just taking out huge trees. This one guy told me, he asked us, we were in a fire investigations class, and he said, 'You know what firefighters are? A firefighter is a pyromaniac with his emotions under control.' And, I mean, when you think about it, when you're trying to do control burns, you try to put out as much fire as you can, to a certain degree, just to see it. See it go. It's neat. I love seeing what it can do. I think it's beautiful, those big ice caps on those big smokes. It's amazing."

A control burn (or a prescribed burn) is a fire purposely lit by firefighters to thin overgrown areas of the forest and to clear out underbrush. When Peter participates in control burns, he tries to light off as much fuel as possible, without allowing the fire to get out of control, simply to see what the fire will do. I have participated in a handful of control burns and several backburning (or burnout) operations, where firefighters fight fire with fire. On these occasions firefighters enthusiastically ignite ground fuels with the white-hot tips of their sulfur fusees, setting loose a wave of flame through a prairie of plain grass or a bed of pine needles. Sometimes they put down too much fire, and things get edgy. On one fire, for instance, Gloria, the highly respected woman firefighter I mentioned in chapter 1, instructed Donald, George, and me to burn out a small section of land between the fireline and "the black"—the burned area encompassed by the fireline. The three of us lit off so much fuel that we created an exuberant and bursting fire that nearly jumped the line our burnout operation was intended to fortify. We spent the next hour patrolling the line and searching for spot fires in "the green" (the unburned area outside the fireline), much to Gloria's annoyance.

A Fading Rush

Besides the beauty of fire, Peter enjoys the rush of firefighting. "Knowing that that thing can kill you kinda gives you a rush," he admits. "It gives *me* a rush. Knowing that it's, it's—I don't consider it playing with my own life or anybody else's life—it's just, I think that everybody else that's in it just looks at it as an excitement, a kind of a rush, an adrenaline rush."[10]

Like George, Peter enjoys the danger of firefighting; but many firefighters, especially veterans, no longer experience a rush while on the fireline. After a few seasons, the electrifying tingle of emergency—that combination of fear, confusion, newness, and amazement that possesses many young firefighters—fades. The frenzied shouts of adventure quiet down, becoming a mild-mannered conversation, then a soft-spoken murmur, and finally only a gentle whisper.

Steve's heart rate hardly accelerates on the fireline anymore. In rank and title he is Peter's counterpart at Elk River, but rank and title are where the similarities stop. Whereas Peter is a cut-loose cowboy, a poker-playing, back-slapping, fun-loving son of a gun who runs his engine with great nonchalance, Steve can be painfully serious, austere, practical, and no-nonsense. Whereas Peter chases after youth, Steve seems to have arrived at adulthood too early. A twenty-four-year-old father of one who has been fighting fire since he was eighteen, Steve has the body and disposition of someone twice his age. He is already balding, wears a mustache, and walks with a mild slouch. And when he walks, as when he drives, jogs, or talks, he does it slowly, carefully, and thoughtfully. He prefers to err on the side of caution, to dot all the *i*'s and cross all the *t*'s. Peter and Steve are both competent operators, well liked and respected by their crewmembers, but their leadership, life, and firefighting styles are very different. Whereas Peter feels an intoxicating rush of excitement on the fireline, Steve experiences nothing of the sort.

"Before, it used to be, you know, I used to like fighting a fire," Steve tells me. "I used to like getting that adrenaline rush. Now it's just more about, you make the money and make sure that everybody's safe. I don't even get the adrenaline rush anymore. It's just the job. Yeah, for the first three or four seasons, yeah, you were on this fire, you get excited about it. Now, it's—the only reason I want fires is 'cause it's more money. I know Allen doesn't get a rush like he used to. Unless it's a big one like the Beaver Creek fire, but these little ones? Nothin'. When I drive to a fire, I start thinking about what do we need to do, the weather, and all this stuff. I had to transfer from, 'Yeah, I get to fight a fire!' to 'How do I deal with this fire?'"

When Steve stepped into his position as engine operator, the responsibility of managing and ordering an engine crew diluted the high of battling the fire, and now fires translate only into larger paychecks (a topic I will address later), not larger thrills. But those in supervisory positions are not the only ones who feel this way. Donald, for example, shares Steve's views. "When I first got into this, it gave me an adrenaline rush. And the more I'm into this, it's not that way so much. It's my job. It's the job I do."

The thirst for action, for the rush, motivates some crewmembers to return to Elk River every year, but stronger is their love for fire itself. Moreover, for those like Steve and Donald, the rush is a rare sensation; the buzz that used to zip through their nerves during their youthful days on the fireline has run its course and been quelled.[11] For them firefighting is not an adventure but a business.[12] Though pyromaniacal passion and adrenaline addiction are significant enticements for the men at Elk River, there is something stronger still. There is something beyond these motivations that draws young men back to the forest each year, and I believe this something is the sanctuary of the fire station itself. Elk River Fire Station—the place itself—is the principal seduction. Veteran wildland firefighter and historian Stephen Pyne, whose nickname, I have been told, is "Pyromaniac," seems to know this: "But none of us is solely interested in fire alone. Smokechasing—the practice of finding and attacking wildland fires—is not just an adventure; it's a life. We relish this place."[13]

Elk River

The Elk River Fire Station nests in the forestland of northern Arizona. Only ponderosa pines, oaks, and mixed conifers neighbor the small commune; the nearest town is fifty miles due west. Herds of elk and deer, snakes, rabbits, squirrels, birds of all colors, and bugs of all sizes are regularly seen at Elk River. But besides the firecrew, people are not. In the early morning, as the crew sleeps beneath dawn's amber glow, the only noise you hear is the *shhh* of the wind cutting through swaying pine needles and the timid peeps of morning birds. The station is in the mountains, well above six thousand feet. You do not need a map to know this. You can tell by the air—thin, cold, crisp virgin air. This is where we live and work, where we play and toil, where we sleep, eat, and exercise. It is a simple place, an isolated place, surrounded only by nature. But undoubtedly, it is *our* place.

The work station is a compound bordered by a chain-link fence. Two parallel strips of buildings, stained in a deep redwood finish with cream trim, face each other fifty yards apart. One strip houses the offices and workshops. Within this strip, the main conference room occupies the building closest to the large swinging gate (the only entrance into the compound). This is where we gather each day during morning briefings and sit around four wooden tables pushed together to form a large rectangle. The building also houses offices for Thurman, Allen, and other fire supervisors. To the right of the main conference room is the saw shop, where most of our woodworking takes place, then the auto shop, followed by the sign shop, where we house Forest Service signs, and last, a large storage area filled with old rusted tools, stacks of tires, old household appliances (like washing machines), rolls of chicken wire, lumber, and boxes of fuses. The other strip of buildings holds our main weapon against fire—the engines. In large bays, four fire engines are parked facing outward, kept filled to the brim with both gasoline and water. Wildland firefighting engines resemble structural firefighting engines only in name. The engines at Elk River are considerably smaller, light green (not red), and equipped with four-wheel drive. Their cabs seat only three crewmembers. The tool cache, by far the most frequented room in the station, where fire tools are stored and sharpened, is next to the engine bays. The cache is lit by a long fluorescent light that shines down on piles of shovels,

combis, Pulaskis, McLeod rakes, files, sandpaper, canisters of spray paint, and a large wooden workbench with several vises.

Between these two building strips is a circle of grass, half shaded by two looming hundred-year-old pines. This is where the crew begins each day with an hour of physical training (PT). Each morning from 8:00 to 9:00, dressed in gym shorts, running shoes, and faded T-shirts, we form a circle in the grass and begin our routine with stretches, jumping jacks, sit-ups, and push-ups. After this warm-up session, our training period can include anything from running five miles to lifting weights. Most days we run two to three miles on hiking trails, although this distance is longer or shorter depending on our workload the day before, which supervisor is running PT, and how angry that supervisor is with the crew.

Some crewmembers take PT more seriously than others. Scott, for example, cannot be beaten on a run. He is a young Hopi in his second season of firefighting. At the end of this season he will begin his junior year in Northern Arizona University's wildlife biology program. Like many of his coworkers, Scott hopes to secure a permanent job with the Forest Service, but, uniquely, he does not want to remain in the fire sector; he wants to be a biologist for the wildlife management division. About five feet five inches tall and weighing approximately 140 pounds, Scott is the smallest member of the crew, but he flies on the trail. Each time we run during PT, he whips the rest of us by at least a minute or two.

Three large tanks used to fuel the engines, two filled with unleaded gasoline and one with diesel fuel, sit at the far end of the station. Beside these large white tanks is a small pump house with hoses that we use to refill the engines' water tanks after they have been drained on a fire. On the opposite side of the compound are two large storage sheds filled with flammable materials such as paints, oil, chain saws, and flares. Because Elk River is equipped with its own gasoline and water supplies as well as hundreds of tools used to repair the fire engines and trucks, the crew rarely has to travel into the nearby town except for groceries and other personal items. (When not on fires, we are required to provide all our own meals.)

Directly behind the work station, outside the fenced border, is another building strip—crew quarters—stained in the same deep redwood finish as the buildings in the station. Three long buildings in a row house four individual units, each shared by two crewmembers. Each room has a kitchen with a small stove and refrigerator and a living room furnished with couches and chairs that look like garage sale rejects. In some couches the foam stuffing has been pulverized by insects or dissolved by age, and when someone sits on them a tan mist rises. The floors are overlaid with pale yellow linoleum, and the wood-paneled walls are sparsely decorated with Forest Service posters from the 1970s showcasing Smokey the Bear pointing like Uncle Sam and repeating his famous line: "Only *you* can prevent forest fires." Each unit has its own bathroom with a three-by-three-foot shower, a white plastic shower curtain (which turns black at the bottom by the end of fire season from dirt and ash), a sink, and a toilet. None of the rooms have air conditioning or heating systems, which does not bother any of my crewmembers. Allen and Vince are the only ones who do not live at crew quarters. They commute to Atwater each day (a fifty-minute drive one way) to be with their wives and children.

Most rooms have two parallel twin beds about five feet apart; some have bunk beds. The mattresses are plastic-covered, and they feel as if they were stuffed with rubber. Whenever Tank, my roommate, shifts in bed, his mattress squeaks. Tank and I don't talk much when we're falling asleep, although sometimes a conversation emerges about girlfriends, the future, or the job, and we lie talking in the darkness until one of us doesn't answer back.

Our room is kept fairly clean and well organized. Steve's room is usually tidy and is sparsely decorated with St. Louis Rams memorabilia; Bryan's room is spotless most of the time and houses a computer and a handful of books including titles by Norman Maclean, Cornel West, and Jon Krakauer. Bryan even burns scented candles. But these are the exceptions—most of the rooms at crew quarters are pigsties. Living rooms are adorned by empty beer cans and spittoons made of plastic water bottles or aluminum cans with their tops pushed in, half full of tobacco juice. Dirty dishes and overflowing trash cans sit next to televisions hooked up to the latest video game system, with red and yellow wires trailing in every direction.

Most of the crewmembers don't go to the trouble of decorating their rooms at all, except for Peter, who has a room to himself. His walls bear wood-framed paintings of cowboys gathering their herds at sunset on the open range. Peter's room also has a deluxe stereo system, a medium-sized television with surround sound, hundreds of movies on DVD, and, to top everything, a small satellite dish mounted on the roof, which brings in hundreds of channels. His room is also one of only two with phone lines. The only other line is in the laundry room at the far end of crew quarters, next to a washer and dryer and a pool table that the crew communally purchased at the beginning of the season. Outside the laundry room, the words "Elk River 2003 Fire Crew" are imprinted in a newly laid sidewalk, traced with a stick while the concrete was still wet. Fourteen right handprints, fourteen sets of initials (including my own), and two Copenhagen lids also mark the sidewalk. To stay at crew quarters, we are charged forty-five dollars a month, including utilities. Rent is taken directly out of our paychecks.

Wildland firefighters are paid according to federal guidelines, and because this is my fourth season, my pay grade is GS-4, step 1: $10.91 an hour. During my first season at Elk River, I made $8.42 an hour as a GS-2. Most of my crewmembers qualify for the GS-3 rate, $9.18 an hour.[14] We earn time and a quarter during fires, aptly called hazard pay, or H-pay for short, and time and a half for overtime. Overtime is not optional for wildland firefighters. When a fire busts, we may be on the blaze until midnight, and in the days that follow, our workdays stretch to ten, twelve, and even fourteen hours. It is not rare for wildland firefighters to work between seventy and eighty hours a week, but this doesn't seem to bother my crewmembers. Hazard and overtime pay translates into bigger paychecks at the end of the month. For many, especially those in dead-end and low-skill jobs, the money they earn at Elk River in three to four months is almost equivalent to (and sometimes more than) what they make the rest of the year. The GS-3 rate that Diego earns as a firefighter is much more than the minimum wage he brings in during the off-season while working at his family's restaurant (or, in earlier years, at fast-food chains). "Money is good," he tells me. "That's probably what everybody says first of all:

the money. But not everybody wants to put their life on the line just for a paycheck." Economic incentives help to draw Diego (and many others) to the profession of wildland firefighting; but economic incentives are not the only motivation, nor are they the strongest.

Diego's economic interests would be better served if he remained in a permanent position in the labor market, where he could take advantage of the benefits that come with full-time employment. Crewmembers who are temporarily employed receive no benefits and no health insurance. And since they are seasonal workers in the summer, they are also seasonal workers in the winter, which means they lose out on benefits from their off-season jobs as well. Because wildland firefighters consistently return to the Forest Service each summer, they forfeit opportunities offered by other employers such as pay increases, promotions, and benefit packages. In addition, they have no guarantee as to how long their positions will last. They could be let go after two months, for instance, if the monsoons come early and the forest does not ignite.[15] If firefighters were only in it for the money, they would secure permanent positions in the labor market that offer better chances of long-term economic advancement. And since firefighting is one of the most popular blue-collar professions in America, often garnering hundreds of applications for a handful of open positions, it is safe to assume that a job as a clerk, a mechanic, or a salesperson would be significantly easier to attain than a sought-after spot on a firecrew.[16]

Although wildland firefighting does not provide my crewmembers with the most profitable means of earning a living, Elk River does give them something of value, something they regard as very precious. It offers them a place of their own, a place where they can carve their names into the sidewalk, an isolated piece of the world where they feel they belong. In their eyes, Elk River is their cleft in the rock, their refuge—from supervision and laws, and from women and city boys and their suffocating civilization.

A Day of Patrolling

On an overcast morning in early June, the Elk River Firecrew stands on top of a steep cliff, peering over jagged rocks and scattered pines hundreds of feet below and allowing the strong updraft scooting up the cliff's face to flow under their chins and through their hair. A large portion of the cliff's soft slope, off to the right, is scarred with dead oaks and downed pines from a devastating fire that raced through this area in 1990, burning hundreds of acres and killing six firefighters. Leafless white trunks rise

from the green undergrowth of wild grass and small shrubs, and as I trace the fire's path (still very visible thirteen years later), I can see where the blaze roared up the cliff wall, barreled across the road where our engines and trucks are now parked, and tore through a large meadow behind us. The fire overtook the crew in a shallow draw not far from here. The fatality report said that some firefighters ran uphill from the advancing flames with their unfolded fire shelters in their hands, tearing at the thin silvery material until the fire chased them down.

But on this cloudy morning my crewmembers are not concerned with such morbid memories. They are engaged in a rock-rolling competition. Donald started it. While his crewmembers stood in silence on the cliff's edge, he picked up a large rock with both hands, a rock weighing sixty pounds, I would guess, and heaved it over the cliff. The others watched excitedly as the rock rolled down the cliff, bouncing off other rocks and over saplings. When that rock had finished its descent, J.J., Tank, Kris, Diego, and others, without saying a word, spread out to look for small boulders that would best Donald's. Crewmembers are now throwing one large rock after another off the escarpment.

With great exertion, Diego carries a weighty rock to the edge and lets it fly. The rock plunges downward and picks up speed. It launches itself over a part of the cliff that juts out. "Yes! Yes! Go rock!" Diego yells. But just as he says this, the rock smashes into the ground, splits in two, and skids to a halt.

"Damn it!" Diego vents playfully.

"Boo," some crewmembers jeer.

Tanks drops a rock; then Kris, then Donald again, then J.J. Rock after rock tumbles down the cliff, rolling farther and farther, to the crewmembers' cheers, which echo over the drop-off. Soon the only way we can tell how far a rock has rolled is by the shaking trees and shrubs near the base of the cliff.

J.J. rolls a large rock to the edge. "I'm gonna try to cause a rockslide," he announces.

He positions his boulder above a portion of the cliff covered with loose rocks and pushes it off. "Go! Go, fucker!" he yells as the boulder races down the cliff. It meets the other rocks and drags a few down with it.

"Yes!" J.J. yells, slightly short of breath. "I'm gonna try it again."

"Man, López, you better cut that shit out," warns Steve, who has abstained from the competition.

"Why?" asks J.J., insolently.

"Because," Steve replies motioning to the rocks below, "those rocks hitting could cause a spark, and, shit, *you* know how dry it is right now. You don't need much to start a fire."

"Good! I hope it does start a fire! I hope it burns up this whole cliff!"

"Fuck around, fuck around, soon you won't *be* around!" Steve chants, using one of his favorite singsongs.

"Shit," J.J. mumbles. He picks up a few smaller rocks and throws them over the cliff, but no other large rocks are sent tumbling down.

After a few minutes, Steve suggests, "Well, we should probably head on out."

The crew walks back to the road and climbs in the trucks, and we start off for somewhere else. We are patrolling today, driving through dirt roads, stopping here and there, and waiting for a lightning bolt to zip down from a rain cloud, strike a dead snag, and send a trail of black smoke curling up against the slate gray sky. After thirty minutes or so of driving, Steve turns his engine off the main road, drives a short distance down a narrow track, and parks beside Paquesi Pit. The two chase trucks following him do the same, and we all lazily climb out and stretch. Paquesi Pit, or simply the Pit, is a shallow stagnant pond, overgrown with reeds and weeds, a stone's throw from Paquesi Perch Lookout Tower. We often spot white cranes standing on one leg in the greenish brown algae-crusted water or see a herd of elk drinking at the edge. Though not particularly pretty, the Pit is one of the crew's favorite spots to hide out while patrolling, not only because it is secluded and an unpopular camping spot but also because it sits just off the intersection of three main forest roads and thus is a good launching point should a lookout call in a smoke.

The air is cold and damp, and most crewmembers have put on hooded sweatshirts. Soon a game of pinecone baseball starts up. Making do with what is at hand, Diego and Kris select a few choice sticks, while Tank gathers cones and places them at an improvised pitcher's mound. J.J., the self-designated pitcher, hurls pinecones at a stick-swinging batter who, if he connects solidly, can send the cone flying twenty feet at best. I sit on the tailgate of the chase truck, chewing sunflower seeds and watching the game, which lasts a few innings until crewmembers grow bored and move on to something else.

Soon J.J. presents a new contest, a trick he learned from the Jameson Hotshots. He takes a dollar bill from his wallet and wedges it horizontally between two small rocks on the ground. Once the bill is secure, he announces, "All right, now watch." He stands on his right leg, gripping his left ankle behind him with his right hand, and tries to lower himself down, without touching the ground with his left hand, and pick up the dollar with his mouth. He bends lower and lower until finally he loses his balance and topples forward into the dirt, leaving the dollar undisturbed. He laughs, jumps up, dusts himself off, and says, "Okay. Anyone who can snag that dollar like that, with one leg up, can keep it."

A rough line forms immediately. The gig is on. One crewmember after another tries to answer J.J.'s challenge, and one after another falls face-first into the dirt. After ten minutes of failed attempts, Peter replaces Washington with Lincoln, for extra incentive, and the game heats up: crewmembers cheer each other on and seem to get their mouths closer and closer to the money with each try. Finally Peter bites down on the bill and lifts himself up, accomplishing what seemed an impossible task. After bowing overdramatically to a round of overdramatic applause, he replaces the bill and the game resumes. A few other crewmembers meet J.J.'s challenge. J.J. then folds the bill in half, to place it closer to the ground and increase the level of difficulty, and contestants line up again.

As the game continues, I slip out the small notebook in the side pocket of my Nomex fire pants and begin jotting down some of my observations and thoughts. I know we are going to be here a while longer, since earlier today the head fire supervisor for Wannokee announced over the radio that all firecrews will stay on until 7:00 in case lightning strikes. I scribble down several pages of notes, losing myself in my writing, until someone slaps my leg.

It's George. "You got five on it?"

I stop writing, look up from my notebook, and ask, "Five on what?"

"On Donald swimming across the Pit!" George answers with a huge smile.

"Oh, hell yes!"

I pocket my notebook, jump down from the tailgate, take five bucks from my wallet, and follow George as he heads hastily for the crew, who has abandoned the money-on-the-ground game and are now standing at the edge of the Pit. J.J. is collecting money, while Donald turns from the Pit to his crewmembers, considering whether the stunt is worth it.

"Thirty-two bucks, Donald!" J.J. broadcasts, after nearly everyone has pitched in. "Man, thir-ty-*twoooo* bucks. That's a lot of money for a little swim."

Donald looks at the bills J.J. waves in front of him. He smiles and scrunches up his brow, still unsure.

"*Maaaaan,* thirty-two dollars," Diego chimes in. "That's like, what, three hours of normal work! You can buy a lot of shit for thirty-two bucks."

"I don't know. I don't know," Donald responds.

"Oh, come *on,*" J.J. taunts. "Before, you said you'd swim it for twenty bucks. Now we have thirty-two dollars, and you're still thinking about this?"

Crewmembers back J.J. Everyone, even Steve, wants to see if Donald will take the plunge. *Shit, I'd do it for thirty-two dollars. That's, like, two DVDs. Didn't you just say you'd do it for twenty? It's not that bad, like swimming in a lake.* Finally Donald caves and starts removing his watch and necklaces. Crewmembers cheer and smile at one another. Donald begins to unlace his boots.

"What are you doing?" asks J.J., loudly.

"Taking off my boots," Donald answers.

"No way. *That* wasn't in the bet. You should have to do it with your boots on!"

"That's like ten pounds on each foot!"

"So! That's the fuckin' deal!" J.J. yells back.

"Come on, López," Peter advises, smiling. "Let him take off his fuckin' shoes, damn."

Most of the crewmembers back Donald this time. So Donald takes off his boots, but not his shirt, pants, or socks. Then, he nods at us spectators, jogs up to the foul water, and dives in head first.

A groan of disgust rises up from the crowd, followed by hearty laughter. I think of leeches.

Keeping his face submerged, Donald swims freestyle through the murky water. Shoreline to shoreline is about fifty yards, and as he paddles and kicks and splashes through the Pit, J.J. runs along the shoreline pointing his finger, and lets out a high-pitched, mocking laugh. J.J. meets Donald as he climbs out of the water on the far bank, dripping from head to foot, and hands him the money.

Donald sloshes back to the crew shivering, with his hair plastered against his head, his clothes soaked and sticking to his body, and his arms folded tightly across his chest. But he greets us with a healthy grin.

"Donald, you are a fuckin' dumbass," Steve observes.

"*Nooooo* doubt," J.J. agrees.

"A major, *major* dumbass," Diego says, still laughing.

As Donald pulls his boots over wet socks, crewmembers walk slowly back to the trucks and talk about how much money it would take for them to swim across the Pit. Most settle on a hundred dollars as the minimum.

By the time Donald makes it back to the trucks and does his best to dry off on his sweatshirt, it's time to head back to the station and call it a day. I climb into a truck with J.J. and Donald.

J.J. starts the truck, stares at Donald, soaked and shivering, and roars with laughter. I join him, and Donald, thirty-two dollars richer, contributes a few chuckles of his own.

"Was it worth it?" I ask.

"Oh, yeah," Donald says, matter-of-factly. "For thirty bucks? Definitely."

"You are the dumbest fuck on the planet," J.J. goads. "You are most definitely the dumbest person I know."

Donald smiles, shrugs, and looks out the window.

As J.J. drives down the road, following Steve's engine, he says, "Man, I act stupid out here. You know why? I act stupid out here because it's fun and everybody laughs."

Donald and I smile at J.J., who loves to make people laugh, especially at someone else's expense.

"So, do you think you feel freer in the forest?" I ask.

"Yes," J.J. and Donald reply simultaneously.

The Freedom of the Forest

The rock-rolling competition, Donald's swim across the Pit, and the brief conversation with J.J. and Donald that followed motivated me to ask all my crewmembers some questions about how they act in the forest compared with how they act in other spaces. Several weeks after this incident, for example, Diego joined me in my room after work for a game of chess. After suffering an embarrassing loss, an outcome I had grown quite familiar with from playing Diego, I asked the self-proclaimed "chess master," "Do you think that you specifically act differently in the forest than you do in town?"

"Yeah. Very much so," he answered. "A good example of that is the cussing. *Everybody* cusses more out here 'cause no one gives a *shit*. . . . I'll cuss around my friends, but not nearly as much, unless I'm drunk, but not nearly as much as out here. I never cussed that much until I came to work out here anyway. I got the *full perspective* of the alternative language."

"So what do you think makes you cuss more—that no one cares or that everyone else does it?"

"'Cause you hear it more. You're engulfed in a new language, basically. Like if you go to Mexico, and all year round it's Spanish-speaking people, you're gonna pick it up quick, and you're gonna be able to communicate. Out here, same way. You're just engulfed in it. Everybody says it. You figure out which phrases to use it in, and if you don't know the word, just use *shit*. That's like the universal adjective. So, it's just, like, like, you could say like your foot pedal thing there." Diego pointed to my dictaphone pedal attached to the tape recorder. "What's that shit? It's an adjective." Then he raised his glass of juice. "This is some good shit. Maybe, I don't know, it's V-8 Splash. See, a universal adjective. So, you're just engulfed in it."

Elk River welcomes a cut-loose flow of vulgarity, whereas the "city," which in this specific context can mean anything from a small town like Atwater to a metropolis like Phoenix, requires bounded, carefully executed, courteous language. As my crewmembers navigate between the two places, they acquire two distinct dispositions with distinct languages. Slippages are bound to occur. After returning from a day off, Tank, still unfamiliar with the bilingual existence of the wildland firefighter, explained that he cursed for the first time in his life in front of his mother. He confessed to a grinning audience during morning PT stretches: "Dudes, I said *fuck* in front of my *mom* yesterday. I was talking to Kris, and it just came out. I have never used the f-word in front of her! I was so embarrassed, and it's *all you fuckers' faults!*"[17]

At Elk River, crewmembers reject the constraining and cleanly requirements of the city through their "alternative language" as well as through their bodies. Whereas the city boy conforms to the etiquette of civilization—delicate, soft, mannered, clean, educated; in a word, feminine civilization—the firefighters at Elk River actively resist it.[18] Unshaven faces complement dirty clothes. Loud voices complement dirty language. Bodily functions are anything but caged. But when my crewmembers leave the forest setting to venture into a nearby town, they clean up their act. They comb their hair, tuck in their shirts, and curb their vulgarity.

When I accompanied the crew to Atwater to close down a sports bar for George's twenty-first birthday bash, I witnessed a transformation of sorts in my crewmembers' appearance and mannerisms.

I walked into Dave's Sports Bar and Grill at 10:00 p.m. with my fiancée Tessa and came upon a group of men I hardly recognized. J.J.'s hair, usually tucked under a baseball cap, was gelled and parted on the side. He wore a tight new gray shirt that you might see at a hip club in Phoenix. His pants had been pressed. Tank kept his hat, as did Donald, but both sported collared shirts and clean blue jeans. The two circled a pool table, eyes locked on the green felt, playing for money. Other crewmembers, with styled hair, shaved faces, and collared shirts, leaned against the bar and arcade games holding pints of beer. A few looked up from their glasses, noticed me, and shouted in unison over the AC/DC blaring from the jukebox, "Hey *Desmondoooo!*"

I smiled as I pulled up a bar stool, thinking to myself that these pretty boys stood in sharp contrast to the rowdies I'd left back at Elk River that afternoon. My smile broke into a laugh when I smelled someone's cologne. I introduced Tessa to the gang. When I got to Peter, he took off his cowboy hat, bowed slightly, and extended his hand almost daintily.

"Two Amber Bocks, please," I told the middle-aged Hispanic woman behind the bar.

"Just put it on my tab," Peter instructed, waving his hand flippantly.

"Well, thank you, good sir," I replied, shaking Peter's hand. "You're looking mighty sharp tonight, boy!"

Whereas week-worn pants and old T-shirts usually hung off his body, that night Peter was decked out head-to-toe in formal western garb. He sported brown Justin boots below snug new dark blue Wranglers, cinched by a brown leather belt with an oversized gold-and-silver rodeo buckle. His long-sleeved shirt, striped in blue and light red, was tucked in and buttoned all the way up, and a handsome black felt Stetson shadowed his clean-shaven face.

I spent most of the night at Dave's on that barstool, taking in the pool games, watching the uncomfortable interactions between crewmembers and their young girlfriends, which reminded me of the timid courting rituals of a high school dance. Peter's girlfriend, for whom he had bought an $8,000 diamond "friendship ring," was anything but timid or nervous. She fed the jukebox quarter after quarter and sang along with Garth Brooks, CCR, the Eagles, and Bruce Springsteen. Everyone seemed to be having a good time, but there was an awkwardness and unfamiliarity to it all. J.J. was quiet and cool-headed; Kris spoke softly and stood up straight; Peter was relaxed but not too relaxed. There was a stiffness to their movements, made even more rigid by their starched and clean clothing, and a polished politeness in their hushed speech.

The only one who actively cut loose was George, who got sloppy drunk because crewmembers kept buying him shots of hard liquor. Bryan and I ordered up a shot that most folks I know try for the first and last times on their twenty-first birthdays: "The Three Wise Men," a disgusting concoction of Jack Daniels, Jim Beam, and José Cuervo. The bartender misheard our order, however, and produced a full shot glass of each inebriant. So we presented George with three birthday presents instead of one, a gesture, I am inclined to believe, that contributed significantly to his headache the next morning.

Except for George, who stumbled out of Dave's at 11:00 p.m., held up by his girlfriend, after giving everybody a hug, my crewmembers were unusually impassive throughout the evening. To them Dave's, though a no-frills sports bar, nonetheless required some control and etiquette. They were no longer hidden deep within the forest but were exposed to the scrutinizing and civilizing gaze of others, some of whom knew them and their parents intimately—and they had to act the part of gentlemen for a night.

But at Elk River the opposite rules seemed to apply. Tidiness and restraint would offend. Crewmembers were not the only ones to uphold such patterns of messiness; sometimes supervisors would reinforce this cultural code as well. I learned this lesson during one of Thurman's "surprise inspections."

One day, near the beginning of the season, I was sitting in the conference room with the rest of the crew when, at 4:55, Steve announced, faking nonchalance, "You *might* think about cleaning your rooms tonight. Word has it that Thurman might pay us a little visit tomorrow morning."

Allen had leaked the information to Steve, and they grinned at each other while watching crewmembers' worried faces. Because I took Thurman very seriously, I marched straight into my room to clean everything once Allen dismissed the crew at 5:00. The inspection came at an unfortunate time for me, since Tank had left the station after work on his day off, so I had to shoulder all the domestic labor. I scrubbed the toilet and shower, polished the sink, and mopped the floor. By nightfall the room was immaculate and begging to be inspected. Allowing my freshly mopped floor to dry, I strolled down the line of rooms. Some of my crewmembers had cleaned up, but not with the same care I had. And to my surprise, Peter, J.J., and Donald, whose rooms needed the most cleaning, had paid little heed to Steve's warning. J.J. and Donald had spent the evening with their girlfriends, who had driven up from Atwater, and Peter had watched a movie in his slovenly room.[19] Their indifference caught me off guard, and as I walked away puzzled, I couldn't help smiling to myself, predicting the spectacle of a Thurman-style reprimand.

Rex Thurman—by all accounts—is a badass. Standing well over six feet, his thick figure looms above the crew he leads. Thinning black-and-gray hair softly folds to the right of his sun-spotted scalp, and an unkempt beard hangs four inches below his pale face, dark near his mouth and ashy at the tips. At forty-seven, he is waiting for retirement from the Forest

Service, where he has served since 1975. When Thurman laughs, so does the crew. When he is stern, we shut up. Although a handful of my crewmembers are not particularly fond of Thurman, they all respect him—and fear him—as do many other firefighters, young and old, in other districts. A firefighter named Jeremy Stocklen, stationed in Jameson, who has been fighting fire as long as Thurman and now serves as a law enforcement officer for the Wannokee Forest, once told me with absolute sincerity, "You know, Matt, there's only *one* firefighter on this forest, only one *real* firefighter, who has been through it all, and who I would trust with my life. And that's Rex Thurman."

The boss pulled into the station at 9:00 sharp the next morning. He summoned the crew to the conference room and explained that he would conduct a surprise inspection of crew quarters. We were instructed to stand outside our rooms while Thurman marched through them. My room was one of the last to be inspected, and because of my placement in line, I could watch Thurman react to J.J., Donald, and Peter.

Thurman emerged from J.J. and Donald's wasteland, casually suggested they try to tidy things up now and then, and moved to the next room. His reaction was certainly not the verbal beat-down I had predicted from a man known for a vituperative tongue that regularly left crewmembers' egos bashed and bruised. I was puzzled, but as the boss nodded at me on entering my room, I was confident that some trophy would be in order.

If J.J. and Donald had only received a few light suggestions, I was surely due for a pay raise.

After spending thirty seconds in my room and whistling as if impressed, Thurman strode out and loudly asked, "So Desmond, you got a woman living there?"

Thurman stared at me, nodding with a closed-mouth grin. His eyes narrowed warmly, wrinkling the corners.

"Uh, excuse me?"

"Shit, that's one clean room! Now, I know *you* didn't clean that up. You must have a woman coming over here to clean it up for you." He leaned in. "Where is she? Is she hiding under your bed?"

I knew my crewmembers were having a ball with this. I felt my face flush.

"Uh, uh, nope," I stuttered. "All by myself." I never could joke around with Thurman.

"Well shit, Desmond, you should come over to my place and clean it up sometime." Then he stopped projecting his voice and mumbled, almost whispered, "Good job." He left me with that and proceeded to the next room.

I glanced down the row of doors, only to be taunted by my crewmembers' smirks and pointing fingers. My cleaning efforts had backfired. Thurman had chastised me for following the "on paper" rules too closely and missing the more important culturally valued rules of Elk River. On paper, the U.S. Forest Service demanded that our rooms be clean, but country masculinity advocated a different set of principles. Thurman wanted our rooms to be neat, of course, but not sparkling clean, not ladylike. I had overdone it. My exaggerated tidiness resembled the polish of the city boy, and Thurman let me know it.

This is not to say that every room at crew quarters is a pigsty or that every crewmember is a clown when Thurman isn't around. Far from it. As I mentioned earlier, Bryan keeps a rather clean room, as does Steve. Because these two men are trying to make a career out of firefighting, they have an interest in impressing Thurman and other Forest Service supervisors with their maturity and responsibility. They also work to distinguish themselves from the younger crewmembers and their juvenile antics. Bryan will sporadically join in wrestling matches and teasing rituals, but he often sits on the sidelines (sometimes rather pretentiously). And Steve, mature—stoic even—tends to avoid such shenanigans altogether. He often grows annoyed by crewmembers' boyish antics, as he did during the rock-rolling competition, and he seems to find companionship mostly with the older firefighters, like Allen and Nicholas, or the most reserved, like Bryan and Scott.

The content of the crewmembers' dialogue is often rude and raw, if only because rudeness and rawness are often funny: I once witnessed an energetic debate between Kris and Tank over what smells worse, a row of twenty portapotties (Tank's pick) or "Peter's ass" (Kris's pick—he won). But many times crewmembers engage in serious and sophisticated conversations on politics, history, and even the arts. Kris and I once carried on a conversation about Machiavelli's *The Prince* throughout an entire workday: during lunch hour, in between tasks, and while riding in trucks. He kept bringing up the subject, insistent on scrutinizing Machiavelli's strategies as a political analyst. On another occasion, the two of us sat on the ledge of a canyon in the middle of the Wannokee Forest and quizzed each other on the details of World War II (Kris won here, too). Donald sometimes spends his nights at crew quarters, and his days off, reading poetry and other literature. In fact, he once recited to me, from memory, "The Cremation of Sam McGee," a sizable poem by Robert Service, while we mopped up a fire.

Because each human being is infinitely complex and full of contradictions, labeling my crewmembers as always boorish or always messy is fundamentally misguided. Luckily, that is not my intention here. I aim to point out that Elk River does not require people to present "perfectly homogenous performances at every point in time";[20] it is not a workplace that expects, in Max Weber's words, a certain "bureaucratization of the spirit"[21] that requires workers to exhibit controlled, calm, and calculated speech and movement at all moments. Of course there are times at Elk River when discipline is demanded—when Thurman is around or when a fire busts—and there are times when supervisors chastise crewmembers for their lack of discipline. Once, for instance, Allen, exasperated because Kris, Tank, and a few others had recurrently showed up for the morning briefing a few minutes behind schedule, sat the crew down before PT for a tart talking-to.

"I'm tired of people coming in late all the time," Allen said, in short, loud sentences. "I'm tired of people coming in to work three, five minutes past nine after PT. And I'm tired of people complaining about PT all the time and walking on the trail. *Lazies!* We need to be in shape in case of a fire, and people are always complaining and being lazy and coming in late. If you keep this up, I will stop *everything*: no more breakfast in the morning, no more welfare, nothing. Got it?"[22]

Although there are moments like this when crewmembers are instructed to shape up, there are numerous other moments, moments of downtime, where they can cut loose. There was the time Kris spent all afternoon in the tool cache, while other crewmembers sharpened tools, constructing a wooden device that would help him shotgun beers, or the time we dropped things off Paquesi Perch to test their resilience; there was the time we spotted a herd of wild cattle that had escaped from a rancher and tried (unsuccessfully) to round them up. There was the time we met at Green Springs Valley to play baseball; the time we hid out at the lowland gully and had a pinecone war; the time we spent a good portion of the afternoon playing on the swing at Jack's Canyon; the time, while washing hoses caked with mud and soot from the last fire, everyone got dunked in the dirty water of the washing trough. There was the time Vince and George engaged each other in a tomahawk-throwing competition using a tomahawk Donald had made at work: the challenge was to see who could stick the tomahawk in a tree trunk first—the wager, a shaved head. George lost and then, under the terms of "double or nothing," he lost again and, accepting "triple or nothing," lost once more. After work that day, he lost his hair.[23]

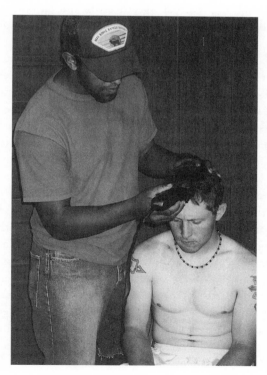

Crewmembers relish these "moments of waiting" lived out on the clock just as much as, and even more than, moments lived out on the fireline. Far from being "killed time" or "wasted time," downtime at Elk River is valued time, important time, in a word, prime time. Elk River—this isolated and country-masculine space—allows crewmembers to act in certain ways that are, in their eyes, prohibited in all other spaces. As such, it should not be surprising that many feel freer at Elk River than anyplace else.

"This job is one of the few jobs where you get to be in the middle of the woods and basically are in control of what you do most of the time," Kris tells me as we both kick back on the dilapidated couch in my room. His uncut thick black hair squeezes out from under a soiled blue mesh cap displaying the logo of the Hotshot crew his father once worked for. The bill shades a goatee under a thick wad of tobacco jammed in his lower lip. An unbuttoned flannel shirt surrounds a thin T-shirt he bought for fifty cents at the Atwater Goodwill store. He continues, "I like being out in the woods. I like being out here. I like the aspect that we're off on our own. I like how we don't have to worry about having to be, quote-unquote, 'perfect' [gestures for quotation marks] for everything we do in our appearances, our mannerisms, and our language, you know.

"You can be yourself in a lot of ways and not have to worry about your presentation to others. . . . Everyone shows up in their green pants and boots and a T-shirt. So I mean, it's not like you have to compete for anything. It's not like your appearance matters. All the little superficial things, how you look, how you shaved, are you clean shaved, are your clothes clean, you know, that don't really matter. . . . I'm going to be sucking down smoke, but that's just a small price to pay to be out here. To be able to see what I see and enjoy what I do."

"Do you act differently in the forest than you do at U of A?"

"Well, in the forest there's less emphasis on society's standards about how you act around others and how you interact around others. Around here I don't have to worry about if my clothes are acceptable. . . . You get away with wearing pants over and over and over again. You get to drive around the woods. Whatever you want to listen to you get to listen to. It's less conflicting here. There are less people to conflict with. . . . There's less of society's rules out here, I would say, because there's less actual laws out here. So, you really get to do what you want to do. It's not like you're constricted. . . . You feel freer. I do feel freer."

"Our Own Little City"

George swore off alcohol the day after his birthday party, but a few days later he fell off the wagon when we shared beers after an excruciatingly boring day of idle patrolling. Usually we patrol on the weekends to talk to campers and inform them of fire restrictions. Another rationale for patrolling is to observe the state of the forest, to get a sense of the vegetation's moisture (and thus to gauge how fire would take to it). But an unspoken purpose of patrolling is simply to get the crew out of the station. When we haven't seen action in a while we get antsy because, aside from the fifty-yard walk from crew quarters to the station, we do not move from an area of approximately fifteen acres for days. Patrolling changes the scenery a bit; plus, it makes us feel more like firefighters instead of painters, loggers, or janitors, though sometimes it too can dawdle on like a bad sermon.

Kris pulled up a chair and grabbed a beer with George and me. Seated outside Steve's room, we yapped away and enjoyed one another's wise-cracks and the beautiful weather. But that serenity didn't last long. Soon our crisscrossing conversation was interrupted by a subtle high-pitched whiz followed by a loud *Pop!* Donald was shooting off fireworks again. He had spent over $200 at the fireworks shop on the border of New Mexico a couple of weeks into the season.

"You better not hit me with one of those, you fuck," Kris yelled. "I'll run over there and whip your ass!"

Donald smiled and sent another one in our direction. I ducked down in my chair, worried I would take a bottle rocket to the face.

After a few more rockets landed at our feet, Kris slammed down his beer and muttered, "All right, that's *it!*" He stomped over to Donald and they scuffled a bit, but pretty soon Kris started shooting off fireworks too. George and J.J. joined the party, and the calm of the cool woods was soon drowned out by a cacophony of whizzes and pops and bangs and whistles. Bodies dived out of the way to avoid being pegged by flying bottle rockets, and we were all drinking and trash-talking each other and having a ripe old time.

Fireworks are illegal in Arizona. They are doubly illegal on the Wannokee Forest, since fire restrictions outlaw anything that could cause a spark. My crewmembers were well aware of this restriction, of course: They were the ones who informed campers about it. A few weeks before the fireworks battle, the crew drove around the forest and mounted large fluorescent orange-and-yellow plastic signs on the roadsides proclaiming

No Fireworks Allowed. But they didn't think that applied to them, not in their "own little city."

"It's kinda like it's our own little city," Bryan reflected. "The way I describe it to people is like, it's like its own country out here. Yeah, you have laws and stuff, blah, blah, blah, but out here, like, during fire restrictions, what are we doing? Having a barbeque when they are saying you can't have one, playing with fire when they say you're not supposed to be playing with fire in the forest. . . . We know it, but we don't care.

"And how often do you think of Phoenix living out here? I mean, how often, sitting out here, do you think, 'Oh yeah, there's a city right over there?' It doesn't feel like that. You're kinda in your own little country out here. And you got people stopping by and you're like, 'Hey you can't touch that! You can't go in there!'"

Many crewmembers delight not only in the freedoms they experience during the workday, but also in the freedoms they experience living at crew quarters. Underage drinking is one such freedom. Crewmembers younger than twenty-one enjoy being able to drink a beer in public. Kris observes, "Living at crew quarters, the rules and regulations are really lax, so it's a good place to find yourself. It's really fifteen guys that pretty much get to do what they want and are out here, like, I refer to alcohol a lot. It's not like I drink a lot or that I'm an alcoholic, but the thing about alcohol is that you get to sit on your porch at nineteen or sit with your boss at nineteen and have a beer with him."

By "boss," Kris is referring to Peter, his engine operator. Though Peter and Steve serve in supervisory positions during the workday, they more or less shed their leadership roles at crew quarters. Peter does this more than Steve, who sometimes tries to make sure crewmembers don't get too out of hand. Most of the time, Steve does not mobilize the power he has at work to control crewmembers' behavior at crew quarters; however, if crewmembers take part in an indulgent drinking party some night, Steve might suggest that Allen make the crew run the five-mile PT course the next morning. But this is a rare punishment, and a weak one at that, so most crewmembers see crew quarters as functioning without repercussions.

If no fires have ignited, then after work crewmembers drink beer, watch movies, play video games, shoot a round of pool, or light fireworks. Sometimes the guys who have the equipment tag each other with paintball guns. Other times, crewmembers grab their real guns and pile into pickup trucks to go rabbit hunting until dark. On nice days they make a quick snack and toss a fishing line into a nearby lake. No matter what they do, the point is that they feel free to do whatever they wish at Elk River.

"I've always liked it out here," Diego says, echoing Kris's reflections. "What better job to do when you're out in the woods every day? You're far away from civilization where you can do what the hell you want, say what you want. You form bonds with your friends out here, just like one big happy family. . . . Whatever job can you say that you live out in a place where you have nobody but your friends around you, nobody tells you you can and can't do this? . . . It's fun out here. You don't got people telling you what to do. You don't got people telling you what time to go to bed. Telling you what you can and can't do, what time you have to be here. You don't have rules. People set their own rules and *we're doing just fine.*"

Like many of his crewmembers, Diego did not leave home to attend college full time. In the off-season he lives with his parents, so it is not surprising that he views crew quarters as a space of liberation and merriment. To many of the younger firefighters at Elk River, crew quarters are what a freshmen dormitory is to first-semester college students: the first place they live outside their parents' houses. Naturally one would expect them to appreciate the benefits of, say, the freedom to set their own curfew or to chug a beer. Yet my crewmembers not only escape parents' supervision at Elk River, they also find refuge from "civilization" itself. As J.J. observes, "I'm not trying to go into Atwater and just act a fool, you know. It's not civilized, I would have to say. And out here I don't act so civilized, and it's okay. It's a release because you have this nine months of the year you have to go trying to act somewhat civilized and out here you can just go crazy. It's okay. I'm trying to be more respectable in Atwater. I'm trying to impress people, and out here you don't gotta do no impressing."

Why does J.J. feel he doesn't have to "do no impressing"? Why do Diego, Kris, and the rest of the crewmembers feel so free at Elk River? Part of the answer, of course, lies in their being isolated most of the time, not only from the direct supervision of overseers but also from that of virtually everybody else in the world—strangers, friends, and family alike. (However, we should not assume that anyone who came to Elk River would experience similar feelings of liberation, and more important, we should not believe Elk River is a place where the only rule is that there are no rules. I will take up this point in more detail shortly.) But a deeper part of the answer lies in the way the culture perpetuated at Elk River mirrors, endorses, and extends the culture most of my crewmembers grew up with. It functions as a country-masculine sanctuary, and *this*—not economic incentives, status, the lure of fire, or the stimulation of action—is the primary enticement that draws them back summer after summer.

Consider the motivations of one crewmember with a serious respiratory condition. He lied about it on his application and somehow managed to fool the doctor who gave him the physical examination that all firefighters must undergo at the beginning of each season. The whole crew knows about it, but no one says a word. The condition is so severe that during a fire last year, this crewmember thought he was going to suffocate from a violent reaction to heavy smoke; accordingly, he pulled himself off the fireline to write "good-bye" notes to his friends and family. And yet he continues to fight fire year after year because he loves Elk River.

"For me, it's not . . . , the fire aspect isn't as big of a deal. Personally, for me, I don't really care about going on fires. Fires make me sick. The day after a fire, I can't sleep that good. I cough up stuff all night and can't breathe for shit. For me, it's not the fire aspect that drives me out here. For me, it's what's out here, you know? . . . Just to be out here and have a beer after work, you know, just to come out here and not have it like being in town. It's just what's out here that's different, you know, that's why I really like it. . . . So for me it's not so much the fire aspect of it, because I'm just as happy working without a fire.

"What is it about this that's that good? What is it that kept me coming back? Like I said, it's one of the places where you can really be free, you know, be happy, at least for me. I don't know what it is out here. . . . I go back to [his location in the off-season] and start thinking about the summer, start thinking about being out here. And it's not the fire. I already told you that, it's not the fire that drives me. . . . If this is one of the few places that make me happy and stuff then, goddamn, I'm gonna come out here if I can. If I have to lie to get out here, I have to lie. If I have to neglect my health a little bit, I'll neglect my health a little bit. And I know I'm not going to be able to do this my whole life, I'm not gonna be able to do this another five years. I'm gonna have to stop pretty damn soon."

For this firefighter, the allure of wildland firefighting is not in the fire or the rush but in the place. Elk River itself beckons him back. But is his love for Elk River just as much a product of firefighting as a cause of joining and returning? After all, people tend to find the good in dire situations; this certainly applies even (perhaps especially) to dominated groups who not only accept conditions that other groups would despise and reject but find ways to remain content—sometimes even happy—in those conditions. Homeless people sometimes claim they chose their lot, and impoverished drug dealers have been known to argue that their trade is superior to better-paying ones in the formal economy.[24] More often than not, rather than resist hardship and oppression, people learn to accept, rationalize, and even enjoy it. As Goffman argues, "Whatever his position in society, the person insulates himself by blindness, half-truths, illusions, and rationalizations. He makes an 'adjustment' by convincing himself, with tactful support from his inner circle, that he is what he wants to be and that he would not do to gain his ends what the others have done to gain theirs."[25] If this is so, should we not expect my crewmembers to partake, like others, in practices of "adjustment" by falling in love with their fate—*amor fati,* as Nietzsche might say—and painting a picture of firefighting with especially romantic brushstrokes?

Absolutely. Indeed, it would be unreasonable not to expect as much. My crewmembers easily forget that wildland firefighting demands that they place their bodies in harm's way, forfeit any control over their time, and work incredibly long hours for mediocre wages. When attempting to comprehend firefighters' motivations, we must not forget the often un-spoken downside of the profession or mistake firefighters' accounts for social mechanisms.[26] The reason individuals become firefighters cannot be found solely at Elk River itself, for it is also found in the economic bleak-ness of American Indian reservations, the land loss taking place in rural America, the inability of small-town communities to carry out economic development strategies in the face of global demands, and the rising costs of higher education. Firefighters' admiration for their craft must be con-ceptualized as molded (in part) by a process of adapting to such socioeco-nomic structures.

But this does not imply that the motivations crewmembers articulate for joining, and returning to, a firecrew are phony or contrived: on the contrary, they run deep and are steeped in sincerity. Rather, it implies that their motivations are partially structured by the social, cultural, political, and economic contexts where they were formed. Nor does it imply that crewmembers would automatically accept other jobs that offered higher wages and job security. I believe most would forgo such opportunities to keep fighting fire, or more specifically to keep living and working at Elk River. Consider how Diego responded after I told him, "If you didn't work fighting fire, if you worked in a permanent job, if you worked at a local dealership selling cars, you'd make more the whole year round and would have benefits."

He replied: "It's boring. . . . Over there [at Elk River], there was never the same day, and if there was a day that was kinda boring, by the end of the day you already had a story to tell about it, 'cause somethin' was going to happen—somethin'! It was different. It was *variety* out there . . . made you want to go to work in the morning. You go work at a car dealership, all you do is sell cars. You tell somebody the same shit you told the last twenty people. . . . Same shit, over and over. That shit gets boring. That's why I like going out there. It might be for three months, but it's the funnest three months. . . . It's the *place*."

Crewmembers trade economic stability for a sense of place, of home.[27] Firefighters are in it not primarily for the money or the rush or the status but for the freedom, a freedom produced when the country-masculine habitus discovers a world where it recognizes itself and can thrive.[28]

Of course, on closer inspection, we see that Elk River is much more structured and constricted than my crewmembers would have it. This space does not operate without rules; rather, it is highly structured by the codes of country masculinity. If it were truly a utopian space of freedom, I would have the liberty to keep a clean room, to drink scotch instead of Keystone Light, or to eat tofu stir-fry without facing ridicule. And more fundamentally, if Elk River were truly some "anything goes" place, some "permanent back region" where people could throw off all social standards, then, ironically, it would not feel so free.[29] If my crewmembers experience a sense of emancipation, it is not because of a genuine lack of rules (a social impossibility) but because they are so well adjusted to the rules of Elk River (the mandates of country masculinity) that they fail to feel the weight of social strictures. Their freedom, to use Émile Durkheim's phrase, is "the fruit of regulation." It is a sensation produced not by the absence of rules but by an abundance of rules: cultural rules governing everyday forms of conduct that are so deeply familiar to my crewmembers that they are taken for granted. To put it crudely, at Elk River one is "required" to curse, to dress sloppily, to trash his room, to drink beer, and to wrestle. Failing at these tasks violates regulations of country masculinity and is punished by withholding something of dire importance: *belonging*. The structure of Elk River, then, is found in its lack of structure; its discipline in its lack thereof.

PART TWO

Training and Discipline

3

A Joke between Brothers

In the middle of a July afternoon, Donald rode in the passenger seat of his purplish Nissan truck while a fifteen-year-old high school cheerleader named Carolyn tried her hand at driving stick shift. Jayme's and Jill's hair whipped their faces as they sat on the edge of the truck bed, gripping the hot aluminum sides, white-knuckled as the vehicle sped down the road from Horseshoe Lake to Atwater at thirty miles an hour. Donald was enjoying his day off with these teenage admirers until Carolyn looked back to see what Jayme and Jill were laughing about and, on hearing Donald yell "Hit the Brakes! Brakes!" saw that she had drifted onto the loose gravel shoulder and frantically over-adjusted, sending the truck cartwheeling into a front flip.

The roll launched Jayme and Jill into the air like crag from a medieval catapult. When they landed twenty-five feet later, their swimsuit-clad bodies skipped and twisted over asphalt sprinkled with gravel and glass. The Nissan slammed back onto its tires, jolting Carolyn, unbelted, from her seat and into the hard plastic steering wheel. Warm blood began sliding off her face.

Planning to meet Donald and the girls, J.J. headed to Horseshoe Lake immediately after work. When he happened upon the accident, he saw the red flashing ambulance lights first, causing him to slow his Mustang to a crawl, and Donald's crumpled truck second. He stopped, pulled the emergency brake, bounded out, and sprinted toward the paramedics. He found Donald, who had been wearing his seat belt, sitting on the back bumper of an ambulance, seemingly unharmed and trying to convince a large woman with a stethoscope that he was fine and needed no further help. The girls were not so lucky. All three were rushed to the hospital, including Jayme—J.J.'s girlfriend of six months.

Assured that Donald was fine, J.J. rushed to his car and headed for Atwater Hospital, steering with one hand and dialing the Elk River Station on his cell phone with the other.

Someone picked up: "Elk River."

"Hey, it's J.J. Donald's been in an accident."

"Wha—?"

"His truck flipped on the way back from Horseshoe. He's okay, but tell everyone. Jayme was with him. She's at the hospital now. Donald's going to the hospital too. I gotta go."

"O-O-Okay. Okay, bye."

Forty minutes later the entire firecrew strode through the automatic doors of Atwater Hospital. Steve asked the nurse staffing the reception desk about Donald and Jayme as ten pairs of muddy fire boots paced nervously across the shiny white-tiled floor.

The crew found J.J. in a small room. He filled them in: Donald was okay and was pulling himself together at J.J.'s parents' house; Carolyn was sent home with a minor concussion; and Jill was scheduled to undergo skin grafts on her arms and back the next day. Jayme had suffered the worst. Severe road burns covered her face, neck, arms, legs, and back, and it would take several treatments to remove all the gravel. "She doesn't look the same, dude," J.J. confessed with a cracked voice. "She's all messed up. This side of her face, it's—" Then he sniffed and stiffened, hiding his tears behind a mask of strength, and walked purposefully out of the room to talk with Jayme's parents.

The crew rushed off, picked up Donald, and took him to La Hacienda, the restaurant owned by Diego's family, to administer their own treatment in the form of red enchiladas, greasy refried beans, Spanish rice, chips and salsa, and several longneck beers. They stayed with Donald well past nightfall and periodically checked in with J.J. Then they headed down the fifty-five-mile pitch-black stretch of open road leading back to Elk River.

A few days later, I asked Donald how the crew's actions made him feel. "I like having people around that actually give a shit about you," he reflected. "I mean, really, people may seem like, 'Oh, they don't really care,' but when I got in that accident, *everybody* was there for me. When something bad happens, everybody was there for me. Whatever happens, *everybody's* there for you. It's really encouraging."

Only a few brief moments passed between the time J.J. phoned the station and the time a caravan of trucks raced out of Elk River, burning rubber toward Atwater. Each crewmember immediately stopped what he was doing and hurried to J.J. and Donald's side that day in an incredible demonstration of solidarity, support, and brotherhood.

Brotherhood—the term has been used to describe firecrews for over 150 years. According to historians, about 1840 America's first organized urban firefighters started to cultivate a sense of brotherhood (within and between crews) that transcended specific locales to form a "national community of firemen." Through fraternal activities such as gift exchanges, public competitions, and complimentary uniforms, firefighters attempted to advertise their presence as a public service.[1] Today few would dispute that fire stations house bands of brothers. We see exhibitions of brotherhood in the gripping words of firefighters' memoirs, such as books like *Last Alarm* and *Strong of Heart,* and in black-and-white photographs of New York City firefighters with cheeks ash- and tear-stained after September 11 featured in several collections, one aptly titled *Brotherhood.*[2] But most of the time, those who write about firefighting fraternity, including those who have experienced it, do so superficially, creating idyllic visions of heroism, beneficence, and purity (even holiness). Many fail to notice power alignments and jagged divisions within the family. By concentrating only on the brothers' innocent eyes and smiling faces, they ignore the flailing feet and bruised shins under the table. While trying to avoid the seductions of sentimentality, this chapter is about the relationships forged between firefighters at Elk River. It is about friendship and trust, power, placement, and pain; it is about how crewmembers see each other and how they show affection and aggression toward one another. In addition, it is about "informal" socialization: about how crewmembers discipline each other and how they uphold the standards of the Forest Service through seemingly innocuous everyday practices. This chapter, then, begins the task of explaining how country boys become wildland firefighters.

To parse these topics—firefighting fraternity and informal socialization—I concentrate on the sometimes *un*fraternal practices of banter. We can learn a lot from jokes. Especially between young men, a joke can be an intimate display of liking. It can constitute a back-slapping hug, but it can also be a fist in the mouth. In jokes, moreover, resistance can hide—a mockery of the master's hand—but so too can the master's stinging whip. If we take humor seriously, we can discern remnants of the social relationships in which jokes occur and through which they gain meaning.[3] Besides, aren't firefighters known to be cunning pranksters? Indeed, several books are devoted solely to the topic of firehouse jokes.[4] As we will see, the crewmembers at Elk River live up to this reputation: each day at the station is jam-packed with playful and not so playful repartee. Alfred Radcliffe-Brown refers to this type of linguistic exchange as "permitted disrespect"; Christopher Wilson coins "abusive derision"; Erving Goffman calls it "aggressive interchange."[5] My crewmembers prefer "shit talk."

Shit Talk and Three Rejoinders

During the middle of a mundane day, a day like many others, some crewmembers and I work in the shade of the tool cache, busily attending to tools dirtied and dulled during the previous fire. Donald and I grind away at the faces of Pulaskis with wood-handled files. Diego and George sharpen combis while J.J., Vince, and Nicholas slowly sand tool handles. We work silently, listening to rock music from a local radio station on a beat-up silver radio with a coat hanger for an antenna.

When a song ends, Vince decides to make an attempt at small talk. "Man, my air-conditioning broke in my house," he says to nobody in particular. "I have to get it fixed soon, because it was real hot last night."

"Yeah, I know, I got all sweaty on your wife last night," J.J. replies without missing a beat. He looks up from his tool and flashes a toothless smile in Vince's direction. Because of his quick thinking, verbal aggressiveness, and unblushing obscenity, J.J. is one of the best and meanest cads on the crew.

I look up from my task and glance around the room, gauging my crewmembers' reactions. All eyes gravitate toward Vince in anticipation of his reply. The game is on.

"Shut the fuck up, J.J.!" Vince blurts out in an exasperated tone. He tilts his head to the side and stares at J.J. with his mouth half open.

"Yeah, *damn* it was hot in your house, man," J.J. replies in a nonchalant, almost sleepy manner. Then he lowers his glance and continues to sand his tool, saying, "We had to take a *cold shower* together."

"Oh yeah, well—"

"Yeah, Vince," Donald quickly interrupts, grinning. "Your wife was so slippery it was like a Slip 'n Slide." Pleased with his comment, Donald chortles and looks at J.J. as if to pass the baton.

Taking his cue, J.J. asks, "Hey Kris, do you want to go to Vince's house tonight? We're all gonna have sex with his wife."

"No, you—" Vince tries to defend himself and his wife but is again cut off.

"*Choo-choo!*" yells George, looking especially amused and tugging at an imaginary lever above his head that triggers the whistle.

"*Choo-choo! The train* is comin'," George yells again, signaling the event of "riding a train" or a "train bang," which is slang for gang rape. "*Choo-Choo! Choo-CHOOOO!*"

"Ahhh! Amtrak is coming!" Kris exclaims, prompted by George's whistle.

At this my crewmembers fill the tool cache with laughter. I shake my head and smile. George doubles over, helpless with the giggles like a child being tickled, and Donald laughs so hard tears form in his eyes. And Vince cannot help laughing with them.

When the laughter dies down Vince forces a sad smile and shoots everyone the finger. And we go back to sharpening tools.

Battles of words, wits, and wills like this take place throughout the workday and carry on into the evening. Trivial things, such as a broken air-conditioner, can be converted into objects of ridicule in a split second.

This is why George often refers to the Elk River Station as "a shit-talkin' institution." Every day brings new derisive clashes, and loud, quick, crude, and abrasive crewmembers like J.J. and Kris prey on the shyer types like Vince, who are slow in response.

"There's a large amount of shit talking that goes on out here," Kris reflects. "There's a large amount of teasing each other and picking on each other and poking fun at each other, and it goes back and forth all the time. You can respond to it and get pissed off, or you could respond to it and brush it off, or you could just join in and talk right back!"

As Kris points out, when someone is verbally assaulted he can respond in three distinct ways: through *engagement, escalation,* or *inaction.* If a crewmember responds to an insult by *engaging* his assailant, as usually happens, he takes part in the repartee and attempts to outwit his opponent through verbal maneuverings. With each exchange, players increase the obscenity and provocative nature of their verbal jabs until someone laughs, gets angry, or doesn't respond and thus loses. To be successful, a player must be clever and mean; his comments must prick. More important, he must retort swiftly and eloquently: a slight pause or stutter can cost him the match. Above all, the competent shit-talker must remain in control at all times. He must never show frustration. When Vince responded to J.J. with a violent "fuck you," he forfeited the match by reacting in anger and thereby revealing a weak spot. And when others saw that J.J. had effectively peeled off a scab, they did not hesitate to pour salt on the exposed wound.

Misogyny often serves as the discursive scaffolding for shit talk. Crewmembers attack one another's masculinity by invoking feminizing epithets such as *bitch, sissy, fag, pussy, pansy,* and *girl,* or they threaten the "purity" of one another's wives, girlfriends, or sisters, usually by confessing fantasy sexual encounters. ("You know what your sister smells like?" J.J. once asked Diego after a morning briefing. Before Diego could respond, J.J. shoved two fingers under Diego's nose and said, *"This, man! This!")* Although sexism structures the content of shit talk, content itself is not enough to win the exchange. A crewmember can label another's wife the foulest name imaginable, but if he does it with a mouthful of marbles, his insult fails. Delivery is more important than content. The successful joker must prove that he can "handle himself better than his adversaries," that he possesses better "footwork than those who must suffer his remarks."[6]

If a firefighter's footwork fails, he can challenge the attacker on another field. That is, he can *escalate* the exchange *a verbis ad verbera,* from words to blows, and silence the assailant by putting him in a painful headlock. Escalation occurs either when a crewmember realizes he will lose at banter but might beat the jokester slap-boxing or when the jokester treads on forbidden ground. Since forbidden subjects vary from person to person, crewmembers feel out through trial and error whose sister they can defame and whose sister they should never mention. And when a crewmember misjudges another by stepping over the line, confrontations often escalate from "friendly" teasing to unfriendly threats—which happened when Bryan made a gauche comment about my (then) girlfriend, Tessa.

One afternoon toward the end of the season, Bryan was slowly driving an F-150 down a two-track dirt road while I rode shotgun and Diego sat in the cab. When Bryan drove slowly, he did not touch the gas. When he drove fast, he kept the pedal pressed firmly against the floorboard. In the same way, he kept his room exceptionally clean, he preferred his Copenhagen exceptionally fresh, and he enjoyed his drinking water exceptionally cold, which was why he froze his water bottles overnight and nursed the chilled melt-off throughout the next day. As we crawled down the two-track, Bryan examined his bottle. About a quarter of the water had thawed, leaving a well-defined ice phallus.

Spinning the bottle in his hands, Bryan studied his ice sculpture with a waggish grin. Then he placed the bottle between his legs, shut his eyes, and bounced his hips violently up and down, moaning lasciviously, "*Oh! Oh! Ohhhhhh!*"

He laughed at himself, then leaned my way: "You think Tessa would like this, Matt?"

Before that moment I hadn't consciously cordoned off my love life as an inappropriate topic, beyond the boundaries of acceptable teasing. But there was something about Bryan's question, something reactive, that made me lose my head. I exploded: "Fuck you, Bryan! *Fuck you*! You *don't* talk about Tessa like that. I don't talk shit about your girlfriend, so don't fuckin' bring her into your shit."

Bryan stopped bouncing, and his large smile shrank to an innocent one. He tried to explain. "Look Matt, I was——"

"*No*. Fuck you," I interrupted. "Don't fucking talk about Tessa like that. If you do it again, pull the truck over."

By giving this ultimatum, I let Bryan know that if he said one more thing about Tessa, he would promptly receive a punch in the face. My eyes locked on his. Blood rushed to my face. I readied myself for a confrontation, though I desperately hoped Bryan would back off. If he continued to slander Tessa, what did I hope to do? If I was foolish enough to follow through on my threat, Bryan, who played college football, would most likely bloody my nose and blacken my eyes—if I was lucky. I felt trapped and stupid.

Bryan stopped the truck and looked at me dumbfounded. After a long pause, he replied in an annoyed tone, "Fuck! Okay! I was only kidding. Just fucking around?"

"All right," I exhaled, relieved. "It's just I don't like people talking shit about Tessa. Anything else, fine, but not Tessa."

"I guess not," Bryan replied sarcastically.

Looking away, he pushed lightly on the gas, and we drove back to Elk River in silence.

Bryan had expected me to respond to his question with normal shit-talking rejoinders—by jabbing back at him, maybe suggesting his boyfriend would be better suited for the ice dildo. Instead, I escalated the confrontation from humor (which creates little offense between joking parties) to conflict. I refused to play the game, for Bryan, it seems, had pricked me deep. That day I lost the match by losing my cool.[7]

If a crewmember refuses to engage his assailant through either verbal or physical reaction, he responds through *inaction* and silently waits for the end of the barrage. Crewmembers usually respond through nonresponse when supervisors rake them over the coals. George often finds himself in such situations. In fact, stories about supervisors' reprimanding George make up part of the local folklore at Elk River, and the one story that tops them all, the one everyone loves to tell and everyone loves to hear—except George, of course—has to do with the time Rex Thurman called George a little bitch.

As the story goes, three years ago, George attended one of Thurman's morning briefings with the rest of the crew. To begin the meeting, Thurman decided to test crewmembers' self-reliance by asking each one, "What are you doing today?" Each person around the table provided some sort of answer, legitimate or fabricated on the spot. George was at a loss. He hadn't been assigned any tasks for the day, nor was he shrewd enough to think up some false duty as many of his peers had done to satisfy the boss's query. Hence George answered with one foolish word: "Nothing."

Thurman glared at George in silence. Then he leaned back in his chair, leaving his hands on the table, and pretended to advise George in a soft, deep voice: "Well, George, if you have nothing to do today you can be our little bitch. George is going to be our little bitch today, guys! George, you can put a skirt on and dance on our table here like a little bitch! How's that sound, George? Would you like to be our little bitch?"

While the room reverberated with his crewmembers' cackles, George looked at Thurman with an abashed grin. He dared not reply.

A Situational Brotherhood

What does a joke do? Most of my crewmembers view shit talk as a form of entertainment, a jovial ritual, and nothing more; hence they believe that if repartee serves a function, it is to build solidarity and friendship ties in a twisted system that fosters alliance through animosity. To be friends, let us act unfriendly. To draw near one another, let us push each other away. To demonstrate our loyalty for one another, let us act treacherous.

"Like family, you can make fun of each other and they're not gonna get mad at you," Peter reflects in his room. Then, he repeatedly stabs at the air with his index finger and continues, "You can just poke, poke, Poke, Poke, *Poke*, POKE, *POKE*! And they're not gonna snap—well, unless you've been on a fire with them for fourteen days and they're sick of your shit. You say 'family,' but, you actually spend more time with them than you do your family, so they actually become your family."

To my crewmembers, shit talk does not create divisions; on the contrary, it ensures fraternal closeness. And the closer crewmembers are to one another, the harder they can *poke, poke, poke*. The more taboo the insult, the rationale goes, the more resilient the friendship. Thus Kris is in the habit of going on and on about his imaginary sexual escapades with Diego's sister: *Diego, me and your sister went out last night. She's freaky! Asked me to use a video camera and shit. Diego, could you do me a favor? Your sister left her panties in the back of my car. Could you return them for me? Hey, Diego, you can start callin' me Uncle Kris.* Diego usually laughs, tells Kris off, or socks him in the shoulder; and although Kris has a younger sister himself, Diego never trespasses on that forbidden subject. Kris teases Diego about his sister's sexual escapades not to hurt his feelings or to disrespect his family but to elicit a setting-specific reaction from Diego that (besides being funny) appropriately lets Kris know he's "in"; and, of course, Kris would not take such liberties if he did not already know Diego was "in."[8] Without a consensual intimacy, derision would be impossible, since jokes are symbols that work to express and uphold cultural structures and relationships; thus, with each taunt Kris and Diego reinforce an alliance between themselves—and a belongingness at Elk River—through "permitted disrespect."[9]

Anthropologists have long observed that derision strengthens interpersonal relationships, since it allows insiders to perform intimacy by responding to insults in ways outsiders certainly would not do. These knowing responses signify insiders' membership in the group.[10] Elk River is no exception: Shit talk, through a strange admixture of fraternity and antagonism, conveys both affection and belonging. It is a secret handshake, a hug and a wink, and it functions as a means of passage into the ranks of the firecrew. For crewmembers who knew each other beforehand, shit talk reaffirms their friendship, and for newcomers it is an initiation rite where they must resist becoming enraged at enraging comments—after all, for initiation rites to be meaningful, as Durkheim once observed, they have to be painful.[11]

Many of my crewmembers think of each other as brothers, and often they act like one big family. Crewmembers cook for each other and perform favors for one another, such as picking up groceries at the Atwater supermarket. They rarely lock their doors, and after work they travel freely from room to room to play video games, borrow this or that, or bum a chew. Elk River functions and feels much more like a com-

mune than a barracks. This leads many crewmembers to observe that ties of brotherly love run deep between crewmembers. Peter's comments are typical:

"When you work with somebody and live with somebody . . . when they're your fuckin' next-door neighbor, even if you don't talk to each other a lot, you build that camaraderie. When you spend that much time together, you grow close together—working with each other all day, going home, fuckin' eating each other's dinner, fuckin' wrestling matches. Like *brothers,* you know, you just grow *tight* with each other. . . . I like the camaraderie, the friendships. That's the main thing. You know, after a good fire, you get in the engine and you're with your friends. . . . We have a camaraderie that's pretty tight around here. We're like family."

"Right, right. Now, do you stay in touch with any of these crewmembers when they leave for the winter?" I ask, sitting in Peter's room.

Peter leans back on his couch. His loose smile tightens into a mellow frown. "Usually we don't talk too much," he replies slowly. "You know, we'll call and see if they're coming back to work. Usually it's a, hey, you're going to school and you're going to be busy. . . . I know they're busy doing their thing, and I hope that they understand that I'm busy doing my thing. And it's not like a couple of freshmen girl pen pal women trying to keep in touch."

He pulls his hand to his ear like a telephone and pretends to talk to another crewmember. "'So you wanna come back and work, you little bastard, or not?' Guys are different than women, *I* think. You don't have to keep in touch to stay friends. As soon as they come back, the camaraderie and the friendship—*snap!*—they're like it was never gone. I've always felt that way."

Like Peter, most crewmembers sever ties when the fire season ends. A few exchange phone calls or say hello when they cross paths at the local post office, but more often than not they simply check out of each others' lives until the next fire season. If my crewmembers are truly brothers, why do their family relationships dissolve during the off-season? Peter believes that maintaining relational ties in the winter is too needy. Exhibiting a masculine style of communication, crewmembers do not need to stay in touch during the off-season like a bunch of giggly girlie pen pals. Indeed, Peter supports many social scientists who argue that men typically convey friendship through instrumental activities, whereas women tend to express their feelings through self-disclosure.[12] While I do not doubt that a masculine ethos is largely responsible for confining the firefighting family strictly to the summer, I know this is not the full story.

The brotherhood created by my crewmembers is real, but it is also *situational*. The firefighting family at Elk River makes sense only because the etiquette of Elk River structures my crewmembers' relationships—so much so that when they bump into each other in different settings (with different rules of engagement), they find themselves grasping awkwardly at communicative straws. They manage to squeeze out only a few clumsy hellos and how you beens before parting ways. Elk River functions as a lifeworld with well-defined rules of conduct and linguistic styles: a shared meaning base that crewmembers draw on when shaping their relationships. And they are slightly unsure how to interact with one another beyond this lifeworld. They cannot fall back on the etiquette of Elk River. After all, one cannot remark, "Yeah, Vince, your wife was so slippery it was like a Slip 'n Slide" anyplace one wishes, especially at Vince's house in front of his wife and kids.

Words as Weapons

Like all families, the firefighting family of Elk River is characterized not only by its intimacy but also by its power dynamics. Once they are inducted into the family, crewmembers often employ abusive language to carve out hierarchical distinctions. By viewing repartee only as innocent joking that marks fraternal inclusion, my crewmembers tend to ignore the way banter sometimes operates as a weapon that intimidates and bullies others—a weapon that J.J. and Kris once used to threaten Vince for no apparent reason.

The threat came unprovoked. It happened in the tool cache, the favored boxing ring for verbal battles royal. Maybe it was the cramped work space that spurred it, or the joylessness of sharpening tools, or the sawdust filling the muggy air. What unseen forces motivated Kris that day remains a mystery to me, but for some reason or other he punctured the perfunctory sounds of our files grinding metal by yelling, "Quit fucking looking at me, Vince!"

Curiously, Vince was not looking at Kris at all. Seated on a plastic crate, he was inspecting a newly sanded combi handle for slivers and rough spots. Of course, after Kris's outburst Vince's head snapped up and his stupefied eyes searched Kris's.

Kris stood over Vince, steadying a Pulaski on the workbench with one hand and holding a file with the other. He glared down at Vince and taunted, "What the *fuck* are you gonna do? *Really,* what the *fuck* are you gonna do about it?"

Vince's mouth moved, but nothing came out.

"Quit looking at me Vince, you fucking bitch, or I'll kill you!" J.J. yelled from the other side of the cache.

Helplessly, Vince turned his eyes toward his new assailant.

Meeting Vince's eyes, J.J. slammed his file down on the workbench with a loud *crack* and screamed invective: "*QUIT FUCKING LOOKING AT ME VINCE, YOU FUCKING BITCH!*"

The tool cache fell quiet. All eyes focused first on J.J.'s exasperated face, then on Vince's discomfited expression.

After a few moments, J.J. snatched up his file and angrily began grinding away at the shovel head of a combi with exaggerated strokes. With his eyes on his tool, he vowed loudly, "I fucking *HATE* Vince. I'm gonna kill him, shove his face in the grinder, and show him who he is."

Vince did not say a word but pitifully lowered his head and inspected the combi in his hands.

Later I approached Kris and asked, "Why do you pick on Vince so much?"

"Pick on *Vince*? I'm not sure that I do," Kris responded with a smile.

"Bullshit."

"Actually, last year Vince and I were on the same engine, and back and forth we would pick on each other. Unfortunately, Vince has a few challenges, so it comes out more of me just picking on him . . . ."

"But why do you gotta be a dick to him?" I prodded. "You're mean, really mean, sometimes."

"My main reason that I say I pick on him is because last year we got drunk as fuck out here, and the dumb fuck decided to drive into fuckin' town after drinking half the damn quarters' beer. So he starts driving off, and so I followed him in, drunk as hell. I had to pull over to sleep on the side of the road because I was too drunk to drive. He made it in safe, so ever since then we have just gone back and forth picking on each other."

I didn't have a chance to pressure J.J. on the issue until several days later.

"It's *fun* to give your coworkers shit," J.J. laughingly explained. "It's like, everybody does it, and I like to piss everybody off, so I do it. It's a fun thing to do. To upset people out here is *hilarious*. To piss somebody off is the greatest thing *ever* out here, dude. When you know you're getting under somebody's skin, it's like, yes, I'm there. I love to do it, it's awesome."

In this incident, Kris was perhaps legitimately fed up with Vince and wanted to put him in his place; J.J., on the other hand, simply enjoyed the thrill of getting under Vince's skin. Their combined threats reflected and reinforced a hierarchy within the crew, in which Vince occupied the lowest rung. As the crew's whipping boy, Vince received much more abuse than he was able to dish out. Consider another time when Vince was subjected to harsh ridicule.

After two weeks without seeing fire during the peak of the burn season, a lightning bolt struck the tip of a dead tree, and the Elk River crew responded in haste. The crew had been chomping at the bit for a fire, and even though the job required only one engine, everyone tagged along to get out of the station. When they arrived at the scene, George, overcome with excitement, leaped out of the engine to check things out, forgetting his personal protective equipment (PPE)—a serious faux pas. The rest of the crew patiently suited up, strapping on their fire packs and securing their helmets, before marching single-file toward the smoke behind Allen and Steve.

When they caught up with George, Allen and Steve severely reprimanded him for his carelessness. Allen assigned him one hundred pushups and ordered him to return to the engine immediately to fetch his gear. George complied, and as he passed the crew, Paul yelled out condescendingly, "*George*! Every time you go to look for a smoke you *have* to have your *PPE*. Shit, damn Space Case!"

George looked at his feet and walked on.

Seconds later, Vince pointed to George's baseball cap and said, "Hey, that doesn't look like a hard hat."

George stopped and spit venom: "Fuck you Vince! FUCK YOU!"

Then he spun on his heel, headed for the trucks, and flipped Vince the finger.

After the fire, the two reconciled. Shaking Vince's hand, George confessed, "Dude, I was pretty pissed. If you'd been any closer, I would have punched you."

George exploded on Vince rather than Paul because he occupied a position between those two within the crew's hierarchy. Although he had to keep his mouth shut when faced with Allen's and Paul's ridicule, George could angrily answer Vince's jeer with impunity since Vince sat at the bottom of the pecking order. In this way George resembled the minister of the court who, after being reprimanded by the king, slaps the tittering jester.

But sometimes the jester slaps back. Sometimes someone occupying a subordinate position decides to orchestrate a coup on someone occupying a privileged seat. This is what happened during what my crewmembers now call the "Twinkie incident."

As the crew worked on random tasks around the station, Kris sneaked into the conference room right before lunch break, opened Vince's lunchbox, and—possessed by some spiteful spirit or maybe driven by that impish impulse to create a humorous scene (which rarely reflects on consequences)—smashed Vince's turkey sandwich, crushed his Doritos into crumbs, and shook his Pepsi but, perhaps to highlight the contrast, left a Twinkie intact.

Now in a corporate setting in the city, this trick would have been mean, but at least the victim could have resorted to a luncheonette or corner store. But there are no such establishments near Elk River, and since Vince did not live at crew quarters, the lunch he had brought was his only source of food.

At noon, Vince found his destroyed lunch. He picked up the plastic bags and looked at his mangled sandwich and chips. Slapping the bags on the table, he slid his fingernail under the pull tab and cracked open his Pepsi, which exploded all over his shirt and face. Vince didn't have to guess who the culprit was. Kris was laughing louder than everyone else.

As he wiped the syrupy soda off his chin and neck, Vince eyed Kris. "Why'd you do this, man?"

Kris shrugged and took an exaggerated bite out of his sandwich. "Mmmm, this is a good sandwich."

After a few seconds: "*Why*? Huh?"

"'Cause I can."

"'Cause you can, huh?" Vince's voice cracked.

"Yeah, 'cause I can! But I left you somethin' there. You still have your Twinkie!" Kris began to cackle again.

"I'm not gonna eat my *fucking Twinkie!*" Vince yelled back.

"Really? Can I have it?"

Vince ignored the mocking question and stared, defeated, at his sandwich. He opened the bag and took a shamefaced bite. The crew looked on, some amused, some, it seemed, feeling sorry for Vince. He finished his pitiful sandwich in silence and closed his lunchbox.

The lunch break ended, and we all left the conference room to go back to work. Kris resumed inspecting the four-wheel-drive system on a chase truck that had been acting up. Lying down in the dirt, he scooted under the truck, leaving his legs exposed.

Vince spied a prime opportunity for revenge. He gathered the other crewmembers, whispering, "Watch this! Watch this!" Slowly and inconspicuously, we all made our way over to the broken truck. We positioned ourselves near Kris and pretended to be working on something. Kris took no notice.

Meanwhile, Vince ran into the conference room and emerged with his Twinkie. Wearing an oversized smile and trying not to laugh, he unwrapped the snack and tiptoed up to Kris. When he was a few steps away, Vince swooped down and smashed the Twinkie directly onto Kris's crotch, rubbing the white filling all over the front of his pants.

Startled, Kris shimmied out from under the truck. Vince sprinted to the engine bays, laughing hysterically; it was the kind of laugh projected for emphasis, the kind that snickers, "nyah-nyah-nyah-nyah-nyaaah-nyaaah." And the crew joined him: we filled the compound with guffaws, some of us holding on to the side of a building or someone's shoulder to keep from collapsing. Vengeance had been served, and it had been served with a Twinkie.

Kris, however, did not take things so lightly. He stood up, the back of his pants caked with dirt, the front sticky with cream filling, looking around. He bit the inside of his check, and the corner of his mouth twisted into an angry grin. Without a word, Kris began walking straight for Vince. If he had sprinted to him, I would have assumed that the rivalry would have ended in a friendly wrestling match: Kris would have chased Vince, and Vince would have run along hooting and hollering. But there was something menacing in Kris's walk: it was the walk of adolescent boys going to settle a score in the back alley—purposeful, serious, and slow. Vince saw what I saw, and he ran and locked himself in an engine cab.

For the next twenty minutes, Kris tried to get at Vince. First he tried prying open the lock with his pocket knife. "Vince," he yelled, pressing the blade against the window. "Open this door. Open it!" When that didn't work, he tried punching through the front window. "Vince! Open this fucking door!" Kris threw his fist into the window. "Open the fucking door, Vince!" He threw it again.

The crew gave the two their space, figuring that Kris would calm down eventually. And he did, once his fists gave out. When Kris finally walked out of the engine bay, his knuckles were swollen and bloody, the engine door was dented, and Vince was terrified.

Vince stayed frozen in the engine another ten minutes until Steve told him it was safe to come out. The supervisors made sure to keep Kris and Vince at opposite sides of the compound. A week later, Kris apologized to Vince, and the two shook hands and reconciled.

That day Vince would not roll over and allow Kris's prank to go un-punished. He rebelled, but he did so clumsily. Instead of patiently, coldly planning how to exact his revenge, Vince pounced on the quickest oppor-tunity. But in doing so he reacted too energetically—touching another man's crotch and ruining his fire pants—and went overboard. But just as Vince was inept at challenging the crew's hierarchy, Kris was inept at confronting such as challenge. Kris could not conceal his humiliation: he erupted and sought to violently shove Vince back in his place. This only exacerbated his ignominy, since he left the incident with injured hands and an engine door to pay for.

The same pattern occurred during a scuffle between Vince and George. The two would regularly wrestle, and George would always win. Once, though, Vince, feeling brash, sneaked up on George, grabbed him from behind, and slammed him as hard as he could onto a concrete walkway, driving his shoulder into the ground. A takedown in the grass is one thing; an unexpected all-out slam onto concrete is quite another. When Vince knocked George onto the concrete with all his weight, he was out of line. His shoulder throbbing and his face beet red, George chased Vince, grabbed his hair, and slammed him onto the ground again and again. What Vince had done to George was not a playful wrestling move but an attack that initiated a fight. Vince did not comprehend this distinction, but George did. And he, like Kris, reacted with ferocity. George would later tell me: "I've never been that mad. And I've never been in a fight in my life. But I was ready to just *go*."

Resistance, displayed by the challenger and the challenged, tended to come out awkwardly. Things functioned smoothly when they were let be, but when someone found the order unsatisfactory and decided to do something about it, his charge tended to be unwieldy and tactless—des-perate—and was met, more often than not, with equally tactless anger and violence.

If Vince did not know how to shit talk with speed, skill, or rhythm; if he did not know how to strike back when victimized with a cunning and clever reaction that would even the score without escalating the conflict; if he did not know how to wrestle with just the right amount of vim, conveying through a squeeze of the shoulder or a tug of the neck that he was out for a serious game, not a brawl, it was because all these behav-iors were new to him. He was not socialized to such boyhood rituals as his crewmembers were. His youth was not spent inside a locker room or on camping trips with friends, brothers, and fathers. It was spent alone, and it showed. Neither his body nor his tongue knew how to play the game. He did not know how to assert himself effectively yet respectfully; hence his unsure challenges to the hierarchy of crewmembers only reaffirmed his position at the bottom. And why did Kris and George react so violently to Vince's challenges? Two reasons spring to mind, the first relating to the doing and the second to the doer. First, Kris and George interpreted Vince's stunts as deserving of recourse, of punishment. Regardless of Vince's intentions, a dangerously forceful slam onto concrete warrants a real fight. This seems clear enough, but does a Twinkie to the crotch merit Kris's stormy reaction? I imagine that if J.J. or Bryan or I had been the culprit, Kris would not have boiled over as he did, knife in hand; that another source of his (and George's) anger is Vince's subordinate position. An attack from an equal or a superior is less threatening and less painful than an attack from below, for when the jester slaps back the sting burns hotter than the king's hand. Order is then restored through a show of force—and the hierarchy is preserved.[13] But both parties suffer a loss. Michel Foucault's words ring true here: "It is ugly to be punishable, but there is no glory in punishing."[14]

Disciplining Each Other

Although my crewmembers sporadically and randomly showered each other with a barrage of insults, shit talk was not simply "spontaneous joking."[15] Certain behaviors and scenarios provoked derision more than others. For example, when crewmembers engaged each other in friendly competitions—wrestling matches, video game bouts, rounds of pool, foot races, rock-throwing competitions—they sprinkled the events with taunts, digs, and curses.

When I finally managed to best Diego at chess a few days before my fieldwork ended, I made sure to rub it in. I wanted to pay him back for all the times he remarked, after checkmating my king, "I thought you were the smart one out here, going to college and all."

"Ahhh, Diego," I said smugly after beating him. "Your lucky streak couldn't last forever. No, no. The chess master has returned!"

Diego and I shared a laugh.

"*I'm* the goddamn chess master," he replied. "And *don't you forget it!* I have my bad days. I only have *one bad day in a year,* and *you* fucking played me on it. . . . We're going to have a rematch soon, *very* soon."

Fully aware that my win was an anomaly, I refused to grant Diego a rematch.

Another situation that invited criticism occurred when crewmembers missed a fire or took too much time off work. I discovered this after taking four days of leave for a good friend's wedding. After strolling into the conference room, rejuvenated from my minivacation and ready to run the PT trail, I greeted Donald.

"Mornin'."

Donald eyed me curiously before asking the other crewmembers, "Who's *this* guy?"

"*Hmmm,*" Steve mused, examining me as if I were an alien creature. "We need to have a new employee briefing."

"Oh, oh, Matt!" Donald blurted out, feigning surprise. "I didn't recognize you!"

"Har, har, y'all," I responded. "Very funny."

To conclude my greeting, Nicholas muttered grudgingly, "It must be *nice* to take *four* days off."

To my crewmembers, one's work ethic was deeply connected to one's pride and sense of manhood. To work and to work hard—not to risk— was to be a man. Like many working-class men, they viewed missing work as a lazy man's vice.[16] In addition, if someone missed a fire call, he usually received a double helping of ridicule, not only for missing work but also for missing the action.

Incompetence, however, served as the most frequent and most potent catalyst for verbal abuse. And when crewmembers responded to incompetence, their words became less humorous and more acid. Shit talk was the primary sanction at Elk River. It was administered from the top down and from side to side. When a crewmember unrolled a hose clumsily, sharpened a tool with an edge crooked, backed a truck into a tree, asked a silly question, or blundered about in any other fashion, he would regularly receive digs from supervisors and crewmembers alike. Consequently, even when supervisors were not around, crewmembers usually performed each task to the best of their ability. They learned how to avoid ridicule by displaying firefighting competence. Just as a strict law professor's gibes scare sensitive students into diligently committing pages of cases to memory, a heckler's tease ensured that crewmembers refined every skill related to fighting fire.

Because crewmembers surround each other day and night, they constantly engage in comparisons of competence and manhood. When they witness miscarriages of competence, they quickly call each other out. All supervise all. Every crewmember becomes an overseer by diligently inspecting others, searching out slippages, mistakes, and imperfections, and correcting them through critical public teasing.[17] Shit talk helps accentuate difference and deviance; it highlights flaws and ensures that firefighters perform at peak efficiency, on and off the clock, supervised and "unsupervised." Thus, although crewmembers enjoy a significant amount of unsupervised time, duties that pertain specifically to firefighting always fall under the watchful eyes of their peers. And far from detaching themselves from shit talk with an attitude of "I don't care what they think," most of my crewmembers invest in it. (Of course, the men at the dominant end of the hierarchy can get away with more than those at the lower end, who tend to approach each action and phrase with trepidation.) Deeply concerned with the judgments of others, they fret over what other crewmembers say and curb their behavior to avoid mockery.

And it works, especially for timid crewmembers like Vince, who often subject themselves to all sorts of pain and discomfort so as not to provoke their peers' harsh words.

As the season wore on, I watched Vince run slower and slower on the PT trail. He had developed shin splints, making running excruciating. Pain shot up his legs with every step. On the days we ran the five-mile trail, Vince finished close to last, choking back tears. He could have requested medical leave or asked Allen to let him lift weights or ride a bike instead of running, but he refused. I began to worry about Vince, and after watching him finish a three-mile run with his face contorted in pain, I decided to advise him to stop running. I quietly followed him into the saw shop after the morning briefing to speak with him in private.

"You know Vince, my friend had shin splints, and he kept running on them," I confided. "And they never went away."

"So, your friend's never went away?" he asked with a worried expression.

"No, but my other friend's did, but only because he didn't run on them for a while."

"Yeah. This sucks, man. I've been running all my life. Well, three years of my life."

"Are you worried?"

"*Yeah*, I'm *worried*. I'm going to get all out of shape because of these stupid things."

"You could ride your bike."

"Yeah, but the guys would make fun of me."

"They might."

Several seconds of silence passed between us.

"But it's not their shins, huh?" Vince asked.

"No. No it's not," I replied, shaking my head.

Vince never stopped running. He knew that if he violated the crew's norms, even reasonably, he would be shamed. And to him that was more painful than the hot daggers that ripped through his legs on the trail each morning.

Vince sacrificed his legs to save his face. Saving face, defending one's self-worth, is always performed in relation to a specific audience and to setting-specific conventions of interaction. "Face" is a relational construct that gains meaning only through the approval or disapproval of others. As such, it is housed not in the body, but in relations between bodies. One quickly learns how to please others (or at least to avoid their scourging), and one can develop a fine-tuned and nearly instinctive ability to comply with the rules of one's surroundings. "Whether or not the full consequences of face-saving actions are known to the person who employs them," writes Goffman, "they often become habitual and standardized practices; they are like traditional plays in a game or traditional steps in a dance."[18] At Elk River, proclamations of and reactions to shit talk are the most readily apparent and powerful steps of this dance.

J.J. once told me, "If nobody likes me talking shit to them, I don't care because I will bare my white ass, and they can *kiss it* if you don't like me talking shit, because *I'm gonna do it,* regardless! . . . When the occasion arises, and I can catch somebody slipping, like when they say something and I know I can just say something, and everybody will laugh at them and make them look like a total jackass, I do. . . . I do it most of the time for entertainment. I probably do it sometimes to piss people off, like I'll say, if someone unrolls the hose wrong, I'll say, 'Man, you fucked up!'"

Despite J.J.'s contention, aggressive teasing serves more ends than mere harmless entertainment, and, despite other crewmembers' observations, it does more than strengthen brotherly ties. Shit talk helps to create an environment that is simultaneously inviting and hostile, familial and critical, affirming and threatening. In fact, at Elk River, it serves at least three interrelated functions: it secures solidarity and friendship by letting crewmembers communicate a shared respect by acting disrespectful; it divides crewmembers hierarchically and allows some to assert their dominance; and it disciplines crewmembers into being competent firefighters who must always perform at their best. One finds brotherhood here, yes, but a brotherhood that is situational, hierarchical, and disciplinary.

What motivates my crewmembers to police one another so intently? Concern for their own safety presents itself as a reasonable answer. Indeed, one incompetent firefighter poses a threat to many. He might fell a towering ponderosa in the wrong direction or put down too much fire while backburning, causing trees to torch. Firefighters cannot afford to suffer incompetents lightly, so they use shit talk to discipline one another. Though there is truth to this thesis, I believe a stronger claim—one supported by more evidence—is that crewmembers police one another because the U.S. Forest Service first polices them. They come to accept an ethic of individualism and search out incompetence because their supporting organization trains them to think that way. To grasp how firefighters are influenced by the Forest Service and how they are educated to think and act in specific and strategic ways, we must examine the processes of organizational socialization that work over and through firefighters. This is the aim of the next three chapters.

4

Real Firefighters Drive Green Engines

"I looked down and saw the fire coming through the trees," Donald recalled in a contemplative voice. His brown eyes stared inward, searching the shadows of his memory. "I ran to the top of the hill and got in the safety zone—luckily. It was right behind us, and it threw spots all over the place. They were all around us. We lost the dozer line, we lost everything. . . . The scariest part of that was we had a rural-metro crew with us that didn't know what was going on. They *did not* know what forest fires *did*. And that was the scary part, because we had to run back out when the crown fire was coming up, and we had to grab them and pull them off. . . . We ran down there because we knew it was coming. We could see the flames coming. The flames were going about 250 feet in the air. We grabbed them and pulled them up, and after we pulled them back, it blew over, burned up the hose right where they were. . . . If we hadn't been there, they'd have been dead. That was the scariest thing."

I met Donald's eyes. A silence hung between us, heavy and thick, perhaps like the silence between Donald and the rural-metro crew after he had pulled them to safety and watched the Moose Print fire "crown out" and consume the area where they had been standing seconds before.

During a crown fire, flames do not move along the ground but go airborne and roll from treetop to treetop—from crown to crown—with incredible velocity. A crown fire can produce flames over five stories tall, vomit up spot fires two miles ahead of its main body, develop a plume of smoke that rises with such heat and intensity that it creates its own wind currents, and chase down retreating herds of deer, leaving black carcasses in its wake. It can suck up all the surrounding oxygen and hold its breath until the winds change and reignite the giant flames. It can burn with such blistering heat that it destroys the very soil beneath its monstrous flames, leaving the land barren for generations.

I saw one once, from a safe distance, during the Rodeo-Chediski fire. It was late afternoon, but the sky was black with the plumes of smoke marking the death trail of the enormous burn. There it was at the bottom of Taylor Hill, stretching, pulsing. It rose and fell, rose and fell, like a pole vaulter who steps back, forward, then back again before sprinting down the lane. And then the fire leaped up with a roar and devoured the hillside, waves of exploding flame leap-frogging each other, building more and more momentum until there was nothing left but smoke and blackness. Groves of mixed conifers and ponderosas, which had stood on Taylor Hill for years, were turned to black sticks in seconds.

I imagine that most people gazing on a crown fire would see a terrifying and monstrous force. But what do firefighters see when they look on their enemy? What did Donald see when he charged toward the Moose Print fire to pull people to safety? If we want to comprehend why firefighters do what they do, we must examine the specific ways they understand fire and danger; we must grasp the practical logic they use to assign order to the disorderly thing they battle; and we must learn how they acclimate to the perils of their profession.

Doing these things requires turning an attentive eye toward the organization that helps shape firefighters' perceptions of risk, inquiring into how the U.S. Forest Service conditions them to face a lethal organism that, as Johan Goudsblom once pointed out, has no purpose other than to destroy.[1] But it requires still more than that, for to fully grasp the logic and practice of firefighting, we must explore how country boys develop into wildland firefighters; we must investigate how the *general habitus* of the country boy transforms into the *specific habitus* of the wildland firefighter. We must study not only the organization but the individual (and his history) within the organization—not only the U.S. Forest Service but the country boy as a member of the Forest Service. Answers to why young men join firecrews and how they become seasoned to the hazards of wildfire are to be found not by examining processes of organizational socialization alone but by analyzing how those processes are specified extensions of earlier processes of socialization that take place during fire-fighters' childhood and adolescence.

Ever since James Coleman pessimistically predicted that the prolifera-tion of organizations in modern society would have unforeseen negative consequences and Charles Perrow published *Normal Accidents,* a path-breaking book that seemed to support Coleman's prediction, sociolo-gists have increasingly turned to high-risk organizations, investigating factors that lead to system breakdowns and successes.[2] Focusing on such things as organizational culture, decision making, emergency protocol, and communication between workers, scholars across the social and or-ganizational sciences have generated considerable research that investi-gates the causes of accidents and disasters, the reproduction of organiza-tional deviance, and how organizations unravel, sometimes with deadly and far-reaching consequences. Yet very few have seriously explored why individuals working within high-risk organizations place themselves in harm's way to begin with and how organizations make sure they stay there. Although social scientists have devoted much effort to document-ing why accidents happen, they have had very little to say about the ways organizations make people deployable by shaping their perceptions of risk and safety or why firefighters, soldiers, police officers, astronauts, nuclear power plant operators, or fighter pilots accept and obey the injunctions of their supporting organizations.[3]

What is needed, then, is an analytical perspective that helps us under-stand not only how organizations prepare their workers for dangerous tasks but also how they shape professional risk takers' imaginations and perceptions to ensure that they place themselves in harm's way and stand firm when things begin to fall apart. For the rest of this book I work toward advancing such a perspective by interrogating the *organizational common sense* of the U.S. Forest Service.

By organizational common sense, I mean the set of unquestioned as-sumptions beneath organizational behavior and dialogue, tacitly agreed on by members of that organization, that buttresses organizational or-thodoxy and ensures consensus between members of the organization.[4] The degree to which people comply with the practices and doctrines of an organization depends, above all, on the degree to which they accept the elementary set of givens, the unspoken common code, that makes organizational thinking and behavior possible. When individuals accept the common sense of the organization—when they begin to think as the organization thinks (without thinking about it), to develop a professional disposition constituted by the culture of the organization, and to accept systems of classification it assigns—they are able to function within it as "productive members" whose productivity, of course, contributes to the reproduction of the organization's common sense.[5]

We have already seen how crewmembers accept the Forest Service's common sense, especially its emphasis on individual responsibility (more on this in the next chapter), through teasing rituals. One other important way they do so is by joining in the symbolic struggles of the organization—"classification struggles," to use Bourdieu's term—through which boundaries of difference and sameness are established.[6] Through these struggles, new recruits quickly learn about the organization's enemies and allies, and soon enough they find themselves joining in the fight. They begin to see how the world looks through the eyes of the organization and start to accept its needs as their own, what Mary Douglas calls the "pathetic megalomania" of institutional thinking.[7] Once this occurs, they launch their criticisms and questions outward at opponents—that is, other organizations and individuals their host organization has classified as "opponents"—and rarely turn a doubtful (and treasonous) eye inward to inspect their host organization itself.

In other words, one way new recruits come to *trust* an organization is by thinking like the organization, and one way they come to think like the organization is by participating in its strivings. When an organization such as the U.S. Forest Service commands its members to stand inches away from a gigantic wall of flame or to stop a rolling crown fire traveling at breakneck speed, it goes without saying that the organization must obtain from its membership a high degree of trust. Firefighters come to trust in the Forest Service, I will argue, by participating in its symbolic struggles. Accordingly, this chapter explains three symbolic struggles through which crewmembers gain a deep understanding of the essence of wildland firefighting and begin to think like the Forest Service. My crewmembers defend the Forest Service against the legal and symbolic attacks of "environmentalists," attacks they classify as tomfoolery. They deride the wildly popular and highly admired activity of structural firefighting as sissy work. And they make distinctions between types of wildland firefighters, from overworked yet respected Hotshots to highly technical yet languid smokejumpers. By joining in these symbolic struggles through hundreds of everyday practices—some subtle, like a slight roll of the eyes or a crossing of the legs, some bold, like a cutting insult or a brash statement of belief—my crewmembers tacitly begin to place their confidence in the U.S. Forest Service.[8] And if they accept its classifications with little question, it is in part because the symbolic binaries pitting environmental groups against the Forest Service and structural firefighters against wildland firefighters align with the symbolic binaries, cultivated within them from childhood, separating city boys from country boys.

Those Damn Environmentalists

I pull into the Elk River Fire Station at 7:30 a.m., reporting to work on the first day of my fourth season, and find Craig Neilson sitting in a lawn chair smoking a Marlboro Red and sipping a cup of jet black coffee. Craig is an old-timer, and I know him from my previous years on the crew. He is forty-five years old, white, with a bushy red-and-gray mustache and goatee. As a "fire prevention officer" (a permanent position), Craig spends most of his time doing public relations work with campers at Wannokee, but he is also fire-qualified and accompanies the crew on burns in the area. Before becoming a wildland firefighter, he served in the navy and drilled in the oil fields of Ohio. His wife Mandy works at the local air tanker base, and she and their three teenage daughters live in Atwater. Although he has a family close by, he stays at crew quarters in the summer and travels home only on his days off.

"Well, I'll be damned!" Craig exclaims with a smile. "You fightin' fire this year, Desmond?"

"Sure am," I smile back. "I couldn't go another year without seeing your ugly mug!"

We greet each other warmly and exchange small talk. Then the conversation slows to the still pace of the morning, and I look around the station with nostalgia while Craig makes a few remarks about last year's fire season and predicts what we are in for this summer. The forest remains dry, he informs me, and "those damn environmentalists" are still a thorn in the side of the Forest Service. I listen quietly as Craig explains that fire is a "natural part of the ecosystem," but that to control it we have to "manage the forest": we need to cut down overgrown areas and burn others. "The environmentalists" are vying for a hands-off approach, no burning or logging, and Craig sees this as pure stupidity. After all, he reminds me after exhaling a long train of smoke, lodgepole pine cones don't open unless they are exposed to extreme heat. They drop seed only during a fire.

Soon my attention drifts from Craig's harangue to crewmembers who begin to emerge from their rooms at 8:00 for PT. Some faces are new; others are familiar. Those who know me come over with sleepy eyes, matted hair, and warm smiles. I shake hands, feign punches, and field comments *about my weight. Hey, ya old bastard, how you been? Ah, shit, Desmond's back, looks like this season's goin' t' hell! I see you're eatin' well in Wisconsin—your ass needs to be on the PT trail. You're on my engine this year. Nah, the season's been pretty slow so far.*

Craig stands up and stretches with a groan. I follow him and the rest of the crew into the conference room. While the crew prepares for the morning run, Allen shows me to the storage room, where I gather my PPE for the season. I select a green fire pack from several hanging on the plywood wall and stuff it with two pairs of dark green Nomex fire pants, two long-sleeved yellow shirts, two pairs of white leather gloves, six plastic canteens, two carefully selected Meals Ready to Eat (MREs)—beef stew and tuna casserole—six fusees, a new shake and bake, a headlamp with extra AA batteries, some parachute cord, a roll of candy-cane-colored flagging, tinted safety goggles, earplugs, and a red hard plastic helmet with reflective yellow stickers on both sides. I bought the most important piece of protective equipment—boots (Georgias)—two weeks back.

I change into my new fire pants, tuck my T-shirt into a brown leather belt holding two pocket knives, and rub sunscreen on my ruddy face. I'm ready by the time crewmembers return from their run, and I join them in the conference room for the morning briefing. George reads "The Six Minutes for Safety"; Donald reads the weather report; I announce my study; and Allen assigns tasks for the day before dismissing us.

Directly after the meeting, Peter pulls me aside and asks, "Have you seen that billboard outside of Jameson?"

"No. What billboard?" I ask, remembering the nearby town that was almost burned over during the Rodeo-Chediski fire.

"Dude, you have *got* to see this!" he replies excitedly and immediately begins logging on to the computer in the main office.

"Oh, man," Donald adds, approaching us. "It's a *cool* billboard."

Peter pulls up a Web site displaying a picture of the sign. A full-sized billboard sponsored by a group called AZFIRE (which stands for Fighting Irresponsible Radical Environmentalism in Arizona) displays the caption, "Thank You EnvironMENTALists for Making the 2002 Fire Season All It Could Be!" against the backdrop of a hillside engulfed by flames.[9]

"Pretty neat, huh?" Peter asks, kicking back in the computer chair and allowing me to lean in and get a closer look.

"Pretty neat," I echo.

During the summer of 2002, Arizona glowed red and orange. Nearly half a million acres were scorched, and over four hundred homes were destroyed. Some people around the state, including those who formed

AZFIRE, blamed "those damn environmentalists" for the severity of the fire season.

Arguments over where the fault lies for a devastating fire season, how best to manage forests, the politics of logging and thinning, the treatment of endangered species, and hunting and camping rights are all manifestations of a power struggle between independent environmentalist groups (such as the Sierra Club or the Forest Guardians) and government organizations such as the U.S. Forest Service. In recent years several organizations that identify with the Green movement have offered hard-hitting criticism of the Forest Service. Whereas the Forest Service generally advocates thinning overgrown areas, selling timber, and administering prescribed burns, some environmental groups see these tactics as too invasive and vie for a less involved approach to forest management. Some critics argue that the Forest Service cares more about the timber industry than about bettering the forest and forested communities; others believe it should "let the forest handle itself," and their efforts have enjoyed some success.[10] Through legislative victories, they have subjected the Forest Service to intense legal pressure and supervision (most powerfully in laws such as the Endangered Species Act), decreasing its ability to thin, burn, and log at will. Some so-called environmentalists argue that the Forest Service destroys wildlife habitats, including those of endangered species, by overlogging and overburning, while members and supporters of the Forest Service retort that a hands-off approach to forestry will only bring bigger and deadlier forest fires.[11]

When my crewmembers commit themselves to the Forest Service each summer, they enlist in this power struggle. To them, "environmentalist" comes to mean "opponent of the U.S. Forest Service," and once they recognize the Forest Service as the rightful overseer of the land, they join in the struggle and caricature environmentalists as misinformed, blindly

Billboard of AZFIRE outside a town nearly destroyed by the
Rodeo-Chediski fire of 2002

zealous, and, indeed, "mental." For instance, Diego believes that all the environmentalists do is tie the Forest Service's hands.

"In your expert opinion, do you think we have the ability to control all wildfire?" I ask.

"Control all wildfire? . . . No, because what we want to do in the fire department area of the Forest Service, they won't let us do because we've got environmentalists, we've got the freakin' timber people, mostly environmentalists," Diego replies, raising his right hand and his voice. "But they won't let us do, like, Thurman wants to do a burnout [to light a prescribed burn] and some things, they won't let us do it because then we are screwing up the National Forest look or we're destroying the *owl habitat*."

Diego rolls his eyes and paints the words "owl habitat" with a thick coat of sarcasm. He is talking about the spotted owl (an endangered species now protected by law), often contemptuously considered the mascot of environmentalist policy. Thurman regularly refers to the spotted owl as "that goddamn bird." "It's pretty scary out there," the boss once barked during a morning briefing. "We can't go in and burn it because of *that goddamn bird!* I apologize for the language, but we put a *bird* over *personnel*." By "pretty scary" Thurman meant that the forest had the potential to ignite with force.

When Diego mentions the "freakin' timber people," who are "mostly environmentalists," he means U.S. Forest Service personnel who are timber specialists. The Forest Service is far from united on matters of environmental practices and wildlife management; in fact, it is fractured by internal disputes between timber advocates, wildlife preservationists, and wildfire specialists, to name but a few groups at odds within the organization. As Peter put it to me, "When people say 'Forest Service,' I say, '*What* Forest Service?' You know, '*Whose* Forest Service?' We got the timber people, who want to log it; the wildlife people, who want to save it, preserve it; and the fire people, who want to burn it. So, there really isn't one, you know, 'Forest Service.'"

Many of my crewmembers classify biologists and timber specialists who work for the Forest Service as environmentalists. Hence the battle between the environmentalists and the Forest Service, at least as my crewmembers see it, is really between the environmentalists and the *wildfire sector* of the Forest Service. And there is just one barrier of separation, for there are only two sides to this fight: that of the firefighters and fire scientists of the Forest Service and that of the "environmentalists" who disagree with them about how to manage the forest. On arriving at Elk River, crewmembers become entangled in crosscurrents of discourse framed by this struggle, and, recognizing that environmental policy has real consequences for them on the fireline, they passionately participate in the fight. For instance Peter, like Thurman, believes that less thinning and burning will result in deadlier fires.

"What they [the environmentalists] do affects me, affects *everybody* to the very lowest point," Peter vents in his room in crew quarters. "What the environmentalists do affects the first-year seasonals. Well, they can't log this, so the first-year firefighters are going to be going into a fire in a dog hair thicket that they can't thin, or can't log or whatever, and that kid's *life is in danger* because they can't thin it. You know? . . . There is such a major, *major* problem. There are thickets everywhere. It's thick as shit."

I nod approvingly as Peter leans forward, resting his elbows on his thighs, his face intense and reddening. "You've got your people that bitch about 'Oh, you're cutting all the trees.' But then they're bitching about these big wildfires. So, you can't thin it. So, then you're like, 'Well, we can control burn it.' But *then* they bitch about the smoke. You know, it's *'cough, cough, cough.'"* He covers his mouth with his fist.

"You know, it's like *fuck!* What the fuck!" Peter throws his hands in the air in frustration. "I can't control burn it 'cause of the smoke when we control burn, can't thin it, can't log it, *what the fuck do you want us to do?* Everything is gonna burn up. Because if it keeps going like it's going, the Rodeo-Chediski fire and all the big fires won't be nothing compared with what's to come."

Peter throws himself back on the couch and stares skyward. I imagine he inherited part of his frustration from his father, a Forest Service supervisor, who might have voiced the same complaints over dinner and on car rides. I begin to wonder if he has ever interacted at all with real advocates of the Green movement or if he is simply parroting a familiar discourse. Following my suspicion, I ask, "So, people have bitched about thinnin' and burnin' to you before?"

He grinningly replies, "Ohhhh, yeah. I was talking to a guy in Scottsdale. This guy named Bob. He's fifty-five years old. He's got money, but I was talking to him, at the bar of course, and, of course, I had had a few beers.

". . . And he was asking me stuff, and I said, 'I think we need to log it, thin it, burn it. We need to do something or it's just going to keep on getting worse.'

"'Oh, you can't log it! You can't log it! When they log it, they only want to cut the big trees.'" Peter erupts, mimicking Bob's nasal voice and frantic gesticulations.

Then he turns into a calm discussant. "Well that's not true. They don't want the big ones. . . . It's like a *garden*. If you don't pull the weeds, you're not going to have good tomatoes or peas or green beans or whatever you're growing because there's only so much water and so much nutrition. Now, if you pull all the weeds, the plants that you do want are going to flourish. They are going to do great."

He nods and smiles at me, confident in his metaphor, before imitating Bob again. "And he's like, 'No, no, no. They only want the big trees!'

"And I said, '*Dude!*'" Peter sighs heavily. "I argued with him for an hour, and I said, 'You just need to come up there. You need to come *up there* and spend a day with me.'"

To Peter, Bob is sorely mistaken. What is needed is a more interventionist, not a hands-off, approach. And the source of Bob's wrongheaded outlook is precisely his lack of country competence and firsthand experience. After all, Bob is a wealthy city boy who needs to "spend a day" with Peter before forming an opinion about how to manage the forest. Peter reacts with such frustration to the Bobs of the world not only because environmentalist policy affects him negatively, but also because as a country boy he is tired of having city folks dictate his fate and the fate of the country.

J.J. shares Peter's sentiments. He remembers a similar exchange with "an environmentalist" he met at his community college.

"I had a person in my computer class this year that was all environmentalist. . . . He'd be trying to ease out of my conversation, like, 'Oh, I disagree with that,' blah, blah, blah," J.J. recalls, shaking his head.

"And I'd say, 'Yeah, you know, shut up! I don't care about your opinion!' We always went at each other because he was always like, 'You know, when you dig, like, it scars the earth, and all you guys do is make things worse.'

"And I was like, 'Shut up, you don't even know what goes on!' They see all the *topical* stuff. They don't see what goes on beneath the surface. We're over here trying to fight fires for good reason. Who wants to let a fire burn and burn all these houses and kill all these snags? And they're worried about, 'Well, you guys kill trees in the ground and all that stuff.' And you're just like, *come on now!*"

Like Bob, J.J.'s nemesis lacks country competence and rural experience. He has only a shallow understanding of the ways of the wild. Most of my crewmembers, however, rarely encounter Bobs or know-it-all classmates. Most do not know any environmentalists personally, and if they do meet advocates of anti-interventionist forestry, it is usually in passing. Nevertheless, all (the word is not an exaggeration) the firefighters at Elk River decry meddlesome "environmentalists," their amorphous enemies, because their fight is not with people but with a specific position within the field of environmental politics, where the symbolic struggle takes place over the best way to do forestry. The fire sector of the Forest Service occupies a certain position in this field, while environmental groups, including groups within the Forest Service such as wildlife biologists, occupy an opposing position. And when my crewmembers commit themselves to fighting fires for the Forest Service, they enter this field and join in its power struggles, struggles as old as the trees themselves. Indeed, since the Bureau of Forestry was transformed into the U.S. Forest Service almost a century ago under the command of President Theodore Roosevelt, at a time when American "progress" speckled the wild landscape not only with steel trestles and steam engines but also with wildfires caused by the sparks flying off the tracks, individuals have fought tooth and nail over how best to handle wildfire and forestland.[12]

Placing faith in the need to ignite prescribed burns or to thin overgrown patches of ponderosas to help protect the forest and firefighters from out-of-control wildfires is a sort of prerequisite for becoming a wildland firefighter.[13] A firefighter who doesn't hold these basic opinions would be like a Trappist monk who doesn't value silence or a police officer who doesn't believe in law and order. However, my crewmembers do not always see eye-to-eye on other environmental issues. For example, they often disagree about how wild animals should be treated. This became apparent to me after some of them, far too literally, ran across a rattlesnake on the PT trail during a morning run.

Killing a Rattlesnake

A few minutes into the three-mile morning PT run, Vince, who was a good distance ahead of the rest of the pack, noticed something lying dead center on the trail. He thought nothing of it and quickened his pace to jump over whatever it was without breaking the rhythm of his strides. Vince was only a few feet away when he realized that what was lying there was a full-grown timber rattler, coiled and vigorously shaking its buttons. Unable to slow down in time, Vince leaped over the snake, which struck at him; then, giving the snake a wide berth, he headed back down the trail to warn the others.

He quickly met J.J., Donald, Paul, Kris, Peter, and George, who all approached the snake cautiously but with interest. Dressed in jogging shorts and sleeveless T-shirts (except J.J., who wore no shirt), the guys gazed at the large snake, which had raised its head and was flicking its tongue to the sandy and steady cadence of its rattle.

Paul picked up the first rock. He adjusted the thick, flat piece of sandstone in his throwing hand, and shouting, "I'll show you how to get this fuckin' snake off the trail," wound up like a pitcher and hurled the stone at the snake. The jagged rock smashed into the snake's side right below its head, opening a small, bloody cut.

The surrounding onlookers let out a triumphant *"eewwww,"* and many searched for rocks of their own. Kris, J.J., and Donald each immediately found the nearest heavy stone and slung it at the snake. George did not pick up a rock. Vince was still shaken by the near encounter with the rattler, not only because its venom-filled fangs had nearly dug into his naked ankle but, more important, as I would later learn, because in the Navajo tradition, snakes are evil omens that cast a gloomy shadow over the near future.[14] It took him a few seconds, but he eventually picked up a rock and, with a nervous smile, smashed it into the snake's head.

The rattler, whose reactions were sluggish in the cold morning air, had no time to escape. It was pelted with one speeding stone after another, and soon enough it lay limp and bloody on the trail. J.J. pushed the dead snake aside with a long branch, and they jogged past. After we finished the run, changed into our fire clothes, and dispensed with the rituals of the morning briefing, Allen told us to clean up the shops. So we headed for the auto shop and began sweeping up dust, scattered screws, and dead insects with push brooms.

"Man, did you see me nail that snake?" Paul asked the group in a loud, excited voice. "Nailed it—*bam!*—right in the fuckin' face. That was awesome!"

"Hell, yeah," Donald answered. "We destroyed it. That snake, yep, that snake pretty much didn't have a chance."

A few other crewmembers chimed in, recreating the stoning laughingly, until George, who had looked uncharacteristically sullen during the morning briefing, dragged down the excited chatter with a charged question.

"Why kill it?" he asked.

"Why not?" Paul shot back.

"Look, we are going on a trail in the woods. That's his home! If he was in here [in the shop], okay, kill it. But there's no reason to in the woods, where he lives."

"That's *our* trail," Paul snapped. "*Our* trail! You don't see the snake puttin' on a bandanna and running, do you?"

"If you say this about the snake, how can you shoot a deer, then?" J.J. asked, knowing George was an avid hunter.

"That's different," George answered. "I eat the deer."

"Some people kill deer just for the antlers," J.J. observed.

"Yeah!" Paul yelled.

"That's, it's, it's different. It's just different," George muttered. Outnumbered, upset over the crew's actions that morning and frustrated with J.J.'s and Paul's reasoning, yet unable to articulate his own views, George withdrew from the debate and started pushing the broom.

"George is a bunny," J.J. said coldly. "A bunny hugger. If he could find a bunny, he would screw it in the ass."

George often found himself protecting animals from what he saw as the cruelty of his crewmembers. Last season Marcos Constañico, an old lookout who lived in Elk River's crew quarters, managed to catch a rattler. He kept it in a large pickle jar. Paul wanted to let the snake out of the jar and "shoot it for its buttons." George protested, and when his crewmembers put up a fight, instead of arguing, he took matters into his own hands. Once he thought Paul was actually going to kill the snake, George ran over to Marcos's room, took the snake, and locked it in his car for the rest of the workday. After work, he hustled to his car, drove into the woods, and released the snake at Jackson's Crossing. George was teased severely for this action, which many crewmembers saw as rash, and Paul was downright pissed off at George for spoiling his fun. But George didn't seem to care. To him, saving the snake was the right thing to do, no matter what the others thought.

That same summer, Nicholas found a nest in a tree within the Elk River compound that was home to three baby barn owls. As other crewmembers gathered around to look at the nest, Nicholas said, without an ounce of humor, "Let's kill them."

"Why?" Bryan asked.

"Because, they're evil omens; they mean that sometime terrible is going to happen."

"So you want to kill them?"

"Yes."

Most other crewmembers thought killing the baby owls was out of the question; but as a compromise, and respectful of Nicholas's beliefs, some of them removed the nest from the tree and drove it to another location, far from Elk River.[15]

Interactions like these show that, although the firefighters at Elk River were united in their fight against "those damn environmentalists" on key issues such as prescribed burning, they held competing opinions on other matters pertaining to wildlife and forest management, such as the treatment of animals. When describing my crewmembers' involvement in the struggle over the best way to manage forest lands and wildlife, we could quote Augustine's famous words: "In essentials, unity; in nonessentials, liberty."

Green and Red Engines

Lights flashing and siren blaring, we pull up to the large campsite, where two full-sized trucks are parked, two large tents are erected, and two large coolers are placed under the picnic table. The two couples playing cards in the shade of a large portable gazebo with mosquito netting grimace and shoot annoyed looks in our direction.

Tank switches off the siren, turns up the loudspeaker, and says into the microphone, "Step away from the cards. I repeat, step away from the cards and come out with your hands up."

His older brother Erik smiles, shakes his head, picks up his beer can, pushes aside the mosquito netting, and walks toward us. Tank had told us that Erik and his wife, Jane, were at a nearby campground with his good friend Bobby and his wife, Katrina, so we decided to pay them a visit while patrolling.

"Wanna beer?" Bobby asks, smiling.

"Uh, yeah, but I better pass," Kris jokes back.

"You enjoyin' yourself out here?" I ask.

"You bet, you bet. Just sittin' around, playing some rummy, drinking some Guinness. What more could you want?" Erik says warmly. Then, pointing to Tank, he asks, "So, how's this punk shaping up?"

"He's a fuckup," Kris teases. "A huge fuckup."

"Yeah, he's been horrible," Peter adds, laughing. "Nah, he's been great so far. It's been great havin' him on the engine."

"Good to hear, good to hear," responds Erik, winking at his brother.

More pleasantries are exchanged, more stories swapped. Jokes are made; dips are sampled; teases are launched; arms are punched. Then, after Bobby asks how we spent the morning, Kris replies, "Oh, it's been pretty slow. We ran four miles this morning, which was a pain in the ass. You, ah, you boys do know what *running* is, don't you?"

Knowing the game, I quickly add, in the serious tone of a teacher, "You see, running is like walking but faster. You actually, uh, exert yourself. You even sweat a little. It's tough. But you boys wouldn't know about that."

"Oh, here we go," Bobby moans.

He and Erik exchange a glance of solidarity, and the two men get ready to defend themselves—or rather, to defend their trade—from our digs. Both Erik and Bobby are structural firefighters in Atwater.

"Man, you think what we do is *easy*?" Bobby asks. "*You* try strapping on twenty-five pounds of turnout jacket and pants and a twenty-five-pound SCBA bottle and marching into a house totally consumed with fire."

"Well, we don't get to wear all that fancy equipment because we actually have to hike," Kris jibes. "We don't get to just plug in to a fire hydrant and walk into a house. No, no, no. We have to chase a damn fire up and down mountains, through canyons. Shit like that."

"No fire hydrants," George adds.

"No, no hydrants," Kris agrees sententiously.

"You know what hiking is? It's like walking but faster and longer. Not as fast as running, but faster than walking. Oh, and it happens outside," I say, resuming my patient teacher persona.

"Oh, is that right?" Erik retorts. "Well, do you know what going into a house filled with so much smoke that you can't see your hand in front of your face is? Do you know what holding on to a hose spraying a jet stream of water with, what, one-fifty psi behind the line, enough to knock you on your white ass, is?"

"Sounds pretty nice, having a fat-ass hose that you can pull out any time you so damn well please and empty a water pipe," Kris observes.

"Well, let me ask you boys something," Bobby interjects. "Any of you boys actually *rescue* somebody from a fire?"

My crewmembers and I begin to mumble stuttering apologies. *Well, uhh, you know we're not interested in, uh. That's not what we, uh . . .;* but Bobby cuts us off: "*That's* what I thought. You see, me and Erik here happen to be in the business of saving lives. How many lives have you guys saved lately?"

Bobby has unleashed the secret weapon, the distinction that seems to elevate structural firefighters above wildland firefighters. But Peter has a secret weapon of his own.

"That's true, that's true," Peter says calmly, completely at home playing this boyish game of banter. "But when's the last time *you* actually went to a house fire and saved a life?"

Erik and Bobby look at each other, trying to remember. Their silent pause, filled only with abbreviated hums, gives Peter the answer he was waiting for.

"'Cause, you see, big-ass wildfires are happening all the time over here," Peter lies. "We're not paramedics, you know, we're *firefighters*."

We carry on the energetic conversation. A cacophony of voices rises up as insults and explanations pile on top of one another like clumsy yet tireless boys playing king of the mountain. The game ends friendly enough. Bobby admits, while patting his beer belly, that he wouldn't want to spend days on end hiking through hills, canyons, and gullies, and Erik nods in agreement. To match this courtesy, I confess that I would never run into a building engulfed in flames with nothing but a hose and the heat to guide me; Peter, Kris, and the rest of my crewmembers nod. After all, my crewmembers and I respect what Erik and Bobby do, and it seems they respect our work as well; and our one-upmanship, our "social game," to evoke Georg Simmel's phrase, has been carried out in a playful spirit.[16] But, as the lyric goes, "everything said in jest contains truth nonetheless," for besides participating in the symbolic struggle over the best way to do forestry, the firefighters at Elk River also engage in a struggle over the very definition of firefighting itself.

Wildland firefighters do not enjoy the cultural prestige that structural firefighters do. They do not wax their fire engines and cruise down the local parade route, lights flashing; they are not the subject of countless popular books and movies; major politicians do not honor their sacrifices on the Senate floor or from the Rose Garden; they do not have bagpipe bands, fancy equipment, enduring icons, or other signifiers of honor verifying the importance of their activity.[17] In retaliation, wildland firefighters claim authenticity. Just as starving bohemians question the aesthetic authenticity of wealthy popular artists and callous-fingered blues guitarists pulling the strings in the dirtiest dives turn up their noses at those who play at venues charging a twenty-dollar cover, wildland firefighters classify structural firefighting as less authentic and more sissified.

"I mean, I'm proud of it, to say, 'Yeah, I'm a firefighter,'" Donald observes. "But wildland firefighters are hard workers. More so than a structure firefighter. I mean, you *really, really, really* bust your ass compared to other firefighters. All the firefighters in town just sit in the station."

Donald believes wildland firefighting is much more physically taxing than the lazy man's structural firefighting. In fact, on another occasion he told me, "They don't go out for days at a time and just pound it out. And that makes them wussy." Wildland firefighters also criticize structural firefighters for battling a weaker opponent. Whereas wildfires can burn for weeks on end, most structure fires are extinguished in hours. This is why one firefighter I met on the Beaver Creek fire (the blaze I discuss in detail in chapter 7), who battles both wildland and structural fires in another district, when asked which is more challenging, replied, "Shoot, we structure firefighters get challenged for minutes, y'all get challenged for *days,* man."[18]

Bryan shares this view: "With structure firefighters, in 'the fire service' they call it, you see a lot of big muscle, and the reason I believe that is, is because they don't have to move around like we do, you know. They're in an isolated incident, where you only have to walk across the parking lot or something. They're not going to be on their feet moving constantly all day, so you see the big and bulky guys there. And on the wildland side of it, you see the people who have the endurance to go all day long."

"What would you say is harder, wildland or structure firefighting?" I question.

Bryan answers immediately, "Wildland firefighters, because I've been through the firefighter academy. I'm a certified structure firefighter. 'Cause there's, in structure firefighting, yeah, you go in and get a good knock-down, it takes about thirty minutes. It's not like you're chasing the thing all night. . . . In wildland, you're not relying so much on water, you know. Yeah, if we had a fire hydrant on every corner, I'll bet we'd be big and bulky too. Just run hose, and not do anything, just spray water, and call it good."

To Bryan, structural firefighting is not easy, though it *is* an easier *kind* of firefighting. Structural firefighters are not "cut out" for the demands of wildland firefighting—they are not prepared for the torturous rigor of digging line—and because my crewmembers see their job as the more manly, they feel cheated out of the two prizes structural firefighters supposedly enjoy: the symbolic goods of heroism and the fleshly goods of infatuated women. Peter explains his frustration with this unequal distribution of rewards with characteristic brashness.

"How does the title 'firefighter' make you feel?" I ask.

"To me, not real strong 'cause people put such a *high fucking level* on structure firefighters."

Then, imitating the voice and movements of a ditzy and sexually interested woman, he continues, "'Ohhhh, you're a firefighter. Eeww, you fight fires.'"

Peter drops the persona and barks, throwing both hands skyward, "Fuckin' structure firefighters don't fight fires! But they're the *'stuuuuds'* man, they're the studs. Why? Fuck, I don't know. They get paid to sleep in a fuckin' air-conditioned building all day and watch TV for three twenty-four-hour shifts. And they go home and fuck their wives and mow their yard for four days and then they go back to work for three days. *Fuck!* Oh, and they go to a car fire, huh, once a month. You know, but those are the stud firefighters, not the ones that *go out* and fucking *hike up and down hills!* And that's the reason when people say, 'Oh, what do you do?'

"'Oh, I'm a firefighter.'

"'Ohhh,'" he says, in his womanly voice.

"Ladies' ears fuckin' perk up. But then when they find out that you are a *wildland* firefighter, they're just kinda like 'oh.'" This time the "oh" is bland and disappointed.

"Fuck man! Fuck you bitch! They fuckin' put out a *house*. I put out a fuckin' house and *all the ground around the house!*" Peter is talking quickly, loudly, and using his whole body. He rocks his legs as if wanting to stand up and flails his arms around his head as if shooing gnats. "They think these structure firefighters are all these fuckin' studs, but you go on a wildfire with structure firefighters, those fuckers are sitting in their engine watching the son of a bitch. You know, they ain't going to walk up the hill. *You* know.

"But, when somebody meets me and says, 'Oh, you're a firefighter? So am I. I'm a structure firefighter,' *that's* where it makes me feel *good* because I'm like, you guys are *fuckin' pussies,* man! But *that's* where it makes me feel good because the people that don't really know what wildland fire involves is pretty much city people that are all, 'Ahh, look at that engine.'

"And they are! Ford F-550 with about three hundred gallons on the son of a bitch—four-wheel-drive dually.

"'*That's* your engine? Isn't it supposed to be a big red son of a bitch?'" Peter asks himself in Bob voice before answering himself in Peter voice: "'Well, fuck no! How am I going to drive that son of a bitch up that hill, around that tree, you know? Fuck! Let's see this son of a bitch drive that big freakin' engine up there!'"

Peter inhales and pauses for a few seconds. He breathes through his nose and begins to calm down. We smile warmly at each other as he takes a sip of beer before concluding his tirade in a hushed voice: "And actually when you start talking to the structure firefighters: *total respect* for wildland firefighters. All the ones that I've seen and talked to. Some of them are dickheads, but now what are the structural firefighters starting to do?

Taking the wildland courses, *getting* more into the wildland stuff because, *shhh,*" Peter lowers his voice to a whisper as if revealing a secret, "*They don't have no structure fires.* Once a year maybe a house burns down, two, three a year. Most of their stuff is paramedic stuff.

"Shit, we've even started calling them in for structure protection cause the [wild]fires are so bad that, shit, they're coming to a town of three hundred residents. The Forest Service can't do it. We can watch a few houses with our small trucks. But that big old *cleeeeean* son of a bitch can get in there, and they can sit on their asses and watch that son of a bitch come. Once the house catches fire they can put it out, you know. . . . We're gonna chase fire this way. *They* can sit there and do that."

He slaps his thigh and laughs, and I join him, aware of the pride that gleamed through his last few sentences. Peter sees structural firefighting as easier, cleaner, and quicker. The structural firefighter is the lesser firefighter; and more, he is the lesser man since he, like the environmentalist, is a city boy. Thus, we are able to see how the fundamental principle of division between the country and the city influences the classification struggle between competing kinds of firefighters, just as it influences the struggle between environmental groups and the wildfire sector of the Forest Service.

Dirt Monkeys, Lawn Darts, Heli-Slackers, and Slugs

But the division separating city folk from country folk cannot explain every classification struggle within the world of wildland firefighting. There are some to which this fundamental principle of division simply doesn't correspond, and the most important one is the debate between different types of wildland firefighters over the definition of the purest form of smokechasing.[19] This struggle takes place, more or less, only between country boys, and of all struggles it is the most lively and charged. Perhaps this is because in relationships marked by similarity and equality rather than by great difference, the slightest variations are more often noticed and contested; what rattles our passions are not the big differences but the little ones.[20]

There are four major categories of wildland firefighters—Hotshots, smokejumpers, helitack crews, and engine crews—allocated varying degrees of respect by their peers.[21] Unquestionably, Hotshots are the most respected. They see more fire, work longer hours, travel to more parts of the country, and hike through more rugged terrain than any other type of wildland firefighter. Further, Hotshots do not use water—the one thing structural firefighters cannot live without. Their primary weapons are primitive hand tools.

Hotshots, or simply "the Shots," do not use fire engines either. They battle blazes only with what they can carry—fusees, hand tools, chain saws—and spend most of the fire season traveling throughout North America. Because they are usually stationed in the most inaccessible and extreme parts of wildfires, Hotshots often hike for miles through mean terrain before they start working each day. Accordingly, they are in top physical condition and know fire well. They work on a fire primarily in two capacities: they can be used for initial attack, where they dig line for ten hours a day, give or take, or for mop-up, where they crawl through the ashes looking for hotspots. The former is physically exhausting. The latter is incredibly dirty work. For these sacrifices, for enduring the foulest, dreariest, and most arduous demands of firefighting, Hotshots are revered by other wildland firefighters.

More important, the Shots are respected for their ability to dig line. A fireline is the *No!* that stands between advancing flames and unburned vegetation or, sometimes, between a monster fire and somebody's property. It is a simple enough invention—a three-foot-wide trail of dirt, a humble force field of mineral soil—but it is an effective one. Firefighters dig "indirect line" away from the main head of the fire, preferred on particularly large or active fires. When they dig line in the teeth of the burn, sometimes only inches from the flames, this is called a "direct line" or "hot line," preferred on smaller or less active fires. A fire needs three ele-

ments to survive: oxygen, heat, and fuel. Digging line steals a fire's fuel, removing all flammable vegetation by plowing into the ground with hand tools. It is grueling work that requires a stalwart back, tough legs, strong arms, both physical and mental stamina, and a high tolerance for smoke and heat.

Firefighters use two types of tools to punch line: furrowing tools and scraping tools. The former lead off, since their primarily function is to break up the soil so it can be scraped away more easily. A Pulaski is the favored furrowing tool: the head of an ax, used for chopping down saplings or trimming branches, married to an adze trenching blade, used for grubbing, uprooting, and digging. The tool is named for its inventor, forest ranger Edward C. Pulaski, who tried (to no avail) to patent it in 1914 in hopes that royalties would pay his medical bills for an injury acquired during the great Idaho fire of 1910.[22] Scraping tools follow behind furrowing tools, and most of my crewmembers prefer combination tools, "combis," because they can be used to dig, scrape, and burrow in small root systems. A combi has the head of a shovel and the tail of a small pick; the head pivots ninety degrees to scrape the ground quickly.[23]

Though digging line may not take scientific precision—"This ain't rocket science, folks," Thurman always reminds us—it does require a familiarity with the tool, a knowledge of fire, and a specific way of being in relation to flames, crews, planes, engines, and the green. "Ground pounders," as they are sometimes called, must know just how much energy to put into each swing, how much dirt to move without becoming prematurely exhausted, how much space to leave between crewmembers, and how to recognize encroaching danger amid whirling fire and blinding smoke. This is why the mark of skilled wildland firefighters rests in their ability to dig.

Thurman has dug plenty of line and seen plenty of dirty work in his time. He was a Hotshot supervisor for thirteen years, and he regularly reminds the Elk River Firecrew (and, by his own admission, everybody else he knows) that in those years he "walked away from more fire than most people see." I enjoy listening to Thurman tell war stories from his days with the Shots, stories that sound crafted and polished, as if he has told them hundreds of times.

On a slow afternoon, I look at Thurman from across his desk and ask a few questions in search of some good memories. I don't have to prod very long before he begins to recall the hardships he endured during his years on the Shots.

"The mental part, *that's tough.* It's, uh, demanding. It's not an eight-to-five job. . . . It's an ongoing all-the-time type thing. It basically took, takes, six months of an individual's life—whether you're a crewmember, overhead, or whatever. You need to be focused, dedicated to that." Thurman explains it all prosaically, in a slow, deep voice. He rests his elbows on his desk and leans forward.

"It wasn't uncommon to get called all hours of the night, morning, whatever, to head off to an assignment. . . . It wasn't unusual to get called out at six o'clock, head back, drive all night to an incident, get there, get breakfast, get briefed, and go out on the line. It's those types of things. You work all day out there. Sleep's minimal. . . . When you get out there, they bed you down right there on the fireline. It's not quality sleep. You get up out of the dirt, these type of things. And it's one of those that you still have a job to do on minimal rest and support.

"It's not like you can go out and sit on no little porcelain toilet. You deal with what's at hand. . . . You get to find out what you're made of. I believe it was '94, we put in 1,100 hours of overtime. It wasn't uncommon then. We'd average about 860 hours a season of overtime on the crew. Considering the crew would come on May 1, and we'd lay them off anywhere between September 30 and October 15, they put in that many hours, it's almost full time equivalent in six months. . . . For the most part, if you got four seasons out of an individual you did damn good considering how they were treated, you know, the expectations that are there."

Thurman's first Hotshot assignment lasted thirty-seven days straight. Another time, he and his crew went without a shower for thirteen days (when he got home, he threw his underwear directly in the garbage can). But long stints like this are a thing of the past, since in recent years the Forest Service has implemented work-to-rest ratios. Now a firecrew can work a fire for only fourteen consecutive days before a mandatory rest period. Many think this protects firefighters, but Thurman sees the fourteen-day limit as too restrictive:

"The way we fight fire today, fourteen days, you really don't even have a good handle on anything and you're gone. When I first went onto a Hotshot crew, you could just go in there and just kick that thing in the butt. You've gone crazy after you were done, you know, we probably did more resource damage than what the fire did, but it was *out*. It was dealt with. There was none of this drag it out for two or three months."

When Hotshots step onto a fireline, more often than not their shirts are tucked in, their helmets are on the right way, their boots are laced up tight, and their tools are not slopped over their shoulders like a coal miner's pick but are carried correctly, with an extended arm holding the tool, blade down, perpendicular to the knee. They tend to care about formation, movement, communication, and stance; they take seriously all the minute details that do not occupy other firefighters' thoughts and actions. And they travel and work as a connected troop, marching single-file or crawling shoulder to shoulder while gridding the ash in a shared tempo, nearly in perfect unison. Someone who overlooks a smoke is assigned push-ups; someone who can't keep up the hiking pace gets little sympathy. Hotshots, then, pride themselves on self-administered discipline and on fighting fires by the book.

Things are different for smokejumpers. This rare breed of wildland firefighter reaches fires by air and parachute—dropping their tools and equipment to the ground before jumping out of planes into the black smoke. Such a spectacular entrance is unnecessary for most fires, so smokejumpers are most frequently used in forests that are largely inaccessible by roads, such as those in Alaska and Montana. The name alone captures the heroic and insane blending of skydiving and firefighting, and it is not surprising that smokejumpers have been portrayed as the icon of wildland firefighting in popular works such as Norman Maclean's *Young Men and Fire* and Nicholas Evans's *The Smoke Jumper*. Journalists have also written about them, and smokejumpers themselves, such as Murray Taylor, tell "the inside story of what it's like to brave the skies and battle raging wildfire in the vast, rugged wilderness of the West."[24]

Smokejumpers enjoy a lore of their own, and other wildland firefighters grant them a decent amount of firefighting capital. They endure a rigorous training academy, which is physically taxing and mentally grueling, and for that they are respected; but although they are the most specialized breed of wildland firefighter, they are not the most tasked, and as such, smokejumpers are not as respected as the Hotshots by fellow wildland firefighters. Smokejumpers themselves realize this: journalist Douglas Gantenbein cites an Idaho-based smokejumper as recalling, "If there's a fire that's getting out of hand, there's not a smokejumper around who won't take a couple of Hotshot crews over two planeloads of smokejumpers."[25]

Many Hotshots disdain smokejumpers. They see their skyward entrance to wildfires as, in the words of one Hotshot I spoke with, "idiotic," and, more important, they see smokejumpers as lazy and sloppy firefighters. Smokejumpers fly out of the sky, but once they get to the ground they are of little value; hence they are often called "lawn darts."

Kris, who transferred to the Jameson Hotshots the year after this study was carried out, told me a story in 2005 about a fire where his Shot crew had to work with smokejumpers. "We get up to the fire, and, you know, the fuckin' jumpers were on it," he recalled. "It wasn't a big fire and yet they wanted us to catch it. . . . It was just us and the jumpers, who put a scratch line in, that [the fire] *jumped,* so, fuck that. . . . Jumpers—they fall, and they're like lawn darts. Jumpers are horrible. They, they get respect because jumpers used to be Shots. You have to be a Hotshot for two years before you can be a jumper. Jumpers are highly trained, highly specialized, they are useful in certain situations, but on a fire that's movin' and goin' they, uh, aren't as much good.

". . . They put in good check line, but they don't put in good handline. Oh, and you want to talk about disregard for safety? Smokejumpers never wear their packs. They just, huh, show up. They, they will put all their stuff next to a tree and go work; go grab their shit and bump it up, go work; you see them a lot of times without their packs on."

Perhaps envisioning a group of smokejumpers going along without their packs, and thus without their fire shelters, in strict violation of Forest Service codes, Kris began to chuckle to himself before he continued, "They'll come get food but only a little bit of food. They'll be like, 'Oh, you know, we don't need that, we don't need that, we don't want this or this or that. . . .' They're like this, 'We're hardcore,' trying to show, 'We're hardcore.' They can't dig line for shit, but they're 'hardcore'!"

Unfortunately, I did not have a chance to talk with any smokejumpers over the course of this ethnography (most of Arizona's forestland is accessible by road), but I believe it is safe to speculate that they have some choice words of their own for Hotshots. I did, however, talk and work with many members of helitack crews. Their primary objective on a wildfire is to use a helicopter to drop water on hotspots, transport firecrews and supplies to areas inaccessible by roads, and serve as eyes in the sky. Hotshots and engine crewmembers regularly criticize helitack crews for their poor line digging. I have been on more than one fire when the Elk River crew had to go over a helitack crew's line, dissatisfied with its quality. In fact, Kris claims, "You can tell what type of crew it is by the handline that's put in. If it's, for example, some of the fires when you were working, if a helicopter crew, if helitack hit it, they would put in check lines. It wouldn't be continuous line; they'll just try to check the main parts of the fire. Engines? Engines are good at diggin' line, but they don't do it enough to get it down right, you know, it's—one, they have fewer people; two, they don't do it enough. If engines had to dig line all the time, it would be a totally different story. Shots crews—*all* they do is dig line. So, you know, they're puttin' in superhighways because that's what they're supposed to do. Smokejumpers rarely dig line, you know, they're puttin' in little lines."

Hotshots and engine crewmembers often view members of helitack crews the same way they view smokejumpers: as firefighters whose work ethic on the ground does not match up to their grand arrival from the sky. Regarding them as slothful, weak hikers, overly concerned with their helicopter, and poor at digging, other wildland firefighters often call heli-tackers "heli-slackers."[26] Moreover, helitack crews are not exoticized the way smokejumper crews are and therefore, while other firefighters recognize that they can get to almost any fire and provide much needed support with transportation and bucket drops, they allot them less firefighting capital than smokejumpers, and far less than Hotshots.

Regrettably for the crewmembers at Elk River, in the competition over the most authentic type of wildland firefighter, engine crewmembers find themselves at the bottom. Unlike other wildland firefighters, they bring their vehicles along: light green four-wheel-drive fire engines that can carry up to six hundred gallons of water. Water is never the primary weapon against wildfire, but engine crews have access to it and use it. But using water associates them with structural firefighters and thus an "easier type" of firefighting. Since Hotshots do not work with water, they see engine crews as possessing a superfluous amenity. Hotshots prefer to fight fire the old-fashioned way—with dirt—and, accordingly, they dub engine crewmembers "ticks" or "slugs" (and, less often, "water whores"). Engine crewmembers retort by standing by their water and calling the Hotshots "dirt monkeys."

Essentially, engine crews are localized firefighting units, whereas Hotshots and smokejumpers are free agents who are dispatched to fires across the country. Engine crewmembers are bound to their vehicles, and if they do travel, they do so within a limited range. Because "when the road ends, so do we," as Thurman is fond of saying, engine crews see less fire than any other wildland firefighting unit. They do not have as many opportunities to earn their keep on the line as Hotshots do, nor are they highly specialized like smokejumpers. Accordingly, they are the least respected type of firefighter under the auspices of the U.S. Forest Service.[27]

Although engine crewmembers distance themselves from Hotshots, many cannot help but venerate them as well. Aware of both the prestige and the misery that comes with being a Hotshot, most of my crewmembers view the Shots with both contempt and admiration, disdain and reverence. As the archetypal smokechaser—dirty, disciplined, primitive, hardworking, resilient, and competent—the Hotshot serves as the measure against which all other firefighters are judged. To think of himself as a capable firefighter, an engine crewmember must prove he is a Hotshot trapped in an engine crewman's body. Some of my crewmembers do this by referring back to times they accompanied the Hotshots on a fourteen-day fire detail. This is the favored strategy of Paul, who, much to his crewmembers' annoyance, too often reminds everyone of his temporary membership on the Shots with stories and references. Others reassure their coworkers (and perhaps themselves as well) that if necessary they could dig line with the Shots on any given fire. They boast that though they are not Hotshots, they very well could be, and when given the opportunity to prove this boast, they eagerly accept the challenge.[28]

New recruits quickly learn their place within the firefighting branch of the Forest Service. Although my crewmembers recognize that they occupy a subordinate status compared with other types of wildland firefighters, they do not dream of being Hotshots one day. Fighting fire on an engine crew suits them just fine, and many prefer this to "going with the Shots," which usually involves grueling work, little sleep, no showers, and lots of blisters. My crewmembers learn that the Hotshots personify wildland firefighting, but they do not aspire to *be* Hotshots. They aspire to be *like* Hotshots, at least on the fireline.

Becoming a wildland firefighter involves much more than simply learning how to dig line, backburn, fell snags, recognize fire behavior, and interpret weather patterns; it also involves learning how to communicate and think like other wildland firefighters and to like and dislike the things and people that wildland firefighters "should" like and dislike. New recruits must learn to answer questions in certain ways and to make arguments around specific issues. They must quickly form opinions on policies that previously didn't concern them and criticize people who previously didn't bother them. In short, they must join in the various symbolic battles the Forest Service engages in, battles over legitimation and classification. Two of the most active and charged battles, we have seen, are the fight against environmentalist groups over the right to manage the forest and the fight against structural firefighters over the title of "real firefighter." Through these symbolic struggles, they are introduced to the common sense of the U.S. Forest Service. By adopting the enemies of the Forest Service as their enemies and its problems as their problems, my crewmembers begin to understand their world through its categories and classifications and aim their critical energies and doubts not at their host organization but at outside organizations and individuals. In other words, through these struggles, they come to identify with and trust the Forest Service. (At the same time, through an intraorganizational classification struggle, new recruits obtain a sense of their place within the Forest Service; they learn to revere—and to emulate—some types of firefighters and to disrespect other types.) If crewmembers have little trouble comprehending the stakes and choosing sides in these fights, it is because the principles of vision and division at work within the Forest Service align succinctly with the principles of vision and division of country masculinity. Thus, though they are not aware of it, most crewmembers have been preparing to trust and to accept the common sense of the U.S. Forest Service since childhood. They began developing a disposition that fits within this organization long before they even knew of its existence.

5

Learning and Burning

On a hot June afternoon in 2002, my crewmembers and I strapped on canvas chaps, hard hats, leather gloves, and earplugs, loaded a dozen chain saws and a few cans of gasoline into the bed of a truck, and headed into the woods. Thurman had ordered us to thin clusters of pine trees that had grown too close together along both sides of a well-traveled forest road. It was the first time that season we'd been given a chance to use the saws, so my crewmembers excitedly looked forward to a day of cutting.

To obtain sawyering certification from the U.S. Forest Service, one must attend both a saw training course and a first-aid class. I had missed the first-aid class, so Allen forbade me to operate a chain saw. I repeatedly asked him to let me cut, emphasizing that I had used a chain saw in earlier years, but he stuck to his guns and relegated me to the lonely position of "radio man." While my crewmembers energetically sank their bars into small tree trunks to the high-pitched revving of the saw engines, I kept my distance and paced back and forth along the dirt road listening to the radio traffic. I watched them drop one tree after another. Each tree required two cuts: a forty-five-degree slice a quarter of the way up the trunk, which felled the sapling in the direction the sawyer chose, and a straight cut at the base to create a smooth stump. After an hour, the air was filled with wood dust and the rich smell of pine sap.

I watched as my crewmembers marched slowly through thickets of saplings, cutting here and there. Wood chips stuck to their perspiring cheeks and necks. Some worked fast and efficiently, cutting with confidence. Others moved at a slower place and didn't pay much attention to where their trees fell. Two crewmembers collected the newly felled saplings into piles that would be burned come fall.

"*Dispatch, Paquesi. Smoke report.*"

Quickly I turned away from the crew and turned up the radio. When Paquesi lookout called in a smoke, there was a good chance it was in our area of response (AOR for short).

"Go ahead, Paquesi," replied the dispatcher.

"Yeah, Dispatch, I have a thin smoke sighted at one-two-four degrees."

"That's 124 degrees?"

"Correct."

"And how far out is it, Paquesi?"

After a long pause, the lookout answered, "Well, Dispatch. It looks quite a ways out there. I would guess it's probably on the Tonto."

"Thanks, Paquesi," the dispatcher answered. "Please keep an eye on it. Dispatch clear."

Because the smoke sounded like it was in another forest, and thereby the responsibility of another firecrew, I didn't mention the smoke report to Allen. But I flipped on the scan feature of the radio so I could monitor all radio channels and learn about the progress of the fire.

After a few minutes, a helicopter located the source of Paquesi's smoke.

"Dispatch, this is Bravo-251," the pilot called out over the radio. "We've located the smoke. It's right below Cibecue Ridge, near the Rodeo grounds."

"Thanks Bravo-251," replied the dispatcher. After a short pause, the dispatcher named the blaze: "We'll call this fire the Rodeo fire."

From the helicopter pilot's report, the fire was not on the Tonto at all; it was on the Fort Apache Indian Reservation, even farther from our AOR. I knew we would not be responding to this call, but I kept my radio on scan anyway to eavesdrop on the unfolding action, action that was sure to be livelier than the weather reports and routine check-ins I'd been listening to all morning.

After roughly ten minutes, the helicopter pilot's voice crackled through the radio waves again, over the deep pulsing of the rotors. "Dispatch, this is Bravo-251. "This fire is starting to get a lot more active. I'd say it's about eight to ten acres now."

After another couple of minutes, the pilot offered an update: "Dispatch, Bravo-251. The fire is now torching out trees and gaining momentum. I'd say the fire is now about thirty acres."

This news startled me. Could he be right—thirty acres in nothing flat?

A handful of minutes passed, then: "Dispatch, Bravo-251. Now I'd put the fire at about fifty acres."

At this I ran over to Allen and told him to kill the saws. The crew gathered around the radio and listened to the updates on the Rodeo fire. Every five minutes or so, Bravo-251 would radio in updates of the fire's size: 70 acres, then 100, then 150, then 200. When the chopper pilot estimated that the fire was more than 300 acres, we loaded up our gear and hightailed it over to the Paquesi lookout tower.

We ran up the aluminum steps and stared at the large black plume rising above the treetops. The column was thick, dense, and dark. We could tell the fire was already plume dominated; that is, it was burning with such violence and heat that it began creating its own weather patterns and wind currents. None of us had seen anything like it, except in training videos, and little did we know we were gazing into the plume of a fire that would eventually destroy nearly half a million acres and burn over four hundred homes, a fire that would cost over $150 million to battle, a fire that would soon be ripping through Wannokee—and that we would soon be fighting.

Whereas the previous two chapters addressed how crewmembers undergo more *informal* processes of socialization (in joking rituals and symbolic struggles), interactions that introduce them to the common sense of the Forest Service, this chapter and the next concentrate on more *formal* mechanisms, analyzing how firefighters are educated, trained, and disciplined by their host organization. This chapter begins by describing the training crewmembers receive for fighting fires, whether those fires are as small as a tent or as monstrous as the Rodeo fire. I focus specifically on the fundamental rules of wildland firefighting—The Ten Standard Fire Orders and the Eighteen Situations That Shout "Watch Out!"—because these mandates are the sacred commandments of firefighters; they are the unquestioned, fundamental doctrines of the Forest Service, which promise to keep firefighters safe. After explaining how firefighters are introduced to the Orders and Situations through training exercises and supervisors' injunctions, I recall a single night on the front lines of the Rodeo fire to show how crewmembers apply these rules in the hot and fast action of firefighting.

A Refresher Course

During my first few days back on the job in the summer of 2003, I sat through Safety Refresher Training with some other crewmembers from Elk River and Jameson. All returning firefighters were required to enroll in this two-day course, where firefighting fundamentals were reinforced. The instructor, Fredrick, a lanky engine operator with a ponytail who chewed flavored tobacco and wore a pair of Oakley sunglasses around his neck, handed each of us a twenty-four-page booklet titled "Think While You Fight Fire," which would serve as our training guide. The booklet began grimly, citing statistics on firefighting fatalities (over eight hundred since 1910), entrapments (seventy a year, on average), and shelter deployments (roughly forty-three a year). Then it turned swiftly to explaining how we could avoid such fates, how firefighters could sidestep the dangers of wildfire and keep themselves safe on the fireline. In doing so, it featured The Ten Standard Fire Orders and the Eighteen Situations That

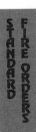

STANDARD FIRE ORDERS

Fight fire aggressively but provide for safety first.
Initiate all action based on current and expected fire behavior.
Recognize current weather conditions and obtain forecasts.
Ensure instructions are given and understood.
Obtain current information on fire status.
Remain in communication with crew members, your supervisor and adjoining forces.
Determine safety zones and escape routes.
Establish lookouts in potentially hazardous situations.
Retain control at all times.
Stay alert, keep calm, think clearly, act decisively.

★ GPO 1992-694-004

PMS 416
September 1987
NFES 2389

SURVIVAL CHECKLIST

☑ **WATCH OUT SITUATIONS**

1. Fire not scouted and sized up.
2. In country not seen in daylight.
3. Safety zones and escape routes not identified.
4. Unfamiliar with weather and local factors influencing fire behavior.
5. Uninformed on strategy, tactics and hazards.
6. Instructions and assignments not clear.
7. No communication link with crew members/supervisors.
8. Constructing line without safe anchor point.
9. Building fireline downhill with fire below.
10. Attempting frontal assault on fire.
11. Unburned fuel between you and the fire.
12. Cannot see main fire, not in contact with anyone who can.
13. On a hillside where rolling material can ignite fuel below.
14. Weather is getting hotter and drier.
15. Wind increases and/or changes direction.
16. Getting frequent spot fires across line.
17. Terrain and fuels make escape to safety zones difficult.
18. Taking a nap near the fireline.

Pocket card displaying the Ten and Eighteen

Shout "Watch Out!" or simply the Ten and Eighteen. These rules were developed in 1957 by the Forest Service to advise firefighters how to prevent injuries and fatalities. Since then they have become the core mantras of wildland firefighting. Firefighters are taught to revere the Orders as rules they must never break and to interpret the Eighteen Situations as dangerous circumstances that they should always approach with extreme caution.

With the exception of cursory lessons on wildland-urban interface fires and downhill line construction, the whole of our refresher course was devoted to the Ten and Eighteen. We began by reading and discussing an article by John Krebs, a retired fire management officer in Idaho. Krebs wanted to rearrange the order of the Fire Orders. Instead of listing each order to create the acronym "Fire Orders" ("Fight fire aggressively but provide for safety first," "Initiate all action based on current and expected fire behavior," etc.), Krebs advocated returning to the original Ten Standard Orders (the first version of the Orders advanced in 1957), which he claimed placed the most important orders first. After a few lines lamenting the loss of the firefighters who died at Mann Gulch and South Canyon—firefighters immortalized in Norman Maclean's *Young Men and Fire* and John Maclean's *Fire on the Mountain*—Krebs began building his case:

First and foremost of the Orders dealt with what the firefighters are there to encounter: "the fire."

1. Keep informed on fire weather conditions and forecasts.
2. Know what your fire is doing at all times. Observe personally, use scouts.
3. Base all action on current and expected fire behavior of the fire.

Each of the 10 Standard Orders are prefaced by the silent imperative "you," meaning the on-the-ground firefighters, the person who is putting her or his life on the line!

My gut aches when I think of the lives that could have been spared, the injuries or close calls which could have been avoided, had these three Orders been routinely and regularly addressed prior to and during every fire assignment![1]

The article went on to catalog the other seven Orders in a specific fashion, first listing three that had to do with fireline safety, followed by three more that dealt with "organizational control." Krebs concluded by observing that the original Ten Standard Orders placed the order "Fight fire aggressively but provide for safety first" not at the beginning of the list, as do the current Fire Orders, but at the end.

After briefly discussing Krebs's recommendations, we focused on the Eighteen Situations That Shout "Watch Out!" and linked each Situation to violations of the Ten Standard Orders.

"Look at the first Situation," Fredrick instructed. "If your fire is not scouted and sized up, what Fire Order does that violate?"

"The second one," a firefighter from Jameson answered, basing his answer on the Original Ten Standard Fire Orders. "Because if your fire is not sized up, you don't know what your fire is doing at all times."

"Right. What else?" Fredrick asked.

"Base all action on current and expected behavior of the fire," Diego responded.

"Okay, good." Fredrick said. "And what about the next Situation, fighting fire in country not seen in daylight?"

"That violates the same two Orders," I answered.

"Yep. And what about the next one, safety zones and escape routes not identified?"

"The fourth Order," a Jameson firefighter responded immediately. "'Have escape routes and make them known.'"

Fredrick walked us through the Eighteen Situations, illustrating that each Situation violates one or more of the Orders.[2]

During the second day of training, we were asked to apply the Ten and Eighteen to various firefighting scenarios taken from previous fire seasons. The first exercise was modeled after a fire in Washington. Fredrick read the instructions aloud: "Run through the risk management process in the Incident Response Pocket Guide. Armed with this information, how would you assign the resources available while adhering to the Ten Standard Fire Orders and mitigating any 'Watch Out' Situations?"

We pulled out our Incident Response Pocket Guides (IRPGs) from the side pockets of our fire pants. I was issued my IRPG on my first day on the job along with my other personal protective equipment. My crewmembers always carried these small notebooks—which detailed numerous safety procedures, first-aid guidelines, and operational procedures for dealing with aviation, dangerous weather conditions, and urban-interface firefighting. The multicolored paper that made up the IRPG was held together by a yellow plastic cover: the front flap displayed a line of firefighters marching single-file next to a helicopter, a fire engine, and a bulldozer; the back flap listed the Ten and Eighteen in bold print.

We flipped through our IRPGs and studied the given scenario. A fire was burning in a steep and narrow canyon on the west side of a creek; some spot fires were burning actively on the east side of the creek; the fuel types were ponderosa, Douglas fir, lodgepole pine, spruce, cottonwood, birch, shrubs, and bushes; the temperature was seventy degrees, the relative humidity 50 percent; winds were calm.

"What would you guys do?" Fredrick asked.

"First, we have to identify safety zones and escape routes," Diego answered.

"Okay. Where would your safety zones and escape routes be?"

"If we were fighting the main fire," Diego responded, pointing to the diagram of the fire, "I would think that our escape route would be the main road and our safety zones would be south of the fire, 'cause if it's in a canyon, then it's gonna travel upwards, like, north."

"All right, good. What else?"

"Well, another thing is that we're getting frequent spot fires across the line," a Jameson crewmember observed, referring to the sixteenth Situation. "So that's something to watch out for."

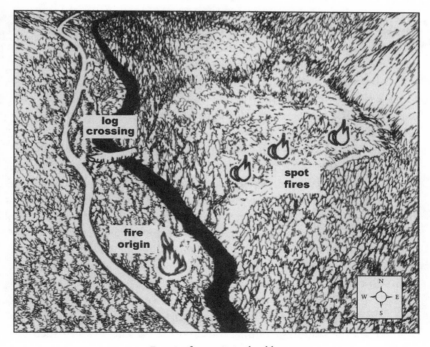

Exercise from training booklet

"And how would you deal with those spots?" Fredrick asked.

"Well, uh, it says that we have a type 2 crew. So, what I would do is send a few guys over to those spots to dig line around them. They could go across this log crossing or whatever. First, I would post a lookout, and then I would have them dig line around each spot. If the spots were big, I would probably dig line around all of them, anchoring in the creek, but if they were smaller, I would probably just dig line around each individual spot."

"Where would your safety zones and escape routes be?"

"Back across the log and onto the road."

"Okay, sounds good." Fredrick affirmed. "What else?"

The rest of the day proceeded like this. We role-played through various scenarios, studying photocopies of fires from last season with different topographies, hazards, weather patterns, and fire behavior, and we always formulated our approach to each on-paper burn according to the mandates of the Ten and Eighteen.

Whereas returning firefighters' training consisted of this two-day refresher class, first-year firefighters attended a basic training course during their first two weeks on the job. The course covered everything from safety procedures, basic fire behavior, and weather systems to first aid and deadly fires. Although an experienced firefighter led the course, most of the information came through interactive videotapes. At several intervals, instructors paused the videos to ask trainees questions or to clarify certain points. In sum, basic training consisted of sitting in an air-conditioned room eating Cheetos or chewing Skoal while an old-timer, long-retired, explained basic fire behavior through a scratchy twenty-year-old VHS tape.

At the conclusion of both training courses, firefighters completed two evaluations. The first was a multiple-choice test that summarized the main points of the course; the second was a timed trial where trainees had to pull a fire shelter out of its plastic casing, climb into it, and secure the corners with their hands and feet within thirty seconds (a difficult task on windy days). The fire shelter test, which all firefighters must pass every year, was the only practice-based training new firefighters received during the introductory course.[3] Once crewmembers passed these two examinations, they had to undergo a physical capabilities trial called the pack test. To pass, they had to hike three miles carrying a forty-five-pound backpack in forty-five minutes or less without running or jogging. Firefighters who passed the training examinations and the pack test were issued red cards. A red card officially certified a crewmember for one fire season; it could also be flashed at the check-out counter of Justin's Western Wear in Flagstaff for a 10 percent discount on fire boots.

The Ten and Eighteen

For the most part, my crewmembers thought training courses were a necessary burden, though one that bore little fruit.[4] New firefighters found basic training excruciatingly boring and believed it could be shortened considerably, while returning crewmembers tended to see the refresher course as something that only repeated what they already knew. Plus, firefighters in training were not on call. If a fire broke out, the rest of the firecrew scurried off to the action while trainees remained seated in a makeshift office. (Returning to the station after a fire, the crewmembers who responded to the smoke were usually quick to gloat to the trainees about the fun they had and the money they made on the line.) Most of my crewmembers did not believe training adequately prepared them for the challenges of firefighting; they felt, as Peter put it, that "most of your experience and training comes on the ground."

"What do you think about training?" I asked George shortly after we finished the refresher course, as we patrolled a forest road in the chase truck. "Do you think it prepares you well?"

"Uh, I mean, the courses, of course, helped, that our instructor put us through, but most of the stuff you have to be able to see on a fire to actually know really what they're talking about. They can say, 'Yeah, this is a crown fire. This is what it sounds like when it's coming.' But until you hear it, you don't really know exactly what they're talking about. . . . Fire's something that you have to see to really know and understand what it's doing."

To George, fire could be grasped only through intimate engagements. To know fire was to experience it, to see it, to hear it, to fight it. He understood "book knowledge" of firefighting to be next to worthless, and many of his crewmembers agreed.

"Do you think that the training you received adequately prepared you for the shit you were going to see?" I asked Bryan during a conversation in my room in crew quarters.

"Nope," he replied. "What prepared me? Well, the stuff they teach you in training, you know, give them the best classroom shit that you could give them and put them out there and tell them, 'Now, deal with this!' You know what would happen?

"The training is good, because it opens your eyes and lets you see what's going on, but it's the experience that you build off of to get to where you are. . . . We could all pick up a book and read fire behavior, and we could all have it word-for-word from a book, but until you see it, you don't know it. . . . You've got to *see it burn to learn.* You've got to experience it. . . . They can preach fire behavior, but until you see it, it's just what you've read."

Many of my crewmembers distinguished book learning from body learning, the classroom from the fireline, science (*episteme*) from craft (*techne*). Thurman often drew a distinction between "paper-qualified" and "experience-qualified" firefighters.

"We're getting bigger fires," he explained to me from his office chair. "They're getting more involved-type thing, urban interface, they are involving a lot more people, and you really don't really have that expertise out there. . . . So we're gonna *continue* to hurt people, we're probably gonna *continue* to kill people. . . . Some of the aspects of the firefighting arena have really improved. Uh, other ends of it have really gone downhill. The expertise that you're seeing on the fireline isn't there. You've got folks in positions that are paper qualified, that have been through all the classes. Their experience level is very minimal, so they can't go out there and be real effective, trying to carry out some of the things that were asked. So you see a decline on those ends."

To Thurman, experience qualification was the *only* type of qualification. Paper qualification must be tempered and tested by fire, by on-the-ground experience. If a novice approached wildfire either as a student (with only book knowledge) or as a maverick (with nothing but guts), he was bound to lose.

Although Thurman believed basic training courses were largely unhelpful, though necessary, he did not have the same feelings for the Ten and Eighteen. On the contrary, he and other supervisors instructed crewmembers that they could avoid injury and death by executing them successfully. Accordingly, he would regularly quiz firefighters on their knowledge of the mandates. If crewmembers missed just one Order, they were severely chastised. I learned this lesson the hard way.

The day I earned the epithet "Deployment Desmond" began like any other day. Thurman drove down from Jameson, as he often did, and summoned the crew to the conference room. We gathered around the four wooden tables pushed together to form a large rectangle in the center of the room and sat quietly and patiently, waiting for the boss to begin.

Fidgeting with his beard, Thurman eyed the crew before breaking the silence. "George, what's the first Fire Order?"

"Fight fire aggressively but provide for safety first!" George rattled off immediately.

Thurman nodded sharply and looked at Kris, who was seated to the right of George. Kris didn't miss a beat: "Initiate all action based on current and expected fire behavior."

My heart dropped as I realized that a round-robin was under way and that I was responsible for the next Order.

"Recall, respond, r-, r-, r-*something*," I clumsily thought to myself.

I had been on the job only nine days, and I hadn't fully recommitted the Ten and Eighteen to memory. My palms began to sweat. All eyes were on me, including Thurman's dark brown ones.

"R-respond to supervisors, no, wait, uh, r-recognize the immediate, uh," I stuttered, failing miserably. My mind blanked, and I stared at Thurman, mute and embarrassed.

Everyone turned from me to Thurman, who glared at me without a word. He let me squirm in my ignorance for a ten-second eternity before snapping, "One hundred push-ups!"

"You got it," I responded with my head down.

Thurman turned from me to Steve, who was seated to my right, and nodded. Steve picked up my slack and answered, "*Recognize* current weather conditions and obtain forecasts." He made sure to accent the word "recognize," giving me a sideways glance.

The chant resumed. After everyone successfully rattled off the Orders, except me and (to my surprise) Nicholas, Thurman paused. His eyes bounced from me to the table, then to Nicholas, and I knew he was thinking up something mean to say.

Finally, looking at the two of us failures, he tersely instructed, "Desmond. Masayesva. If you don't want to practice your Fire Orders you can practice with your fire *shelters!*"

The comment stung. What Thurman meant by "practicing with our fire shelters" was that ignorance of the Ten and Eighteen would land us in a deadly situation. At that very moment we were the weakest links, and my crewmembers let me know it. After the meeting, I avoided Thurman by rushing into the kitchen to fill my water bottle. Peter, J.J., Donald, Kris, and Tank followed close behind to twist the knife further.

J.J. laid his hand on my shoulder and sighed loudly, feigning sympathy, before folding over with laughter and confessing, "Better you than me, Matt. Better *you* than me."

Surrounding crewmembers erupted with hoots and hollers. They pointed fingers and offered more wisecracks, which I tried to ignore. I scurried out the door and struggled through my push-ups. When I returned to the group, my crewmembers welcomed me back as "Fire Shelter Boy" and "Deployment Desmond," referring to the act of "deploying" a fire shelter. It was Donald who came up with "Deployment Desmond," an epithet that would stick with me throughout my fieldwork. Immediately after work, I memorized the Ten and Eighteen forward and backward.

Thurman and Allen administered such tests throughout the season. Allen liked to quiz the crew by asking them to write down the Ten and Eighteen in five minutes. To prepare for these pop quizzes, crewmembers often reviewed the Orders and Situations from their IRPGs. They studied during the workday and afterward, refreshing their memories over dinner or before falling asleep. By midseason, crewmembers could recite the Ten and Eighteen just as easily as they could pledge allegiance to the flag. Again and again, supervisors reminded their subordinates that the Ten and Eighteen were a firefighter's safety net, his parachute, his bulletproof vest—a promise of protection in bold print. As Thurman put it, while leading a meeting in the conference room toward the end of the season, "We can send you to training until we fill up this room with certificates, but unless you know these things, these Ten Orders, these Eighteen Situations, then you're gonna fail. And you're gonna drag down those who are with you to fail. . . . It's proven that shelters save lives, but if you know these types of things, you won't need them. Damn it, we want you here tomorrow. We want you here next year, and it's pretty simple what you have to do to stay safe: know your Ten and Eighteen."

The Rodeo-Chediski Fire

In the middle of June 2002 two strangers, a man and a woman, through two disconnected acts of desperation, created something terrible, something that would scar the landscape of Arizona and the memories of its citizens for generations. The man was poor. At twenty-nine, Leonard Gregg was struggling to make ends meet for himself and his family. He was a member of the White Mountain Apache Tribe employed on a Bureau of Indian Affairs contract firecrew (a crew that makes money only when fires bust). Facing the dire poverty that affects many people living on Native American reservations, Gregg played the role of arsonist in order to play the role of breadwinner. On June 18, he lit two fires with stick matches in a deserted area outside Cibecue, Arizona, in hopes of fighting them later that day and collecting a paycheck later that week. The first fire, the Pina fire, burned a single acre; the second, the Rodeo fire, torched over 1,000 acres in a matter of hours. The next day the Rodeo fire, aided by a severe drought and strong winds, scorched over 55,000 acres. The day after that, it doubled in size.

The woman was stranded. On the same day that Leonard Gregg touched a few matches to dry grass, Valinda Jo Elliott, a thirty-two-year-old white woman, ran out of gas in the middle of the White Mountain Apache Indian Reservation, where she was trespassing on a back road. She abandoned her car and stumbled around the deserted hills, trying to establish cell-phone reception. After being lost for two nights, she was hot, hungry, and dehydrated. So when a news helicopter sped her way, Elliott didn't think twice about lighting a signal fire. She pulled out a cigarette lighter and ignited a desert bush right below Chediski Mountain. The fire didn't stay in that bush for long. By the time the news chopper picked Elliott up, flames had raced up a hill, consuming all vegetation in sight. The next morning, the Chediski fire covered over 14,000 acres. It pushed east while the Rodeo fire pushed west. Barreling toward one another, seemingly drawn together by some primordial attractant, the two colossal burns joined forces on June 23.[5]

In what follows I do not offer a full-bodied description of the Rodeo-Chediski complex, a play-by-play of unfolding events; nor do I explain the various dynamics of fire camp, the diverse strategies employed while fighting the fire, or the countless hours of mop-up and rehabilitation work we carried out after the smoke had cleared. Rather, I analyze a single night on the fireline, paying special attention to how the Ten and Eighteen were employed on the ground.[6] I have described how crewmembers encounter these firefighting fundamentals through training exercises and supervisors' drills; now I turn to analyzing the "relationship of the formal plan to actual conduct" and show the extent to which firefighters apply these rules among torching trees and billows of black smoke.[7]

We had been fighting the Rodeo-Chediski fire for about a week before we received orders to go to a small mountain community five miles or so off the main highway. The fire was quickly encroaching on the community, which had been evacuated days before, and we were instructed to save as many homes as possible. I rode in the chase truck with George, while J.J. rode in the engine with Arturo Mata, a Hispanic engine foreman nicknamed "Chubby" (though he wasn't chubby at all) who fought fire at Elk River for seven seasons before being promoted and moving to Jameson. The engine lumbered into the threatened mountain community past an old man whose gray beard hung down to his chest. He stood alone beside a pile of smoldering rubble that the day before had been his aluminum trailer, holding a garden hose that arced a pathetic stream onto the steaming remnants of his life. He shook his fist at us and cursed. Too late for him, we drove on, into the flames.

"Engine Seven-one, Two-seven-two," Thurman called us over the radio.

"Go 'head, Rex," Arturo answered.

"Location?"

"We're driving down the forest road into the development. We just passed over the bridge."

"Okay. I want you guys to hold up in the safety zone a little up the road there. You'll see where we flagged it off. It's in a huge meadow off to the left side of the road. You can't miss it."

"Copy."

"Uh, things are starting to heat up in here, Arturo, and I want you guys to hold up in that safety zone until the temperature drops and the RH starts to rise. Hold up there and wait for my instructions."

"Copy."

"Two-seven-two clear."

"Engine Seven-one."

After using wire cutters to snip the barbed-wire fence that encircled the meadow so the engine could get though, we parked in the middle of the safety zone. Piling out of the truck, we watched the forest ignite around us. The main fire rolled with force across a group of hills three or four miles away. But auxiliary fires caused by launched spots were beginning to ignite in all directions. Torching trees and racing ground fire nipped at the borders of our safety-zone meadow, a meadow filled with dead plain grass that would welcome flames the way water welcomes electricity.

"All right guys, listen up," Arturo instructed. "If it looks like the fire is going to jump in this safety zone, what we are going to do is dig line around the engine and light off from here. We'll backburn and kill all the fuel before the fire reaches us. Cool?"

"Cool," we answered simultaneously.

We watched the phantom flames weave through occluding smoke, sometimes crawling stealthily among the shrubbery before spinning up the trunks of ponderosas and consuming entire trees from trunk to tip. Other times the flames formed themselves into a ball and rolled on top of the treeline, scorching the top half of trunks but leaving the bottom half undisturbed. Still other times, the flames followed the charcoal smoke column fifty feet above the treetops before lashing out at the sky with a flash of fleeting orange in search of something else to burn.

We admired the firestorm from the safety of our meadow. Arturo seemed fascinated. Sporting a pair of thick-rimmed glasses, a goatee, and a black ponytail that trailed down to the small of his back, he fixed on one spectacle after another. "Damn! Look at that!" he exclaimed again and again. J.J. and George looked serious and purposeful. They did not goof off or tease one another. They abstained from their usual antics and resolutely studied the movements of a blaze much bigger and much more violent than any fire they had ever seen. I stood silently beside them, nervous and ready, cautious but eager. The fire was having its way with the forest; so when Thurman called ninety minutes later and instructed us to proceed down the road, I jumped in the chase truck with a yell. But then I swallowed hard.

As the sun sank below the smoky horizon, the coolness of night began to pacify the fire. I stared out the truck window while George drove slowly behind the engine into an area we had never seen. As we approached the community, fire surrounded us. Both sides of the road were ablaze: flames towered above our heads, consuming the branches of mixed conifers and pines, and sped beneath our tires on the backs of dry leaves and pine needles.

After a few minutes we reached the small development, a circular scattering of thirty or forty homes, varying in size, connected by a small grid of dirt roads. Thurman drove an ATV beside the engine and told us where to park. We hopped out of our trucks and strapped on our fire packs, pulling them snugly around our shoulders and buckling the waist and chest straps: *click, click*. I twisted my waist and back to adjust the twenty-pound sack, shifting its contents: MREs, fusees, a headlamp, batteries, flagging, and water bottles. I cinched the wristbands on my leather gloves and reached behind me to tap my fire shelter. Arturo and I strapped on chest harnesses and turned the volume on our hand-held radios all the way up.

"Gentlemen!" Thurman greeted us with a half-cocked smile as we gathered in front of him. "How's everybody doing?"

"Good," we replied.

"All right. Some fire we got on our hands here, huh? All right, what we are going to do here, folks, is structure protection. We are going to try to save as many homes in here as we can. But we *aren't* going to be *stupid* about it. We aren't going to put ourselves in any type of danger out here. Understand?"

"Yes, sir," we answered.

"Now, your escape route is that route you just came in on, and your safety zone is that same clearing you were just at. Understand?"

"Yes."

"All right. Now, what I'm gonna do is walk you around these houses and show you what we're gonna do."

We stepped quickly behind Thurman as he marched up and down the dirt roads surrounding the houses, pointing out propane tanks, stacked woodpiles, power lines, and other hazards that awaited us. Thurman showed us the location of two "pumpkins," fold-out plastic water tanks that each held three hundred gallons, where we could refill the engine, and described the terrain surrounding the community.

"The fire is headed right this way, folks," the boss observed. "It will probably run through this place. So what I want all of you to do is to prepare the houses for the fire. Dig line around the propane tanks, scatter the woodpiles, uh, rake the pine needles away from the houses, and spray the houses down with foam. These type of things. Understand?"

"Yes, sir," we answered.

"All right. Arturo, you're gonna come with me. We're gonna keep an eye on the fire and formulate the best plan of attack in here, work with the dozer to push some stuff through. The rest of you, take the engine, start

over here on the west side, closest to the main fire, and start protecting them houses. Understand?"

"Yes."

"Desmond," Thurman addressed me.

"Yes, sir," I answered.

"That radio work?" Thurman asked, pointing to my chest.

"Yes, sir."

"Okay. What I want you to do is spin the weather every thirty minutes and make sure everyone on the line knows what the weather is doing out here."

"Got it."

"Okay, folks. Be safe out there. I know I don't have to tell you this, but this is no time to get complacent. If you feel that the fire is getting too close, back the hell off, head out to the safety zone using the escape route I just told you about. But, uh, let's work hard out there. We've got a chance to do some good in here. Save some houses and be heroes. Uh, been getting pretty tired of sitting on our ass at base camp all day, now we have a chance to do some good. But, uh, let's be safe. Any questions?"

"No, sir," we answered.

"All right. Let's get to work."

J.J., George, and I marched back to the engine. Once there, we unzipped our fire packs and pulled out our headlamps, single-bulb lamps connected to thick rubber bands, and strapped them onto our helmets like coal miners. We did not turn the lamps on yet, for though night had fallen and slow-rising smoke hovered above the community, an orange-and-yellow glow rose above the surrounding hills like the dawn and illuminated the smoke, casting light on our surroundings and reminding us of the threat racing our way. We could hear the fire rumbling in the distance.

J.J. parked next to a group of houses and began to prime the gasoline-powered water pump mounted on the rear of the engine. The pump mixed the four hundred gallons of water in the engine's tank with a flame-retardant foam mixture and allowed us to shoot a stream of water with up to 300 psi behind it. While J.J. prepared the pump, I climbed on top of the engine and unhooked the canvas tarp that covered dozens of nozzles, gated wye valves, hosepacks, and several rolls of hose. The engine carried many sizes of hose, but on most fires we used only a lateral and a trunk line. The lateral was a cotton-jacket hose, one inch in diameter, used to spray the water. It was the hose firefighters held. The trunk line was an inch and a half thick, used to encircle fires. Because our task didn't require a trunk line, I grabbed fifty feet of lateral hose and climbed down.

After snapping off the rubber band that secured the hose roll, I tossed the hose down a slight incline, allowing it to unroll as it went. Then I hooked the female end of the hose up to a one-inch adaptor that George had already fitted to the engine pump. George screwed a forester nozzle onto the male end of the hose.

"We should probably use a foam nozzle, since we're gonna be trying to foam the shit out of these houses," I told George.

"You think?" George responded.

"Yeah, plus those foam nozzles put out *a lot* of foam."

"All right," George agreed. He unscrewed the forester and headed for the engine cabinet to switch nozzles.

By the time George had replaced the forester with a bright orange foam nozzle, made out of an eighteen-inch length of PVC pipe, J.J. had cranked up the pump, which sputtered and coughed on its mounting brackets—the rusted contraption was nearing the end of its days. With the old pump primed and the hose secured, we were ready to get to work.

George held the hose and let fly a sudsy stream of foam and water onto an abandoned house, spraying the roof, walls, and porch. The foam coated the house, drying slightly and leaving a slippery film that would make it harder for the fire to penetrate the building. George was laying it on thick, soaking every inch of the house.

"George!" J.J. yelled from the engine pump, where he was monitoring the water pressure. "Don't straight stream everything continuously, man. We need to conserve some water."

"All right," George yelled back, cutting off the hose.

After we foamed down a few houses, I stepped away to spin the weather. Under a pine tree, I took off my fire pack and pulled out a belt weather kit. Unsnapping the button of the kit, held together in a soiled and worn red nylon pouch, I pulled out a sling psychrometer (we called it "the sling") used to obtain readings of temperature, relative humidity, and dew point. The sling had two bulbs—a "dry bulb," which is a basic thermometer, and a "wet bulb," used to obtain the relative humidity (RH)—secured to a rectangular aluminum mount roughly six inches long and one inch wide. The mount was attached to a thin chain connected to a pencil-sized round metal handle. I unscrewed the cap from a small bottle of distilled water in the weather kit, dipped the wet bulb in the water, turned away from the wind, and spun the sling, rotating my wrist to circulate the bulbs. After sixty seconds of spinning, I glanced down at the reading on the wet and dry bulbs: forty and sixty-five. Next I reached into the weather kit and unfolded a large paper table with wet bulb readings listed in the far left column and dry bulb readings on the top row. The many intersecting squares between these axes each displayed two numbers: the top number was the dew point, and the bottom number was the RH. I placed my index finger on the box created by my two measures and found the RH reading. After jotting the numbers on a small pad, I radioed in the update:

"Rodeo fire, Desmond. Weather update." I took my thumb off the button and paused for two seconds before continuing, "Dry bulb sixty-five, wet bulb forty. Relative humidity is ten. Winds out of the south, southwest, five to seven miles per hour."

After I heard Thurman, Arturo, and a few firefighters from other crews respond with a reaffirming "copy," I packed up the weather kit and marched back to rejoin George and J.J. I found my two crewmembers quickly dismantling a pile of wood leaning against the side of a house. I joined in, hurling the juniper logs as far from the house as I could. After we dispersed the woodpile, George sprayed the house down with foam, and we moved to the next structure. The three of us scurried around several houses, working fast and purposefully. We knew the fire was closing in.

The fire didn't roar into the community like a Mack truck or advance like a unified military formation. It didn't barge in through the front door or kick down the rear; instead, it sneaked in through every window, every crack and opening, every vulnerable spot, quietly and cleverly invading the community from all directions. It came from the air, since the main fire had topped the surrounding hills and sent embers and charred pine-cones pouring over roofs and onto wooden porches. And it came from the ground as lines of flame jumped playfully from dry leaf to dry leaf until they found their way into the mountain community. Drunk and disorderly, the fire skipped over houses and through backyards. Groves of trees between houses caught fire here and there; then a shed ignited and a house went up in flames, followed by another, then another. The fire had caught up with us. J.J., George, and I could no longer proceed in an orderly, preventive manner. We now had to react to the whims of the flames.

We jumped in the engine and sped to the first house we saw burst into flames. By the time we arrived, the entire structure—a two-story log cabin with a wraparound porch—was engulfed. Knowing there was nothing we could do, we saved our water and drove on.

"Desmond, Thurman," the boss called over the radio.

"Go, 'head, Rex," I answered.

"I want you guys to head over here to the east end of the community, across from the second pumpkin."

"Copy."

Thurman was waiting for us. We hustled out of the engine to meet him.

"How's everybody doing?" Thurman asked.

"Good," we all responded.

"Okay, you guys got to be real heads-up in here now. Really be aware of things that are going on in here. Remember your LCES, your Ten and Eighteen, your look up, look down, look all around. Understand?"

"Yes, sir."

"You really want to be heads-up with this urban-interface type of thing. Don't extend yourselves. Don't put yourselves in a situation that could harm you. Understand?"

"Yes, sir."

"Good. Now, see that house?" Thurman asked, pointing to a medium-sized house next to a small barn in an open prairie at the far end of the community.

"Yes."

"That fire is gonna come sweeping through that plain grass and take that house. What I want you guys to do is to dig line around the house and burn out from there. Don't spend a whole hell of a lot of time doing it. Get in there and get it done. We can save this house. So, dig a good line, and then light off. Understand?"

"Yes, sir."

"Good. Desmond, you still spinning that weather?"

"Yes, sir," I answered quickly.

"Okay, good. Let's keep doing it. Let's go."

At that, J.J., George, and I turned and jogged to the engine. J.J. slung open the engine cabinet that held the hand tools. He handed me a Pulaski and took combis for himself and George. We hiked as quickly as we could to the house and barn, which were not yet threatened by flames. We didn't ask why this house should be saved while another one burned; we didn't quibble over the size of the dwellings or guess what kind of people lived there; we simply did what the boss told us.

We lined up. I took the lead, and George took the anchor.

"George, make sure the line is good," I said. "And let me know if I need to take more. We don't want the backburn creeping up on this house."

"Check," George answered.

"Shit, guys, this is the real deal," I observed with a smile.

"Hell yeah, it is," J.J. responded resolutely.

"All right, you guys ready?" I asked.

"Ready," my two crewmembers answered.

"All right. Movin'," I announced before slamming my Pulaski into the ground.

After I had swung my tool two dozen or so times, George yelled, "Take more!"

This meant I needed to bust up more ground, to narrow the space between my hits. A line-digging crew of three was a small crew indeed; essentially, each of us would have to pull the dirt of three crewmembers.

I hastened and deepened my swings. Luckily the ground wasn't stubborn. It wasn't rocky or full of gnarled roots, and the grass was not clumped in tight bunches that glued themselves to the ground through intricate root systems. Our tools cut through the dirt quickly, and after ten minutes or so we had surrounded half the house and barn. Still, my body quickly grew tired. We had been fighting the Rodeo-Chediski fire for roughly a week straight, sleeping in tents at a base camp in the parking lot of an abandoned town's high school. We were running on little sleep and had been worked hard. But having never before been called to defend someone's home, we dug with heart, with determination, tenaciously swinging our tools around some stranger's home within which, perhaps, were someone's books, someone's picture albums, someone's children's drawings.

It took roughly twenty-five minutes of hard digging to encircle the house and the barn. When we finished we took a short breather, wiping the sweat from our faces and chugging some water from the canteens strapped to our fire packs.

"Let's inspect it," J.J. suggested.

We paced around our line carefully, searching out weak spots and making repairs. Satisfied with our craftsmanship after one lap, we unzipped our fire packs and pulled out our fusees to backburn.

"Desmond, Thurman," the boss's voice crackled through my radio.

"Go 'head, Rex," I answered, still breathing heavily.

"How's it comin'?"

"Good. We just finished the line and are about to burn out."

"Okay, good. I want you guys to hold off on the burnout operation. I want to get you in here and get you working the engine on some of these houses like you were doing before."

"Damn," George said, after I directed a disappointed glance in his direction. "I wanted to light this motha off."

"No, Rex, we are going to light this motha off," I said into the radio without pushing the transmitting button.

"*Shiiiiit,*" J.J. laughed, calling my bluff.

"Okay Rex," I answered, clicking the button this time. "We'll head over there right now."

We climbed back into the engine and sped down the dirt roads. We sprayed down a handful of houses with foam, dug line through someone's backyard and around several propane tanks, scattered more woodpiles, and drove on to look for more vulnerable areas.

"Look at that!" J.J. shouted, pointing out the window.

George and I snapped our heads to the left and spotted the house J.J. was pointing at. Fire was creeping up the porch steps and wrapping itself around the wooden columns that supported the porch roof.

"Let's chop it off!" J.J. yelled, slamming the engine into park.

George, J.J., and I bounded out of the engine and swooped around to the tool cabinet. After each of us grabbed a Pulaski, we ran over to the porch and proceeded to demolish the burning steps and railing. Surrounding the porch steps, we synchronized our Pulaski swings so one hit would

come directly after another. *Slam, slam, slam!* Our ax heads fell hard onto the burning wood, splitting the steps into pieces. Each time we separated a piece of smoldering wood, someone would pick it up with his gloved hand and heave it away from the house. As flames teased at our shins and knees, we kept at it, chopping at the porch ferociously.

Suddenly we heard Thurman's voice behind us: "Fuck yeah! Fuck yeah!" he yelled over the splitting wood. "Chop that mother fucker! Get on it boys!"

Thurman came rushing over to us, pumping both arms skyward, cheering us on: "Come on! Fuck yeah! Fuck yeah!"

Thurman's shouts made us swing harder and faster. Our rhythm sped up, and we started grunting and yelling with each swing, pounding away at the porch. *Slam!* The step split, and the flames jumped through the new crack. *Slam!* The piece fell, and George threw it to the side.

By the time we had cut all the engulfed wood away from the porch, Thurman had primed the engine pump and was ready with the hose. He handed the nozzle to George, who foamed down the porch while J.J. and I knelt on the ground and rubbed dirt into the pieces of wood we had scattered, suffocating the flames. When the task was completed, the house, for now, was saved. And as I stood with J.J. and George, lungs heaving and shoulders weighty, exhausted and muddy, I raised my arm to receive a high five from Thurman and felt satisfied and proud. We didn't save every home in that community, but we saved that one—we three and our Pulaskis.

Fighting Fire on Paper and in Practice

If I were to analyze the Rodeo-Chediski fire in accordance with the organizational thinking of the Forest Service, I would juxtapose every event to the bylaws of the Ten and Eighteen. I would study the fire retrospectively—just as I was taught to do in basic training courses—evaluating how well each action satisfied the Orders and Situations. This way of proceeding, so the logic goes, would allow me to expose any chinks in our armor of safety. Such an analysis would look something like this: When fighting the Rodeo-Chediski fire, my crewmembers and I satisfied many of the mandates listed in the Ten and Eighteen. We initiated our action in compliance with Thurman's description of the fire's behavior; we paid attention to weather conditions by obtaining temperature and humidity readings every thirty minutes; we were given clear instructions by Thurman and followed them without question; we stayed in communication with Thurman and other firefighters at the site by handheld radios; we determined safety zones and escape routes; I believe each crewmember retained control. And to the extent that these judgments can be made, we stayed alert; we kept calm; we thought clearly; we acted decisively. Although most of the Ten and Eighteen were "obeyed" when we battled the fire that night, there were moments of transgression, moments when we failed to follow some of the Orders or to avoid some of the Situations. Consider the eighth Order: "Establish lookouts in potentially hazardous situations." Although Thurman and Arturo served as our lookouts throughout the night, they could not be everywhere, carefully observing each "hazardous situation." We worked with lookouts sometimes and without them other times. When we chopped off the porch, Thurman was there to watch our backs (and cheer us on); but when we dug line around the house and barn, no lookouts were posted.[8] Several "Watch Out" Situations were compromised: We fought the fire "in country not seen in daylight" (a breach of the second Situation); we dug line without a safe anchor point (a breach of the eighth Situation); we foamed down houses with dry, unburned fuel between us and the flames (a breach of the eleventh Situation); and we chased frequent spot fires (a breach of the sixteenth Situation).

This way of proceeding emphasizes the question of fault; it defines "competence" as the successful and responsible execution of the Ten and Eighteen and "deviance" as the failure to follow these rules; and it understands firefighters' actions only through the retrospective application of a set of regulations. Although the standard practices of the Forest Service follow this kind of thinking—manifest in basic training courses and instructional materials, supervisors' actions and opinions, and (as we will see in chapter 8) fatality investigations—on closer inspection such seemingly reasonable and commonsense logic is fundamentally flawed.

The practice of analyzing crewmembers' actions on the fireline through the Ten and Eighteen assumes that crewmembers actually can fight a fire without violating an Order or a Situation. In reality, however, this assumption is not viable. It is impossible to fight a wildfire without violating at least one Order or Situation.[9] If we compromised some of the Orders and Situations while fighting the Rodeo-Chediski fire, it was not because we fought the fire irresponsibly or haphazardly. On the contrary, we took special precautious (e.g., waiting in the safety zone until the temperature fell; spinning the weather every thirty minutes) to "provide for safety first," as the first Order advises. Rather, it was because the Ten and Eighteen are unachievable standards, realistic only on paper. In order to engage wildfire in a meaningful way—that is, to *fight* it—no matter what its size or intensity, firefighters must sidestep portions of the Ten and Eighteen.[10] In principle, the Ten and Eighteen should never be violated; they are revered as life-and-death ultimatums: "Follow these rules, and no harm will come to you; break them, and you will invite harm upon yourself." But in practice the Ten and Eighteen are too much to ask of ground-pounding crewmembers engaged in the controlled chaos that is firefighting. These rules are "ideally possible but practically unattainable."[11]

Explanations that rely on the mechanical notion of following a rule, of "obeying" or "violating" the Ten and Eighteen, do not help to illuminate the actual practices of firefighting.[12] On the contrary, such rule-based investigations obscure the thousands of dynamic and subtle strategies firefighters employ while battling a blaze. Those who regard a crewmember's craft only as adherence to regulations, only as a "yes" to the Ten and Eighteen, blot out the immense intricacy inherent in every act of firefighting. Consider the complexities of digging line. Although some Orders and Situations stipulate the nature of digging line—or, better yet, stipulate the nature of *unsafe* line digging—they do not come close to capturing the essence of digging line, an essence uncovered only when we concentrate on the practice (not the rules) of ground pounding.

During the Rodeo-Chediski fire, George, J.J., and I put in motion dozens of practices (some tacit, some conscious) when digging line around the house and barn. We positioned our bodies next to one another in a specific order and with specific spacing requirements (making sure we did not stand too close or too far from one another). Each time we slammed our tools into the ground, we paid attention to the angle of the blade, the kind of soil and vegetation we were busting through, the curvature and width of the fireline, and the "purity" of the line (that is, how much our mineral-soil-only line was contaminated with roots, pine needles, grass, and other flammable vegetation). We held our tools in such a way that we could swing with strength, gripping the handles tightly enough to squelch the vibration caused when the metal head hit a rock but loosely enough to avoid hand cramps and aching knuckles. We bent our backs at a forty-five-degree angle, low enough to dig line but upright enough to watch our surroundings, and shuffled our feet side to side after every hit, dragging our boots, not lifting them. We scraped off the top layer of the soil but did not dig deeper than was necessary. I made sure to bust up enough ground to allow J.J. to scrape the dirt away quickly, while George took time to perfect the line and kick down the small berm created by J.J.'s pulls. All the while, we exchanged curt statements: *Take more. Take less. How's it looking? Got some roots here. Tied in.* When I needed to fell a sapling in the path of our line, I stood erect, spun my Pulaski 180 degrees, and chopped at the trunk with my ax head, announcing, "Swinging!" To confirm that he'd heard my pronouncement, J.J. echoed, "Swinging." George followed, "Swinging." When I ran across a grouping of slippery, moss-covered rocks, I yelled, "Watch your footing!" "Watch your footing," repeated J.J. "Footing," George acknowledged. As we swung our tools, our eyes concentrated not only on the construction of the line but also on the surroundings—crewmembers' actions, the house in front of us, the plain grass to our rear, the looming smoke, the surrounding flames—and our ears attuned themselves to the radio traffic as well as to the crackles and bellows of the fire. Although such practices are structured and constrained by the Ten and Eighteen, they cannot be adequately explained by these rules.[13]

Furthermore, the Ten and Eighteen do not apply themselves; they must be applied by firefighters engaged in action. Applying a rule is a practical accomplishment in itself, one that depends on an actor's interpretation.[14] In every situation, the actor must decide when to apply the rule, how to apply it, to what degree, under what conditions, and with what stipulations; as a result, in every situation a rule is applied "for another next first time," as Harold Garfinkel would say. Because the application of rules relies on the whims of interpretive actors, these actors' actions cannot be explained by the oversimplified notions of "following a rule" or "violating a rule," for an explanation of this nature would lead to nothing less than an infinite regress. For example, if firefighters wished to follow the fifth Order—"Ensure instructions are given and understood"—as accurately as possible, they would need to create more rules to satisfy the questions this Order generates. What are instructions? Do they come from supervisors or crewmembers? Do we need to acquire them for each activity? If not, when are instructions necessary and when are they superfluous? How will we know they are understood? Behind each rule are dozens of "unstated conditions" like these, conditions that can be satisfied only by the formulation of still another rule.[15] Thus, because applying a rule depends on another rule, which depends on another rule, and so on ad infinitum, practical activity cannot be adequately explained as following rules.[16]

For these reasons, analyzing firefighting only as the (successful or failed) execution of the Ten and Eighteen is thoroughly misguided, only limiting our understanding of the many minute techniques employed on the fireline. To best make sense of firefighting, we should not proceed mechanically, evaluating crewmembers' obedience to a set of rules; rather, we should pay attention to "the only evidence that counts," as Bourdieu would have it: the on-the-ground practices of firefighting.[17] Skilled firefighters employ bodily and practical knowledge; they attune their bodies to the rhythms and rushes of wildfire and literally "embody competence."[18] One cannot get by simply by "knowing" the Ten and Eighteen cerebrally or mnemonically or by "following" these rules; rather, one has to live and breathe the Ten and Eighteen, to condition one's movements and decisions around them, to acquire a habit of making decisive and quick choices when fighting fire that align (to varying degrees) with these safety guidelines. This "experience qualification," this *phronesis* of firefighting, lets firefighters act with swiftness and competence on the fireline; their practical knowledge helps them coordinate their actions and work efficiently, and it allows them to sense (to feel, to predict) the fire's next move.

The Source of Firefighting Competence

If this is so, then how do firefighters acquire this deep-seated bodily competence that they employ on the fireline? If their practical knowledge does not come from a strict application of the Ten and Eighteen, contrary to what our basic training lessons hold, then what is its source?

To my crewmembers, as we saw earlier, the answer lies in their experience on the fireline. Yet, though crewmembers claim they "had to see it burn to learn," in truth many lack extensive exposure to wildfire. Aside from old-timers like Nicholas and Allen, most have seen only a couple of fire seasons. Some have not been on a wildfire larger than twenty acres. Of course, firefighting experience helps to condition firefighting competence; however, if most of my crewmembers are new to the world of wildfire but nonetheless can perform proficiently and coordinate their actions impeccably on the fireline, then experience is not the only, or primary, source of competence.[19]

George, J.J., and I had never experienced anything like the Rodeo-Chediski fire. We had never faced flames of that magnitude or guarded houses against a fire's wrath. I had only two seasons under my belt, while both J.J. and George had only one. While navigating the perils of the fireline, we were not simply following rules or relying on years of firefighting experience. And though our training certainly informed our decisions and practices, it was only a brief and rather mnemonic education transmitted through videotapes and was not the primary basis of our know-how. If firefighting is not easy, and if the principal source of our firefighting competence was not to be found in training, experience, or obedience to the Ten and Eighteen, then how were we able to synchronize our actions on the fire and to work together seamlessly, safely, and efficiently?

The answer lies in the fact that we were already ready for the Rodeo-Chediski fire before we set foot on the fireline. As country boys, we came to the Forest Service already acclimated to the tasks of wildland firefighting; we possessed shared histories and competences, a country-masculine habitus, that helped us adjust to the demands of firefighting and coordinate our actions vis-à-vis one another. As Bourdieu observed in *The Logic of Practice,* "The habitus is precisely this immanent law, *lex insita,* inscribed in bodies by identical histories, which is the precondition not only for the co-ordination of practices but also for practices of co-ordination. The corrections and adjustments the agents themselves consciously carry out presuppose mastery of a common code; and undertakings of collective mobilization [such as firefighting] cannot succeed without a minimum of concordance between the *habitus* of the mobilizing agents [such as incident commanders like Thurman] . . . and the dispositions of those who recognize themselves in their practices or words [such as seasonal firefighters], and, above all, without the inclination towards grouping that springs from the spontaneous orchestration of dispositions."[20]

During the Rodeo-Chediski fire, J.J., George, and I worked side by side, quickly coordinating our actions and acclimating to different scenarios. To foam down houses, the three of us separately worked toward a shared goal: J.J. primed the pump, I fetched the hose, and George secured the nozzle. These independent (yet corresponding) actions allowed us to get water on the houses as soon as possible. We didn't intentionally coordinate each action; we didn't formulate a game plan; rather, our actions seemed to coordinate themselves. This process involved offering and accepting suggestions (*Let's use a foam nozzle instead of a forester, Don't use too much water*), always delivered in a hasty and forceful manner. If we were able to understand and act on these minimal suggestions, changing direction and making adjustments in response to words that barely formed sentences, it was because we shared a linguistic habitus, one formed in past pressure situations. Growing up, we took orders from a football coach who barked terse commands as Thurman did, and we orchestrated plays on the gridiron based on pithy phrases (*Forty-five is the Mike, Shift left, Watch the draw, Wing-right, thirty-eight sweep*). We knew the language of firefighting, so to speak, because we shared a linguistic disposition formed (and informed) by a shared country-masculine history. Because we possessed a similar history, we also possessed a common code that allowed us to communicate meaningfully and seamlessly even though we had never been in a situation like the one we faced that night.

J.J., George, and I adjusted our movements to one another on the fireline. When we stood heel to heel lopping off the porch, or dug line close together, or ran and jumped into the engine, or threw woodpiles away from threatened houses, our bodies harmonized with each other. Again, this was possible because we shared a country-masculine history that predisposed us to such actions.[21] When my country-masculine habitus encountered itself in the postures, movements, rhythms, gestures, and orientations of my crewmembers, it recognized something familiar, something known deep down, and accordingly it synchronized with other manifestations of itself, creating a chemistry of sorts that coordinated action.

Country competence served as the foundation for wildland firefighting competence. My crewmembers easily found the isolated mountain community, though they had never been there before, because the roads they drove to find smoke in the summer were the same ones they drove to find deer in the winter. Since many crewmembers took their driver's license test in the seat of a four-by-four pickup, it was not difficult for them to adjust to driving the chase truck or the engine. J.J., George, and I knew how to swing an ax to destroy a half-burned porch because we had been chopping our parents' and grandparents' wood since we were children. We knew how to observe the forest because our eyes had been searching the tips of pines and the trunks of oaks for years. Our ears knew what to listen for; our noses knew what the forest was supposed to smell like. Our footing and balance, posture and hiking style, sense of touch and movement were attuned to the forest, and this heightened awareness, this woodsy know-how inscribed in our histories and in our very bodies, allowed us to adapt quickly to the challenges of the fire.

When J.J., George, and I returned to fire camp after doing battle on the line, our faces, necks, arms, and legs were caked with a thin crust of dried sweat, ash, dirt, and hardened foam. Our filthy fire shirts and pants bore evidence of the dirty work of firefighting; globs of mud stuck to our boots; and we smelled of body odor and smoke. But we were used to getting dirty. As children, we were encouraged to muck around in the outdoors, and as teenagers, we were urged to muddy ourselves on the football field.

This is not a trivial point, for if one chooses to fight wildfire, one must not mind being coated in dirt, ash, and sweat for days on end. One crewmember returned to Elk River from a fourteen-day fire stint, where no showers were available, with large puss-filled swellings in his armpits that had to be lanced and drained. The doctor told him the swellings were brought on by the thick layer of dirt and ash that had clogged his pores, drastically hindering his ability to sweat. Stories like this are not uncommon, for wildland firefighters must function under extremely primitive conditions, stripped of amenities like running water, hot food, and, in Thurman's words, "little porcelain toilets." Far from shying away from such discomforts that affront cleanliness and the ways of civilization, crewmembers embrace them. They take pride in the soot that covers their faces, arms, legs, and even teeth after a full day's work on the fireline, and more to the point, they have known the taste and feel of dirt ever since they were children.

When we attempt to identify the source of firefighters' practical knowledge, when we pursue a trail leading back through young adulthood, adolescence, and childhood trying to put into words the unspoken intuitive competence that allows firefighters simply to do what they do, we discover that neither organizational socialization nor direct experience within the organization can lay full claim to being the source of this knowledge. The Forest Service accounts for firefighters' competence through training courses and the Ten and Eighteen, and firefighters tend to attribute their know-how to their time on the fireline, but there is a deeper source. There is something in the background, something alive, though invisible, and present in nearly every action of wildland firefighting; this "something" is the country-masculine habitus. Crewmembers' shared history manifests itself in their very bodies. It is brought to life through their skillful actions, but it usually resides under the surface, the unnoticed bond that holds everything in place. Firefighters are practical actors, who have adapted to the demands of firefighting not through a drastic transformation (after all, the training new crewmembers receive is meager), or by following the ordinances of the Ten and Eighteen, or even through direct experience fighting fire, but rather through subtle modifications of already established dispositions and skills. The skills for battling a wildfire come almost naturally because firefighters' rural working-class masculine upbringings have already laid the groundwork. "The machine required can be constructed," Foucault once remarked about the eighteenth-century soldier.[22] But unlike Foucault's cadet, molded out of "formless clay," the wildland firefighter comes to the setting preformed, preconditioned, and thus, in the root sense, *prepared*—from the Latin *praeparare*, literally meaning "to previously procure"—for the demands and dangers of firefighting.

6

Taking the "Wild" Out of Wildfire

A large chunk of a wildland firefighter's life is spent in the seat of a truck. Firefighters drive for hours down dirt roads in search of elusive smokes or lost campers. When they are sent off-district, they spend days riding in engines (Hotshots ride in small buses called "buggies"), making the long haul to Montana, Idaho, California, or New Mexico. Over the span of a single day, my crewmembers may drive to the grasslands at the north end of the forest to repair a fence before heading south into the piñon junipers to thin saplings; then they might head west to talk to campers at Rompart Lake and end the day planting grass seed at an old burn site on the east end of Wannokee. Sometimes crewmembers spend the entire workday in the engine, as when they hang signs advising campers of fire restrictions or patrol the forest to inspect campgrounds and to observe fire conditions. Firefighters get used to being a passenger or driver. Some pass the time chewing sunflower seeds or Copenhagen; some entertain themselves by punching the buttons of portable videogames. Some like shooting the bull and teasing one another, while others search the trees for elk, deer, or wild turkey.

I used to wonder how Rex Thurman passed the time when making the ninety-minute commute to Elk River from his house outside Jameson. Thurman didn't chew (he quit cold turkey many years ago after one of his daughters, then a toddler, mistook his spit cup for grape juice); he wasn't much of

a hunter, so the elk's favorite spots and the turkeys' migratory patterns
didn't interest him; and I couldn't picture Thurman singing along to the
radio or letting his mind wander in a daydream. But I believe I discovered
what the boss did when he woke up early and drove alone through the
pale morning sunlight on his way to our station: he planned speeches. He
had to, for when he arrived at Elk River and summoned the crew to the
conference room, Thurman delivered powerful, well-crafted, and highly
polished lectures, usually revolving around his views of firefighting and
safety, reflections on recent firefighting fatalities, and reviews of our performance.

One day Thurman delivered a two-hour monologue to the firecrew,
who sat still and quiet in the conference room. Dressed in a buttoned-up
khaki Forest Service shirt (with a badge pinned above his left pocket) and
sitting at the head of the table (where he always sat), Thurman leaned
forward. Resting his tanned and burly forearms on the table, he began his
speech with a few casual observations and jokes before growing serious
and reflecting on the grim dangers of firefighting.

"Remember, folks, step back, take a deep breath, and look," Thurman
advised, projecting his baritone slowly and steadily. "You want to *act* on
things and not *react*. The Forest Service is great on this knee-jerk reaction
shit; this is why we have all these regulations [that is, regulations other
than the 'basics']. . . . I keep emphasizing that we need these Eighteen,
we need these Fire Orders. It don't matter if you're on the bottom of the
totem pole or in a position like me, if you're recognizing things you will
always be successful out there.

"One of my goals when I first started out was to never get in a fire shelter. That's still a goal. And you know, don't trust anyone to watch out for
you folks. Realize that our fire seasons are continuing to get worse every
year. Realize things are getting worse and more complicated.

"It's not like you're flippin' burgers at McDonald's," Thurman observed in a no-nonsense tone, leaning back in his chair. "What's the worse
thing you can do there? Maybe burn a burger or two. Here, we burn individuals. . . . Don't wind up like that poor kid that came out of the Thirtymile abatement stuff. Kid went through seventeen days of training, all
the bullshit we have to tell you, and went on his first fire and dies.

"The government is real good at setting you up for failure, folks.
Don't fail. The Eighteen don't change, the Fire Orders don't change. We
keep switching them around, but we continue to kill people. . . . Don't
let somebody control your destiny when they don't know what they're
doing. The crew bosses [on the Thirtymile fire] violated all ten of the Fire

Orders and eleven of the Eighteen. We have not held anyone accountable. Guy kills four people and he's still out there fighting fire. . . . This guy kills four people because of his stupidity, and we have yet to hold him accountable. Just something to think about, folks."

Thurman paused and studied his crew. It seemed he wanted his message to sink in, to settle on us with a heavy weight, before he returned to his original point: "*Acting* on things, we come home safe; *reacting*, we bring people home in bags. It happens to the best of them, and who they say *aren't* the best. Like I said, no one is safe from it. . . . Nobody is exempt from these types of things. South Canyon, we burned up smokejumpers, Hotshots, and helitack. In the investigations, every [fatal] fire there was a violation of the Ten and Eighteen and LCES."

After discussing safety, fatal fires, recent changes in Forest Service policy, and his outlook for the rest of the fire season, Thurman brought his speech to a close: "We're not going to outsmart the good Lord. So, anyone who thinks they know everything, I say bullshit to that individual. . . . Does anyone know when their time is? Don't let anyone else control when your time is. . . . We continue to kill people. We continue to have shelter deployments. . . . Who's responsible? It's right here in black and white: the firefighter himself. You are responsible for your own safety, folks. Don't assume that anyone else is taking care of you."

Thurman delivered each word with precision and care. He knew how to use timing and silence; he was adept at turning phrases ("burning hamburgers" and "burning individuals") and structured his message so the main point was emphasized several times. We all listened.

Although Thurman sharply criticized his host organization, he did so by invoking the organizational common sense of the Forest Service. He rebuked the Forest Service because it had lost sight of its own essential rules by implementing new regulations (in reaction to fatalities) that overshadowed the importance of the Ten and Eighteen. But Thurman's primary concern centered on something more fundamental; he dug below the basic rules of firefighting to underscore certain institutionally sponsored principles that support and are supported by the Ten and Eighteen, principles such as personal accountability and individual responsibility. These principles, as we will see, are the cornerstones of the Forest Service's conception of risk, safety, and death.

If we search for the bedrock understanding on which the Ten and Eighteen rests, if we "reach *through* the text," to borrow a phrase from Dorothy Smith, we soon discover that accepting these rules, seemingly innocent and straightforward, requires accepting unspoken institutionalized principles that influence the way firefighters understand risk and death.[1] This chapter unpacks and analyzes these institutional principles, uncovering not only how the Forest Service constructs danger and safety but also how firefighters develop a specific professional disposition toward risk taking. This chapter, then, is about the meaning of "risk" to the Forest Service and to its firefighters.

Making Luck

As I reach across the table to shake Jack MacCloud's hand, I feel compelled to squeeze firmly and call him "Sir." As fire deputy, Mr. MacCloud oversees all the firecrews on the Wannokee Forest. This year marks his thirtieth season with the Forest Service. He began working directly after high school as a grunt on a seasonal helitack crew and worked his way up to dispatcher in the main forest office before being promoted to fire deputy two years ago. But that isn't what impresses me. It's not MacCloud's extended years on the fireline or his title, which makes Thurman himself stand a bit straighter, that compels me to call him "Sir." It's his mustache. My crewmembers call it "the badass 'stache," and for good reason. MacCloud's mustache is a thick brown handlebar that completely conceals his upper lip. Individual whiskers rebel against the overall form of the 'stache, darting out in a jumble of directions, and MacCloud tries in vain to discipline the wild hairs by repeatedly rubbing his hand over his mustache, his mouth half open.

He wears broken-in Wranglers with a Copenhagen ring worn into the back left pocket and a large bracelet watch made of silver and turquoise in traditional Hopi style, perhaps a keepsake from the days when he used to make "Indian jewelry" between fire seasons to get by. His hirsute skin is weathered with sun spots from a lifetime of working in the Arizona heat. Sliding his scuffed cowboy boots under Thurman's desk, he removes his dark sunglasses, revealing a slight tan line from the wrinkles around his eyes to his temples, and lets them hang from an elastic lanyard. He settles into the chair with a sigh, taking a pinch of Cope that disappears behind the badass 'stache, and I think to myself, right before I ask the first interview question, that Jack MacCloud makes Sam Elliott look like Philip Seymour Hoffman.

MacCloud was on the great Marble Cone fire in 1977 that burned on California's Big Sur coastline. "At the time it was, you know, we used to always sit around while we were waiting for a fire, like you guys are today," he recalls in a soft voice, almost a mumble, laced with nostalgia.

"And a son of a bitch says, 'What are you guys doing today?' 'Well, we are saving ourselves up for the big one!' Well, when we got the Marble Cone fire, that was the big one."

When he traveled west to fight the Marble Cone burn, MacCloud went without the protective gear that all wildfire crews use today, such as a fire shelter, Nomex flame-resistant pants, eight-inch leather boots, and flame-retardant shirts. In fact, most of the PPE used today was developed within the past fifteen years. Although MacCloud welcomes these technological advances, he also believes they are producing an unforeseen negative consequence.

"We hire eighteen- and twenty-year-old kids to fight fire, and they're already at the age where they're *invincible,* and we give them all this PPE and the fire shelter, and so now they're just *bulletproof.* So a lot of times they are putting themselves in positions that they shouldn't. Where, if we gave them Bermuda shorts and a pair of tennis shoes and said, 'When it gets too hot, get the hell out of the way,' well . . ."

MacCloud smiles, perhaps envisioning the scene.

"You know, we gotta have people out there with all the protective gear they can have, but it's more of a *mind-set.* I mean, you know the machoism of the firefighter. And, uh, I was the same way. Smokejumpers, Hotshots, they're *all* the same way. They feel a little on top of the world, you know what I mean? And sometimes that gets us in trouble. PPE isn't always the answer."

"So have you even been in a situation on a fire or seen a situation on a fire where you were injured or someone else was injured or hurt very badly?" I ask.

"Hmmmm, no." MacCloud answers. "I've been in quite a few positions and places that, uh, were a little hairy, but, uh, never been in a position where I had to pop a shelter. Of course, we didn't have shelters in the seventies. But, uh, yeah, a few hairy situations, but I've never been out on the ground when somebody cut their leg with a saw or anything like that."

"Why do you think you stayed safe all those years?"

"Not that we had a South Canyon or a Thirtymile or anything like that. Just lucky I guess. But you make your own luck a lot of times."

"You said you can make your own luck a lot of times. Could you expand on that point?"

"Well, it's like, take Rick Lupe, for example. On the Rodeo-Chediski fire, he was in, *definitely,* in harm's way trying to stop that fire from going east on Highway 60, and, uh, probably had a good plan, well thought-out, and it worked, and everything went right. And uh, here he goes on a *dang prescribed burn,* and uh, shit, makes a mistake, basically. And costs him his life. And he just wasn't so lucky that time.

"And, you know, we didn't get to talk to him or ask him any questions, so what happened for sure, who knows? But it just appears that he went down in a hole and got himself in a bad spot and fire came up around him, and it was in a place that he couldn't get out of. So he didn't make any luck for himself that day. . . . The bottom line is that when we are out there fighting fires, we're responsible for our own safety, and we have to make good decisions."

I nodded in unreflective agreement when MacCloud repeated this last refrain. I'd heard it hundreds of times. Thurman reminded us of this during each morning briefing he ran. At the close of each meeting, just when the crew was ready to rise and start the day, he would remark matter-of-factly, just as he did at the conclusion of the speech recorded earlier: "You are responsible for your own safety, folks. Don't assume that anyone else is taking care of you."

This idea, as MacCloud said, is the *bottom line* of the Forest Service's thinking. If a firefighter falters, it is his own mistake. If he is injured, it is due to his lapse of judgment. If he dies, it is because he departed from a rational, right decision. Each firefighter is responsible for his own safety. There are no exceptions to this unassailable rule, which is repeated over and over in basic training videos and official documents as well as by supervisors. The firefighter makes his own luck by making well-placed, competent decisions. He masters the fire by mastering himself. Those who fail at this task, like Rick Lupe (according to MacCloud)—by relying too much on their PPE or pushing their limits too far—pay the ultimate price.

This hearty emphasis on personal responsibility and individual competence undergirds the Ten and Eighteen as well. These rules say little about actions that involve trust, teamwork, or solidarity.[2] Commands dealing with collective behavior, such as "Never go into a fire alone," "Be aware of your crewmembers' actions and whereabouts on a fire," or "Do not separate from your fire buddy," are strikingly absent from these fundamental guidelines concerned with the (necessarily collective) act of firefighting. Instead, the Ten and Eighteen are individualizing rules, rules that rank a firefighter's competence as an individual over his involvement in a larger collective endeavor; after all, each of the Orders and Situations is prefaced, as John Krebs instructs, "by the silent imperative 'you'": *You* must "fight fire aggressively but provide for safety first." *You* must "initiate all action based on current and expected fire behavior." *You* must "recognize current weather conditions and obtain forecasts."[3]

The Forest Service is marketing a message of individual competence, personal responsibility, and reliance on the Ten and Eighteen. But how much of this message do firefighters buy? Do they believe, as their supervisors do, in the fundamental importance of the Ten and Eighteen? (After all, just because crewmembers memorize these rules and can rattle them off like well-tuned cadets does not mean they respect them.) Moreover, do these firefighters believe that their own competence, their own special knowledge, ensures their safety?

Faith in the Fundamentals

As Bryan relaxes with a can of beer in my room in crew quarters, I ask him a question that has been tapping on the inside of my head ever since I learned of Rick Lupe's death: "So do you think that if someone, anyone, gets seriously hurt on a fire, like burned, or dies on a fire, that most likely they made a serious mistake?"

He nods and replies, "Yeah. I mean, you look at the research now, and they give you the Ten and Eighteen, and I'm not trying to sound like Thurman here, but in the research they have shows that something was broke among those guidelines. I wouldn't call them rules, well, I guess they are rules. Whatever you want to call them. They're like *guidelines,* you know. Stuff that you have to pay attention to."

I pose the same question again, this time using positive phrasing: "Do you think that if everyone acts properly, acts exactly how they should, that no one should *ever* get seriously hurt on wildfire?"

"Sometimes you have to break something," Bryan replies knowingly.

"Break some of the Ten and Eighteen?"

"Yeah. Like, if you're building fireline downhill, you're trying to hook it or something like that. Like, you can *mitigate* it though, and put your lookout in a proper position, and you can set it up so that even though the risk is there, you take away from the risk factor. You know what I'm saying?"

"Yeah."

"As long as everybody's informed on what's going to happen, 'cause, I mean, if you *break* something, you better know where your escape routes and safety zones are, because if shit goes to shit you gotta get out of there. . . . That's why *I* say, and I'm not speaking on behalf of the Forest Service or anything, that's why I say, this is just my opinion, why I say they are more like guidelines. You better have somebody who knows what they're dealing with if you're gonna do something like that."

"What's the difference in your head between mitigating and violating?" I ask skeptically.

Bryan sets his beer down on the coffee table and extends both hands, demonstrating "on the one hand, on the other hand." "*Mitigating* is where you come up with, uh, you *know* what you're dealing with. Everybody understands the risk. If they are *violated,* to me, when they say 'violated,' it seems that they were ignored. You know, they weren't even looked at or thought of, because if you look at it and you see that it can't be done, then you don't need to do it.

"So, that's what I'm getting at. If it can't be done you have every right to turn down an assignment. . . . Maybe I have broken some of the stuff. I've done a frontal assault and shit that, you know, I felt that, at the current situation, if it starts really blowing up, we could get out of there."

"What percentage of fires have you been on where you or your crew have broken at least one of the Ten Fire Orders?"

"I don't know." He looks down at his beer and rubs his forehead. "It's a good question. I mean, we've dug line downhill more than once. You know, we've hot-lined, done a frontal assault on a fire, cut off the head. With the fire behavior, it wasn't fifty-foot flame lengths coming off of it. Yeah, we've had ten-foot flame lengths, and we just pulled back, and we knew how we were going to get out of there."

"I see. And what percentage of fires that you've been on has there been a lookout posted?"

"It all depends because, percentagewise, we're talking like every fire, it's not a high percentage. But there was *no need* for a lookout to be posted, and, you know, some of your smaller fires, like the ones we deal with, you'll see the whole fire standing there. But, well, I've been on fires on the district that we've had to put a lookout because we couldn't see the fire that was below us."

Although Bryan admits to regularly "mitigating" Fire Orders, he still blames fallen firefighters for "violating" them. On one hand, that Bryan reverts to the Ten and Eighteen when addressing the question of fault is not surprising. The idea seems clear enough: if a firefighter violates the unquestioned rules of firefighting, he will reap the consequences. On the other hand, Bryan's unwavering faith in the Ten and Eighteen is curious since he knows, as well as any other firefighter, that it is impossible to fight a wildfire without circumventing, to varying degrees, some of the Orders or Situations.

Peter employs a similar logic when making sense of firefighting fatalities. "When they *do* kill people," he explains with a glum look, "and they look in the investigations, that's the first thing they look at: the Ten and Eighteen. They look at how many they broke. Almost always: no lookouts, no escape routes, no safety zones, no communication. And that's why they came up with those. They killed people, and they looked, and what's killing them?"

He bends back a finger for each violation: "They don't have lookouts; they violated the Ten and Eighteen, LCES. So now every time a fatality happens, they go back to that. 'Okay, did they have lookouts? Yes/no. Did they have escape routes? Yes/no.' And usually it comes down to that. They don't have to look any further than that. It was right there in what they'd been taught."

". . . How many fires have you been on that you actually violated the Ten and Eighteen?" I ask.

"It's actually, what they say is not 'violate.' You, uh, mitigate it. You can get by it if this is in place. . . . They are kinda like guidelines. Okay, we're gettin' frequent spot fires across the line, but we're pickin' 'em up. . . . Just 'cause the wind is changing direction doesn't mean, 'Oop! We gotta stop fightin' the fire!' Just 'cause you're startin' to get some spots doesn't mean, 'Oh shit! We gotta quit fighting the fire!' Hell, we get spot fires all the time. . . . You don't always need a lookout. If you're on a tenth acre, you can see the fucker right there. . . . Safety zones and escape routes? Yeah, there are times when it's not such a big deal. But if a fire's moving, you definitely need 'em."

Peter and Bryan share an institutionalized vocabulary ("mitigating," "violating," "guidelines"). They also share the opinion that Orders and Situations can be mitigated on smaller fires. After all, why post a lookout when the fire is the size of a swimming pool? Why establish safety zones and escape routes when the fire is moving lethargically through ground fuel and is easily corralled? Although this seems reasonable, Peter and Bryan also know that most firefighting fatalities do not occur on large, violent fires. Smaller, childlike fires are the deadliest and therefore are the ones that require *extra* (not mitigated) precautions. According to a handout I received during basic training, "Most [fatal] incidents happen on the smaller fires or on isolated portions of larger fires. Most fires are innocent in appearance before the flare-ups or blowups. In some cases, tragedies occur in the mop-up stage. Flare-ups generally occur in deceptively light fuels."

Sociologists usually are quick to draw a line separating the formal perspective of an organization from the perspective of its members, the official perspective from the perspective of "lower participants," the "manager's eyes" from the "worker's eyes."[4] Many have found that bureaucrats (the higher-ups, the managers) have a vision of the organization that has little in common with the vision of workers on the ground. Following this logic, we might assume (especially after highlighting, in the previous chapter, the discrepancies that arise when the Ten and Eighteen are taken from the quiet and comfort of the training room and placed in the middle of a half-million-acre crown fire) that firefighters have little faith in these core maxims, that they notice the inconsistencies between the rules on paper and the rules in practice and come to look on the Ten and Eighteen with cynicism and doubt. But this is not true for Bryan and Peter; nor is it true for other firefighters. On the contrary, they respect and value the Ten and Eighteen, and stickers bearing these rules adorn bathroom mirrors, lunchpails, and hard hats. Moreover, crewmembers explain violations of the Ten and Eighteen not by employing a "worker's perspective" fundamentally at odds with the perspective of the Forest Service, but by more or less adopting the organization's perspective as their own.[5] Consider, for example, how Bryan answered a brief sequence of Thurman's questions that revolved around risk and responsibility during a morning meeting in the conference room.

"Mr. Keeton," Thurman bellowed, as the firecrew sat around the table.

"Yessir," Bryan answered, in a relaxed tone.

"If you go out here on a fire and get hurt, who's responsible for it?"

"I am!"

"Are they [the Forest Service] going to do anything to me if y'all go out there and get killed?"

"No."

"Why not?"

"Because it's our responsibility."[6]

Why does Bryan believe this? And why does he (along with his fellow crewmembers) value and accept the Ten and Eighteen even though these rules can't be fully satisfied in practice? Why don't they look on the regulations of firefighting with disbelieving eyes? The answer, I think, is that they have internalized the organizational thinking of the Forest Service. When crewmembers are asked how they stay safe in the midst of a raging inferno, the Forest Service already has provided an answer: the Ten and Eighteen. And when crewmembers are forced to bypass some of these rules, their host organization has supplied a discursive loophole with the concept of "mitigation." Although the Ten and Eighteen do not fully explain crewmembers' actions on the fireline, as I demonstrated in chapter 5, they do function as a language crewmembers can use to make sense of their actions when considering them retrospectively. The Ten and Eighteen, then, are preformed, satisfactory responses to questions, responses that firefighters rely on to comprehend firefighting as orderly and safe. In a word, these rules are what C. Wright Mills called "vocabularies of motive"; they are institutionally sponsored justifications for action, accepted by members of the institution, linking anticipated consequences (such as safety or harm) to specific actions (such as following or violating an Order or a Situation).[7] Crewmembers draw on these vocabularies of motive to interpret, analyze, and justify their actions on the fireline after the smoke settles, and in so doing, they alter these actions by replacing the logic of practice (based on practical strategies) with the logic of procedures (based on rules), by replacing the "acting agent" with the "reflecting subject."[8]

To be sure, my crewmembers are not "organizational dopes," to augment Garfinkel's phrase, who treat the Forest Service with reverence and passively accept each mandate without question. Many have very critical things to say about the institution and its rules, as I document later on. However, most crewmembers believe wholeheartedly in the importance of the Ten and Eighteen. They do not endorse their organization's mandates uncritically or simply because they were told to do so; but they *have* decided to place their faith in these fundamentals, they *have* chosen to trust their host organization, and they have done so because, as we saw earlier, the organizational common sense of the Forest Service aligns with deep-seated dispositions cultivated within crewmembers from childhood.

When firefighters commit the Ten and Eighteen to memory, they accept something besides a litany of dos and don'ts; they accept an amalgam of commonplaces that focuses their understanding of firefighting through the narrow prism of individuality and personal responsibility. Once crewmembers accept the organizational common sense of the Forest Service, they begin to develop a certain disposition toward firefighting, a disposition through which they place their faith not in supervisors, fellow crewmembers, or deities, but in their individual abilities alone. And if they are competent, so goes the logic, if they know and observe the Ten and Eighteen, they have nothing to fear from fire. As Thurman put it: "After all these years, does fire still scare me? No. I respect it, but it doesn't scare me. You're scared of the unknown. . . . So, if you cover your basics, then you shouldn't be scared."

What Is Risk to a Firefighter?

The day before I had planned to take Tessa on a weekend getaway to pop the question, a monstrous lightning storm descended on the Wannokee Forest and delayed my plans. The lookouts began reporting one smoke after another, and my crewmembers and I chased dozens of small fires all around our district. About 10:00 p.m. I accompanied Allen, George, and Vince to a small fire a hundred yards off a heavily traveled dirt road. A bolt of lightning had struck a dead oak tree, which had toppled and was engulfed in flames.

The rain had moistened the ground, so the fire moved slowly. It didn't take us long to dig a quick line around the fallen snag and the smoldering ground surrounding it. But then we had to deal with the snag itself. Molten orange coals covered the thick oak trunk, which had been burning for hours. It radiated waves of blistering heat: when I approached the log, swells of heat stung my face and eyes. I shielded myself with my arms and stepped back, feeling as if I had received first-degree burns on my cheeks.

I yanked the hard line from the engine and began spraying the log down with water, but that didn't buy much. The log was burning so hot that it was vaporizing the water before it could penetrate the wood.

"This is taking too long," Allen said after a couple of minutes. "Hey, George!"

"Yeah," George answered from the engine, where he was monitoring the pump.

"You know how to run a saw?" Allen asked jokingly.

"Uh, yeah."

"Good. Then come over here and do it. Buck this log up."

"Who-hew!" George exclaimed, always eager to cut.

George dashed around to the side of the engine and removed the chain saw from its cabinet. Knowing how hot the log was burning, he took a thick canvas face mask from his fire pack, secured its Velcro tabs to the inside of his helmet, and wrapped it around his neck and face. Then he revved up the chain saw and got to work.

Standing in a thick bed of coals, George sunk the saw into the burning snag, maneuvering it in a slow seesaw pattern. A flurry of bright sparks shot out from behind the saw and bounced off George's shirt, pants, and face mask; it looked as if he were cutting metal. The fresh slits in the wood brought oxygen to the sealed snag; the smoldering coals inhaled the fresh air and exhaled a powerful burst of heat. George was able to stand only short spurts of the heat: He would cut for a few seconds, then pull the saw out of the trunk and jump off the coals to cool off. After a few gulps of cool air, he would return to his task. Holding the hose, I stood behind George and sprayed down the areas he was cutting, but the heat was over-whelming. After a few minutes, George began to rethink Allen's plan.

"Allen," George asked, stepping away from the log, "Do you think we should be doing this? It's really, *really* hot in there. I'm burning up, man."

George breathed hard, sweat pouring off his bright red face. His boots were smoking.

Allen glanced at the burning log, then back at George and huffed, "So! If you're good, you'll do it. I've had to cut stuff like that, stuff way hotter than that!"

George hesitated, looked backed at the snag, and asked again, "Are you sure? It's really hot, and the water's not doing anything."

"I know it's hot," Allen replied with a tinge of frustration in his voice. "But I've cut hot stuff like that lots of times, all the time. It's not that hot."

"A-a-all right," George agreed, indecisively. He strapped his face mask back on and returned to the log. Sweltering next to the red-hot snag, George continued to cut. He managed to buck it up—slicing the thick trunk into a dozen pieces, which were then separated and watered down—but only after partially melting the soles of his boots and replac-ing the saw's chain when it overexpanded because of the heat.

On this particular occasion, George displayed uncertainty. He was re-luctant to cut the log and might have abandoned the plan if Allen hadn't pushed him.[9] He felt threatened by the blistering log; he was not sure he could (or should) expose himself to that kind of heat, so he pulled back and reevaluated his approach, as firefighters are taught to do when they feel uneasy or in harm's way.

There are moments like this when firefighters hesitate, moments when things get too hot, when the flames get too violent, when the smoke is too thick, or when something doesn't feel right. Sometimes they push forward, as George did, feeling disconcerted and edgy. Other times they step back and let the fire calm itself. Once, for example, Bryan, Diego, and Scott tried to cut off the head of a fast-moving grass fire by punching a scratch line in front of it. As they punched line, the flame lengths grew and the intensity increased. They soon found themselves in front of a powerful wave of heat and five-foot flames. All three pulled back and ran to a safe spot. They let the fire die down before returning to the line.

Sometimes when firefighters encounter fire in all its mystic power, they feel helpless and realize it is not completely within their control. As Peter explains it, reflecting on the Moose Print fire: "Fire is a natural thing. . . . Why I wanted to see a fire on the rim of the canyon was because that's Mother Nature doing her thing and, you know, the rim hasn't been logged, it's too steep. The rim hasn't been thinned, too steep. When there's fires on the rim, they *go big*. You can't put them out. That's pretty much Mother Nature right there, there's no human influence on it at all."

He waves his arm, tracing the contours of an imaginary roller-coaster, and continues. "Go up. Back down. Go up. Back down. That's Mother Nature doing her own thing, and there's really nothing people can do to prevent it. There's really nothing people can do to avoid it."

And when Mother Nature "does her thing," all firefighters can do is pray for rain.

J.J. shares similar opinions: "I would never say that you can catch it every time, 'cause you can't, even if you act properly, follow everything by the guidelines. There's a lot of times when you can't catch it. I mean, Mother Nature and the Lord above is the only one who can tell you what's

going on with the fire. You know? . . . Acting properly, you still wouldn't catch every fire. Ain't no way."

In Peter's and J.J.'s eyes fire remains, as in Prometheus's day, a secret of the gods. Referring to large burns, they admit to feeling outmatched at times by a powerful and unpredictable element.

I ask Kris: "Do you believe that we have the ability to control all wildfire?"

"No," he responds. "You can *recognize* a lot of the aspects of fire and *predict* it to a certain degree of accuracy, but I don't think that you can *control* every fire every time. We're talking 'bout one of the most powerful forces of nature. You don't get to control it every time. And that's why you have to respect it, you know. And that's my outlook on it. You won't be able to control fire. You can establish and set up so you can gain control, but once you start having that mind-set that you can actually control it, and that mind-set that you are in perfect control of everything, then that's when stuff starts happening."

When confronted with wildfire, sometimes crewmembers doubt their ability to corral it; they realize that fire is bigger than they are and that it punishes those who test it. But what is surprising about the moments when firefighters doubt their own ability is not the doubt itself—a reaction that seems completely reasonable given their opponent. What is surprising is the rarity of such moments. Much more often than not, firefighters do not doubt or hesitate; although there are times when they are more cautious, firefighters usually march forward with marked confidence. And this is because, although they recognize that fire is not completely within their control, that it is majestic and violent, that sometimes it cannot be harnessed or defeated, they believe they can rely on their knowledge to steer clear of the deadly flames.

"To a point you can control all fire," George elaborates in jerky, uncertain sentences. "But in some cases, like last year with the Rodeo-Chediski, that fire was burning so hot, nothing we could do was going to put an immediate stop to that fire. . . . That's one of those cases where you know that if you get in front of it, even on the sides of it, I mean, you're gonna get hurt. And that's one of those things that we know. We knew from the way it was burning, there was no way we could get in there and do, do any good. . . . So, to a point on fires, you can stop it in certain ways, but when it's burning hot, there's really nothing you can do. You just gotta let it burn, and it's gonna do what it's gonna do."

"Were you scared during the Rodeo fire?" I ask.

"No."

"Why not?"

A few seconds pass as we mosey down a dirt road in the F-150, windows down, seat belts off, country music coming quietly from the radio.

"'Cause, personally," George begins, looking me in the eye, "I don't consider my life in danger. I think that the people I work with and with the knowledge I know, my life isn't in danger. . . . If you know, as a firefighter, how to act on a fire, how to approach it, this and that, I mean you're, yeah, fire can hurt you. But if you know, if you can soak up the stuff that has been taught to you, it's *not* a dangerous job."

Although George cannot always control fire, he can always control his own safety. And he must, for "each firefighter is responsible for his own safety." Though he might not extinguish every blaze, he can at least escape unharmed. Thus, George marvels at the power of the Rodeo-Chediski fire, but he does not fear it.

Though fire cannot always be tamed, the firefighter can always tame himself. Though the flames might lash out in a rage, he can always step back (and should always know when to step back). When my crewmembers look at wildfire, they see something that can kill them but almost certainly will not. Thus many come to understand their job as no more dangerous than any other. "Well, any job is dangerous," Kris explains. "People die in factories. People die building cars. People die making boots. They make the job seem more dangerous. . . . But knowing the situations and knowing the Ten and Eighteen that they preach to us, not going in closed-minded to what's going on, drastically reduces the chance of being harmed."

Peter agrees: "I think, yes, it can be dangerous, but if you watch your ass, and you're smart to the tactics and strategies that you go after, yeah, it can still be dangerous, but not more dangerous than walking to school. Fuckin' car can run you over. Well, a tree can fall on you. There's more cars driving around than there are trees falling, I think. Shit, somebody can get killed walking to school or walking to work or driving their car to work. How many people are killed in car accidents going to work every day?"

The thought of dying on the fireline is so distant from firefighters' imaginations that they find the idea comical. My crewmembers attempt to top each other's stories of times they've used the line "I'm from the Elk River Firecrew; I put my life on the line each and every day" to impress people, especially single women. Peter currently holds the title; he fed Arizona Diamondbacks player Matt Williams that line when he spotted the baseball star in a bar in Jameson. Williams handed Peter a napkin inscribed, "To the Elk River Fire Crew: Keep fighting fires, saving lives, and being heroes." Peter framed the napkin and hung it in the conference room. When they saw it, crewmembers keeled over in laughter because Williams actually thought wildland firefighting is a dangerous profession whereas my crewmembers don't see it that way at all. Whereas those outside the firefighting world believe firefighters "put their lives on the line every single day," that they are "paid for their bravery," as William Goode expressed it, most of my crewmembers conceptualize their profession as devoid of danger.[10] To them there are no heroes, for there is no risk.

"Do you ever think about the danger of this job?" I ask J.J.

"Not really," he replies. "Not hardly ever I think about it. It's there, but that's like the last thing on my mind. 'Hey, I might die today.' I probably only think that once a week, if that; once a month maybe I'll think about it. It's like you wake up in the morning, you know what you have to do, you get it done. . . . I don't wake up thinking, 'Hey, I might die today.' That's a bummed-out way to start your morning." Beginning to laugh, J.J. adds, "'Hey, I might die today.' The risk is there, but I don't ever think about it. It's not a big deal to me."

While analyzing crewmembers' perceptions of risk, some might be tempted to determine the "reasonableness" of these perceptions. To do so, they may investigate how well firefighters' perceptions of risk align with the objective hazards of firefighting. On learning that crewmembers rarely consider the perils of their occupation, they might pronounce, "Indeed, it is reasonable that they do not worry much about such things. Wildland firefighting is not *that* risky. Wildland firefighters suffer fewer fatalities per year than those in other high-risk occupations such as timber cutting, soldiering in times of war, farming, roofing, or mining. Driving a truck actually is more dangerous than fighting a fire, and so is giving birth, for that matter."[11] (It is conventional to measure the "danger" of occupations by yearly death rates, a practice that excludes from analysis any measure of short-term and long-term injuries.) This kind of mechanical thinking confuses the matter. Instead of focusing on how firefighters think, *how* they assign order and meaning to their job, this approach wants to determine how firefighters *should* think; it proclaims their fear (or lack of fear) either "rational" or "irrational." Regardless of whether firefighters actually have such knowledge—as we will see later, they do not[12]—analysts in hot pursuit of "rational risk taking" try to quantify danger in order to determine if the risk taker's *image* of danger aligns accurately or inaccurately with the "actual" danger of the activity. In the social-scientific literature on risk taking, this Kantian distinction between objective danger (*noumena*) and perceived danger (*phenomena*) can be found in the distinction between "hazard" and "risk," where the former term connotes a measure of objective danger and the latter connotes individuals' perceptions of that danger.[13]

My purpose is not to gauge how frightened firefighters "should" or "should not" feel; I do not desire to infuse calculations, proportions, and time-series analyses into their heads, for doing so would distract from my primary purpose: to explore the way firefighters' risk perceptions are formed. In this book I seek to approach the logic of firefighting on its own terms, to understand exactly what risk is to firefighters (never mind what it is to the analyst, and never mind its "accuracy"), and to identify the source of this logic. And as I have shown, firefighting, to firefighters, is not so risky an endeavor at all, and the foundation of this belief is to be found in the organizational common sense of the Forest Service.

One final consideration is that mechanical thinking overlooks the qualitative components of danger in its hunt to discover exactly how risky some occupation truly is. I have already listed firefighting's "danger by numbers": its annual averages of fatalities and entrapments. But I do not need these numbers to know that wildfire is dangerous. I have seen it; I have run from it; I have been burned by it. Comparisons between objective hazards and subjective perceptions of risk cannot adequately capture the essence of a dangerous activity. After all, just because only two people are chomped to death by sharks each year does not mean swimming with great whites is a walk in the park.

The Illusio of Self-Determinacy

A week after hundreds of firefighters "contained and controlled" the Rodeo-Chediski fire, my crewmembers and I were required to endure a mandatory "stress debriefing." Apparently someone in the top office thought those long days and longer nights on the fireline, foaming down roofs and chopping off porches, were traumatic enough to warrant group therapy.

We sat in the conference room with firecrews from surrounding forests who had also helped fight the Rodeo-Chediski fire and listened to a supervisor from Jameson introduce the Phoenix-based psychiatrist. A middle-aged woman with a fixed smile studied our faces with eyes camouflaged beneath a heavy layer of mascara. Large gold earrings, which matched her large gold necklaces, pulled on her earlobes and glimmered brightly against lacquered black hair, which matched her black blouse, black belt, black pants, and black shoes. It would be difficult to imagine a person easier for wildland firefighters to ignore, which was precisely what we did. Focusing not on the psychiatrist but on the supervisor from Jameson, firefighters began posing questions about the way the Rodeo-Chediski fire was fought and criticizing overhead decisions. The objects of inquisition became the inquisitors.

The firefighters did not complain about the long hours, the food rations at base camp, or leaving their families for weeks on end. No one was concerned about paychecks, lack of benefits, or the immediate threat posed by the Rodeo-Chediski fire. Rather, crewmembers were angry that they were not used more. They wanted to be placed in *more* dangerous settings. They wanted to be worked *harder* and *longer*. Soldiers ready to defend their neighbors' homes, men willing to stand surefooted in front of a crown fire, the firefighters let fly a frontal assault of disparaging remarks, which the supervisor from Jameson fielded with frustration.

"We are *not* a paramilitary organization!" the supervisor vented. "You weren't fighting a war. No one died or was seriously injured while fighting the Rodeo fire, and that's something we are very proud of."

"But over *four hundred homes* were burned to the ground!" a Jameson firefighter shot back. "I knew some of them folks who lost their homes, and we could have *done* more. We spent too much damn time *waiting around,* watching the plume build, when we could have been in there *fighting* the fire!"

The meeting lasted roughly two hours, and if group therapy was its purpose, I believe that goal was met, though perhaps not the way the woman in black would have predicted. On reflection, the reason those crewmembers were angry, the reason they demanded to be exposed to more harm, was that they stared into that large cloud of smoke and saw no threat. The "paper-qualified" supervisor believed that extinguishing a fire so portentous and massive without losing any firefighters was something to be proud of, but the "experience-qualified" ground pounders did not see such loss as possible in the first place. And they did not consider it possible because at the center of the logic of firefighting lies not the lust for danger, or even the recognition of danger, but something Goffman once referred to as "the illusion of self-determinacy."

In "Where the Action Is," tucked away in a corner of Goffman's text, lie the following overlooked sentences: "When we meet these stands [of resolve in the face of danger, demonstrated by professional risk takers], we can suspect that the best is being made of a bad thing—it is more a question of rationalizations than of realistic accountings. (It is as if the illusion of self-determinacy were a payment society gives to individuals in exchange for their willingness to perform jobs that expose them to risk.) After all, even with chancy occupational roles, choice occurs chiefly at the moment the role itself is first accepted and safer ones forgone; once the individual has committed himself to a particular niche, his having to face what occurs there is more likely to express steady constraints than daily re-decidings. Here the individual cannot choose to withdraw from chance-taking without serious consequences for his occupational status."[14]

Two things are regrettable about Goffman's phrase "the illusion of self-determinacy." First, it is unfortunate that he devotes only one pass-ing parenthetical sentence to this concept, for I have found no better term to capture how my crewmembers understand risk. Second, and more im-portant, Goffman's reliance on the notion of an "illusion" to describe the logic of professional risk taking is regrettable. When he refers to profes-sional risk takers' perceptions as illusions, Goffman (explicitly or implic-itly) invokes images of unreflecting, duped actors who go about their business with a thick layer of wool pulled over their eyes.[15] To avoid this pitfall, I will give Goffman's phrase a Bourdieuian modification and trim "illusion" to "*illusio*." Whereas illusion denotes a state of hypnotism and false consciousness, illusio implies an investment in the organization, a belief in its rules, and an ingrained feel for its dynamics.[16] My claim is that my crewmembers (to varying degrees) possess an *illusio of self-determinacy,* an acceptance of and investment in the organizational common sense of the Forest Service, through which they approach danger as un-danger, risk as un-risk.

The illusio of self-determinacy cannot be fully equated with the purely psychological process of denial. In denial, the subject suppresses the object of danger (or grief, or anxiety, etc.) and classifies it as nonexistent in toto. The actor who denies recognizes the harm and suppresses it. Hence the harm retains its original shape, though the subject denies its existence. Con-versely, for those operating with the illusio of self-determinacy, the object is transformed, not suppressed, by subjects' collectively (mis)recognizing it in a certain fashion. The firefighters of Elk River do not *deny* the harm of fire. In their epistemological horizons, there is nothing to be denied. The actor who functions under an illusio of self-determinacy transforms the harm into a malleable object (or transforms himself into an invincible subject) and thus erases the harm altogether. Hence this illusio escapes the rigors of risk by anticipating it.[17] Furthermore, whereas denial tends to be an individual process, the illusio of self-determinacy is cultivated through collective means. It is a self-evident "truth" shared by young and old fire-fighters alike, one that codes safety as always achievable and death as always preventable; it is a truth that effortlessly extracts the "wild" from "wildfire."

My arguments diverge from the way most scholars, following Goffman, have thought about professional risk takers. Wildland firefighters are not danger-lusting heroes who laugh in the face of death, as they are commonly depicted. Firefighters do not respect the fearless but fear those who disrespect fire. Nor do my crewmembers consider book learning, or "paper qualification," as anything but worthless, as I pointed out in chapter 5. Wildland firefighters reject both rashness and calculation. They dismiss the former for its stupidity and the latter for its impracticality. The logic of firefighting finds refuge between compulsion and calculation, courage and rationality, release and restraint.[18] Thus Goffman's fundamental argument concerning risk taking—that the more one risks, the more masculine character one acquires (an argument that has been accepted and applied by dozens of other scholars who have sought to understand dangerous work and dangerous play)—simply does not hold up at Elk River.

"What qualities do you think a good firefighter has to have?" I ask Donald.

"*Hmmm,*" he hums, staring upward, before turning to me and answering, "Common sense, a great big one. If you've ever watched fire, you look at it, see how it works. Like the fire triangle, that's pretty much common sense. You have to have fuel, have to have oxygen, and have to have heat, because it cooks oxygen! You look at it and so, the fire's gonna burn."

Donald chuckles to himself at the simplicity of his deduction and continues, "Stuff that you look at, other things, like how much, how much precipitation you have, or how much humidity you have and stuff like that, and start adding in these environmental factors. How much wind do you have? And what wind does to your fuels, and just stuff like that. And, I mean, it's pretty cut-and-dried what's going to happen. It gets hotter and the wind's blowing, you *know* that thing's drying out and it's gonna *take off,* so you have to have that common sense.

"And you have to have your wits about you *all the time,*" he explains soberly. "You can't relax. You can't be sitting in the smoke and just concentrating on that one thing here. Be like, 'I'm digging line, I'm digging line.' You *have* to have your wits about you and say, '*Hey!* This smoke's getting *heavier* and the fire's getting *hotter* and we have to back off a little bit, or whatever.' You have, *have* to have your wits about you."

"Have you had an example where you were on a fire or in a sticky situation where you felt that this person, you wouldn't want to listen to that person?" I ask.

"Yes, I have had that," he explains, and reconstructs a representative scene. "We'll be fighting fire, and a tree will be torching, and you say, 'Okay, let's move back,' and someone's saying, '*No.*'

"The other person is thinking about it, you can see the wheels working in their head, saying, '*Hmmm,*' and the person's saying, '*We can do it!* We *can* do it!'

"And *you* say, 'No. Let's get the *hell* out of here!' Now, that's not a break of trust. That's just someone saying, 'Yeah, I think we can do it.' But you're saying, 'I *seriously* doubt it.'"

Donald disrespects firefighters who value bravery over prudence, who think with their guts instead of their heads. If given the choice, my crewmembers would rather fight fire with a thoughtful coward than a rash paladin, since they believe aggression and courage are *negative* qualities in firefighters. They despise the heroic, macho, gung-ho, balls to the walls, all or nothing, go big or go home firefighter. Donald and his crewmembers rank their heroes not by courage but by competence. A good firefighter knows, not tests, his limits.

In fact, crewmembers sometimes criticize women firefighters, not for their unwillingness or inability to take risks or for their lack of courage, but for being too daring.[19] Consider, for instance, Peter's comments:

"Some of them ladies," Peter tells me, after a few rounds of beer, "they think that since they're women, people look at 'em like, 'Oh, they can't do the job since they're women.' So they, some of them, try to make themselves tougher than they are when all they're going to do is *hurt* themselves."

Then, as he often does, Peter starts a conversation with himself to illustrate his point: "But I think that men are more like, 'Fuck that shit! I'm a fat lazy fuckin' slob. I'm not going to fuckin' hike up that goddamn hill!'

"'Why, because you are a fat lazy fuckin' slob?'

"'Well, *fuck yeah,* because I'm a fat lazy slob!'

"You tell that to another *female,* and she——" Peter squeals in a high-pitched voice, "'*Oh fuck it, 'cause I'm a female!'*

"And *whooom,* there she *fucking* goes. . . . There she goes."

Peter slows down and rubs his chin contemplatively. He continues, chuckling. "They're a—they're a dedicated breed. . . . This one female firefighter I know wants to fuckin' hike up with an eighty-pound pack on her back and smoke jump. *I* ain't gonna fuckin' do it! It's gonna fuckin' kill *me*. I mean, yeah, you can work at it and work at it, and, yeah, you can set goals. I'm not saying you can't set goals and try to accomplish something, but don't fucking *kill yourself* trying to do that. Don't hurt yourself trying to accomplish your goals."[20]

If the men at Elk River prize competence above all else—not courage and daring, as previous theories have predicted—it is because they come to understand their enemy as undeserving of their courage. By examining something Goffman overlooked—organizational socialization—I discovered that the Forest Service does not train firefighters to be confident when facing wildfire; it trains firefighters to perceive wildfire as something so innocuous (for the competent and capable) that confidence is superfluous. A central organizational given of the Forest Service is the belief that fire should never injure or kill those competent souls who challenge it. And when crewmembers accept this given (transferred to them through training courses, supervisors' advice, the Ten and Eighteen, and official documents), they develop a professional disposition toward firefighting, an illusio of self-determinacy, that cleanses fire of all danger. Accordingly, firefighters value accuracy, precision, and embodied competence above all else, for these qualities protect them from the flames. As Kris puts it, "But if you go in with an emphasis on really being alert and really trying to be able to accept if not control your situation and respond to that situation, then I believe you are perfectly safe. Well, not perfectly safe, but you're very safe in a profession such as firefighting."

My crewmembers are not confident on the fireline, because to be confident one must recognize the challenge. Because they understand the challenges wildfire presents as unchallenging and construe the flames as harmless through a collective agreement based on their illusio of self-determinacy, my crewmembers are much more than confident on the fireline. They are comfortable.

PART THREE

Fire and Death

7

The Beaver Creek Fire

Two events more than any others temper and test the firefighter's illusio of self-determinacy: a fire that rages out of control and the loss of a fellow firefighter. This chapter deals with the first, the next chapter with the second. It is only by following firefighters through these vexatious tests (trials by fire, one might call them) that we acquire the deepest understanding of how they (and their supporting organization) comprehend safety and risk, fire and death. Only in these trying times when firefighters suffer defeat can we sufficiently gauge the durability of the illusio of self-determinacy. Beaver Creek was no ordinary fire. It was an especially violent blaze that forced me and my crewmembers to drop our tools and run for our lives. As such, this fire—presented here in narrative form—provides a rich opportunity to observe not only the extreme danger and fast action of firefighting but also the way firefighters make sense of their world when it spins out of control.

: :

George, Donald, and I step drowsily out of our rooms at 7:59 a.m. and stroll the fifty yards to the station through sticky air brought on by the monsoons. Even in my basketball shorts and a sleeveless T-shirt, the sun feels noontime-hot already, and I assume, surveying the cloudless sky, that by midafternoon the temperature will reach the high eighties.

The rains have been drowning the fire season, and we have yet to fight a blaze over ten acres. The season has been slow, too slow—especially compared with last year, when the Rodeo-Chediski fire stampeded through our forest. On the highway leading out of Jameson, for miles and miles only barren trunks that once were vibrant ponderosas loom pathetically over the blackened soil. Grass has begun to spring back, but it will be generations before it looks pretty again. Jeremy Stocklen, the law enforcement officer, had his name drawn to hunt elk in that area; he bought a new camouflage outfit—shirt, pants, and hat—all jet black.

Steve and his crew have been sent off-district to lend a hand on the Aspen fire that is torching homes near Tucson, and Peter and his crew are taking the day off. So, today only Donald, George, Allen, and I guard Wannokee.

Donald, George, and I sit quietly in the conference room, sleepy-eyed and yawning, while Allen dawdles from office to office, trying to get some forms in order. At 8:10 he gives the signal and we head out for PT. After a quick stretch, Allen tells us to lift weights so he can catch up on paperwork.

"Woo-hoo!" George responds enthusiastically.

Donald and George happily hustle over to the engine bays—they both hate to run in the morning—and throw open the bay door closest to the tool cache, which houses a bench press and some free weights donated by crewmembers. George climbs into the fire engine parked next to the bench press, rolls down the windows and cranks up the hard rock station, and we get at it.

"You wanna bench?" Donald asks me.

"Uh, okay," I answer, trying to hide my nervousness. I haven't lifted weights since my freshman year of college.

Donald and I trade sets, working up to two hundred pounds. After a few rounds, my arms and chest pulsate and burn. I stop at two hundred, but Donald pushes upward.

"What do you want?" I ask.

"Uhhh," Donald eyes the plates as if to gauge their weight not by the labels on the side but by their mass. "Let's throw on another forty-five."

"All right."

After removing the smaller weights, I slide a forty-five-pound plate onto each end of the bar with the echoless *clank* of iron against iron. As Donald lowers himself onto the bench, I assume my spotting position, standing directly behind his head and gripping the bar with my hands in opposite directions in anticipation of his signal. After a silent meditation,

Donald nods, and I help him lift the bar off the rack. I let go, and his arms remain steady. He lowers the bar, keeping his triceps close to his torso, and allows it to rest ever so briefly directly below his pecs before pushing up, exhaling steadily, and raising the bar with ease. He completes two more presses and racks it.

"Nice lift."

"Thanks."

"We done?"

Donald sits up, breathes in deeply, and then, in a cheerful tone, says, "Nope."

He climbs off the bench and picks up two ten-pounders. He's going for 250. I glance over at George, who is not taking this as seriously as Donald. He curls two dumbbells to the beat of rock music, focusing on his tattoos, which scrunch up and extend as his biceps flex.

Donald is ready. He lowers himself onto the bench without announcement, as if he didn't need a spotter at all, but I take my place behind the bar nevertheless. After placing his hands in just the right position, he nods, we lift, and I let go. When met with the full weight of the bar, Donald's arms begin to vibrate. Previously unseen tributaries of veins rise beneath the skin of his forearms. He breathes shallowly and rapidly. His eyes focus on a single spot in the center of the bar, then all of a sudden the shaking stops. Donald lowers the bar, pauses, and hoists it back up, groaning. He locks his elbows and racks the weight with a purposeful *whack*! With his hands resting on the bar, Donald exhales and informs me with a smile, "*Now,* I'm done."

Impressed, I shake my head and whistle.

George turns off the music, signaling the conclusion of our workout, and we march back to crew quarters to wash up. After a quick shower, I change into the same getup I wear every day at Elk River: my dark green Nomex pants, held up by a leather belt securing two pocket knives (a Leatherman and a single-blade Buck), and a faded T-shirt. I rub sunscreen on my face before sitting down to lace up eight-inch leather boots pulled over wool socks. I grab my lunch with one hand, slam the door with the other, and walk over to the conference room.

I hope we're going to patrol today. We haven't left the station for three days, and it's been at least two weeks since we've seen fire.

Perhaps sharing my sentiments, George pulls a chair up to the conference room table and eagerly asks, "What are we doing today, Allen?"

"Staining," Allen replies with a smile.

"Ahhh, shit," groans Donald.

"Hell," agrees George.

The buildings do not need to be stained; most were given a fresh coat just last year. But that doesn't matter. Allen is behind in his paperwork and needs to keep us busy while he catches up.[1]

After George reads the morning reports on weather and safety, we three grudgingly peel ourselves out of our chairs and get to work. We gather rollers, a drop cloth, and a five-gallon bucket of stain from the flammable materials storage shed and begin restaining the back side of the conference room. The thin redwood stain drips down the rough wood walls as we paint in silence, concentrating on the slow motion of the rollers and trying not to breathe in the acidic stench.

After an hour, George puts down his roller without announcement, and walks over to his car at crew quarters. Then he parks the teal Honda Civic next to the stain bucket, rolls down the windows, and cranks up Metallica's "Justice for All." On hearing the first guitar riff, Donald and I look at each other, nod in agreement with the selection, and continue working without a word. Our rollers now move swiftly with the intense beat, and our bodies rock to the pounding bass and screaming guitar solos. We lip-synch our favorite parts into brush-handle microphones.

At 12:30 we stop work and gather in the conference room for lunch. Donald, George, and I say very little, since Tom Joppa, the bulldozer operator, is doing most of the talking. A forty-five-year-old single father of two boys, Tom spends half his week at Elk River and the other half at Jameson. My crewmembers welcome Tom's happy-go-lucky spirit and his virtuosity with the dozer blade. But today Tom is anything but happy.

"The Forest Service is screwing us man," Tom vents. "*Screwing us!*"

More and more, he tells us, the Forest Service is filling specialized positions, like bulldozer operator, with private contractors, and Tom has spent this fire season worrying that he might be out of a job next year. Donald, George, and I listen attentively, munching sandwiches and potato chips, as Tom protests and searches job listings on the Internet.

The lunch break ends at 1:00, but none of us move. The clock ticks on as we sit, talking quietly. At 1:20 Allen tells us to get back to work. Happy that we were able to milk the lunch break for an extra twenty minutes, we step outside and pick up our rollers. George throws Taproot's "Welcome" on the car stereo, and we go back to work.

Firefighters drag their feet through most days, longing for a fire. They pray for fire, literally, asking God to summon back that destructive force.[2] They miss the terror of the heat and the strike of the flames not only because they adore fire passionately and because their hourly pay rate shoots up when it comes, but also because the alternatives—staining, patrolling, sharpening tools, pouring concrete, washing hose, cleaning the office, itemizing the trucks, on and on—are such drudgery. So when firefighters receive a call, when the chute springs open, the tempo of their universe flips upside down. Their bodies violently accelerate from monotony and inaction to fervor and speed, like someone who stands in line for hours at the carnival until she suddenly finds herself strapped in and whirled away as the coaster zips and loops along its tracks.

"Dispatch, Paquesi. Smoke report."

Our rollers freeze to the wall. Donald and I snap our heads down and stare at the handheld radio on the ground. George dashes to his car and kills the music. My heart rate picks up.

We put down our rollers and gather in front of a forest map in the conference room, eagerly anticipating the coordinates.

"Go ahead, Paquesi," replies the dispatcher.

"I'm pickin' up a tall blue smoke at fifty-eight degrees, six minutes," Clarence Kraus answers in his thick Carolina drawl.

Our eyes focus on Paquesi Perch's spot on the map, a dark dot surrounded by a large circle displaying 360 degrees, numbered every tenth degree. Donald draws a line across the map with his finger, showing that 58 degrees passes directly through our AOR.

"That's five-eight degrees and six minutes," repeats the dispatcher.

"Affirmative."

"And how far out is it, Paquesi?" the dispatcher asks in a cool, soft tone.

"Uh, Dispatch, it's hard to say. Maybe five to eight miles from the tower," Clarence guesses, his voice crackling through the radio static.

"Thanks, Paquesi, please keep an eye on it. Dispatcher clear."

Donald's finger adjusts to Clarence's estimation. "Five to eight miles out," Donald mumbles, "fifty-eight degrees . . . *that's on us!*"

A scurry begins. We bust out of the conference room in a controlled rush. Donald and George throw their gear in the bed of the chase truck, a new Ford F-250 four-by-four with a V-10 under the hood, and climb in. I jump in the engine with Allen; he has already started the rig, and it rolls out the gate before I can shut my door. Tailing the engine, Donald spins the chase truck's tires as we leave the station. A cloud of dust and gravel falls over the open buckets of stain.

"Dispatch, Hartman. Smoke report."

"Go ahead, Hartman," answers the dispatcher.

"Yeah, I'm picking up that smoke that Paquesi Perch spotted. I've got it at 105 degrees."

With this cross-bearing (if the lookouts are sharp), we can pinpoint the fire's location fairly accurately. I pull down a forest map from behind the visor and quickly unroll it as my body bumps and sways in the passenger seat. Laying the map on my lap, I place my left index finger on Hartman and find 105 degrees while my right pointer rests on Paquesi's 58 degrees. Then I slowly move my fingers toward each other like attracted magnets, creating a bearing.

My fingers meet and I report, relying on the map's grid system, "Allen, that puts it at the 25/115 junction, 12 north, 12 east, section fifteen."

"Okay," Allen replies, reaching for the radio. He clears his throat, keys the microphone, and perfunctorily says, "Dispatch, Engine Seven-one."

"Go ahead, Seven-one," the dispatcher replies, expecting our call.

"Yes, we are en route to Paquesi's smoke."

"Copy, Engine Seven-one, fourteen-thirty."

Allen hangs up the radio and steps on the gas while I roll up the map and slide it back in its spot. Then I reach in my pocket for a red bandanna and tie it snugly around my head. I'll be sweating soon. The engine careers down the dirt road at fifty miles an hour, lights flashing. Allen guides the heavy machine over bumps and around turns with a graceful agility earned through twenty years of practice.

The feeling of emergency possesses me. I'm responding. I'm among the ones called; called when it all blows up and everyone else runs away, called when shit needs to get done. Twenty minutes ago I was a painter. Now I'm a firefighter.

: :

As Allen parks the engine at the 25/115 junction, I survey the tips of ponderosas for the slightest wisp of smoke while listening to the cacophony of voices instructing, directing, reporting, questioning, and answering over the radio waves. Organizing all these voices is the dispatcher, the master of ceremonies who directs crews, summons supplies, asks for reports, and relays information. I lean out the open window and sniff deeply, hoping to catch a whiff of smoke.

Craig pulls his F-150 up to the engine on Allen's side. Leaning over his bench seat, he yells out the open window, over the gurgle of the diesel engine and ceaseless radio traffic, "I say that son of a bitch is down a way, past the four-six-nine road."

His vowels cheat and ebb, competing for space with an oversized wad of chew that sloshes inside his cheek. "Follow me!" Craig shouts, stepping on the accelerator.

Allen obeys. Following Craig's truck, the engine speeds up and down the four-six-nine road, turning down minor offshoots leading to rusted tree stands, water tanks, or nothing at all. But our smoke eludes us. After ten minutes of silent watching and smelling I begin to feel frustrated. Smoke can be phantasmal. It can crouch below the treeline and cover itself in shadows, or it can dissipate, unnoticed, into the stratosphere; it can blend in with ashen storm clouds on an overcast day, or it can hold steady and low until your back is turned, then vanish into a sapphire sky. Sometimes lookouts spot a smoke one minute and lose it the next, and sometimes firefighters look for a reported fire for hours before calling it a night. Most of us who have fought wildfire know precisely why Norman Maclean called it "the Black Ghost." I know this takes time and patience, but I want to get there. I want to see what we're up against.

"Paquesi, Dispatch. What's the condition of your smoke?" the dispatcher inquires over the radio.

"Uhhh, Dispatch, it's building," Clarence replies. "*Definitely* building. It's getting bigger and blacker."

Allen and I exchange a quick glance but keep quiet. Bigger and blacker? It sounds as if the fire is picking up. Most of the time we fight smaller fires—a lightning-struck tree or a quarter of an acre on the ground burn from a fugitive campfire—but sometimes we spring a big one. Sometimes it's a real emergency.

"Engine Seven-one, Nine-four-zero," Jeremy Stocklen calls us.

Allen keys the mic. "Go 'head, Jeremy."

"Yeah, Allen, I'm at the smoke. Go to channel seven."

Jeremy has found it. Allen turns the radio dial to seven, and Jeremy gives us directions. Craig pulls up as Allen starts to turn the engine around.

"You told us to go the wrong way!" Allen yells out the window, tongue-in-cheek.

Craig shrugs. "All right," he yells. "I'll meet ya there. Sounds like this thing is shittin' 'n' gettin'!"

"*Yeaaaaah,* buddy!" Allen yells back as Craig speeds off.

Allen follows Jeremy's directions and turns the engine onto a rutted old logging road (which most likely hasn't seen a logging truck in ten years) marked by candy-cane striped flagging tied to a tree. Allen guides the engine down the washed-out, bumpy road, slow and steady. Leaning on the oversized steering wheel, his body tilts and pauses with the engine as if flesh and steel were one. He taps the gas as the engine struggles over a slight hill and immediately leans on the brake after topping it. The rig gracefully rumbles to the scene, and all the while I'm looking for it.

At a fork in the road Allen turns right, following the flagging, and lifts a finger off the steering wheel to point out a paper plate nailed to a tree splitting the intersection, with "RANDY TEQUILA →" written in black marker. Campers. A smoldering campfire? Discarded cigarettes? Fireworks? I don't care. I am grateful to Mr. Tequila and his carelessness, in whatever form it may have come, for he has brought fire back to the forest.

There it is.

I see the smoke and smell it simultaneously. I point, and Allen nods silently. The fire pulsates at the bottom of a hill, vibrant and powerful, emitting a thick ring of smoke that hovers over ponderosas and mixed conifers like a black halo. Whenever a fire is at the bottom of anything—a hill, a canyon, a ravine—it is especially dangerous. Fires travel uphill. Radiant heat moves upward, drying out and heating up the vegetation above, which welcomes the ascending flames. A fire gains momentum as it climbs, just as an avalanche grows larger and faster as it slides down a mountain slope.

Allen steers the engine down a road and parks directly above the fire. I spring out and meet George and Donald. We gear up by first pulling from our green fire packs our yellows—our fire shirts, stained with soot and slurry, wrinkled and smelling of two-week-old sweat and smoke—and buttoning them up. They haven't seen a washing machine since the beginning of the season, not because of any superstition but because it's a disgraceful thing to wear a clean yellow. (When a firefighter marches into a blaze in a clean shirt with creased sleeves, it tells others that he hasn't seen fire, that he hasn't gotten his hands, or his shirt, dirty. Thurman hasn't washed his fire shirt in over ten years.) After hastily tucking these putrid shirts into our fire pants, we strap on our fire packs and crown ourselves with bright red helmets.

Allen, geared up as well, grabs a handheld radio from the engine's cab and marches toward the Jameson crews. George, Donald, and I head to the side of the engine. I fling open the cabinet housing newly sharpened and freshly painted fire tools.

"Get me a Pulaski," Donald says.

I comply and look at George.

"I smell *money*," George says, grinning and rubbing his hands together. "Uh, hand me a combi."

I take two combis from the cabinet, handing one to George and keeping the other. Now we're ready to face this thing. As we hustle over to meet Allen and the Jameson crews, I listen to the fire. *Giocoso* eighth notes of staccato crackles, hisses, and pops skip unevenly across the five treble clef lines while a whole-note rumble—guttural, a continual clearing of the throat—stretches across measures on the lowest ledger.

When we meet the Jameson crews, we realize there was no need to hurry. No one is doing much besides watching the fire grow. We join them, studying the flames as they fly to the top of pines, other conifers, and oaks and swirl along the ground engulfing pine needles, duff, leaves, dead wood, and sapling thickets. An inversion of smoke fogs the area and my vision, obscuring the true size of the burn. I can't see through the flame front, and I can't pinpoint the flanks of the fire. But I can see that it's building—and that it's heading straight for us.

An aroma of burning oak and boiling sap fills the air. Because we are standing a good fifty feet from the head of the fire, the smoke is not overwhelming but pleasantly allusive. It's the smoke of fireside chats and hot dogs on whittled sticks, of barbeques and Boy Scouts and hunting trips.

Silently, I begin to "assess the fire." "Be aware of things before you go in there, folks," Thurman always tells us. "Assess things. You want to *act*, not *react*."

Fuels? This fire has moved from the ground and is consuming smaller trees. Burning in light fuels (pine needles and grass) and heavies (downed trees and slash). Lad-

der fuels? Yes. Weather? Hot and dry. Seventy-five, maybe eighty degrees. Relative humidity definitely below 10 percent. Fire has room to grow in this kind of weather. Topography? Hilly. A canyon behind us. A narrow road between the fire and the canyon. I've never been back here before. Vegetation? Pines (burn hot and fast), oaks (burn long), mixed conifers (in between). Thick. Overgrown, lots of dog hair thickets. Duff. Intensity? Hot and fast. Torching out. Shittin' 'n' gettin'.

"This is fucking stupid," Donald whispers in my ear, breaking my concentration.

Before I can respond, he walks briskly toward Allen, who has left the main group and is priming the engine's water pump.

"Allen, we are right *in front* of the fire. I think we should move the engines back," Donald says.

Allen pauses, looks at the fire, and replies, "No. Let's lay a quick line and knock it down."

"Are you sure? I mean, the fire is *right there*," Donald questions with an outstretched arm.

"*Yes!*" Allen snaps back. "Start a quick line. I'll prime the pump."

I comply at once by scaling the ladder on the back of the engine. I begin to unhook the canvas tarp covering the hoses and nozzles. Allen is in charge here. He is the incident commander (IC), the one who lays out the plan of attack, and if he wants to shoot water on the fire as quickly as possible, then hosepacks are the way to go. I toss down five army green hosepacks to the waiting firefighters below—backpacks that hold a lateral and a trunk line packed in a careful zigzag pattern so that firefighters can pull them out quickly and avoid tangles. But they only continue to wait, tools in hand, because Donald and a Jameson engine operator named Tyson Brenzel start arguing over how best to lay the hose.

"Let's just *go!* Tie this end of the hosepack to the engine and go!" Donald asserts.

"No. No. We should lay a *trunk line* first, *then* pull out the packs," replies the middle-aged Tyson—bald, white, stocky.

"Why? You're just waiting time."

"What's *really* gonna waste time is if you start with a pack and run outta hose. Look, if we lay a trunk line, we can reach the fire easily and then start pullin' out the hosepacks."

The fire is growing. As I stand on top of the engine waiting for Donald and Tyson to agree on a plan of attack, I can feel the heat on my face, and I know we'd better lay this hose and lay it fast. My eyes dart nervously from the meaningless argument below to the frozen and anxious crewmembers to the building black smoke.

This delay is trying my patience and my mettle. We need to make a decision—or rather, Allen should make a decision—and pronto. But Allen is tangled up in radio traffic. The dispatcher wants an assessment of the fire's size and intensity: *How big is it? Is it going anywhere? Do you need more crews? Should I order an air tanker? Should I order a dozer?* Two helicopter pilots keep calling in updates and asking questions: *The west flank of the fire is picking up. There's significant torching on the bottom slope. The fire is making a run up a hill on the southeast border. Where do you want us to administer bucket drops? Do you want us to keep an eye on anything in particular?* And other firefighters dispersed around the fire, such as Jeremy Stocklen, have questions and observations of their own. Allen is trying to communicate with all these parties and pull-start the engine's water pump at the same time. Overwhelmed, he doesn't even know about the dispute.

Others join the exchange between Donald and Tyson, but I refuse to wait for its resolution with this fire nipping at our heels. Climbing down from the truck, I side with Donald and grab a hosepack. I screw the hose into the engine's water pump with exaggerated twists to convey my frustration. The water is ready. Allen has primed the pump. He darts around to the front of the engine to release the valve and yells, "Can I turn it on?"

"No! No!" I shout back from the rear, "Not yet!"

I heave the hosepack onto my shoulders and march into the flames. The

hose unravels behind me, and as I kneel to secure the nozzle, my whole body grows hot. Feeling too close, I quickly turn back toward the engines to tell Allen to release the water.

The situation is maddening. We're like a body without a head. Donald and Tyson continue to bark at one another. Allen dashes around the engine, his demanding radio in hand, checking the water level and pressure. Some crewmembers adjust their packs, while others collect more hose.

Then we hear it. A ferocious rumble fills the air. The gluttonous fire releases a sonorous vibration as if a fighter jet has just broken the sound barrier. The force reverberates in my gut. Scuffling bodies and arguing voices stop, held in a silent trance, as the fire rises with a roar. My breathing stumbles. It's upon us.

Everything falls quiet. Movement dies. In this moment the frenzy of action inhales, freezing all sensation, before bursting forth to rend the air once again.

"*Pull back! Pull back! PULL BACK!*" Allen yells, breaking our short silence.

Everyone obeys in a unified swoop. We drop everything—our tools, the hose—and run.

I drop my combi and sprint to the engine yelling, "*Move! Move!*"

We all scatter to the trucks. Donald and George fly into the chase truck and slam the doors. Donald throws the gearshift into reverse, speeds backward into a clearing, slams it in drive, and leads the retreat. I jump into the engine with Allen, and we speed away.

As we race down the dirt road, I look back through the cloud of dust in our wake. The fire has savagely topped the hill. It is crowning out and barreling forward in combusting waves. Everything is ablaze. Flames engulf the area where we stood moments before, burning up all our equipment. I watch as the fire sprints to the road and bounds across.

"We lost *the road*!" I tell Allen, between short gulps of air. "We—lost the road."

Allen speeds a few hundred yards down the dirt road and parks the engine next to the chase truck in a safe clearing. The Jameson crews pull in close behind us. Everyone is safe. Following Allen, I jump out of the engine, assuming he will gather the troops and formulate a new plan of attack. Instead he marches straight back toward the fire without a word, leaving us in the clearing with no instructions.

Jarred and rattled, I grab another combi, since my old one is now charcoal, and stand next to Donald. We both watch George tramp hastily after

Allen, followed by Tyson and some of his crewmembers. Others stand their ground. Leaning on the handle of my tool, aware of the heavy rising and falling of my chest, I wait in silence and study the fire from a safe distance. A few wordless minutes pass before Donald picks up his new Pulaski and begins walking toward the tree-length flames.

"You going in?" I ask, remaining still.

Donald turns and shrugs. "Might as well," he answers.

My glance bounces from his eyes to the fire and back again. "Might as well," I echo and join him, stepping cautiously.

: :

The fire has doubled in size and is showing no signs of slowing down. It glides up, around, and over trees with enormous heat and power. Donald walks ten steps ahead of me. My head swivels as we enter the fire and slowly pick our way between fallen logs alive with red-hot embers. "Look up, look down, look all around," the mantra goes. Out of the corner of my eye, I notice something falling fast.

"Watch out!" I yell.

Donald stops and ducks as a thick burning branch zooms past inches from his head and lands with a *thud* by his feet. Donald stares down at the branch before turning to me. He raises his eyebrows and cheeks in a relieved smile.

"Holy shit!" he chuckles.

"Yeah," I answer, nodding upward. "Widow maker."

My gaze scales a large dead pine and stops fifteen feet from the top, where a ring of fire has burned through its trunk. Donald and I watch as sparks and embers fall on uncooked ground.

"It's gonna go soon," I observe.

"Yeah. Let's dig line around it," Donald suggests.

"All right," I agree, lowering my head.

But after only a few swings of the Pulaski, Donald abandons his plan. "Look," he says, whipping his finger all around us, "there are spots everywhere. When it crowned out, it threw fire everywhere."

I follow Donald's finger and notice cupcake-sized fires smoldering on top of unburned beds of pine needles and below young dry saplings—"spots in the green." Soon, these minifires will combine to form another head of fire that will combust with a vengeance. Donald and I take a few steps back to discuss a new plan.

"Look, Tom's laying a dozer line," I say, pointing to the yellow Cat a few hundred yards away maneuvering busily around flames and fallen trees to create a six-foot-wide road of dirt between the black and the green. Tom's efforts are paying off. But if we don't take care of these spots, another wave of fire will swoop behind Tom's line and escape down the canyon, where we might never catch it.

Donald turns from the burning snag to Tom's new dozer line and back again. He bunches his mouth sideways, thinking.

"A lot of damn spots," I offer.

Donald nods and, after a brief silence suggests, "Yeah, look, I think we should dig line from here to the dozer line. From here, right through there." He motions with an extended arm, tracing the path. "That way we can head off these spots and maybe backburn from there."

"Sounds good. Let's find everybody."

Donald and I walk farther into the bowels of the fire and find Tyson, his crew, and George bent over, scouring the ground for spots like children hunting Easter eggs. Donald explains our plan, they agree, and we head back to the burning snag.

Once we're there, someone shouts, "*Line out!*" First come those with Pulaskis, who break up the virgin ground with their tools' grubbing ends, followed by those with combis, rhinos, and vipers, who scrape back the dirt the Pulaskis dislodge.

"Watch your spacing!" George yells out.

Crewmembers comply by shuffling away from one another, maintaining a five-foot cushion between themselves to ensure that no one gets clobbered once we start digging.

"Ready?" Donald asks from the head of the line.

We nod.

Donald lowers his body, yells, "Movin'," and begins by slamming the grubbing end of the Pulaski into the ground. He thrusts the tool deep into the dark soil, past the pine needles and duff, and pulls back. Again, again, and again, Donald's arms and back pulse up and down, and the Pulaski punctures the earth at one hit per second, leaving behind a jagged crease of dirt and roots.

After a dozen or so swings, the next in line begins to dig: "Movin'!"

Then the next: "Movin'!"

"Movin'!"

"Movin'!"

I am last and responsible for the line's perfection. I cannot leave any trace of fuel behind; there must be no branches, or leaves, or sticks, or roots—bridges the fire can cross on. Only mineral soil can remain. After the Jameson firefighter ahead of me does his part to widen the four-foot trail of dirt, I begin. I bend toward the ground with my combi. Leaning forward, left leg extended, I place my left elbow on my left thigh. The gloved fingers of my left hand wrap upward around the mid-section of the handle as my right hand grips the back end in the opposite direction. I straighten my vertebrae from my neck downward and stare at the tip of my combi, noticing my crewmembers' movements at the edge of my vision. After placing the head of my combi on the far bank of the line, where there is still fuel left, I pull back with my whole body. My right arm leads the tug, followed by my torso and hips, which drop and sway backward. My weight shifts from my left leg to my right as I drag the combi's sharp perpendicular head and the dirt it gathers across the line, away from the fire. I shuffle, dragging my feet to the side like a defending basketball guard, kicking up dust, and repeat, and repeat.

I pay close attention to where my tool's head lands and to the effectiveness of each pull. Every few seconds I look down the line to the firefighters in front of me and then up at the flames. Fire surrounds us. It hovers above us on the branches of conifers, rains down upon us as trees combust, vomiting up embers with loud *pops,* and charges toward us, overwhelming everything in its path: rolling, climbing, and tossing about in a radiant rabid seizure. The heat blasts me, burning my face. Beads of sweat sprinkle the line with every lunge I take. I want to stop, to cool off, to catch my breath, but I push on. *Dig, dig, dig.*

"How's it look, Matt?" Donald yells.

I stop and look back on a solid barrier of dark brown soil, a four-foot-wide force field.

"Goo—," I yell back, my chest heaving, "Goo—, good. *Good!*"

Donald offers a curt nod and resumes. I follow. *Dig, dig, dig.* After a few minutes the wind shifts abruptly, sending a wall of smoke crashing over the line. Immediately, I turn away, shut my eyes, and cough violently. My mouth turns to felt, my eyes to vinegar. But I can't stop digging. The line is all that matters, and I can't cheat. I face the smoke and squint down the line. I can only faintly make out a few of my crewmembers through the thick black haze, but I can hear them all coughing and wheezing, trying to get the smoke out of their lungs. I continue to dig with my face turned away from the oncoming smoke as much as possible. And when I can no longer stand the acrid stinging in my eyes, I shut them and dig blind for a few hits.

"Tied in!" bellows Donald as he reaches the dozer line.

Beautiful words. This agony will end soon. I inhale desperately, sucking in a mixture of warm oxygen, smoke, and gasses, and push on with my body worn and aching. Sharp pains shoot from my legs through my back; the joints in my fingers and my wilting arms vibrate with each hit; tears try to protect my eyes from the biting smoke. I feel there's nothing more left in me. But I've been here before. My body knows these pains, and it knows its duty.

A few more grueling minutes, and I join my crewmembers at the end of the line. I step onto the dozer's path, painfully wrench myself upright, and join the others in a chorus of coughing. As I wipe my eyes with a clean part of my sleeve and take a long drink of water, spitting most of it on the ground, I stare down the three hundred yards of nothing but dirt and at my crewmembers' sooty, sweaty faces and ash-caked lips and teeth, thinking to myself, "This is what it's all about."

: :

I catch my breath in the heart of the fire. Now that the line is dug, the question of "what now" lingers. Still shaken by our initial retreat and this fire's fierce advance, I need to reorient myself, to find my way back to control. The Ten and Eighteen will be my compass. Inwardly, I summon up the familiar acronym. *Initiate all action based on current and expected fire behavior.* Violated. We received no information to predict the fire's behavior and no report on its current status. *Ensure instructions are given and understood.* Violated. Instructions were never given. *Obtain current information on fire status.* Violated. We have not received a size-up. How big is this thing? What is the rest of the fire, the part I can't see, doing? How much, if any, is contained? *Remain in communication with crew members, your supervisor, and adjoining forces.* Violated. I have no idea where Allen is, and I haven't heard his voice over the radio.[3] *Determine safety zones and escape routes.* Violated. We used a safety zone and escape route during the retreat, but now the escape route is flooded with fire. If that route no longer exists, what is our new escape route and, for that matter, our new safety zone? *Establish lookouts in potentially hazardous situations.* Violated. I'm on red alert.

Tyson, his crew, and George wander off to chase spots. Donald and I trek off in the opposite direction to do the same. We work quietly and tediously, combing the ground for embers in the green and burying them under mineral soil. Hundreds of miniature smokes surround us, and we dash from one to another to another in a seemingly endless game of connect-the-dots. It is worthless work. There is no chance we will find all the spots, and it takes only one to kindle a fresh start.

We carry on like this for twenty minutes. Then, out of the smoke, the man himself approaches. Thurman is here. His tall, commanding figure startles me. Immediately, Donald and I stop working and look up at Thurman. His eyes hold mine for less than a second from under his slurry-stained hard hat before darting to the tips of trees, the ground flames, the spots, and other crewmembers. A thin yellowish gray fire shirt wraps his thick torso and arms, and a two-foot plastic antenna protrudes from a handheld radio belted to his chest by a fraying harness.

"Let's go," he says, turning away.

Donald and I follow without a word. As I walk behind Thurman, I feel in trouble, caught. But I also feel comforted and safe, shepherded by a trusted leader.

We walk behind Thurman as he gathers Tyson and his crew, George, Craig, and Allen. He leads us away from the fire to an open clearing and lines us up, shoulder to shoulder. Thurman paces patiently in front of the quiet group with the fire to his back. "No need to rush," he likes to say, "the fire will still be there." After a long silence, he addresses us, rocking his head back toward the fire every few seconds.

"The fire isn't doing anything, folks," he advises, projecting that baritone voice of his. "It ain't going nowhere. We've been running around this damn thing, but it ain't going nowhere. We're not going to waste our time running around and chasing these spots, folks. We're gonna have the dozer push the line behind them, and we'll burn it out. Take all damn day to chase all these spots and it won't do a damn bit a good."

He pauses, searching our faces to gauge how well we understand his point, and continues, "Allen, take your crew and grid the east side of the fire, down the canyon face, and check for spots. Tyson, head for the west side and do the same. I'll have Tom finish pushing line around this thing, and then we'll burn out from there. Any questions?"

Silence.

"Okay, let's be heads-up out there, folks. This fire ain't going nowhere," Thurman concludes, before repeating one of his favorite sayings: "Still, this is no time to get complacent."

We march to our new assignments. Donald, George, and I spread out along the canyon bluff and begin surveying the ground. "If there's a fire in the bottom of a canyon, keep it in the bottom. If it's up on top, keep it on top," as Thurman always says. In a parallel line, we creep back and forth along the precipitous slope, finding only one lonely smoke. My boots slip sideways over moss-covered rocks and piles of brush. Fresh blisters forming and tearing on the balls of my feet and the backs of my ankles add their salty sting to the deep soreness already moving through my shoulders, arms, and back. As I stumble along, I consider breaking our silent

search to complain about how much I hate this fire. But George beats me to it.

"Ohhh, *shit*," he exclaims in a soft, anxious tone.

I look up and notice that George is not looking down at the ground. He is staring at something far away, something across the canyon. My eyes follow his gaze, and I spot what struck him. At least half a mile away, on the opposite canyon rim, a lanky gray smoke snakes gracefully above the treeline.

George sprints up the canyon face to tell Thurman the fire has bridged the chasm. Donald and I follow, stopping at the top to watch. Fighting a fire in a canyon is like swimming away from a shark in the ocean: it has an incredible home-field advantage. It is agile where we are clumsy, fast where we are slow, and powerful where we are at the mercy of the jagged rocks. Flames twirl and skip and run and pounce through the steep terrain; they explode like cannon balls up vertical formations called chimneys. Thirtymile, South Canyon, the Dude burn—when they found the bodies, they found them in canyons.

"Looks like it's gonna be a long night," Donald predicts, fixing his eyes on the new smoke.

"Yep, yep," I agree, nodding. But I also know it's nothing we can't handle. Our fire isn't going anywhere. Thurman told us so, and Tom is making sure by encircling it with a freshly bulldozed highway of dirt. The temperature is dropping, the humidity is rising, and I'm confident Thurman will know what to do with this new start. I don't remember when I made the decision to trust Thurman. (Perhaps it was the first time we met, when he told me, "Don't fuck up! I don't want to be bringing you home in a body bag." Perhaps it was after I saw him command crews on a fire with uncompromising leadership; perhaps it was his thirteen years on the Shots; or perhaps it was his stained fire shirt and spotted helmet.) But somewhere along the line I'm sure I did.

I sit on the edge of the canyon with the rest of the crew and watch the slurry bombers Thurman has dispatched to the new smoke kiss the treetops with their bellies and drop clouds of maroon mist, which turns neon red against the setting sun. Thurman also has ordered several crews to the new start, and judging from their radio traffic, they're getting a handle on things.

Soon Allen's voice crackles over the radio, instructing us to "monitor the line." We get up and return to the fire, spreading out thirty paces apart along the fireline. We walk back and forth looking for spots in the green and weaknesses in the line. But as nightfall descends, we spend less time with our heads bent and more marveling at the bright oranges and yellows, their full splendor luminous against a black backdrop. Small flames sway and flutter on branches like dancers, exhausted but entranced. Drops of fire cling like phosphorescent dew before slipping off to the glowing ground below. Ground coals permeate the smoke with a yellowish hue, making the fire look deep and long. Skeletons of trees are silhouetted against this gold canvas, outlined in orange. I meditate on this beautiful destruction of familiar shapes and colors, which always present themselves anew.

At 10:00 p.m., after an hour of pacing, Allen tells us to burn out. I join other crewmembers and take two fusees and my sunglasses from my fire pack. Donald, George, and I exchange smiles. We love burning out. Stepping over the dozer line, I crack the sulfur tip of one fusee against its strike pad, causing a glaring white flame to shoot out from the tip with a *Pop!* My eyes shielded by sunglasses, I point the concentrated flame downward, lighting off the unburned fuel inside the dozer line.

Tossing our fusees into the fire, we hurry back to the line to admire our handiwork. My fire meets up with Donald's, then George's, and on down the line. The backburn rises up and recedes into the black. It sprays an orange glow on our cheeks before slowly dying down and finally joining the heavy smoke. We search the green for embers from the burnout. After a few minutes, Allen calls Donald, George, and me over the radio and tells us to meet him on the east flank of the fire. We suspect we are heading home for the evening, but instead Allen presents us with one more task. He has found an especially hot spot on the cusp of the fireline and instructs us to reinforce the line with our hand tools. We suppress our pain, stiffness, and exhaustion and grudgingly bust ass for another twenty minutes. Satisfied, Allen tells us to head for the trucks.

I lift my heavy body into the cab of the engine and roll my sleeves to my elbows, baring soot-caked forearms. My stomach grates, since I haven't eaten since lunch. My boot soles feel like lead, and my back, legs, shoulders, feet ache. I smell of sweat, dirt, and smoke, which is all I can taste. I feel worn down, beat up, accomplished, and seasoned. As Allen slowly pulls away, I lean back and sigh, staring at the clock blinking 11:15 p.m. Allen steers the engine back to Elk River as I gaze out the windshield with drooping eyes and reflect on the fire. This one was serious.

After Allen backs the engine into its stall, I slump back to crew quarters. I go immediately to my refrigerator, heat some leftover pasta in the microwave, and eat it straight out of the container. Tossing the empty bowl in the sink, I head for the shower, dropping my smoke-saturated clothes. As the warm water washes over me, I scrub the ash and dirt from my arms, face, legs, and hair, watching the black water swirl down the drain. I collapse in bed at half-past midnight and set my alarm. Thurman wants us at work by 6:00 a.m. and back on the line by 7:00.

The Incompetent Dead

Thurman would never have found out about our retreat if someone hadn't left the charred tools and hose exposed in the bed of the chase truck. George, Donald, and I kept our mouths shut, mostly for Allen's sake. The burned equipment snitched. Thurman pulled Allen aside, asked what had happened, gave him a stern talking-to, and told him to take the crew back to the scene of the Beaver Creek fire and conduct a safety meeting called an after action review (AAR). So a week after the last smoke of the fire was laid to rest, the entire crew returned for a reenactment safety briefing. Standing in the precise spot where the fire had overtaken the crews, Allen led the meeting by reconstructing the day's events, skillfully trimming the narrative of the most embarrassing details.

"I told them to get their IA packs on," Allen slowly reflected. "The first thing I told them was that the escape routes and safety zones are up the road. It wasn't really doing anything at the time. I was thinking that we could probably stop it, but I don't know. . . . Then, all of a sudden it started flaring up and torching and, uh, Cutter [a firefighter from another district] yelled, '*Get out of here!*'

"So I yelled, '*Get out of here!*' So me and Desmond jumped in the engine and took off. . . . By that time, the fire was right here when we took off. . . . After that, I told the guys to stay down there, and I ran down here to get Stocklen's truck. . . . So, anyways, that's what happened. We caught it down there on that ridge."

Crewmembers nodded and tried to follow the fire's path with their eyes, skimming over the black and gray ground, across the wide dozer line, and up tree trunks charred and brittle like the insides of dirty chimneys.

"We had some hot, windy fuckin' days," Peter added. "I'm surprised it didn't blow up earlier."

In Allen's version of the events, the fire didn't sneak up on a group of fussing firefighters parked in a foolish place; it exploded suddenly, owing to an unexpected wind shift, right when we were organizing an approach. Allen didn't leave his crew without instructions after the retreat; he told them to stay put in the safety zone while he fetched Jeremy Stocklen's truck. By the time Allen concluded the safety meeting, it seemed as though the crewmembers who did not fight the Beaver Creek fire believed it was ferocious and erratic, that we did everything right, and that the initial evacuation was no big deal—except Bryan. And Bryan doubted Allen's story because he noticed me doubting it.

The fire didn't sit well with me. It chased us, drove us back. I had never run from a fire before. I had never felt so threatened by a blaze. But I certainly didn't feel responsible for that. I blamed Allen, and when he painted what I thought was too pretty a picture of the fire at the safety meeting, I grew irritated, then angry. My frustrations increased the more Allen talked, and my body soon began betraying my feelings. I kicked the dirt and sighed. I smirked knowingly and shook my head slightly, staring at the toes of my boots. Bryan caught on. After the meeting, he approached me with a grin, put his hand on my shoulder, and whispered in my ear, "So, what's *your* take on this? Or am I gonna have to read about it?"

"Later," I whispered back. "Later."

I avoided Bryan for the next week. I was confused, bitter, ticked off, and jarred, and I didn't want these feelings to influence my crewmembers' interactions or Allen's reputation. Plus, I was beginning to wonder if there was anything to be confused, bitter, ticked off, and jarred about, since neither Donald nor George thought much of the Beaver Creek fire. They agreed that it was heavy on confusion and light on leadership, but they didn't think their lives were threatened. Nonetheless, pessimistic "what if" questions occupied more and more of my thoughts, and when Bryan stopped by my room for a beer and pressed me for details about the fire, I released a deluge of emotionally charged criticism. I presented an alternative history of the Beaver Creek fire and included the countless violations of the Ten and Eighteen, the fight between Tyson and Donald, and Allen's virtual absence during initial attack. I concluded by pointing out that neither safety zones nor escape routes were identified—a fact, I thought, that would force Bryan to join me in pointing the finger at Allen.

"We didn't know where safety zones and escape routes *were* till Thurman told us one hour later!" I confessed, leaning forward on my sofa.

"Well, see, *that's* when you guys should of asked for them," Bryan replied, pointing upward. "And, I mean, I don't know, I feel that that's partly your responsibility to ask for them, because, I mean, like last year on the Buckingham fire, we had to sit up on top most of the day, and I didn't get to go down till they started burning at night, and I brought up the point and said, 'Well, where's the escape routes and safety zone?' And the message had to get bumped all the way up to Wilson [the supervisor], by the whole crew.

"Then Wilson came up to me after that and was like, 'You know what?' He's all, 'Nobody else brought that up the whole day while they were down there.' I mean, they *knew* where it was, they told them before, but *I didn't know* where it was. So I asked. And he complimented me on asking because I wasn't informed out there."

"So, if I got seriously burned or died on the Beaver Creek fire, whose fault would it be?" I asked, cutting to the chase.

"Ahhh, that's a tough question because it could go either way. Because you, as a firefighter, have the right to know stuff, and you have every right to ask questions, you know. If you don't know what's going on, *find out what's going on*. But then again, you should have been informed about what's going on and what needs to be done. See what I'm saying?"

"Yeah. I think. So, do you think it would be *both* my fault and Allen's fault?"

"In a way, yeah. If something like that were to happen. Because, I mean, you're an intelligent person. . . . It's not like you go out there and they tell you, 'Shut up. Don't say anything. Do as you're told,' you know. 'This is what you're going to do *whether you like it or not*.' You can say, 'Well, you know, I'm not sure if this is a good idea.' You can bring that up. And you should *not* feel uncomfortable bringing that up, you know. It's your safety, but then it's also the responsibility of people in charge to inform you."

Bryan finished his beer and went to bed. I poured myself another glass of Glenfiddich. *My* fault? Why did Bryan think *I* was to blame? If the Beaver Creek fire had claimed my life, would Bryan blame me? Would others? But the trajectory of these broodings soon reversed itself. Why did I feel the need to blame Allen? Wasn't I just as culpable as he? Bryan had a point: I can think for myself. If "no" is a word in my vocabulary, then wasn't my silence just as pitiful as Allen's lax leadership? Then again, why must we blame anyone at all?

The death of a firefighter poses a significant problem for the organizational common sense of the U.S. Forest Service because at first glance it seems to contradict its fundamental tenet: that fire is safe and controllable, that properly trained firefighters should never incur harm on the fireline. If the Forest Service strives to cultivate within firefighters an illusio of self-determinancy, how does the organization react when this illusio faces its biggest challenge, the death of a firefighter? What happens when the body of an experienced firefighter is "burned beyond recognition" and is brought before firefighters as evidence that the illusio of self-determinancy might be nothing more than a chimera?[1]

To address these questions, I parse the organizational process through which the Forest Service manages death. I first return to that awful summer afternoon on Sawtooth Mountain with which I began this book and describe the fallout surrounding Rick Lupe's burnover. I then broaden my scope by analyzing the Forest Service's approach to all deaths.[2] Finally, I explore how firefighters themselves react to death, how their reactions are influenced by the common sense of the Forest Service, and how this affects their illusio of self-determinancy.

Two Eulogies

Two days after Rick Lupe died, a small article titled "Firefighting Warrior Led Crew That Saved Pinetop, Show Low" appeared in the opinion section of the *Arizona Republic*.[3] The columnist, Jim Paxton, a firefighter with over thirty years of experience and a public relations spokesperson for the Forest Service, recreated the Sawtooth burnover:

> On May 14, Rick went in to check a hot spot. Suddenly, there was a flare-up that surrounded him with fire. Rick had trained for this moment a thousand times. He attempted to deploy his fire shelter, but turbulent winds blew away the shelter. Rick went into the dirt face down, sticking his nose into the ground to protect his lungs from the hot air and flames, but when the firestorm passed, Rick had severe burns over 30 percent of his back, legs and arms.
>
> Rick is a fighter, and he knew what to do. The battle wasn't over. He pulled himself up and walked out of the woods about a half-mile and found

help. The medical helicopters took over, transporting this warrior to Whiteriver Hospital and then to Maricopa Burn Center. That was five weeks and two days ago . . . but the battle ended at 8:50 a.m. on Thursday. The firefighting family lost a brother and a son.

Through Paxton's eyes, Rick Lupe (or just Rick, as Paxton called him, emphasizing first-name intimacy) died because he was in the wrong place at the wrong time when the fire unpredictably intensified ("*Suddenly, there was a flare-up*"). Lupe "knew what to do." He fought the good fight yet still lost out to the overpowering flames. To Paxton, Lupe died a heroic, innocent, warriorlike death at the hands of a deadly force of nature.

Arizona grieved its loss and poured out its thanks. Governor Janet Napolitano commemorated Lupe by lowering all American flags flown over state buildings to a sorrowful half-mast for seven days. The Fort Apache Tribe topped the governor's gesture by declaring a thirty-day mourning period. The Bureau of Indian Affairs set up a donation fund for Lupe's wife and children, and strangers gave. Over five hundred people attended

his funeral. Later that year Lupe was named "Firefighter of the Year" and recognized by Congress (HR 237) for "his dedication to the United States, for his long and essential service in fighting wildfires and caring for the environment, and for ultimately sacrificing his life for the people of Arizona." And on September 19, 2005, the citizens of Pinetop, Arizona, dedicated a life-size bronze statue of Lupe, which now stands outside the public library.[4] (A Boy Scout, Richard Genck, collected enough money from local businesses and private donors to commission the statue, thus completing his final service project for the honor of Eagle Scout.) The bronze Lupe, dressed in full fire gear, a helmet, and sunglasses, confidently carries a Pulaski and marches ahead with a ready face. The plaque at the foot of the memorial reads:

RICHARD "RICK" GLENN LUPE

MAY 18, 1960–JUNE 19, 2003

A TRUE AMERICAN HERO, RECOGNIZED AS ONE OF
OUR NATION'S GREATEST FIREFIGHTERS,
DIED IN THE LINE OF DUTY.

*"LITTLE DO THEY KNOW OF OUR LONG LABORS ON THEIR
BEHAVE FOR THE PROTECTION OF THEIR BORDERS . . .
AND YET, I GRUDGE IT NOT." J. R. R. TOLKIEN.*

This *external eulogy* was the one most people witnessed after Lupe died.[5] Hats covered hearts. Gruff men hugged. Politicians sighed over clusters of microphones. A solo bugler played Taps on a cool morning. And a starched American flag was draped over a closed casket. The Forest Service presided over many of these ceremonies, but it also presided over another kind of eulogy, one observed by those who had to return to the line the next day. This *internal eulogy* served a wholly different function and constructed an entirely different picture than the external one.

In earlier chapters I described scattered observances of Lupe's internal eulogy—in my crewmembers' shrug-of-the-shoulders reaction to the news of his death, discussed in the introduction, and in Jack MacCloud's observation that Lupe "did not make enough luck" for himself. But one other instance of this ritual deserves attention here because it was led by Ronald Crasser, the top forest supervisor.

RICHARD "RICK" GLENN LUPE

MAY 18, 1960 - JUNE 19, 2003

A TRUE AMERICAN HERO, RECOGNIZED AS ONE OF
OUR NATION'S GREATEST FIREFIGHTERS,
DIED IN THE LINE OF DUTY.

"LITTLE DO THEY KNOW OF OUR LONG LABORS ON THEIR
BEHALF FOR THE PROTECTION OF THEIR BORDERS...
AND YET, I GRUDGE IT NOT." J.R.R. TOLKIEN

Fifteen days after Lupe was burned, Thurman called Allen and told him to skip PT and clean up the station. Three top Forest Service supervisors were headed our way to inspect Elk River. The crew scurried about the conference room emptying trash cans, vacuuming the thinning carpet, polishing the windows, and scrubbing the toilet bowl. These men were Thurman's bosses, so we paid extra attention to our chores. I mumbled the Ten and Eighteen under my breath as I dusted the large conference tables and window sills.

At 10:30, a brand-new white Forest Service truck followed Thurman's dirty green one into the station. Three older white men in khaki uniforms shook hands with Thurman and Allen before beginning the inspection. Crewmembers avoided the supervisors by looking busy at the opposite end of the station but were soon summoned to the conference room to hear the results. Jack MacCloud sat near the head of the conference table next to his boss, Ronald Crasser, a short man with a full head of gray hair neatly parted on the left. Crasser smiled cheerfully at each crewmember as we took seats around the table. An oversized silver and turquoise bracelet weighed down his left wrist, and thick steel-rimmed glasses framed his light blue eyes. He had an air about him, a posture of authority; it was something about the way he sat and folded his arms, confidently, knowingly, that made me feel he was comfortable in most places and had grown used to giving orders.

After complimenting the crew on the cleanliness and order of the station and suggesting some minor changes, Crasser began discussing two recent shelter deployments in a nearby forest.

"These guys were trapped, but they managed to escape, thankfully," he observed with his elbows on the table and his hands folded neatly in front of him. "These things out there are telling us that things are not okay. Things are not good in the woods right now."

Then he turned his attention to Rick Lupe. After explaining vague bits and pieces of the scenario on Sawtooth, he remarked, "There are some things he did wrong, uh, but we don't know what it was because we can't talk to him."

There it was. Lupe did some things wrong. His incompetence landed him in a messy situation. This idea could not have been further from the veneration and praise poured out during Lupe's external eulogy. The external eulogy held Lupe to be an innocent hero whose altruistic and sacrificial death could be explained simply by the violent and volatile nature of wildfire. The internal eulogy held him to be a failure whose fully preventable death was the outcome of incompetence. These two disparate eulogies did not take place in a vacuum, isolated from society. On the contrary, the external and internal eulogies connected to larger cultural structures and webs of meaning operating throughout the society that envelops the Forest Service. As Mary Douglas once observed, "Any institution that is going to keep its shape needs to gain legitimacy by distinctive grounding in nature and reason: then it affords to its members a set of analogies with which to explore the world and with which to justify the naturalness and reasonableness of the instituted rules, and it can keep its identifiable continuing form."[6] Whereas the external eulogy gained meaning by connecting to widespread convictions of symbolic honor and masculine sacrifice, convictions linked to ideas of nationalism and heroism, the internal eulogy borrowed from ideas of American individualism, autonomy, and self-reliance. Through the former, the Forest Service maintained legitimacy with the surrounding community; through the latter, it hoped to gain legitimacy in the eyes of its workers, those ground-pounding grunts who could end up on a side slope like the hillside near South Canyon, a hillside now speckled with fourteen white crosses, or in the guts of some canyon like the guts of Thirtymile, or in some bowl, innocent to all appearances, like the bowl at Sawtooth.[7]

Crasser's pronouncement was not based on any sort of evidence—he had not spoken with Lupe, and the fatality report had not yet been released—and he did not know exactly how Lupe failed. Nevertheless, he had been around long enough to know how and when to preside over the ritual of the internal eulogy. He knew that all dead firefighters, in one way or another, were incompetent firefighters and ultimately were responsible for their own burns. And I should point out that during his short stint at Elk River, Crasser presided over Lupe's internal eulogy not as someone who needed to rationalize death so as to assuage his own fears—he had not been involved in dangerous initial attack operations in years—but as an elite supervisor and spokesman of the Forest Service who helped to reinforce and reproduce the common sense of his host organization.[8]

Crasser assumed that the findings of the fatality report would support his bold prediction, and he didn't have to wait long to find out. Twenty-four hours after Lupe was burned, a twelve-person investigative team was assembled by the Bureau of Indian Affairs. Two days later they descended on the burn site. Determined to discover what circumstances led to the entrapment, the team interviewed all the fire supervisors, the helicopter pilots, and many of the crewmembers at Sawtooth as well as the hospital nurses who first treated Lupe. Team members took pictures of the area where the fire overtook Lupe as well as aerial shots of surrounding topography; they collected official documents and weather readings, following a paper trail all the way back to 2001, when the Sawtooth prescribed burn plan was originally drafted. The investigators finished drafting the first report on May 21, just three days after they began their work, but did not officially submit the document because they planned to interview Lupe, who was then comatose. That chance never came, and after Lupe died, the team presented its findings in a document authoritatively titled *Sawtooth Mountain Prescribed Fire Burnover Fatality Factual Report*.

When I first read the report, almost immediately after the 2003 fire season ended, I initially believed it supported Crasser's assumption that Lupe had erred in some serious way. I didn't believe Crasser was right, necessarily, but I did somehow believe that the fatality report backed him up. I read the fifteen pages of the report's key findings as well as the ninety or so pages of supporting documents attached as appendixes. I used a highlighter. But the only part of the report that resonated with me, the part I took to be the core finding of the investigation, was a paragraph-sized checklist that seemed to document Lupe's mistakes:

1. It was unclear on May 14 who was to serve as lookout, and where the individual was to be located in order to observe the activities of the burn.
2. The individual serving as lookout on the afternoon of May 14 was unable to see all the areas where the holding crews (Apache #2 and Apache #8) and Rick Lupe were working.
3. Escape routes were not pre-designated for the holding crews.
4. Specific safety zones were not pre-designated, except for "the black."
5. Anchor points for control lines within the burn area perimeter were not established.
6. Wednesday, May 14, was Rick Lupe's first day on the burn site.
7. Rick Lupe was not specifically assigned a position on the prescribed burn, but showed up at the burn site of his own accord, and then was assigned duties by Burn Boss #1.[9]

I had found what I was looking for, and in an earlier draft of this very book, this is what I wrote: "Violations of the Ten and Eighteen served as the center point of the report. By working without clearly established safety zones and escape routes, Lupe violated the seventh Order, and because he did not attempt to secure the firelines to safe anchor points, he violated the eighth Situation. Two pages later, the report recorded that Lupe was not properly equipped: he had rolled up his sleeves and had forgotten his gloves. The overarching conclusion of the fatality report, then, was that individual decisions made on the ground by Lupe (and, to a much lesser extent, by his supervisors) were to blame for the entrapment."

I then attempted to cast doubt on these findings and the internal eulogy of the Forest Service. However, I did not do so by marshaling any evidence, any documentation showing that Lupe in fact had done nothing wrong. I merely speculated that predictable discoveries of fault were not discoveries, that the "fact-finding" investigative team was really a "fault-finding" team that could always and easily charge a fallen firefighter with violations of the Ten and Eighteen. Thinking I had successfully broken with the organizational common sense of the Forest Service by simply looking at it with disbelieving eyes, I stopped there.

Little did I know how truly blinded I was by the common sense of my host organization, how effortlessly and thoughtlessly I had adopted its way of thinking as *the* way of thinking. Though I had taken the resistant baby step of saying no to the internal eulogy, I had not yet taken the next (generative) step of constructing a new way of conceptualizing the death of a firefighter, one not molded and conditioned by the dominant thought categories of the Forest Service. I thought that most, if not all, fatality reports found that entrapments and burnovers were brought about by incompetence. I had been trained to think in such a way, just as I had been trained to dig line, to sharpen tools, and to recognize wind shifts.

But in March 2006, while working on the final round of revisions for this book, for no reason in particular, I reread the *Sawtooth Mountain Prescribed Fire Burnover Fatality Factual Report* cover to cover and came to realize that I had been completely wrong. Lupe's violations of the Ten and Eighteen were virtually absent from the report, and those violations that were highlighted were supported by flimsy and contradictory evidence. This realization, this moment of unanticipated reflexivity, forced me to reevaluate why I had originally overlooked all the evidence that contradicted Crasser's proclamation and instead had assumed with him that the report found Lupe to be at fault. It forced me to delve deeper, through the obscuring organizational common sense of the Forest Service, to arrive at a sounder understanding not only of that awful summer afternoon on Sawtooth Mountain but also of the opaque and complex way the death of a firefighter is managed. Analysts, after all, must struggle against spontaneous and false ways of thinking not only at the inception of the research (in its design) or at its conclusion (as an afterthought, a regretful navel gazing confession) but during absolutely all stages of the research.[10]

I scrapped the bulk of the chapter. I brought up from my basement a dusty box that contained fatality reports, handbooks, and stacks of other official documents I had previously collected, read, and filed away and began poring over them with renewed motivation. I had to turn the tools of socioanalysis on myself, to objectify myself as (still) a member of the organization I sought to objectify; I had to break with self-evident organizationally sponsored rationalizations deeply entrenched in my own way of thinking. I had to keep digging.

What really happened to Rick Lupe? The next section draws on the meticulous (and sometimes self-contradictory) fatality report, and its supporting documentation, to answer this question as thoroughly as possible.

Returning to Sawtooth

Our story begins in April 2001, when members of the Fort Apache Agency of the Bureau of Indian Affairs (BIA) sought the approval of the BIA Western Regional Office in Phoenix for a proposal titled "Prescribed Burn Plan: Sawtooth Mountain Habitat Improvement Burn Project." The sixteen-page proposal advanced a plan to burn two thousand acres on the Fort Apache Indian Reservation. According to the plan, "The primary objectives [of the prescribed burn] are to improve up to 2,000 acres of existing decadent wildlife habitat; to open-up existing closed canopy overstories; and to disturb approximately 25 to 50 percent of the mountain mahogany in the project area." Furthermore, the prescribed burn was intended to clear out ladder fuels, such as low-hanging branches, brush stands, timber slash, and thick clusters of high-growing shrubbery, that would allow a wildfire to climb into the crowns of surrounding trees. To accomplish this goal, the control fire would need to "burn with sufficient intensity to top-kill 50 to 75 percent of the brush species less than 8 feet tall. It is expected this objective can only be attained in dense (greater than 60 to 70 percent canopy cover) shrub stands and stands with at least moderate quantities of dead fuel, particularly where they occur on steep slopes." The plan, then, called for a fire that would burn hot.

The fire would be lit in two phases. The first was referred to as the blacklining operation. During this phase, firefighters would use matches and drip torches to ignite vegetation on the east and north sides of the burn. The black line would stretch for about five miles and extend about fifteen to twenty chains into the burn area. (A chain is sixty-six feet, or fifteen to twenty paces, depending on your stride.) This would produce a mildly burned boundary around the area, a boundary that was designated as a safety zone, to pretreat the area for the second burning phase, the helitorching. During this phase, a helicopter would fly over the interior of the targeted area and dispense large amounts of fire from an underslung torch that would drop burning gelled petroleum on the ground below. The helicopter pilot, the plan advised, should target pine stands and dense clusters of shrubs.

The plan described the topography of the burn area in detail: the ridgetops and valleys were marked by gentle rolling terrain, and numerous cliffs and drop-offs, including the summit of Sawtooth Mountain, as well as steep slopes and zigzag drainages, cut through the landscape. However, when the plan described the types of vegetation in the area, it downplayed the threat of explosive fire. The plan made no mention of chaparral—an obstinate, drought-resistant, and highly flammable shrub—which littered the prescribed burn area. Moreover, although the plan estimated that 60 percent of the vegetation in the targeted area was classified as fuel model 6, "shrubs, shrubs with sparse timber," it was quick to point out that "most shrub lands in the project area lack an herbaceous or litter layer and do not have sufficient fuel loading or continuity to support fire spread except under extreme conditions. Therefore, model 6 tends to over predict fire behavior for these types in most instances." This dismissive observation, based on fuel density and type, which cautioned against inflated predictions of fire behavior, would have been justified if the burn plan had not specifically targeted dense shrub stands. But while most of the burn area consisted of sparse shrubs with weak fuel-loading capacity, the areas to be set ablaze were precisely the thickest and densest areas of the landscape. The statements on fuel loading, then, functioned like a red herring, perhaps leading the architects of the burn plan to predict that, during the blacklining phase of the burn, the fire would not produce flame lengths over fourteen inches and that during the helitorching operation flame lengths would not exceed ten feet in the shrubbery (unless torching occurred) or eighteen inches in the heavy timber. In hindsight, we know such predictions were gross underestimates.

Perhaps most important were the plan's weather requirements, its "prescription parameters," which instructed as follows: For the blacklining phase, ignition must not begin if the temperature exceeds eighty degrees or the relative humidity falls below 20 percent; for the second phase, ignition must not begin if the relative humidity falls below 10 percent (the temperature limit remained the same). And for both phases, the fuel moisture for one-hundred-hour fuels—that is, the amount of moisture in fuels one to three inches in diameter, represented as the percentage of the weight when exhaustively dried at 212 degrees Fahrenheit—must not drop below 8 percent. Finally, a spot weather forecast, a forecast crafted to the specific topographic, temporal, and environmental elements of a fire, must be obtained before both burning operations.

Regarding the proposed schedule, the plan read: "The burn may be conducted anytime prescription conditions are met in the fall, winter, or spring. The preferred burning schedule is March 1 through May 15."

The plan was approved by the Phoenix-based BIA Western Regional Office, and the "low-intensity" blacklining phase was set in motion in April 2001. Things did not go as planned. The prescribed fire escaped and required suppressive efforts: holding crews had to fight the fire they had initially lit, a fire that had been predicted to act predictably, to scoot along the ground with puny fourteen-inch flames. As a result, the Western Regional Office rescinded its approval for the burn on May 9, 2001, an action that brought all future prescribed burning at Sawtooth to a standstill.

The burn operators' hands were tied, and they were not happy about it. On May 24 Ben Nuvamsa, the superintendent of the Fort Apache Agency, responded to the Western Regional Office's decision with a detailed memorandum addressing the concerns raised by his administrative overseers in Phoenix. Judging by the tone of the memorandum, Nuvamsa thought the actions of the Regional Office were rash and based on an exaggerated version of what had happened during the blacklining. For one thing, he did not think the fire had "escaped," a notion "prompted by some erroneous information about the size, location, and potential of the fire, as well as an automatic assignment of a fire number when someone is sent to a fire." Moreover, he claimed that because the so-called escape was accounted for in the burn plan, withdrawing support for the prescribed burn and demanding that the plan be modified before support would again be offered was an unnecessary complication. Nevertheless, Nuvamsa agreed to change the burn plan, if only because, by his own admission, the Regional Office called for some sort of change. He decided to make the prescription parameters more conservative, lowering the maximum temperature to seventy degrees, in hopes that these stricter parameters would win back the Regional Office's favor and get the burning operation—stalled before even the first phase was completed—up and running again.[11]

He would have to wait seven months to find out. Finally, on December 10, the BIA Western Regional director responded with a curt note: "We have reviewed your memorandum and attachments regarding the Sawtooth Rx Burn project. We concur with your decision to use the alternative of black lining in the fall. . . . The revised burn plan, which we have not received, should include sufficient resources on site to avoid exceeding 2,000 acres. . . . The tribal resolution included in the burn plan has expired; therefore, a new tribal resolution is required." The Sawtooth Mountain Prescribed Burn operation was a go once again.

What happened the next year is unclear. I assume the Fort Apache Agency resumed phase one of the operation and finished putting a black line around the perimeter of the targeted area in the fall. When the operation resumed in May 2003, it was time to initiate phase two, the helitorching. The Western Regional Office never received the revised burn plan for this phase, and, crucially, those who orchestrated the final phase of the burn did not abide by the prescription parameters set forth in 2001.

At 7:30 a.m. on May 12, 2003, the sky weather reading—the official forest and fire weather report most likely to be read at the preignition morning briefing—predicted that the maximum temperatures for the Sawtooth burn site and surrounding weather zones could reach eighty-five degrees and that the minimum relative humidity could drop below 5 percent—conditions that exceeded the limits established in the 2001 burn plan. Little change was predicted for the proceeding days. (No spot weather forecast was ordered.) There was zero chance of precipitation, which was not surprising, since some weather stations on the White Mountain Apache Reservation had gone over a month without rain. Moreover, the fuel moisture reading for the one-hundred-hour fuels was 4 percent, four points lower than the driest percentage the plan allowed. In fact, historically, between mid-May and mid-June, fuel moisture levels in northern Arizona reach their nadir, dropping, on average, below 10 percent. But 2003 was no average year. It was a drought year, and the fuel moisture levels were lower than average. The graph below, based on readings gathered from a weather station that accurately represents climate patterns on the Apache reservation, displays the average, maximum, and minimum fuel moisture content for one-hundred-hour fuels, as measured over thirty-three years; it also shows the readings for the beginning of 2003. On May 12, 2003, fuel moisture levels were breaching record low percentage readings.

On May 12, only three days before the deadline of the "preferred burning schedule" set forth in the plan—a plan, remember, that authorized the burn only during fall, winter, and spring—the forestlands surrounding the summit of Sawtooth Mountain were primed to explode with fire. Under such weather conditions, arrangements to ignite the burn area should have been abandoned. In fact, the "Go-No-Go Checklist," a form the burn boss had to fill out at the beginning of each day, conveyed the same warning. The checklist consisted of thirteen yes/no questions and, at the top of the page, instructed "A **NO** RESPONSE TO ANY ITEM MEANS STOP." The first question on the list asked, "Is a burn plan complete and approved?" The second, "Are all fire prescription parameters within burn plan requirements?" The third, "Is the current fire weather forecast favorable for burning today?" All three questions deserved negative responses, but when we glance over the checklist filled out by the fire management officer on May 12, we see nothing but a row of thirteen *x*'s, marking "yes" on down the line.[12]

It was dry—drought-stricken Dust Bowl dry. The air was that waterless Arizona air, air that cracks your lips and knuckles, that sucks the moisture out of your skin, leaving you sunburned but not sweaty, with a headache from dehydration. There was no moisture in the slash and timber either. Downed logs were rotting from within: termite-infested deadwood that would crumble into a light yellow-brown powder if you rubbed it between your hands. The stuff that was not eaten up was wood that an ax could split in one swing with a clean *crack*. And it was hot: a lookout would later record that it got up to eighty-nine degrees around lunchtime. Arid, rainless, and hot, oven hot—but they lit it off all the same.

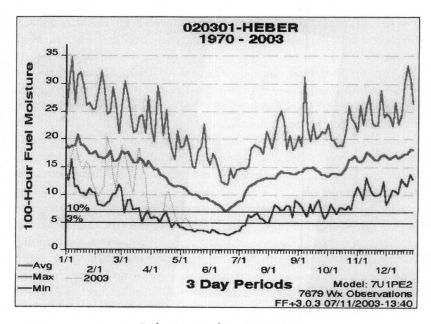

Fuel moisture readings, 1970–2003

According to the log sheets filled out by the burn bosses, things seemed to go well during the first two days of the burn. The fire was manned by two burn bosses and over forty BIA firefighters. On the first day, about six hundred acres were set ablaze. The fire grew active in dense brush clusters, causing many flare-ups and burning with average flame lengths of twenty feet (a shade higher than the 2001 burn plan had expected, but not much). Scorching and torching were observed in pine stands. The temperature remained in the mid-eighties most of the day, dropping below seventy-five degrees only after 6:00 p.m.; and the relative humidity stayed below 10 percent most of the day. Live fuel moistures were recorded between 6 and 9 percent.

The next day, the fire began heating up. Another six hundred acres were ignited. High temperatures and low humidity persisted. Again, when the fire hit dense brush, it produced flare-ups, but this time the average flame lengths were fifteen to thirty feet. And the fire started to rip through the piñon junipers, at times producing flames up to eighty feet. The 2001 plan never predicted such extreme fire behavior.[13]

The next day, May 14, Rick Lupe showed up at the 7:00 a.m. briefing for what would be the last fire he ever battled. No one knew why Lupe showed up. He was not scheduled to work the Sawtooth burn. It was his day off.

Lupe was more than qualified to do so, however, and his help was welcomed. In fact, hearing Lupe's voice and call number over the radio gave Ralph Thomas, one of the two burn bosses overseeing the operation, a distinct "feeling of comfort."

The other burn boss, Ralan Hartzell, an extremely qualified fire behavior analyst and burn specialist, ran the morning briefing. The fire, he reported, was threatening to back down into the Holy Grounds. Accordingly, crews were instructed to keep the fire from invading the sacred site. There would be no new ignition that day; their objectives were strictly protective, preventive, and, if necessary, suppressive. Instead of helitorching, the helicopter, H-355, operated by Orville Pahe, would administer bucket drops on the particularly active and threatening parts of the fire.

After the briefing, the two burn bosses climbed into H-355 and took a quick reconnaissance flight over the fire. Identifying two particularly active areas that could mean trouble for the Holy Grounds, they instructed two ten-person handcrews—Apache #2, led by Gerald Banashley, and Apache #8, led by Cheryl Bones, Rick Lupe's cousin—to head to the troublesome areas and construct a handline to prevent the fire from burning through the sacred site.

Around 11:00 a.m., Rick Lupe met up with Ralan Hartzell at the Holy Grounds. Hartzell instructed Lupe to work with the two handcrews and to help them identify how best to control the approaching fire. "Instructions were given and understood," as Lupe worked with the crews for thirty minutes until Hartzell asked him to work with H-355 to direct bucket drops onto hot areas. So as the two handcrews continued to punch line on opposite sides of a drainage that they predicted would carry the approaching fire to the Holy Grounds the way a fall gust carries a scattering of leaves, Lupe worked alone, directing the helicopter pilot here and there. The helicopter, guided by Lupe's signals and instructions (by radio), hovered over slash and dead trees, burning heavy and hot, and released buckets of water onto the blazing orange-and-black ground below.

At 11:45 the two handcrews took lunch. Lupe skipped it and kept working. After a few minutes he called the handcrews: "Move up the drainage, tie into my flag line, and begin line construction when you get there." When lunch was over, the crews followed Lupe's instructions.

Two hours pass. The temperature rises. The humidity drops. Orville Pahe calls Lupe from H-355 and tells him the helicopter must refuel. On receiving this message, Lupe radios the lookout, Harry Lupe (no relation), and requests a weather report. The lookout responds within minutes. Dry-bulb temperature, eighty-five degrees; relative humidity, 13 percent.[14]

The fire starts to grow violent.

Twenty minutes pass, and Lupe calls H-355. He tells Orville Pahe to get a move on: "The fire's heating up. We need more bucket drops."

H-355 is on the way.

Then a large black column of smoke rises from the southeast end of the burn. Lupe does not see it, but the lookout does. He radios Lupe and tells him about the new burn.

"I'm going down to check on the smoke," Lupe responds.

"Copy," answers the lookout, who can't see Lupe. "Be heads-up."

Lupe drops down into a shallow drainage facing a steep slope. In fact, he is standing in a "bowl," a subtle sunken-in spot at the intersection of three descending drainages at the foot of the western aspect of a hill. Sixty-foot ponderosas and piñon junipers surround him, along with several kinds of brush, including chaparral. Lupe summons a bucket drop, but H-355 does not receive his message. So he radios Cheryl Bones at Apache #8 and asks her to relay the request. She does.

Ten minutes pass before Lupe's loud voice comes across the radio again: "Get out, get back into the black!"

The two handcrews heed Lupe's order and retreat into the black, the pretreated area ignited during phase one of the operation and designated as the official safety zone. No crewmember or lookout can see Lupe.

The radio traffic hushes, and everyone waits.

Then an explosion: it sounds as if an enormous quantity of air is being either sucked in or shoved away by some ominous force; the noise is at once a deep, booming shudder and a high-pitched sizzle. The new smoke column, the one Lupe went to check out, tells the tale. It has more than quadrupled in size and is rising a thousand feet into the air. It is not the thin gray column of a spot fire but the fat, black mushrooming plume of a crown-out.

In the black, in the safety zone, the handcrews wait.

They call it a blowup, "a sudden increase in fireline intensity sufficient to preclude immediate control or to upset existing suppression plans, often accompanied by violent convection." That's the official name for what happened. Five acres of land comprising the steep slope on the east side of the bowl, and the bowl itself, disintegrated under crowning flames lashing out over a hundred feet into the air.[15] The fire burned the sixty-foot pines in their entirety, leaving nothing but gray ash on the forest floor. The gray ash is how you know it burned hot—"moon-faced" is what my crewmembers call it, and when you see it, you don't need to ask why.

"Help, this is Rick. I've been burned. I need medical assistance, feet burned in hot ash." Lupe's voice crackles over the radio. It's 2:45.

Orville Pahe hears him. He unhooks the bucket from H-355 and speeds toward the site of the blowup.

Gerald Banashley and Cheryl Bones hear him too. They start hiking toward the bowl. Heavy black smoke fills the drainages, and as the two crew bosses push their way through the haze, coughing and stumbling, they faintly hear Lupe cry out for help. Gerald makes out a figure stumbling toward them and runs to him.

"I deployed my shelter. But if I would have laid on the ground, I would have never have made it."

Cheryl catches up.

"I'm burned, my hands, legs. It got me from behind. I don't know what happened. I tried deploying my shelter, but the fire took it away from me. I walked through it. It happened so fast, so fast. It came from behind me."

"Do you want some water?" Gerald asks.

"No."

Gerald calls H-355 and reports that Lupe is injured and needs to be flown to the hospital.

H-355 responds that the closest place to land is at the Holy Grounds.
Lupe starts walking.

"It happened so fast. I'm hurting."

Leaning on Gerald and Cheryl, he makes it to the landing spot.

Once the chopper lands, Orville Pahe bounds out and rushes to Lupe.

"You need to fly me to the hospital. I'm hurt real bad."

Someone wants to drive Lupe to the hospital.

"No. I'm hurting. Fly me in."

At 3:13 two nurses are enjoying a cigarette break outside the White River Indian Health Services Hospital when an unauthorized helicopter lands in their heliport. They're not expecting Lupe, since H-355 had no way to communicate with the hospital. The frazzled nurses throw their cigarette butts onto the pavement and rush into the hospital for a stretcher. By the time they find one, Lupe has already walked from the chopper through the emergency room doors.

Ten minutes later, Lupe is only able to mumble two or three words.

One hour later, he is evacuated to the Arizona Burn Center in the Maricopa Medical Center in Phoenix.

Thirty-six days later, Rick Lupe dies of adult respiratory distress syndrome and severe inhalation injury with cardiovascular compromise.

The hot air got him. He burned from the inside out.

Processing Death

Did the fire really sneak up on Lupe just as he claimed? There is no evidence that causes me to think otherwise. In fact, when I examined the burn pattern left by the fire, I was immediately struck by the fact that the blowup that claimed Lupe's life seemed to start virtually where he stood. Flames swept through the bowl from the south end and overran Lupe on the north edge of the drainage before exploding up-slope and destroying all vegetation in its path. The fire's run was tumultuous and fast, but it was also concentrated and uniform, almost rigid. The vegetation surrounding the moon-faced slope and bowl was left unscathed, as if a giant branding iron had seared a rectangle against the western aspect of the slope, killing everything underneath it but leaving the adjacent land unharmed. A pilot who happened to fly over the Sawtooth burn precisely at the moment of the blowup would later tell investigators that the flame front looked strange to him: it was very square and tidy in appearance, unlike a "typical slope driven spot fire." To him it looked prescribed and "appeared to have been lit." Jim Paxton was right: *suddenly,* there *was* a flare-up.

And Lupe cannot be faulted, even under the overweening gaze of hindsight, for observing the spot fire from the bowl. If he had stood on the summit of the slope while fire torched pines in the drainage below, then it would be indisputable that he had placed himself in a bad spot. But Lupe stood in a relatively safe area, one not yet threatened by flame, a secure distance from the spot fire. Although Lupe knew the fire was heating up—he did instruct the handcrews to retreat to safety zones—it is reasonable to conclude that he had no idea, and could have had no idea, that a blowup of that magnitude, velocity, and intensity could (and would) occur in the drainage.

Was Lupe properly equipped? We know he had a fire shelter, a helmet, fire boots (which, according to an observant emergency room nurse, were left in "surprisingly good condition" after the burnover), Nomex fire pants, a fire shirt, and a fire tool. But the fatality report states: "Medical reports and reported observations of firefighters and medical personnel indicate that Rick Lupe was not wearing any gloves, and had the sleeves on his Nomex fire shirt partially rolled up." Things are not this cut-and-dried, however. Lupe's gloves were never found. This could mean he did

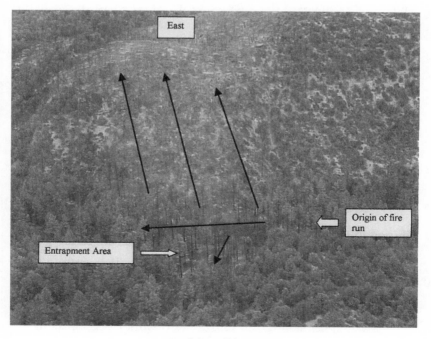

Aerial shot of blowup

not bring them to Sawtooth that morning, or it could mean he tossed his cumbersome gloves aside when trying to unwrap and deploy his shelter. Or Lupe may have set his gloves down somewhere while feeling the fuel moisture of timber with his bare hand to gauge how the fire would take to the surrounding vegetation—a standard practice. No one interviewed by the investigative team reported seeing Lupe without gloves.

On the question of Lupe's sleeves, a question that looms larger than one might expect in the fatality report, answers are mixed. Orville Pahe, the helicopter pilot, reported noticing that Lupe "had no clothing from the elbows down" and that his forearms were severely burned; a helicopter crewman who flew with Lupe in H-355 claimed that only Lupe's right sleeve was rolled up; and an emergency room nurse recalled that neither of Lupe's sleeves was rolled up. Thus, although the main findings of the report propose, sanitarily and authoritatively, that Lupe was not wearing his personal protective equipment correctly, a closer examination of the documents attached as addenda to the report reveals a much muddier picture. The truth is that we simply do not know whether Lupe was wearing his gloves or his fire shirt properly during the blowup.

Is there any proof, then, that Lupe made some egregious mistake? There is none. Lupe conducted all his actions by the book, and to the extent that the Ten and Eighteen can be obeyed, Lupe obeyed them. Lupe recognized current weather conditions and obtained forecasts; he even requested extra weather readings from the lookout. By attending the morning briefing and following Ralan Hartzell's orders, he ensured that instructions were given and understood. He was aware of the fire's status and behavior, which led him to request extra bucket drops. He remained in constant communication with crewmembers, burn bosses, and H-355. We know he had determined safety zones because he instructed the two handcrews to retreat to them, and although the report claims that "escape routes were not pre-designated for the holding crews," it offers no evidence that confirms this finding. Since the two handcrews effortlessly retreated to the safety zone, it is sensible to assume that escape routes were in fact identified. The report also finds that "the individual serving as lookout on the afternoon of May 14 was unable to see all the areas where the holding crews (Apache #2 and Apache #8) and Rick Lupe were working." If this is true, it is because Lupe was acting as a lookout himself: in volunteering to check out the smoke column, Lupe was establishing himself as a lookout in a "potentially hazardous situation."[16]

Lupe was alone, but he was instructed to work alone, or more specifically to work with H-355. In the hours before the blowup, Lupe had worked autonomously, connected to crews only by radio. Acting alone on a wildfire is not against the rules. On the contrary, it is encouraged by the individualizing common sense of the Forest Service: *Trust only one person: yourself. You are responsible for your own safety and actions on the fireline.* If anything is to blame for Lupe's death, perhaps it is this individualizing organizational ethic, an ethic that several organizational scientists have found contributes to breakdowns and simply does not square with the actual practices of firefighting (more on this later).[17] Moreover, the Sawtooth Mountain Prescribed Burn should have never been lit. It was too hot and arid, and the fuel could hardly have been drier. Under such extreme conditions, conditions determined to be hazardous and beyond the prescription parameters of the 2001 burn plan, a torch should have never been put to Sawtooth on May 12.

What is certain is this: If we have any respect for truth, we cannot in good conscience blame Lupe's burnover on his incompetence. But if this is the case, then why did Crasser claim Lupe must have "done some things wrong"? Why did MacCloud believe Lupe did not "make enough luck"? To answer these questions, we must examine the unfolding processes through which the Forest Service seeks to manage death—dynamics that come into view after close examination of many official documents such as fatality reports, press releases, and training booklets.

After any firefighting fatality, and many nonfatal entrapments, an interstate and interagency team of fire behavior analysts, safety officers, chief investigators, and fire operations specialists is dispatched to investigate. Each team bases its investigation on guidelines established in manuals distributed by the U.S. Forest Service, the Department of the Interior, and the Bureau of Land Management.[18] Its job is to identify the causes of the accident in order to generate recommendations—"lessons learned," as they are often labeled—that one hopes will help prevent future accidents.

All the manuals developed to guide accident investigations emphasize the need to identify multiple causes of fatalities. For example, one often-cited manual instructs investigators to organize the causes of an accident into four categories: "people causes," mistakes made by those injured or killed in the accident; "management causes," oversights or blunders made by fire supervisors or top administrators; "equipment causes," mechanical breakdowns or failures that in some way caused the accident; and "environmental causes," how fire weather or fire behavior functioned as a factor in the accident.[19] Another manual advances a similar typology of causes through examples: "Direct causes may include such items as failure to follow the *10 Standard Fire Orders* [people], extreme fire weather or fire behavior [environment], lack of adequate communications equipment [equipment], or inadequate briefings on expected fire weather and behavior [management]."[20]

Although such accident investigation handbooks stress the importance of different factors, they devote significantly more attention (and pages) to people causes than to the other types. "Human factors play a large role in most accidents. Investigators need to be able to identify the human factors that contribute to the accident," one manual instructs.[21] We can gain a sense of the emphasis these handbooks place on the errors of the injured simply by comparing the number of examples given for people causes with those given for the other types. Whereas only a few paragraphs are allotted to examples of management, equipment, and environment causes, accident investigation handbooks devote several pages of examples to people causes. One manual provides a nine-page list of ways the dead or injured can err, while devoting only one page to managerial causes and no pages to environmental or equipment causes.[22]

Moreover, accident investigation manuals not only coach investigators to downplay management, equipment, and environment causes, they also instruct them to think about them as somehow linked to people causes. For instance, one guidebook directs: "Environmental causes *occasionally* are the cause of an accident. A lightning strike is the classic example. When this occurs, *look for human errors* that may have exposed the employee to the environmental hazard."[23] Therefore, if investigative teams follow the instructions set down in their manuals, manuals almost always cited in the introductory pages of fatality reports as providing guidelines for the investigation, then while scrutinizing the burn scene they will actively and ardently look for evidence of incompetence by the dead or injured. They will search for other causes as well, but they will look for rule violations, ground-level misconduct, mistakes, and insubordination—that is, people causes—above all else.

Given these guidelines, it is not surprising that many fatality reports focus on the incompetence of the dead, manifest in violations of the Ten and Eighteen or some other "evidence" of people causes. But I am not aware of any fatality report that does not also identify management, equipment, or environment factors as consequential causes of the accident. Consider, for instance, the report documenting the investigation after fourteen firefighters were burned over by Colorado's South Canyon fire in 1994. Although the report claims that a "can do" attitude led crewmembers to compromise the Ten and Eighteen, it also claims that "fuels were ex-

tremely dry and susceptible to explosive spread" and that the fire strategies developed by supervisors were grossly inadequate.[24] Or consider the
investigative report for Washington's infamous Thirtymile fire of 2001,
a report that begins with a dedication to the four firefighters who lost
their lives—as well as "to those who will be saved." This report explains
the entrapment in terms of forty-two environmental causes, thirty-four
equipment causes, forty-two people causes, and thirty-six management
causes. The temperature and humidity readings were nearing historical
extremes; the crew experienced several operational problems with water
pumps and hoses; the fatigued and sleep-deprived crew failed to recognize the severity of the encroaching fire; and leaders were confused and
reckless.[25] Or last, consider the report examining the deaths of two helitack firefighters on Idaho's Cramer fire in 2003.[26] It was a scorching day,
ninety-five degrees by early afternoon with wind gusts up to thirty miles
an hour—conditions that nurtured an explosive crown fire. (The report
estimates that temperatures at the burnover site exceeded two thousand
degrees Fahrenheit.) Besides these extreme environmental causes, skimpy
resources and too few personnel assigned to the blaze, as well as "inadequate leadership," played a large role in contributing to the burnover.[27]
Of course, violations of the Ten and Eighteen receive significant attention
in each of these reports—after all, as another report put it, they "serve as
an analytical tool to help assess what errors might have occurred during an
incident"—but such violations are always accompanied by other causes of
the accident.[28] In fact, these three fatality reports, as well as many others,
identify a managerial or environmental cause as the *primary cause* of the
fatalities.[29]

Sometimes, however, as the saying goes, what matters is not the message but the messenger. Because, as one accident investigation handbook
instructs, "it is imperative that information about specific entrapments
and the 'Lessons Learned' from these situations be disseminated to all firefighters in a thorough and timely manner," information about fatalities is
speedily circulated throughout the wildland firefighting community once
the investigation is concluded.[13] This is primarily accomplished through
truncated reports widely distributed within firefighting organizations in
memos and press releases. But as information about fatalities is selectively
harvested from the prolix and scholarly fatality reports (rarely read by
firefighters) to produce small, friendly, and manageable minor reports, a
trimming and erasing occurs. Despite the emphasis fatality reports place
on the role of poor leadership, broken equipment, or extreme environmental conditions, in the truncated reports these causes regularly (though

not always) fade into the background—and sometimes out of existence—while the mistakes of firefighters and low-level supervisors are accentuated. The news release that followed the Thirtymile fire, for example, listed only five "key conclusions" about the causes of the four fatalities: "There were inadequate fire and safety briefings; potential for extreme fire behavior was not accurately assessed; firefighters disregarded 'watch out' situations and the ten fire fighting rules; fire suppression tactics were not reassessed once problems arose during the incident; and there was inadequate preparation for the deployment of fire shelters."

Trimming and erasing continues as this institutional message makes its way into training pamphlets and other official handbooks distributed throughout the Forest Service. These documents (regularly read by firefighters and assigned in training classes) overlook all other causes and treat people causes as the leading *and only* causes of accidents. Thus, even if memos and press releases were to emphasize, say, extreme weather conditions, firefighters would be predisposed to find blameworthy neither the environment nor their supervisors (and never the blazing fire itself) but their counterparts: the fallen firefighters. For in response to the question, What caused these deaths? these pamphlets and handbooks, one after another, offer but one answer: the incompetence of the dead.

For example, the authors of a fourteen-page booklet *Wildland Fire Fatalities in the United States: 1990 to 1998* observe, "Many of the wildland fire fatalities from burnovers can be directly attributed to the failure to follow the basic guidelines that are the basis for all wildland fire strategy and tactics: 10 Standard Fire Orders, 18 Situations that Shout 'Watch Out.'" A few pages later they continue: "All firefighters are ultimately responsible for their own safety and well being. . . . Self-discipline can reduce fatalities. When individuals adhere to Agency policies . . . they help ensure a safe operation and the successful completion of the fire mission. . . . Firefighters need to understand the hazards of steep, winding, unpaved roads; live and dead vegetative fuels whose flammability varies with the season as well as the time of day; and fire behavior that is directly and immediately affected by both the terrain and the weather."[31] Another document, which I acquired during basic training, boldly makes the same case: "Fire shelter deployments have always been attributed to violations of the Ten Standard Fire Orders or the Eighteen Situations that Shout Watch Out. . . . Shakespeare was correct—'There is nothing new under the sun'—when we violate BASIC SAFETY STANDARDS AND RULES—BAD THINGS HAPPEN! BASICS, BASICS, BASICS—There is no excuse for not doing what we are trained to do, yet we continue to do just that."

We can therefore identify four stages in the organizational process of managing death: *investigation*, in which a team of professionals advances several factors that led to the fatality, including managerial, equipment, and environmental causes; *dissemination*, in which trimming occurs, as fatalities often are attributed to the mistakes of firefighters and low-level supervisors; *generalization*, in which trimming continues, as causes of accidents are reduced to people causes and universal claims about the incompetence of the dead are advanced in widely circulated training materials and small handbooks; and finally *reproduction*, in which the organization's elite reinforce the internal eulogy of the Forest Service and group every fallen firefighter with the not-good-enough dead who met their maker on the rocky hills of Idaho, the barren wilderness of Alaska, the vast expanse of Montana, the logged and slashed forests of Oregon and Washington, and the windblown woods of northern California. The multifarious and complex causal factors behind fatalities presented in investigative reports are filtered through the individualizing screen of the illusio of self-determinancy, and this sanitizing process produces only one clear, consistent, and convincing cause: incompetence.[32]

This, then, is why both Crasser and MacCloud claimed that Rick Lupe did something wrong.[33] They were performing an often-repeated ritual, the internal eulogy, based not on the factual findings of the fatality report but on the organizationally sponsored belief, upheld by abridged and widely read secondary documents, that fatality reports regularly, if not always, find the dead inept or reckless. I had uncritically accepted this belief, which was why after reading the fatality report for Sawtooth Mountain, I had initially concluded, though pages of evidence that proved otherwise were right in front of me, that the report found that Lupe's death was his own doing.

As we have already seen, many crewmembers would agree with Crasser and MacCloud in perceiving fallen firefighters as incompetents. But I have not yet fully sorted out crewmembers' perceptions of death. To understand their complex perceptions—and, moreover, to apprehend their deep acceptance of the organizational common sense of the Forest Service—we must explore this topic in greater depth. It is to this task that I now turn.

Thinking Like the Forest Service

"Listen up," Allen said to a restless firecrew sprawled around the conference room table on a gray and misty morning in late July. "Listen up, goddamn it! This just came in from over there in Jameson. It's a 'critique of the incident' about two firefighters that died, uh, died up in Idaho."

He put on his bifocals and squinted as he pulled the white pages closer to his face. He began reading: "During the afternoon of July 22, 2003, an incident occurred on the Cramer Fire, a Type III incident on the North Fork District of the Salmon-Challis National Forest. Two firefighters were involved in the incident resulting in two fatalities. . . . At this time, we cannot confirm what took place but will do so as soon as it becomes available. . . . The Forest Service has requested a National Serious Accident Investigation Team be sent to the incident to determine what took place on the ground. This team is a 'fact-finding' team not a 'fault-finding' team.'"

Allen cleared his throat and continued: ". . . The Cramer Fire, located thirty-four miles west-northwest of Salmon, Idaho, on the Salmon-Challis National Forest is approximately two-hundred-and-twenty acres. It is burning in extremely steep terrain on the Salmon River front below Long Tom Lookout. . . . At approximately seventeen hundred hours on Tuesday, July 22, the Intermountain Regional Office was notified of an incident on the Cramer Fire where the extreme fire behavior was experienced causing 'blowup' conditions. Two firefighters were involved in the incident resulting in two fatalities. Names of the indiv—"

Allen skimmed the page silently before concluding, "Oh, this just says what I read before."

He gently placed the papers and his glasses on the table, rubbed the bridge of his nose, where his glasses pinched, and looked around the table at a group of somber faces.

"That sucks," J.J. said.

"Someone fucked up," Donald responded immediately. "I'll tell you what happened: Someone fucked up. That's what Thurman will say. Someone fucked up."

Heads nodded.

Craig Neilson added, "Their communications might have been fucked. . . . The fire was under them and burned up."

"They probably weren't paying attention," Donald said.

"Were they informed on the current weather conditions?" Craig wondered out loud.

"They're probably stupid. Probably weren't talking to their crew," Peter guessed.

"Yep. They're fuckin' stupid, not talking to anyone. They should've known better than to build a helispot on top of the fire," said Donald.

Heads continued to nod. Then Paul cocked an eyebrow and asked loudly, "Hey, Diego, what you got over there?"

"Nothing," Diego answered quickly with a mischievous smile. He was holding something underneath the table.

"What is it?"

"Don't worry about it."

"A *Playboy*?"

"Nope."

"A girlie magazine?"

"A *Maxim*," Diego answered, raising the magazine only inches above the table to reveal the cover model's blonde hair.

"Eewww," Paul responded with interest. All eyes were on Diego in anticipation of the unveiling.

"And not just any *Maxim,* I might add, but one *featuring* . . . Anna Kournikova!"

Diego pulled the magazine from under the table and held up the cover, which displayed the tennis star clad in a dark maroon string bikini.

Several crewmembers let out a pleased moan. Paul, along with Tank and Kris, rushed to Diego's side. Other crewmembers quickly followed.

Rising, Allen gathered up the papers and slid his glasses back into their case. No crewmember spoke a word about the Cramer fire for the rest of the day.

Although Craig suggested that communication and command failure may have led to the entrapment, Donald and Peter quickly shifted the blame back onto the shoulders of the "inattentive" or "stupid" dead. In this instance, crewmembers transformed equipment causes ("Their communications might have been fucked") and management causes ("Were they informed on the current weather conditions?") into people causes ("They're fuckin' stupid, not talking to anyone").

A few days later, Thurman brought up the incident during one of his morning speeches. Once again, crewmembers wore somber expressions and shook their heads as the boss said, "Couple fatalities this past week. Information is real sketchy. They're not sharing a whole lot. People are continuing to die out there. . . . Whether the pilot was in error or the weather contributed, the pilot still should have known better. With the fire in Idaho, if you look at the report, it shows that *they blew it*! They were in a situation when they shouldn't have been."

And once again heads nodded in agreement.

When news of the Cramer fire reached Thurman and his crew, they did not seem to resist the internal eulogy of the Forest Service; on the contrary, they reproduced the common sense of their host organization. To the extent that they cared about the two firefighters who died on the Cramer fire, they cared about the question of fault.

A few days after Thurman's speech, I asked Peter if he thought all injured or dead firefighters were faulty firefighters.

"If it's a single death, just one person, it's that person's fault," Peter replied assertively. He continued to state his case by referring to the two firefighters who died on the Cramer fire. "They're down there cuttin' this thing. This fire blows up and kills them. You know, I haven't read the investigation, but my guess is that they probably didn't know the fire was coming. Hell, their helicopter's right there. Maybe they didn't have communication. Well, if you don't have communication, you don't have a lookout. They obviously didn't have an escape route and a safety zone, being on a side slope. There's *four* things right there.

"It will come out in the report," he predicted. "But I'm just guessing that they didn't have good communications or had no communications with their helicopter. They should have been able to know, 'Hey this fire's coming up on our ass.'

"If nothing else, if *I* was on that damn helicopter crew, it was a rappela-crew, so they rappel out of their helicopter, if nothing else I would have said, 'Throw my damn rope down, I'm gonna tie it around my waist and get me the fuck out of here,' which totally could happen. Yeah, you may get your ass in a sling but at least you would *have* an ass *to get* in a sling. Fuck, fire my ass! I don't give a fuck. I'm still here to be fired."

Peter paused and hushed his voice before he continued. "But sometimes I think, actually *more* than sometimes, I think, hey, sometimes shit just happens. Shit can just fucking *happen,* man, and that's what scares me. They teach us all this stuff, and what if you *do* have your communications in place? What if you *do* have all this shit in place? What if shit *just fucking goes nuts*? And that scares me. Yeah, shit can just, just. . . . Sometimes shit happens, period. I really try to pay attention on fires. . . . But, who knows, that son of a bitch, it's Mother Nature, that son of a bitch can do anything. . . . I don't know. I believe in God, and I think that there's a time for everybody."

At first Peter responded to my question by employing the organizational thinking of the Forest Service, blaming the dead. After all, as one official Forest Service document puts it, "Firefighters need to be responsible for their own destinies."[34] Peter even went so far as to put himself in the shoes of the two firefighters killed by the Cramer fire and boast that if he'd been there he would have escaped. (Peter didn't know that in fact there was no helicopter, although the two victims repeatedly called for one, that there was no way out but up, and that they very much foresaw their hellish fate. One helitack member called over the radio, "Oh, God. We just got fire down below us. The smoke's coming right at us. Just make them hurry up.") The two who died at the Cramer fire, according to Peter, fouled up. Many of his crewmembers would agree with him. For example, when I asked Donald the same question I posed to Peter, he didn't mince words: "If we keep our wits about us, we have a pretty damn good chance of not necessarily controlling it, but keeping people safe. I believe that *deep down* in my heart, that we can keep firefighters or whatever personnel on the fire or around the fire, that we have the ability to keep them safe. We have the knowledge. We have the brains. We have everything that we need. . . . Firefighters that die? Someone made a bad decision."

But what if shit just happens? What if firefighters do not foul up and still lose to the flames? What if sometimes nature is bigger? While Peter reaffirmed the internal eulogy, he also doubted it. Though he responded to my question by first blaming the dead, Peter backpedaled as suspicions of powerlessness, manifest most clearly in his reference to a "time for everybody" dictated by a divine sovereign, pushed their way through the dominant thought categories of the Forest Service.

George understood risk and blame through a similar tension: "If someone dies, usually it's, it's their fault. It's something that they've ignored, that they've done wrong. . . . They've put themselves in a bad situation. So, yeah, most of the time when you get hurt it will come down to you doing something wrong."

"Why don't you tell me what you think happened on the Thirtymile fire and who's to blame for that?" I suggested.

George sighed and thought for a few seconds before answering. "That's, it's hard to say *exactly* what happened. But the people that were there, they should have known what to look for, they should have known their escape routes. Like the road they took, they should have known it was a dead-end road, I mean, from the very beginning. I mean, you know that if a fire's moving, that you don't go into a road to try to get to a spot 'cause if it crosses, you have no way out. And that's the *major* thing that they did wrong. . . . It's everybody's fault but, the main people that should have known that stuff were their operators that were actually driving into the situation. They should have known, after they looked at roads and stuff, that they shouldn't be going down there. A lot of it comes down to the people who are in charge. . . . But it was a lot of the crewmembers' fault not bringing it up to him."

"What? The dead-end road?"

"Yeah. When you're driving an engine or what not, you have to know what you're going into. And that's something that they obviously didn't think much about. They *should have known* what they were taking their crew into. So a lot of it is *everybody's fault,* 'cause with that many people someone should have realized it, but to actually put them into that predicament, it was the operators' fault. . . . It's basically everybody's fault."

George's commentary reminded me of one of my first days on the job when I sat through a training course and watched scenes from the Thirtymile fire flash across the television screen. A deep-voiced narrator attempted to piece together the day's events: exhausted crews, unclear instructions, many ran, some deployed, four dead. Our instructor stopped the videotape and further reconstructed the fire and the crew's "fatal mistakes," regularly asking, "Now, if you guys were on the crew, what would you have done differently in that scenario?" Subtly, the instructor found fault with the four dead firefighters and their supporting crew; he drew our attention to their inadequate preparation and multiple violations of the Orders and Situations. And following his example, we began offering criticisms of our own. *They shouldn't have driven up that road without a map. I wouldn't have deployed on that side of the hill. If I'd been there, I would have challenged those orders since the crew worked too long. There was no LCES. They should have recognized the weather getting hotter and drier and the wind shifts.* The instructor nodded in affirmation. We would have done better, we assured him; we would have adhered to the Ten and Eighteen—and survived. (We didn't know the fire had ripped through that drought-stricken Washington canyon so fast that the crew, running on only a few hours' sleep, had little chance of anticipating a crown fire so ravenous and large; that they had water but couldn't use it because the pumps were broken; and that the incident commander lost control of the fire and his crew before the burnover.)

I was about to ask George if he had undergone the same training, but instead, I decided to ask something else.

"Do you know how many wildland firefighters die every year?"

"No. I don't," George answered matter-of-factly.

"If you had to guess, what would you say? I mean, in the United States."

"I think it's under a hundred," he guessed, hesitantly. "I would *definitely* say it's not over a hundred. I would even say its maybe, *maaaybe* fifty, and not that many people die on fires. . . . You *really* have to do something wrong, when you're dealing with fire, to be in a situation where it takes your life. You *really* have to violate more than one of the Standard Orders or the 'Watch Out' Situations. There's just stuff you know to watch out for, and if you don't do it, it's gonna get you. But not that many people die on fires."

"But people still do die, right?"

"Yeah. I mean people, in dealing with fire, in something so wild and with the gasses that it gives off and all that, injuries are very common, and people are gonna lose their lives dealing with something so extreme. But it's something that, you know going into it that something can happen. You know that you're dealing with something that breathes on its own and it's gonna do what it's gonna do, and you know, you're basically putting your life in danger when you're going into a fire."

George blamed fallen firefighters for their incompetence, just as I was taught to do in basic training classes, but as with Peter, a small "what if" nagged quietly in the back of his mind. To him, to get hurt on a fire, someone would have to violate multiple Orders or Situations, implying that fire is more or less tamable or, at the very least, escapable. Yet George immediately contradicted himself by claiming that fire is a wild, violent, and deadly force that causes many injuries. Despite this similarity, I noticed a significant difference in how the two firefighters distributed blame. Whereas Peter hinted that some fatalities might be the work of Mother Nature, suggesting that the Forest Service should blame *less,* George believed that, although Mother Nature was a wild woman, the Forest Service should blame *more.* And when I spoke to more of my crewmembers about their perceptions of blame, I quickly discovered that Peter's views were anomalous. Far from questioning the blaming process, most of my crewmembers believed we should expand its scope—especially to incompetent "paper-qualified" supervisors—which was a sermon that Thurman himself often preached.

Erasing Risk by Exaggerating Deviance

"We've held nobody accountable," Thurman argued to me from behind his desk. "Until you actually go out there and hold people accountable for mistakes that have killed somebody, we're gonna just continue to operate like we are. It's one of these that some people shouldn't be in positions that they are. They're not *dealt with.* If something happens, uh, while they're in that position, again, there is no accountability. It's, uh, what continues to happen. It's pretty simple. . . . When you look at some of the investigative reports, and it always falls back to your Fire Orders, Eighteen Situations, LCES, these type of things, and you figure that one or more have been violated, and we do nothing to the individual that's done this. We move forward. No big deal. Again, it's what price can you put before you made these changes? Are they really qualified to be there? A number of folks aren't even *in fire*. And they go out there and do these positions. . . . We should be filling these positions on not '*I'm only qualified because I'm book smart*' but '*Here's where I've been.*'

"Coming up in the ranks of the fire end of it . . . if you are not involved in fire, how current are you in what the *hell* is going on in the fire world? If you look at it, very few firefighters, it was the actual grunt that made the decision that either killed them or severely burned them. It was an *overhead decision*. So, uh, have we dealt with the overhead? I don't think so. Until we do, these things are going to continue to happen."

As Thurman built his case, his voice grew louder and his speech sped up. He was growing more and more frustrated—and angry.

"And how would you suggest that we hold these people accountable?" I asked, nervously.

After looking me dead in the eye for a couple of seconds, Thurman replied, "I go out here on the highway, and I've been drinking, and I get involved in an accident, and I kill somebody, they're gonna *deal* with me. I go out there and take somebody and make a bad decision on a fire and kill somebody, I walk free. . . . You ain't gonna kill somebody and say, 'Ah shit, it was an act of God.' It wasn't an act of God. *You blew it!* Whether you're training, whether it was, whatever the case may be. To give him the death penalty? I don't think so, but it's not something that, uh, we're gonna go ahead and just move forward and call it good. . . . Punishment? I'm from the old school, an eye for an eye; but you know, it's not my decision."

Thurman wanted the feet of incompetent supervisors held to the fire. More, he came close to suggesting they should be thrown in the fire themselves! It is important, however, to notice that he levied his protest not against the Forest Service's convention of blame itself, but against the unequal distribution of that blame. Thurman did not suggest the dead be let off the hook; instead, he wanted the Forest Service to blame upward, to hold top administrators responsible for putting firefighters in deadly situations.[35] Rex Thurman did not suffer fools gladly. He regularly assured his crew that the day he placed them in a situation where they had to deploy their fire shelters would be his last day as a firefighter. He readily accepted great personal responsibility for his actions on the fireline, and he expected other firefighters to do the same—high office administrators, veterans, supervisors, and rookies alike.

As an engine operator, Steve felt responsible for the welfare of his crew: "They're listening to you. If they get burned, it's your fault. It's not something *they* did. It's something *you* told them to do because you're the supervisor. . . . I'd rather myself be the one to get hurt, injured, whatever, than to have somebody else. It'd be so much more difficult to deal with me hurtin' or killin' somebody."

"You said that if someone got hurt, it wouldn't be their fault, it would have been your fault. Is that true?" I asked.

"That's how it's set up. That's how this system is set up. If it goes wrong, if something goes wrong, yeah they're gonna be at fault, but who put them in that position? If it's the supervisor that did it, now if they went out and they just started doing stuff on their own—not talking to anybody, not letting anybody know—hey, that's their fault. But if myself, Peter, whoever, as a supervisor you're in that role to make sure they're in the spots, the safest spots, getting the job done, and not putting them in harm's way where they're gonna get hurt. . . . But if you go down there, and you think it's safe, you put 'em down there, it's your fault."

"And you agree with the system, how the system is set up?"

"No, I don't agree with it. I think the fault lays on *everybody*. . . . It's like Thurman was saying, 'You're responsible for your own safety.' . . . I think the supervisor should have more responsibility than the crewmember. If something was to happen I think they, the supervisor, told that person to do something. The supervisor should have more responsibility for what happened. But these people aren't stupid. They should know, especially if they've had three or four seasons, they should recognize some situations. . . . You're responsible for your own safety."

"So if someone dies on a fire, they probably made a serious mistake?"

"Serious mistakes? I mean, people make the same mistakes on other fires and get away with it, and some people make those same mistakes and they end up getting killed." Steve raised his voice. "They always, it's always, *really,* what's always *really bugged me* is they say these Ten and Eighteen, to follow these Ten and Eighteen, and *this one* was violated, *this one* was violated, and *this one* was violated. That's because on those Ten and Eighteen, no matter what happens, *no matter what,* you can trip or fall or whatever, and they can say that you violated one of those. There's not been *one* instance where some of those wasn't violated, and still—"

He paused for breath and lowered his voice. "I don't think they really preach those enough. I mean, obviously, those are basically everything in the fire. I mean, everything in the fire is said there in that Ten and Eighteen, what you need to watch out for, pretty much everything. And it just kinda bugs me that if something happens they go back to that and then they say, 'Ah, do these people know these and can they apply them?'

". . . I mean, obviously they made some bad choices, they violated one of those rules, those 'Watch Out' Situations, but people make mistakes. It's just that these mistakes, it's just, I mean, a hundred people could have made the same mistakes before and they've got away with it. People aren't perfect. People are gonna make mistakes, and that's what I don't understand. I mean, yeah, we're involved where people can get killed, but they're sending us through these trainings, then they're shoving us out there on these fires, where people make mistakes, and they ask why. 'Why didn't they know this? Why didn't they do this? Why are these Ten and Eighteen mitigated?' And it's just, the more I, each year it goes on, the Forest Service gets *frustrating*. They do some funky stuff."

Along with Thurman, Steve believed that supervisors should be held accountable for faulty actions. But unlike Thurman, he mildly criticized the usefulness of the Ten and Eighteen. Although he observed that violations of the Ten and Eighteen can be documented everywhere for anything—which suggests they are vacuous—Steve went on to reaffirm the importance of these firefighting fundamentals by arguing that the Forest Service should stress the Ten and Eighteen even more. He knew that the Ten and Eighteen were impossible standards, but he continued to place his faith in these fundamentals. He saw no other way. When Steve attempted to escape from the common sense of the organization, he ended up returning to it and reaffirming it.

J.J.'s reasoning exhibited a similar circular pattern. "You can't put the blame on one certain person because, as firefighters, we know what to look for," he told me regarding Thirtymile. "And as supervisors, they know what to look for. And there were a lot of the Ten and Eighteen that were broken. But why didn't the firefighters, uh, so why *did* the firefighters break them? I know they were tired, fatigued, but I wouldn't use that as a reason or excuse to say, 'Hey, the supervisors *burned them up*,' because it's as much our job to see what's going on as it is theirs.

"Like *I'm* gonna leave *my* life in my supervisors' hands," J.J. expounded in a tone that sounded as if he were speaking of leaving his child in the arms of a stranger. "You know, I trust *one person,* and that's myself. It's *all* their fault, from the people that burned up to the supervisors. . . ."

"Right, but have you ever been in a fire where the Ten and Eighteen were broken?" I asked.

"Can't say that I have."

"On *every fire* that you've been on, has there been a lookout?"

"No. I think on a lot of fires they don't post lookouts. I think more than half the time they don't post lookouts on the fires."

"So does that violate a Fire Order?"

"I guess it does. It does. Lookouts not established or whatever."

"Do you think that you'd ever know if instructions were not given clearly or understood?" I questioned, referring to the fourth Fire Order.

"At the time it happened, if it actually didn't concern me, I don't think I would."

"So would you concede, then, that you've been on fires where Fire Orders were broken?"

"I guess I'd say I would, more than once. And we are breaking them too!"

"On the Beaver Creek fire," I disclosed, "we must have broken like ten of the Eighteen, dude."

"No joke?"

"No joke."

"You're lucky that they didn't burn anybody up, you know. I guess it probably happens a lot like that in the Forest Service. I bet more than 90 percent of the time you're probably breaking a Fire Order on a fire, but you don't hear about it if somebody doesn't die, you know."

"So why do you think we have the Ten and Eighteen?"

"For reasons to fall back on," J.J. observed. "Say somebody got burned, well, there's an excuse. 'Oh, it was broke,' you know. 'That's why they burned up, 'cause they broke the Ten and Eighteen.' It's an excuse to fall back on. You'll never hear them say, you know, so and so burned up, you know, because of the *truth*. They're not gonna say, 'Well this person burned because *we fucked up*.' They are gonna say, 'Ah, they burned because there are all these rules, and they didn't abide by the rules, therefore he burned.' They're not gonna admit *they* messed up, you know. No, they are gonna find an excuse. That way, they can get their ass out of trouble. . . . When you die they're gonna say, 'Well, it's his fault. They should have known the situation.'"[36]

J.J.'s views resembled a labyrinth of mirrors that always reflect back on that which is most familiar. In no more than two minutes, J.J. claimed always to abide by the Ten and Eighteen, retracted that claim by guessing that these fundamentals are violated on most fires, placed his faith once again in the Ten and Eighteen in response to my observation about the Beaver Creek fire, then renounced his newfound faith by describing the

Ten and Eighteen as empty rules useful only to supervisors for insurance purposes. For J.J., thinking about fire without the Ten and Eighteen was like thinking of a brand new color that no one has seen before.[37]

When J.J., Steve, and other crewmembers tried to resist the common sense of the Forest Service—when they attempted to challenge the thought categories provided to them in all the vehicles of organizational socialization (reports, pamphlets and brochures, training, supervisors' injunctions, and daily interactions with one another)—they quickly discovered that their universe made little sense. If they did not believe that fire was controllable, that harm was preventable, that the dead were ineffectual, then crewmembers found themselves staring into an abyss of disorder. To be sure, they did not accept the common sense of the Forest Service without raising skeptical questions and retaining stubborn doubts, but they accepted it nonetheless, because without it fire is a dangerous chaos. Firefighters learn to think within the categories and classification schemes of their host organization; it becomes extremely difficult for them to arrive at an understanding of risk, death, and fire without employing the principles and assumptions provided to them. Thus the serious characterization of dead firefighters as something other than incompetents exists only as a "discarded possible" (to borrow Bourdieu's expression), as a thought that resides beyond the periphery of firefighters' imaginations.[38] Although this skeptical and heretical thought trespasses their minds from time to time, it lingers but a short while before the thought categories of the Forest Service shoo it away.

Is crewmembers' reaction to the death of a firefighter predictable and commonplace? Do other professional risk takers react this way? If we base our response on current psychological research, we must answer in the negative. Many researchers have found that police officers, firefighters, soldiers, and other professional risk takers are often overwhelmed with feelings of helplessness and fear on learning of the death of a fellow officer, crewmember, or infantryman. Police officers, as one psychologist put it, "individually and collectively feel tremendous empathy for fellow officers who are killed or seriously injured in the line of duty."[39] Some researchers have claimed that soldiers have similar feelings, which is why they go to great lengths to recover their dead and bury them honorably. And firefighters, others have found, tend to identify with their burned and fallen colleagues and sometimes feel a dark guilt over their deaths. If these accounts are valid, we can assume that firefighters' reactions to death are not psychologically "normal" or predictable; rather, they are reactions cultivated by their supporting organization.

That said, since the organizational structure of Forest Service is grafted into the social structure, its processes of socialization are grounded in processes of socialization at work within society writ large.[40] Although organizational socialization can never be completely disentangled from cultural socialization, an organization can *select* which aspects of the larger culture it wishes to mimic. Within the organization, then, we can identify specific practices and beliefs that mirror practices and beliefs operating throughout the organization's sociopolitical environment; however, we must bear in mind that the organization labors to endorse certain elements while rejecting others. The Forest Service chooses from a vast repertoire of culturally-appropriate responses to death and selects certain principles (individualism, self-reliance) over others (solidarity, collectivism, honor) when crafting a firefighter's illusio of self-determinancy. It provides firefighters with a cognitive winnowing device, a "focus of attention" to use March and Simon's term, that espouses a definite response to death (one that harmonizes with American individualism) while discouraging other responses (which would correspond to equally appropriate cultural beliefs).[41] Indeed, if this were not the case, if firefighters "naturally" responded to death by blaming the victim, why would the organization need to dedicate so much energy and resources to socializing its workers to think in such a fashion?[42]

The death of a firefighter does not take the Forest Service by surprise; far from it: the organization is prepared to manage death, and it trains its firefighters, from their first days on the job, long before they experience death firsthand, to think about death as a consequence of a mistake. New recruits pick it up fast: I once heard a rookie firefighter from Jameson exclaim, on hearing that a snag had fallen and killed a firefighter sleeping in a tent at fire camp, "What was she doing sleeping under a tree!"

Rituals of blame are not a minor component of this universe; they reside at the very core of the logic of firefighting. By framing the death of a firefighter as the result of that firefighter's individual mistakes, an approach that diverts responsibility from the organization and places it squarely on the shoulders of the dead themselves, the Forest Service makes death seem palatable, fire manageable, and firefighters invincible.[43]

It has been said that burning to death on a mountainside is dying at least three times: "First, considerably ahead of the fire, you reach the verge of death in your boots and your legs; next, as you fail, you sink back in the region of strange gases and red and blue darts where there is no oxygen and here you die in your lungs; then you sink in prayer into the main fire that consumes, and if you are a Catholic about all that remains of you is your cross."[44] But on closer examination we see this is incomplete. There is another death, where the firefighter dies not in his legs, lungs, or skin but in his soul. Here the memory of the dead becomes a memory of wrongdoing. This does not happen in front of the whole world. Most of the world witnesses a different ceremony where the firefighter's memory is made precious; it is lauded and cherished. But at the same time the dead firefighter is being exalted in front of weeping family members and sorrowful strangers, he is also being brought low by those who may have known him best. He is hallowed by most but humbled by some, for during the fourth death of a firefighter, his legacy is blotted out by the black stamp of incompetence.

By exaggerating individual deviance, the Forest Service erases risk. This allows firefighters to rub out the dangers of their occupation by concluding that firefighting is dangerous only for the idiotic and the irresponsible.[45] As Donald put it to me once, "Is it dangerous? Sure it's dangerous, if you have *stupid* people working with you. If you know what's going on and you have other people that know what's going on, it's actually not that dangerous."

What happens to a firefighter's illusio of self-determinancy when confronted with death? Something magical: the illusio does not weaken in the face of death, it only grows stronger. That is, although we might assume that death has the potential to shatter firefighters' illusio of self-determinacy, the opposite occurs. By inscribing all dead firefighters with the mark of incompetence, the Forest Service helps firefighters maintain this belief even when faced with the reality of death. Lest they slip their feet into the shoes of a corpse, firefighters must distance themselves from fallen friends and crewmembers and clutch the belief that, as George puts it, "people are gonna die, but just because *stuff happens,* I mean, it doesn't necessarily mean it's gonna happen to *you.*" And so the dangers of the flames fade away like plumes of smoke rising above the treetops.

Conclusion

I have divided this conclusion in four parts. The first summarizes the main arguments of the book and explains how they challenge various currents of sociological knowledge. The second deals with the advantages and limitations of the theoretically driven methods I employ—those of an ethnography of the habitus—and suggests how others might use these methods to advance our understanding of risky work, professional socialization, and social reproduction. Returning to the substantive findings of this book, the third part addresses how my arguments may better inform our understanding of risky work and argues for the importance of a sociology of risk. The final part highlights the book's practical implications and advances several concrete recommendations for the U.S. Forest Service, workable ideas that support the organization's goal of making firefighting as safe as possible. These recommendations, I think, will also interest administrators investigating ways to improve worker safety in other high-risk organizations. Thus this conclusion proceeds from the theoretical to the practical, from implications and recommendations of interest to social scientists to those of interest to administrators of high-risk organizations and, specifically, supervisors and firefighters of the Forest Service. Selective readers can discriminate accordingly.

Why Do They Risk?

The reason firefighters risk their lives when other means of earning a living are available, some say, is the same reason everybody risks: to gain recognition and honor. To risk is to be a man. Professional risk takers endanger their lives day in and day out because they accept the rules of masculinity and thirst after honor.[1] But in the case of Elk River such beliefs are completely wrongheaded. In this dangerous world made up almost entirely of young men, a world where, by all previous accounts, I should have witnessed many daring and courageous acts, I discovered exactly the opposite. The firefighter who tested the flames was labeled not a hero but a fool. My crewmembers did not value bravado; they loathed it, and the firefighters who were accorded the greatest esteem had the greatest competence.

By working with a dispositional theory of action, I was able to uncover how the country-masculine habitus "helps to determine what transforms it."[2] I was able to break with current accounts of risk taking and to demonstrate that crewmembers gravitate "naturally" to the ranks of firefighting not in search of manly honor but because the country-masculine habitus seeks out a universe in which it can recognize itself, an environment in which it can thrive. Wildland firefighting offers a specific and salient outlet for the reproduction, reaffirmation, and reconstitution of the country-masculine habitus; it offers a space and culture that corresponds to, confirms, and amplifies crewmembers' skills and dispositions, a habitus rooted in the rural, working-class world where they grew up. For the men at Elk River, the decision to fight fire was not a bold leap into a new world but a small step into familiar territory.

By tracing the conversion of a general habitus into a specific one, I was able to show that the process of becoming a wildland firefighter starts long before young men join firefighting crews; in fact, it begins with thousands of experiences specific to working-class rural backgrounds. Most of my crewmembers acquired the dispositions and skills needed to perform their job long before they become employees of the U.S. Forest Service. As country boys, they came to the organization already ready to fight fire and took to the rigors of firefighting *secundum naturam,* with nearly instinctive proficiency. Thus the Forest Service did not need to exert much effort in sculpting the deployable firefighter. The rookie didn't need to be broken down and rebuilt. His dispositions and skills needed only to be tweaked slightly, since the country boy was "adjusted in advance" to the requirements of wildland firefighting. And if this conversion seems like a totalizing one, leaving little room for resistance, it is not only because the world of wildland firefighting is a quasi-totalizing world, but also because the preformed dispositions of my crewmembers align succinctly with the organizational common sense of the Forest Service. The final products of this transformation are firefighters who do not think twice when the alarm sounds but who, on the contrary, run headlong into the clutches of danger not pursuing manhood but guiding their own destiny.

The main problem plaguing traditional theories of risk taking is a tendency to decontextualize risk. Grouping all types of risk takers (firefighters, soldiers, bullfighters, drug dealers, downhill skiers) into a single class—"puddles of people on the edges of society who apparently find it reasonable to engage directly in chancy deeds of an honorable life," in Goffman's words[3]—analysts proceed to assign a single master logic, a grand narrative, to explain risky behavior. In doing so, they pass over the specific logics of the different settings they classify as "risky" and shroud the context-dependent practical logic of these settings in the context-independent blanket of scholasticism. This obscures our understanding of what kinds of people are taking these risks and, moreover, how individuals' social positioning has somehow predisposed them to do so.

Such context-independent theories also ignore organizational socialization. This book has shown that if we want to comprehend how professional risk takers understand risk and how they acclimatize themselves to the perils of their professions, we must dissect the internal logic of their host organizations. Accordingly, I have attempted to parse the ways the U.S. Forest Service motivates individuals to fight fire. The Forest Service trains firefighters to conceptualize risk by cultivating within them an illusio of self-determinancy, a deep-seated belief that their job is no more dangerous than the next one. This project of organizational socialization centers on the successful execution of the Ten and Eighteen, rules that, as we have already seen, cannot be fully obeyed during the action of firefighting. And when the illusio of self-determinancy meets its ultimate challenge—the death of a firefighter—the Forest Service reacts by erasing risk and exaggerating deviance. As a result, the illusio does not weaken in the face of death; it fortifies, leading firefighters to distance themselves from the dead as well as from the objective dangers of their job.

This strategy is possible only because crewmembers more or less agree with and help to reproduce this illusio, this rational myth connected to the larger cultural ethos of individualism and personal accountability. Consider, for instance, what Kris told me over a cup of coffee in Tucson, after reading an earlier version of this book: "It's a collective building but an individual fall. . . . I don't know. It's hard for me to wrap my head around changing that, though, because, I mean, maybe I'm just too entrenched in that mentality, but when I do look at it . . . when something does happen, you can look back on it and be like, 'This is where it went wrong.' . . . That's how you rationalize what happened. To get rid of the individual would be to get rid of the investigation, you know, in the end. That would be like, in a sense, saying, 'The Forest Service fucked up again,' not 'Let's find out how.' We would have to investigate the Forest Service, how the Forest Service fucked up. To me, that's not feasible."[4]

Ethnography of the Habitus

This book has shown that answers pertaining to why young men join fire-crews and how they become seasoned to the hazards of wildfire are found not by examining organizational socialization alone but by analyzing how it is a specified extension of earlier processes of socialization taking place during firefighters' childhood and adolescence. To comprehend how firefighters acclimate to the dangers and demands of their occupation, I first had to understand what dispositions and skills they brought to Elk River. In the same way, if researchers want to reconstruct the practical logic of executives, Marines, street hustlers, or nurses—in short, if they want to understand how people become "experts"[5]—then they must explore the interface between individuals' general habitus and the culture and practices of the office building, the military, the street, or the hospital. As Durkheim observed, "In each one of us, in differing degrees, is contained the person we were yesterday, and indeed in the nature of things it is even true that our past *personae* predominate, since the present is necessarily insignificant when compared with the long period of the past because of which we have emerged in the form we have today."[6] And it is this person of yesterday who helps or handicaps our present-day actions.

Examining the emergence of a specific habitus from the configuration of skills and dispositions that constitute the general habitus requires much more than simply researching personal histories.[7] Otherwise, investigations into the transformation of a habitus would be no different from the pursuits of bread-and-butter anthropology, a discipline built on the examination of kinship patterns and genealogies. What makes a habitus-driven approach distinct is its insistence on ferreting out *specific links* connecting personal histories with present-day social contexts (such as the link between country competence and firefighting competence). It requires rigorously examining the origins of acquired dispositions and skills as well as the precise ways they advantage or disadvantage individuals in various organizational, educational, cultural, social, or political settings.[8]

Rather than view individuals as suspended in a single context within a single time frame, balancing themselves on the knife-edge present, ethnography of the habitus forces researchers to view them ontogenetically, as developing agents and inheritors of a specific social history. To quote Durkheim once more, "What we need to understand is not the man of the moment, man as we experience him at a particular point in time, influenced as we are by momentary needs and passions, but rather man in his totality throughout time. To do this we need to cease studying man at a particular moment and instead try to consider him against the background of the whole process of his development."[9] If the habitus is internalized and forgotten history, as Bourdieu claims, then the aim of ethnography of the habitus is to *historicize the habitus* in an effort to externalize what has been internalized and bring to mind what has been forgotten.[10] And because personal histories are constituted by social histories, searching out the social genesis of dispositions and skills can yield insights beyond those solely pertaining to individuals' development: It can shed fresh light on the ways the social order reproduces itself through everyday microlevel mechanisms. Thus ethnography that is determined to understand the transformation of a general habitus into a specific one presents new and exciting ways to discover the workings of "specific macro determination in the micro world."[11]

By employing the concept of habitus in my fieldwork, I was also able to reconstruct the logic of firefighting on its own terms. Instead of reducing crewmembers to rational calculators who supposedly not only practice the same mode of thinking as the analyst but also possess the same understanding of "risk" as the one who observes their risk taking, I treated crewmembers as practical actors. This enabled me to avoid what Bourdieu called "scholastic ethnocentrism." Bourdieu observed that the ethnographer often becomes trapped in this form of ethnocentrism when he is "confronted with a difference between two socially constructed modes of construction and comprehension of the world: the scholastic one which he tacitly sets up as the norm, and the practical one which he has in common with men and women seemingly very distant from him in time and social space, and in which he cannot recognize the practical mode of knowledge . . . . Scholastic ethnocentrism leads him to cancel out the specificity of practical logic."[12] Adopting an Archimedean stance that shoves the messy data of everyday life into spic-and-span categories of scholastic thought, the ethnographer guilty of this fallacy presents the social world "as he thinks it," as opposed to how people live within it.

As I said at the outset, when it comes to the sociology of risk taking, many analysts have fallen victim to scholastic ethnocentrism. Assuming that rational agents can base decisions on a clear and accurate measure of risk, analysts falsely suppose that all risk takers conceive of risk in the same way. Yet this is far from the case. I hope I have shown that even in a universe that threatens individuals with extreme, immediate, and deadly harm, risk is not a self-evident thing but an organizational construction formed through the cultivation and duplication of the illusio of self-determinancy. And throughout, I have attempted to place the practical logic of firefighting above the analytical logic of social science—to reconstruct as fully as possible firefighters' logic of practice (its creation, cultivation, and challenges), articulating the quasi-bodily skills, half-articulated perceptions, and deep-down know-how that crewmembers apply on the fireline.[13]

Hence, instead of succumbing to the temptation to judge the concept of habitus by the theorist's gauge, by its philosophical sophistication, I have tried to *use* the concept of habitus and measure its effectiveness by the pragmatist's ruler, by its practical application. When I used the concept in my fieldwork, I did not find it to be, as many scholars would have it, an unhelpful "black box" that does little to advance our conceptions of action.[14] Rather, I found that the concept allowed me to harvest fruitful analytical insights.

That said, this approach does have certain disadvantages. First of all, if the analyst attempts to grasp the practical logic of a group of individuals, she must do so by means of socioanalysis, an endeavor that distorts the very practices she wishes to capture. The logic of practice always mutilates what it intends to apprehend; that is, articulating the inarticulate (and visceral, fast and fleeting, and habitual) practices of firefighting, no matter how rich and "thick" the description, renders on paper only a partial and frozen picture of what is lived out in practice.[15] This poses a vexing problem for the analyst who is forced to freeze time and to create a textual existence for action that does not define itself through texts. Like the curious but clumsy child who can explore the shapes and colors of a butterfly only after rendering it flightless by touching its wings, the ethnographer who analyzes practical logic can do so only by imposing on it a theoretical logic that simultaneously acts as its clarifier and its solvent.

I have tried to remedy this tension by giving sustained attention to the pace, sound, and dynamics of practice, whether lived out on the fireline or in the crew quarters. I have also attempted to interrogate the body of theoretical knowledge that helped me comprehend such practices while not allowing (it has been my hope) theory to trample on practice. However, the tension remains unsettled; I have not overcome it here. It remains to be seen if future studies can effectively reach beyond this tension (between action and science, between fast practice and timeless theory) by developing new concepts, methods, and approaches to research, or if we will come to discover, with Bourdieu, that this tension is an immutable irony built into the very idea of the logic of practice.

Second, a thinker influenced by the "second Chicago school" might object that casting a searching eye toward the past blinds the ethnographer to the ongoings of the present.[16] The thinker would refuse to grapple with history and social position because such "why" questions would distract her from "how" questions. "Seeking after why people do what they do," she might argue, "forces you to overlook some of the minute and complicated details that inform precisely how people do what they do, how they create and maintain social order, how they structure their interactions and daily lives." This thinker would have a very good point. (After all, Bourdieu, whose experiences as an ethnographer are largely confined to the very beginning of his career as a soldier turned renegade ethnologist in colonized Algeria, never paid much attention to the minutiae of interaction.) However, the ethnographer does not commit intellectual treason by remaining loyal to both phenomenon and explanation.[17] As I see it, "how" and "why" questions enrich, inform, and overlap one another. Explanations for why firefighters risk (the why) are couched in descriptions of specific historical and organizational processes of socialization (the how).[18]

Despite these limitations, Bourdieu's logic of practice does offer much to analysts. If the ethnographer's task is to elucidate the inner workings of social life, and if social life is "essentially practical," as Karl Marx observed, then ethnographers must search out theories, concepts, and methods that can help them reconstruct the practical logic of social life and put them to work in the field.[19] As I have hoped to show in this book, the method of ethnography of the habitus is ideally suited for such a purpose. In my research it has allowed me to account for how firefighters become acclimated to their universe, and it has made it possible to avoid the snares of scholastic ethnocentrism. Because the idea of habitus rescues our theories of human action from "the icy waters of egotistical calculation," to employ Marx's phraseology once more—that is, because it privileges the "hot logic" of practicality over the "cold logic" of rationality—this concept can be of great value to ethnographers.

Beyond This Book

Do other high-risk organizations work this way? Is the illusio of self-determinacy specific to these wildland firefighters, or might we be able to identify its presence in the minds of astronauts, coal miners, police officers, or soldiers? Wildland firefighters differ from other professional risk takers on at least one important score: they can abandon their tasks if they feel threatened, and they are frequently encouraged to do so. Wildland firefighters are not at the mercy of machines as are astronauts or fighter pilots, who have little control over their destinies if their equipment malfunctions. Nor do they resemble soldiers, who abandon their posts only at peril of dishonor and sanction, running from the battlefield into the military prison. And they are unlike structural firefighters, who risk their lives for others and whose professional identity centers on altruistic sacrifice. Thus, we might say that wildland firefighters have more individual agency in the face of danger than their counterparts in other risky professions—they are not dependent on their equipment, bound to their service by a contract, or committed to saving lives—and they can and do take full advantage of this freedom.

Perhaps, then, professional risk takers who do not enjoy such great discretion in the face of danger do not feel as much in control as wildland firefighters do. We can imagine a continuum of control, so to speak, where on one end are astronauts and fighter pilots, who have very little agency in the face of danger and cannot survive without their machines, and on the other end are wildland firefighters, who have a high degree of control and can retreat if things start to go wrong, at the relatively meager cost of a few more acres burned. We can further imagine a continuum of professional dispositions mapped onto this continuum of control, ranging from the fatalism of the astronaut to the illusio of self-determinancy of the wildland firefighter, from a sense of powerlessness to an abundance of confidence in one's power to control one's own destiny. Given this, the critic might point out that I have captured not a professional disposition possessed by most professional risk takers but one idiosyncratic to those who can exert great control in the teeth of danger.

However, this train of thought assumes a robust correspondence between "actual" danger (or control) and perceptions of risk, a correspondence that several studies have disconfirmed.[20] Moreover, what little evidence there is seems to suggest that the illusio of self-determinancy is not necessarily congruent with the objective control the risk taker is able to exert. Even in the extreme case of astronauts and fighter pilots, whom we might expect to adopt a fatalistic attitude toward death and risk, the illusio of self-determinancy, upheld by the pervasive doctrine of the incompetent dead, is marshaled to make sense of danger. According to Tom Wolfe, Navy fighter pilots believe that there "are no *accidents* and no fatal flaws in the machines; there are only pilots with the wrong stuff. . . . When Bud Jennings crashed and burned in the swamps at Jacksonville, the other pilots in Pete Conrad's squadron said: *How could he have been so stupid?* . . . [Once pilots accept this way of thinking,] the Navy's statistics about one in every four Navy aviators dying meant nothing. The figures were averages, and averages applied to those with average stuff."[21]

Thus, if the illusio of self-determinancy is neither something found only in those high-risk organizations where workers exert a high level of control nor a "normal" psychological reaction to death, as I argued previously, then perhaps it is a generalizable trait developed by other high-risk organizations and at work within the minds of other professional risk takers. If so, then previous theories grappling with questions of worker compliance, organizational conduct, and perceptions of risk must be overhauled and refashioned. For one, theories of risk taking and risk perception must impose contextual limits on themselves; they must take seriously variation between types of dangerous activity and avoid creating a false category of "risk" into which they can shove all ostensibly edgy behavior. In addition, this book suggests that we should rethink our conceptions of the beliefs and practices of professional risk takers, for the axiom "to risk is to be a man" was turned on its head by the young men at Elk River. Finally, the concept of an illusio of self-determinancy can serve as a generative alternative to current conceptions of risk taking by requiring analysts to scrutinize organizational socialization. I hope this concept can shed light on questions that have baffled risk analysts and students of dangerous work. Consider, for example, "Why do workers faced with immediate danger throughout the workday regularly disregard safety procedures and protective equipment?" Many researchers have been befuddled by this question,[22] but I suggest that workers might disregard safety precautions not because doing so would violate a code of manliness but because their supporting organization actively strives to shape their perceptions of risk in such a way that they erase the perils of their profession from their minds and thus come to view safety precautions as superfluous.[23] Ultimately, however, a statement like this can be validated only through further empirical pursuits. Future studies should devote themselves to understanding how the military, the police academy, the construction firm, the mining company, and other high-risk organizations successfully cultivate, condition, and motivate cadets and workers to expose themselves to deadly harm.[24]

Social scientists should devote more attention to risk and dangerous work. Sociologists in particular have paid far less mind to these questions than have economists and risk analysts, even though questions of risk directly inform one of sociology's oldest and most important questions, that of social order. In a world where maintaining order can be very dangerous, where order means policing the lawless, waging war against the threatening (or the vulnerable), or rescuing the helpless, professional risk takers are the keepers of social order. In this respect, order succeeds or fails according to how effectively organizations can motivate individuals to risk their necks to keep order. In light of this, it is curious that sociologists have expended virtually no effort to understand how organizations secure a high level of compliance from workers for life-threatening activity that many might reject outright. Sociologists must research not only how organizations unravel, the causes of accidents and disasters, and the reproduction of organizational deviance—topics that have enjoyed considerable attention over the past twenty years—but also how organizations make workers deployable, how they train, educate, motivate, and discipline them to ensure that they place their lives on the line when "duty calls."

Sociologists should also devote more attention to risky work in order to better understand worker compliance. If we want to know why a worker goes when an organization says go, if we want to understand "the often neglected relationship between the broad pronouncements at the top levels and the day-to-day activities of those who perform the physical tasks of an agency," then we should set our sights not only on the factory floor, as has been the tradition, but also on high-risk organizations.[25] This is because the most extreme form of worker compliance is the one that requires workers to comply with their entire bodies, with their lives and their health. If we can understand the compliance of soldiers, police officers, firefighters, loggers, fighter pilots, or miners—a compliance of flesh and blood—would this not help us to better understand the compliance of lawyers, marketing executives, teachers, clerks, and social workers? In other words, by studying workers in high-risk organizations, could we not generate deeper insights into worker compliance in all occupations, those that demand much as well as those that demand little?

Finally, sociologists should study risk because the world is getting riskier. Wildfires burn hotter and longer today than they did twenty years ago, and wildfires have recently threatened major metropolitan areas such as San Diego, Denver, and Tucson, exacerbating the dangers for firefighters. The twentieth century claimed more soldiers' lives than all other centuries combined, and weapons of warfare grow more efficiently lethal by the day. And as Perrow predicted, scientific advances in fields such as nuclear energy, chemical manufacturing, and aeronautics (to name a few) are increasing in complexity much faster than are advances in safety.[26] As technological and occupational dangers increase in intensity and weapons of warfare increase in proficiency, high-risk organizations face the problem of securing significant obedience from their workers for lethal action. What is dramatically perplexing is that most organizations have very little trouble motivating their workers to expose themselves to virulent hazards; in fact, some of the most dangerous jobs are also the most sought-after. As sociologists, we must understand how this is possible. We must figure out why workers deploy themselves in dangerous environments and how organizations fashion deployables to serve their own ends.

And we must do so if only because questions of risk illuminate questions of inequality, poverty, and power. As the world grows increasingly dangerous, we must never forget that it will be the poor and the working class who bear the heaviest loads. When mines cave in, they cave in on poor men. When a fire overtakes some poor soul, that poor soul usually had blue-collar parents. When a tree smashes a logger, when a fishing boat tosses a deck hand overboard, when a high-steel ironworker slips on the rail and falls to his death, when the roof gives and thick beams and cinder blocks crash onto the construction workers below—the ones killed are rarely from wealthy, educated, privileged homes. When soldiers come home in coffins, more often than not they come home to working-class families. High-risk organizations can exist and thrive only if they succeed in exposing lives to the power of the grave. But not every kind of life is exposed to such threats. We must avoid the decontextualized fallacy practiced by earlier theorists of risk who ignored the class composition of high-risk organizations. Professional risk taking is a reflection of the social order—the ordering of people—which is why, I repeat, that to study risk is to study power. Questions of risk taking, then, should not be treated as innocent ones, pursued merely to appease the intellectual curiosity of a marginalized group of specialists, for they strike at the very heart of questions of social order, of organizational performance, of worker compliance, of power, inequality, and privilege, and indeed of life and death.

Recommendations for the Forest Service

In my opinion, though some of my crewmembers might disagree, the U.S. Forest Service has done an admirable job of keeping firefighters safe. It has made safety a top organizational priority; it has dedicated millions of dollars to safety research and development; and with an eye toward improving the safety of its workforce, it has been willing to take steps that many other high-risk organizations have yet to initiate, such as scrutinizing its "organizational culture."[27] In fact it is so concerned with safety that many wildland firefighters I have met believe the Forest Service is *too* safe. Nevertheless, there is room for improvement, and in these concluding pages, I advance several concrete recommendations that I hope will contribute to the goal of keeping firefighters as safe as possible. These recommendations, which primarily confront the consequences of an organizational ethic of individualism, may also prove useful to practitioners in other high-risk organizations.

Many students of organizational behavior, as well as many administrators overseeing risky systems, have focused almost exclusively on how individual mistakes cause accidents. Psychologist James Reason, for example, has devoted most of his career to explaining how human error leads to system failures.[28] Reason's research has directly informed some of the Forest Service's developments and policies: drawing on Reason's "Swiss cheese model of human error," the Forest Service has adopted a system to identify "the root causes of human factors" that contribute to accidents, labeled the Human Factors Analysis and Classification System.[29] Advocates of this system claim that it "is well known in the world of accident investigations that approximately 80 percent of accident causes are directly linked to human factors," and they argue that accident investigations need to focus more on individual blunders.[30] Recently, investigation teams have begun to use this system when researching firefighter fatalities.

Yet social scientists have long criticized human-error approaches for obscuring "the complexities of interaction between humans, machines and organization" and for misdirecting our attention so that we end up "blaming the wrong people and the wrong factors."[31] Stressing that this way of thinking blinds us to how malfunctions in equipment and failures of leadership also contribute to system failures, social scientists have gone on to suggest that to fully understand the causes of accidents, we need to pay attention to such things as organizational culture, the actions of elite administrators, and glitches in system design.[32] Although this is true and important, I would like to push the point further by arguing that ardent concern with human error actually encourages organizational practices that may themselves contribute to system breakdowns. Put another way, proponents of human-error approaches fail to realize that the problems they purport to address—in this case, firefighting fatalities—are actually exacerbated by such approaches precisely because they necessarily emphasize and reinforce an organizational ethic of individualism. This institutionalized irony, or "unanticipated consequence," is at work within the Forest Service today.

As this book has demonstrated, the organizational common sense of the Forest Service is an individualizing one, and it urges firefighters to "command their own destinies." Leadership is important, of course, but firefighters are explicitly taught to question supervisors and to turn down assignments more than they are explicitly taught to listen to them. Training materials and other documents that minimize hazards by exaggerating individual deviance, explored in chapter 8, along with organizational initiatives such as the Human Factors Analysis and Classification System, only reinforce this organizational ethic of individualism.

A culture of individualism can lead to miscommunication, poor teamwork, a devaluation of leadership, and breakdowns in the chain of command. In fact, it has been identified as a leading cause of firefighting fatalities. Sociologist Jon Driessen, in a document prepared for the Forest Service, discovered that "accidents in field crews were inversely correlated with the cohesion in the crews. In other words, the greater the crew cohesion, the fewer the accidents." Karl Weick, an organizational scientist and psychologist who has studied the burnovers at Mann Gulch, has argued that fatalities are caused in part by "a culture emphasizing individual work rather than group work." And several investigators have attributed the deaths of the firefighters at South Canyon to crewmembers' "can do" attitude.[33] These studies focus on the shortcomings of particular firecrews, arguing that trapped crews are somehow more individualistic than others. But the real source of the problem, I argue, resides at the organizational level and is pervasive throughout the wildland firefighting community. Individualism is not simply a trait plaguing at-risk firecrews, one that is discovered in this crew but not in that one; rather, it is the supreme value of the organizational common sense of the Forest Service. If crews who experienced burnovers are found to exhibit a high degree of individualism and a low degree of teamwork, this might be because they adopted the Forest Service's common sense as their own.[34]

In a word, an organizational ethnic of individualism, unknowingly supported by human-error approaches to accidents, stokes the coals of danger. What can be done about this? For one thing, members of the Forest Service should continue to think deeply about how its "organizational culture" may be making firefighting situations ripe for accidents.[35] More specifically, we need to think of ways the common sense of the Forest Service can shift away from an individualizing ethic emphasizing autonomy and competence to a communal one emphasizing communication, leadership, and teamwork. Of course firefighters should be taught to be competent and responsible, but they should also be taught communication strategies, ways to strengthen intracrew cohesion, and practices for obeying and challenging leaders. These lessons should be included in basic training courses and incorporated into all areas of the Forest Service. The organizational ethic of individualism at work within the Forest Service does not match up with the necessarily collective action of firefighting. Since firefighting is a collective enterprise, firefighters should be trained to act as members of a collective.

By the same token, practical exercises should be incorporated into basic training. If firefighting is essentially a practical activity, why is basic training so mnemonic and nonpractical? Basic training could better prepare trainees for firefighting through applied exercises. For instance, trainees could fight "pretend fires." Under supervision and working alongside veteran firefighters, they could engage in the craft of fighting fire—digging line, observing hazards, procuring weather readings, and so forth—without being exposed to flames and smoke. During this exercise, certain scenarios could be role-played: *A spot fire ignites on the east end of the fire; a slurry bomber drops low to dump a load; trees are beginning to torch out in front of you; the incident commander instructs you to backburn; the incident commander drops to his knees and clutches his chest—what do you do?*[36] During such imaginary fires, new recruits not only could be taught how to react to different challenges and how to employ different strategies, they could also be taught how to do so *as a team*. Through such hands-on exercises, new recruits would gain a physical sense of firefighting, one much more true to life than lessons offered in videotapes, before they ever set foot on a real fireline.

In addition, firefighters not only should be instructed on how to avoid entrapments, they should also be thoroughly taught how to act *during* an entrapment: how to assess the situation, how to communicate with each other, how to listen to and quickly evaluate leaders' instructions. Such lessons are strikingly absent from training courses (the individual practice of shelter deployment aside). And firefighters should be taught that entrapment is a reality for all wildland firefighters, not just the incompetent, the deviant, or the irresponsible. The dangers of firefighting must be made fully transparent to those who choose to challenge the Black Ghost.

Staying on the topic of fatalities, accident investigation teams must continue to stress how a number of interacting factors—environmental, equipment, managerial, and people causes—contribute to burnovers and entrapments, and they must try to disseminate their findings throughout the wildland firefighting community *in their completeness*. Currently, people causes are emphasized as the primary reason for fatalities; but as I have shown above, overemphasizing human error can indirectly have harmful consequences.

Furthermore, investigation teams should determine if and how decisions made by elite administrators are responsible for accidents.[37] As was the case with Rick Lupe, the administrative decision to breach prescription parameters of the Sawtooth Mountain Prescribed Burn Plan and to light the fire during record-high temperatures and record-low humidity readings was in many ways the primary factor that led to the burnover. We should hold lead administrators responsible for organizational deviance and think of ways to deter such behavior.

My final recommendation has to do with those fundamental guidelines on which both training and fatality investigations are based: the Ten and Eighteen. Organizations will go to great lengths to propagate institutionalized rules that have little to do with increasing efficiency and much to do with maintaining legitimacy.[38] This begs the question: How useful are the Ten and Eighteen to firefighters on the ground? Accident investigation teams seem to have found them "useful analytical devices," and the Forest Service seems to rely on the Ten and Eighteen to maintain legitimacy in the face of fatal accidents. But do these rules actually benefit firefighters engaged in the act of firefighting?

The Eighteen Situations That Shout "Watch Out!" strike me as perfectly legitimate, so long as they are not marshaled post mortem as evidence of incompetence. (As we saw in chapter 5, even on a fire fought with the utmost care and precision, the Ten and Eighteen must be violated. Accordingly, we gain little purchase from pointing out how crewmembers violated the Orders and Situations on fatal fires. We would surely count a similar number of violations on nonfatal fires.[39]) The Situations are specific and pointed; they offer firefighters tangible reminders of hazardous conditions that call for heightened awareness and caution. The Orders, on the other hand, are vague and elusive: Exactly what is a "potentially hazardous situation"? What does it mean to "remain in control"? What is it to "fight fire aggressively"? The Orders, then, would prove more useful if they were sharpened, if they were made more explicit and concrete.

On balance, the vagueness and impossibility of the Orders is not that troubling: most organizational rules are vague and impossible, but this does not mean they are unhelpful or should be abandoned. What *is* troubling—and here we circle back to a point just made—is that the Ten Standard Fire Orders, perhaps more than any other device of the Forest Service, uphold, reproduce, and fortify an ethic of individualism. As I have demonstrated, the Orders say very little about teamwork or communication. There are Orders that deal with such issues, but since each Order is "prefaced by the silent imperative 'you,'" these rules reinforce an emphasis on personal responsibility and individual competence much more than they promote cohesion or solidarity. For this reason, it is perhaps time to rethink the essence (not simply the order) of the Orders. For example, the Orders could be recast to stress collectivity, communication, and leadership. Firefighters could be instructed to link up with a "fire buddy," someone who must accompany them at all times and who is responsible for watching their backs. In addition, firefighters could be advised to listen to leaders unless they have egregiously violated some Orders and Situations. More thought could be put into how the Fire Orders can be made more specific and collectivist so that they are more useful on the ground.[40] As they stand now, the Orders may be doing more harm than good.

A Coda for My Crewmembers

I fear you have taught me far more than I have taught you. But just as your lives have informed this book, I hope this book can also inform your lives. I hope you will find in these pages some ideas, some critical tools, that might help you reflect on the risks you take day in and day out.

"Do us justice" were the last words Rex Thurman said to me while shaking my hand at the end of my final day at Elk River. I have tried to satisfy his command by representing our lives honestly and with complexity, by suggesting ways to make firefighting safer, and by rendering apparent what we so often take for granted, that weightless common sense ingrained in our thinking. Perhaps, then, you will gain here some insight, as I have through this process, into what games we play and what games play us.

They are growing hotter and bigger. Fire season is starting earlier and ending later. Greater dangers await. Tomorrow will bring new smoke to chase, and someone must be there to put a stop to it all. But if the line must hold, then let us fully know why it is we who hold it.

Appendix: Between Native and Alien

Although for quite some time now anthropologists have turned themselves into "indigenous observers" and conducted studies of their own culture, they have done so primarily by employing the same research techniques and assumptions they employed for decades when studying "strange peoples in strange lands."[1] The homeland, they have found, is just like the exotic locale: different settings, same paradigm. But this seems problematic, since the dominant paradigm in anthropology is based on the premise that the field is foreign. The discipline, after all, grew out of travelogues, and the word "ethnography" is derived from "ethnic," which comes from the Greek translation of a Hebrew word, *goyim,* meaning foreigners, strangers: gentiles (to the Jews) and, later, pagans and primitives (to the Christians).[2] Images of anthropology's leading figures, its "fearless spectators," cannot be severed from the far-off places where they earned a name for themselves: Malinowski on his lonely island, Radcliffe-Brown in his war-torn jungle, Geertz hypnotized by his spectacular Balinese cockfight.[3] The same can be said of sociological ethnographers, who often temporarily abandon their privileged social positions to embed themselves in the most marginalized and dilapidated areas of American society: Whyte in his Italian slum, Liebow drinking canned beer on the corner, Gans stationed in Boston's West End. In both sociology and anthropology, ethnographic practices are riveted to notions of "the encounter." Here the problem, one on which many have ruminated, is getting in: learning the language, understanding strange rituals, protecting the culture from the toxicity of modernity, assuring lawbreakers that you are not a cop, struggling against society's barriers separating, say, the educated from the uneducated. The problem facing the indigenous ethnographer, however, is getting out.

Of course the ethnographer who is already "in" (re)enters the field with several advantages. Because of my insider status, I enjoyed unparalleled access to all aspects of crewmembers' lives, and I could participate in all their practices, from relaxing at crew quarters to fighting fire. By taking the "participant" in "participant observation" seriously, offering up my mind and body, day and night, to the practices, rituals, and thoughts of the crew, I gained insights into the universe of firefighting, insights gleaned when I bent my back to thrust a Pulaski into the dirt during a direct assault on a fire or when I moved my fingers through new warm ash to feel for hot spots. My body became a fieldnote, for in order to comprehend the contours of the wildland firefighting habitus as deeply as possible, I had to feel it growing inside of me.

Moreover, being a firefighter before I was an ethnographer allowed me to gain entrée and to earn the trust of my crewmembers, some of whom at first were strangers to me, much more easily than had I been new to the profession. That is, I had already accomplished most of the crucial labor of establishing trusting relationships with my crewmembers in seasons past, and this trust was established through *reputation* as well as through *presentation*. It was secured not only from relationships formed in previous years but also by conveying an essence of genuineness, one presented through an intimately recognizable (better, mirrorlike) patina, a "silent language," that I carried with me: in my body (attuned to the rhythms of the setting), my speech (familiar with crewmembers' phrases and tones), and my style (used to the clothing, gear, and posture of the wildland firefighter). My bodily presentation allowed crewmembers to sense, perhaps at a molecular level (a sensing without sensation), that I belonged there.[4] Accordingly, when I asked permission to carry out the study at the start of the morning briefing my first day back at work in 2003, I was greeted with an enthusiastic response from each crewmember.[5]

To the men at Elk River, I was primarily a firefighter and secondarily an ethnographer; hence I rarely met the wall of suspicion that confronts many outside fieldworkers who are known only as fieldworkers to those they study. And I am inclined to believe that my crewmembers were more open and less defensive in my presence than they would have been in front of a stranger.[6] (In my mind an outside ethnographer cannot win this level of intimacy simply by spending more time in the field; it must be cultivated before the fieldwork proper begins.[7]) Some crewmembers articulated this in so many words. After reading an earlier version of this manuscript, Steve told me, "Since you worked with us, there's that comfort level. 'Hey, this is Desmond. He's worked with us for four seasons.' . . . There's a comfort level knowing that it was you. 'Cause if somebody else came over to Elk River and asked us, I would have said, '*Heeeeck* no. You're crazy! I don't want you hanging around here.'" Because they knew me and trusted me, most crewmembers believed that I had their best interests in mind, that I wanted to do right by them.[8] This led many to act freely in front of me and to tell me things that perhaps they would have not told an outsider.

This was not always the case, however. For one thing, the reputation I had earned in previous years at Elk River—as someone who was fairly intolerant of sexist and homophobic comments—may have curbed some dialogue of this nature.[9] Two interactions with Donald illustrate this point.

After extinguishing a small fire, some of my crewmembers were leaning against a pickup, waiting for Allen to release them. As I walked toward the group, I saw that Donald had tied the front of his T-shirt in a knot, exposing his stomach. He let his arms go limp and was dancing around on tiptoes saying in a high-pitched voice, "Look! I'm a queer! I'm a queer!" Some of the guys were chuckling, but when Donald noticed I had arrived in the circle, he immediately stopped dancing and said, "Oh, I'm sorry, Matt. I'm a *homosexual*." Then he started up the flamboyant dance once more. Donald felt that his mocking dance, and especially the word "queer," might offend me, so he slightly altered his behavior.

On another occasion, Donald, Kris, and I were driving down a dirt road, and for one reason or another we were acting silly. As a small truck rounded the corner, I joked to Kris, who was driving, "Ram that truck!"

Waving, we passed the truck and noticed that an attractive young woman was driving.

"I'd like to ram her!" Donald remarked, playing off my words.

"Oop! That's going in the book!" Kris remarked.

"Uh, well, I take that back," Donald answered. "First I'd get to know her a little. Then I'd ram her!"

Although my presence in the truck didn't seem to affect Donald's behavior, it might have affected Kris's. Perhaps, then, there were times when crewmembers did not relax in front of me, when they refrained from acting a certain way for fear it might "go in the book." I think this was more the exception than the rule, but since one can never be sure of such things, I must let the reader be the judge of that.

Sometimes crewmembers did not fully articulate their thoughts to me, not for fear they would be portrayed negatively in the book, but because they saw me as "one of them" and assumed I already knew what they were talking about. This occurred, for instance, when I asked Clarence the lookout to tell me more about his distinction between the "Buick crowd" and the "pickup crowd." Clarence answered in one sentence and knew he didn't have to explain himself any further. Friends and family members have a kind of communication that does not easily lend itself to ethnographic reproduction.[10] And veterans of any occupation need not carefully articulate the ins and outs of their trade to one another, though they certainly would need to for some ignorant and inquisitive outside ethnographer.

Undoubtedly the biggest challenge facing the native ethnographer, however, is breaking with unquestioned ways of thinking internalized from previous experience and forgotten. When the field is familiar, when the "informants" are friends, one is more likely to leave unexplored commonsense ways of viewing the world. Although a new language need not be mastered, one's mother tongue must be spoken anew, with hesitancy and doubt; although one's surroundings are comfortable and recognizable, they must become uncomfortable, disconcerting and curious; and although one's informants are intimates, familiar and friendly, one must look on them with searching eyes. In a phrase, the task of the native ethnographer is to "exoticize the domestic," to resist relaxing in the comfort of familiarity.[11]

Like my crewmembers, I came to Elk River with a country-masculine habitus. To the extent that we can divide ethnographers into insiders and outsiders, I was of the former sort, not simply because I was a man with a rural working-class upbringing (not all such men would be considered insiders in this setting) but because I had previous experiences at Elk River, having shared in the life of the firefighter before I set out to study it.[12] As such, I was quite comfortable in the field—it would have required no great effort to "settle down and forget about being a sociologist"[13]—and, as I already mentioned, I believe my crewmembers were, more or less, comfortable with me. What's more, my country-masculine habitus predisposed me to take crewmembers seriously, to invest in the things they invested in (distaste for the vanity fair of urbanity, the skills and knowledge that make up one's country competence), since I too invested in such things, and to piece together how crewmembers' rural upbringing mattered in the context of firefighting. The question of organizational socialization, however, eluded me during the introductory phases of the study.

Going Alien

The question of organizational socialization confronted me only after I had sufficiently distanced myself from my crewmembers and the Forest Service, only after I had broken away from familiar self-evidences. In this distancing, this getting out, I was helped by three factors. First, the up-tight reputation I earned in previous seasons separated me from my crewmembers. I already was used to listening to their conversations with a critical ear, and it was not difficult to employ this posture on behalf of sociological inquiry. Second, my status as an ethnographer, as unceasing recorder, put distance between me and other crewmembers. My tape recorder, my proverbial notebook, my jotting, my objectifying curiosity, my many nights monopolized by copying and developing my fieldnotes, my interview questions—all these tools, practices, and demands of the fieldworker—made it clear to my crewmembers (and to me) that I was not simply at (or of) Elk River but was there to represent and write about the place.

Third, my education set me apart from other crewmembers. My tastes had been altered, and my language (which, like most academics, I cared very much about) had been refined. As I described earlier, Paul often referred to me as "the genius" or "the doctor"—half-flattering and half-pejorative nicknames—and other crewmembers told me I talked in "school talk." Since I identified as a sociologist, I was regularly asked my opinion on the Iraq war, Indian gaming, affirmative action, and other political issues. At first I avoided answering these questions out of an adolescent fear that I might somehow "contaminate the setting." But I quickly learned that dodging the questions or answering only with a question ("I don't know, what do you think?") stifled conversation. Plus I quickly sensed that crewmembers were growing annoyed by these fake responses and by the one-way flow of inquiry. Kris once teased me, "So, that's what ethnography is: you can ask us questions but we can't ask you nothing?" I therefore began answering their political questions honestly and with passion. I argued with George about the "natural differences" of the sexes, talked with Vince about economic sustainability on American Indian reservations, and debated Kris, who had a knack for rhetoric, on one topic after another. This increased my otherness in relation to my crewmembers, but at the same time I believe my honest opinions drew out my crewmembers' honest opinions at least as effectively as did my questions.

So while I was in the field, my reputation, my ethnographic commitments, and my education all pulled me away from other crewmembers. A pressure had been building, so to speak, but the break—a break against common sense—came only with the news of Rick Lupe's death. I had entered the field with a set of research questions that had to do with the relation between masculine status and risk taking; I had read Goffman and other social-psychological accounts on this topic, but at the time I had no real interest in the study of organizations. However, when I witnessed my crewmembers' reactions to Lupe's death, I immediately began questioning how we made sense of risk and death, what the latter had to do with the former, and how my thinking had been influenced by the Forest Service. The sad news of Lupe's death, or rather, my crewmembers' apathetic reaction to this news, produced a double effect in me: I began thinking of ways to reconstruct the logic of firefighting and processes of organizational training and discipline; and I grew skeptical of crewmembers' and supervisors' opinions and injunctions. The question I began asking myself again and again was, "Why do they (and I) think that?"

Reflexivity did not come to me softly and gently, like a hand gliding over bent heads of grain. No, it flung itself at me forcefully, violently, not in the quiet comfort of my study but in the isolated wilderness of Elk River. Many fieldworkers have experienced similar encounters, unexpected ethnographic episodes that forced them to reevaluate their own ways of thinking.[14] Full-immersion fieldwork—the demanding method that requires investigators to become, as deeply and completely as possible, what they wish to understand—not only allows one to grasp the *inponderabilia of actual life,*[15] the unscripted, unrepeatable, and often unutterable stuff of existence beyond the grasp of interview-based inquests, it also presents the embedded ethnographer with reflexivity-inducing situations, conceptual crises, that raze underdeveloped ideas and replace them with new ways of understanding. "So, the way to get it is to need it," Goffman advised young fieldworkers. "And the only way to need it is to not have anything of your own. So you should be in a position to cut yourself to the bone."[16] Embedded in Elk River, I was in such a (vulnerable) position, and when my crewmembers reacted to Lupe's death, I searched after the understanding that is recorded in the pages of this book because I had to, because I needed it, because life as a firefighter could no longer make sense without it, and because questions about firefighters could in no way be severed from questions about me.

The reflexive moment ushered in with news of Lupe's death led me to inquire into many things I had taken for granted. Such a process, I learned, can look and feel quite ridiculous: I certainly felt silly asking my crew-members what a cotter pin was and how they came by such knowledge. (But didn't Goffman tell us we "have to be willing to be a horse's ass"?[17]) More than silly, I felt distant and alien. An insider would never ask such a question; but I was beginning, day by day, to become less and less of an insider. Unlike the ethnographer of a foreign culture, who proceeds (sometimes quite literally) from the outside in, I proceeded from the inside out. I did so by transforming my comfortable surroundings into strangeness, by viewing familiar practices—both the jarring (reactions to the death of a firefighter) and the mundane (knowledge of a cotter pin)—as curious things.

I do not pretend to believe that this process, this break, was accomplished in toto. As I pointed out in chapter 8, when it came to understanding the death of a firefighter, I learned that I was still thinking with the organizational common sense of the Forest Service when I was more than two years removed from my fieldwork.[18] The outsider ethnographer can never fully graft herself into the foreign culture no matter how "deep" she gets, but the indigenous ethnographer can never fully detach himself from the world that in many ways created him. If "going native" is nothing more than a chimera for the outside observer, then so too is "going alien" for the inside observer.

But can we fashion a virtue out of this necessity? In principle, the native fieldworker who went alien, who severed all ties to her homeland and assumed the aloof and objectifying gaze of the outsider, would be just as ill served as the outside observer who went native, abandoning all theoretical training and erasing all memories of his mother country, resources one draws on to know how, what, and why to observe. Why? Because the optimal ethnographic vantage point sits between indigenousness and foreignness. The ethnographer who is too close risks becoming oblivious to the "practical achievement" of interaction and may accept subjects' explanations and rationalizations at face value. But the ethnographer who is too distant passes over the rich details of practical life and may give in to the temptation to typify individuals, to hastily impose rigid theoretical concepts, and to snuff out the delicate complexities of social action.[19] Both researchers will produce naive arguments, the former because he is too quick to accept the world and the latter because he is too quick to ignore it.

The trick, then, is to float somewhere in the middle. Between native and alien is precisely where we want to be. Here I am reminded of Evans-Prichard's words: "One enters into another culture and withdraws from it at the same time. . . . [O]ne lives in two different worlds of thought at the same time, in categories and concepts and values which often cannot easily be reconciled. One becomes, at least temporarily, a sort of double marginal man, alienated from both worlds."[20]

As doubly marginalized, simultaneously "stranger and friend," the ethnographer must work to create a tension, a space of ambiguity; he must be informed by both social science and social setting but fully loyal to neither.[21] For the insider ethnographer, this requires going quasi-alien through a twofold epistemological break. First, she must break with scholasticism—with the shaky assumptions of our discipline; with the impulse to reason the world away without actually listening to it; and for some of us with a "fascination with metaphors, signs, and symbols."[22] Second, she must break with parochialism—with our unscrutinized common sense; with our anti-intellectualism that renders useless (or, a blasphemy, unpractical) a rich and diverse body of sociological theory that is anything but; and with our tendency to accept uncritically the accounts of intimates as always accurate, replacing knowledge with ad-miration.[23]

George Orwell once quipped, "To see what is in front of one's nose needs a constant struggle."[24] Accordingly, when the ethnographer chooses to exoticize her homeland, it is imperative that rituals of rigorous reflexiv-ity—self-objectification, self-scrutiny, and even self-mockery—be built into *every step* of the investigation.[25] Breaking with self-evidences carries on long after the indigenous ethnographer leaves the setting. Many people who read parts of this manuscript, or who witnessed pieces of this work being presented, contributed to this process by revealing to me the value of "scientific treasures" (to use Malinowski's phrase) tucked away in a pass-ing comment or a brief observation, treasures I had treated as insignificant. One sociologist, born and raised in New York City, found it fascinating that firefighters had to buy their own boots. "That would be like asking soldiers to buy their own rifles," he told me. Comments like this—and I was the beneficiary of many—prompted me to reevaluate things I had uncritically accepted as unworthy of evaluation. This is just one of many reasons all ethnographers, but especially those running reconnaissance in their homeland, should gather an audience and share their work at vari-ous stages. Set a mess of ethnographic data in the middle of a table and ask others (especially those you usually disagree with) to pick at it with you.

But can the insider ethnographer ever be objective? This is the question that refuses to go away. Lévi-Strauss, for instance, held that objectivity is "freely granted" only to the outside observer, who stands "sufficiently lofty and remote" above the foreigners.[26] While it is true that the indigenous ethnographer must struggle against "immediate knowledge," deeply familiar yet rarely dissected, objectivity does not come only to the ethnographer who puts miles between herself and her "subjects," nor is it inversely associated with the fieldworker's moral commitments, as at least one anthropologist has argued.[27] Objectivity, rather, comes to the ethnographer who "knows herself," who can critically expose and assess her position in relation to her field site, whether it is right down the block or in the center of the Amazon jungle, by exploiting the instruments of socioanalysis and self-analysis. In fact, Bourdieu's excursions into intimate universes, his hometown of Béarn as well as the French intellectual field, demonstrate how sociology of the familiar can spur practices of "participant objectification," revealing to the analyst his own commonsense ways of thinking that do not obstruct objectivity but increase "epistemological vigilance."[28] Objectivity comes by way of reflexivity, not by way of indifference.

Recording and Representation

Many ethnographers have had great luck using a tape recorder to capture everyday interactions. I did not. I made several attempts during working hours, but each time I tried, my crewmembers only clammed up. My last attempt came during a fire call. Paul, Vince, and I were riding in a truck. Paul was driving, Vince was riding shotgun, and I was in the back cab. We had spent the afternoon walking the line of a newly extinguished fire, searching for smokes and signs of reburn. Since we found none, we were headed back to Elk River when the lookout in Paquesi Perch called in a smoke. Vince pulled out the map and pinpointed its estimated location, which happened to be in our AOR. We were off: Paul stepped on the gas and grabbed the steering wheel with both hands; Vince flipped on the lights and sirens and let out a yell; the radio traffic sped up: *Paquesi, what's the color of your smoke? Dispatch, Engine 7-1 en route. Engine 7-3 en route. Dispatch, this is Chopper 976. I've located the fire.*

Paul, Vince, and I were reacting to the radio traffic and trying to find the best route to the fire. As the action unfolded, I thought to myself, "This would be a perfect time to use the tape recorder. I could capture the exciting scene of rushing to a fire." I dug the device out of my fire pack, pushed "record," and loudly announced, over all the ruckus, "All right guys, I'm gonna turn on the tape recorder now!" before setting the device in the middle of the front seat.

The reaction was immediate silence. Paul and Vince stared at the tape recorder but didn't say a word. Vince began to say something, but Paul quickly cut him off. "*Shhhh,*" he hissed, pointing to my machine. Then, he whispered, "What were you going to say?"

I sat annoyed and baffled in the back seat as Paul and Vince whispered to each other. Here we were rushing to a fire call, speeding down a dirt road with sirens blaring—a scene that moments before had evoked whoops, hollers, loudly barked instructions, and curt responses to questions—and my crewmembers now had hushed their voices till they were barely audible. After a couple minutes of whispering and a couple more minutes of my trying to explain that only I would listen to the tapes, I reached over the seat and switched the recorder off. Having interfered violently in that moment, derailing its rhythm and natural sequence, I never again used the tape recorder in daily interactions (though I did use it during interviews).

Later, Paul told me he did not want to incriminate himself on tape. He was unlawfully *speeding* to the fire, as nearly all firefighters do, and did not want to leave any evidence of his mild infraction, nor did he want to be recorded saying something senseless while caught up in the exhilaration of the moment. After talking with several other crewmembers, I learned that this was why my tape recorder smothered conversation. Crewmembers didn't want to get caught on tape cracking a dirty joke or making fun of other firefighters or supervisors. To them a tape recorder was threatening and invasive; it could be used against them, and they reacted accordingly, buttoning their lips when the red button was depressed.

Some fieldworkers believe one can gain ethnographic precision only by using a tape recorder. However, my failed experience led me to wonder what we mean by "ethnographic precision." A tape recorder (almost) guarantees that the fieldworker will be able to *reproduce* conversations verbatim, but it might also lead the folks the fieldworker hopes to understand to *produce* different conversations than had the device not been used. The ethnographer with a tape recorder might capture the words perfectly, but are they the perfect words? If people change their language and actions in the presence of a tape recorder and the ethnographer does not pick up on this, then the finished product might be nothing more than an accurate representation of a misrepresentation. While ethnographers who do not use a recording device need to worry about "fictionalizing fact," those using one need to worry about "factualizing fiction." This is not true for all ethnographers and their "subjects." Some ethnographers, especially those who hold vastly different social positions than the people they intend to study, might be well advised to use a tape recorder so as not to present a distorted picture of people's words and actions.[29] And some people may not flinch when the ethnographer pushes "record." But my crewmembers certainly did. In all cases, ethnographers must ask how their methods of data collection might affect the field they want to know, and they must consider not only how their practices capture, with precision, what was said, but also how these practices influence the precision—the authenticity—of what was said in the first place.[30]

After my experience with the tape recorder proved unfruitful, I relied solely on recording interactions in fieldnotes. I carried a notepad at all times and jotted things down throughout the day. Sometimes I would take notes in front of crewmembers during ongoing conversations; other times I would dash into an empty office room or engine bay and record my observations immediately after they occurred. I took notes every chance I could: while riding in engines, during breaks on fires (my dirty and scuffed notepads smelled like smoke months after my fieldwork had ended), and while morning meetings were under way. (My crewmembers did not seem to mind this, and I was asked what I was writing only a handful of times.) Once the workday had ended, I would transfer my fieldnotes from my small notepad to a larger journal and fill in the details.

Because most interactions used in this book were recorded in my fieldnotes either when they were taking place or shortly afterward, I was able to report conversations accurately, in most cases capturing crewmembers' sentences word for word. As a rule, I have avoided relying on interactions I failed to capture in the moment. This has not been possible, however, for the moments of high intensity, namely firefighting. My depictions of firefighting (besides those of the Rodeo-Chediski fire, which I address below) are based on notes taken during breaks and after my crewmembers and I were dismissed from the fire. I took extensive notes on fires—often over several days—in an attempt to capture as many details as I could, and I double-checked my representations with each crewmember involved.

Since I was a firefighter, required to participate fully in the duties of the job, I did not have the luxury of stepping away every few minutes to record this or that. I was bound to overlook thousands of details in the heat of action. And yet it is questionable whether the ethnographer who does not participate in the interactions and settings she wishes to understand can fully capture the habitual how-ness, the "incarnate intelligence," possessed by individuals who have grown familiar and comfortable in the worlds they help to order.[31]

Embedded, I was able to access that deep knowledge that comes only from full-fledged membership, from gripping the thing with your own two hands. In my opinion it is not enough simply to ask these professional risk takers to articulate their experiences on the edge in hopes of grasping their passions and perceptions through their canned utterances. In fact, many risk takers have described their activity as unutterable. "In the early stages of the study," laments one researcher, "I was constantly frustrated in my attempt to get sky divers to talk about the jump experience. The typical response to my probing was, 'If you want to know what it's like, then do it!'"[32] As these sky divers well knew, the body has a language of its own, a language that cannot be fully articulated through responses to questions or observations of interactions but can be grasped only through corporeal investigations. This is why Loïc Wacquant argues that "it is imperative that the sociologist submit himself to the fire of action *in situ;* that to the greatest extent possible he put his own organism, sensibility, and incarnate intelligence at the epicenter of the array of material and symbolic forces that he intends to dissect."[33] To fully know the game we must play the game. We must eat their food, speak their language, walk on their sidewalks, work in their jobs, fight in their struggles, teach in their schools, live in their houses; and we must do all of this until their things, their life—its smell and taste and temperature, its way of reasoning and psychology, its rhythm and tempo and feel—become our things, our life.

My recounting of the night I fought the Rodeo-Chediski fire might be called "retrospective ethnography."[34] It is gleaned from my experiences as a firefighter, not my experiences as an ethnographer. Except for a handful of minor events,[35] this is the only instance when I used this kind of data. I did not take systematic notes during the Rodeo-Chediski fire, nor did I intend to use those experiences in this book. I hesitated at length to include this event, but in the end I decided to do so for a specific theoretical reason. Recall that I draw upon my experiences fighting the Rodeo-Chediski fire to illustrate that even during fires that are fought "by the book," portions of the Ten and Eighteen must be sidestepped. When illustrating this point, I wanted to rely on a fire that was battled with the utmost precision and care, a fire where special precautions were taken to increase firefighters' safety. More than any blaze I had ever fought, the Rodeo-Chediski fire lent itself to this purpose. Because the fire was so monstrous and because we were carrying out urban-interface tactics, Thurman and other supervisors were extra careful, and my crewmembers and I had our guard up. Thus the Rodeo-Chediski fire was "the toughest nut to crack," as a teacher of mine likes to say: it was the hardest case to prove. If I wanted to make my argument most effectively, I would have to make it with this fire.

Luckily, the event was a memorable one. I worked with crewmembers involved in the incident to carefully put the pieces together. I wrote the story and my crewmembers confirmed the particulars, adding comments that only better developed or slightly augmented the events. In the end, we all agreed on the details of the narrative. However, I do not defend retrospective ethnography as a practice that should be taken lightly or as one that ethnographers should use regularly. For one thing, the memory plays tricks on us; it cannot be trusted. And though a collective remembering of the story can improve accuracy, nothing is as precise as data recorded in the immediacy of the action. In the case of the Rodeo-Chediski fire and my arguments regarding the application of the Ten and Eighteen, however, analytical obligations were given primacy over ethnographic precision.

Moreover, retrospective ethnography raises an ethical concern. During 2003, when I was "out" as an ethnographer, crewmembers could choose what to reveal and what to conceal; but in previous seasons, when I was just one of the guys, crewmembers acted without considering that their deeds might one day end up in a book. Should the ethnographer be permitted to use interactions that occurred before the ethnography proper, before announcing a study? The only way to answer, in my view, is to put it to those involved in such interactions, to request their permission post factum. This is what I did, and my crewmembers allowed me to include these events.

One final note about the interviews: I waited a month and a half after starting work to begin conducting my interviews.[36] This not only allowed me to (re)establish friendship and trust before beginning the interviews, it also brought to mind questions I had not considered asking beforehand.[37] Although I had entered the field with a set of interview questions in hand, many were tweaked or discarded altogether as more interesting and more important ones began to emerge from my interactions with crewmembers.[38] My crewmembers imposed a new set of questions on me, and I returned the favor by imposing these questions on them during the interviews. After all, ethnography is never fully inductive or fully deductive. Fieldwork is a determined search (sometimes ham-fisted, sometimes nimble) in which deductive orientations, with loyalties to theory, and inductive orientations, with loyalties to the field, join in a dialectical fashion. It is a dynamic process of following out and tying together the strings of one's curiosity, "poking and prying with a purpose."[39]

Audiences and Anxieties

If the ethnographer is to straddle two worlds, the setting under investigation and the science helping the investigation along, it follows that she should have something to offer each. Soon a question appears: For whom should I write? To whom should I hold myself accountable? Some ethnographers, following Schutz,[40] have suggested that there is an unbridgeable gulf between the student and the studied, and since the ethnographer can never please both, she should "segregate her audience" and address one or the other (usually other students).[41] But this option is not available to the insider ethnographer, who must answer to friends and family members, nor is it desirable, since fieldworkers, by employing, challenging, and advancing scientific knowledge, can (and should strive to) give much to those who offer up their everyday lives to benefit her craft.[42]

While writing this book, I always kept wildland firefighters ("the toughest audience," I called them) in the forefront of my mind. There were two other audiences as well: social scientists, of course, and the reading public. I attempted to write *On the Fireline* for all three, employing the "three languages of the sociologist" that Hughes described: the language of the people one studies; that of the professionals one belongs among; and that of the public one hopes to inform.[43] But each of these audiences has different needs and desires. In my mind, the firefighters wanted a fair, if slightly flattering, representation along with practical implications;[44] the sociologists wanted depth, critical scrutiny, and theoretical innovation and intervention; and the public wanted honesty, rawness, vitality, and broad comments that reach beyond the fireline. Pulled in three competing directions, I was sometimes pestered by a feeling of anxiety. Multiple audiences meant multiple accountability.[45] And I knew, as Joan Didion knew, that "writers are always selling somebody out."[46] I recognized, too, that the same fate that befell William Foote Whyte, a double rejection—from sociologists (who refused, at least at first, to accept his core conclusions about slum organization) and from those he studied (North End residents who felt they had been poorly represented)—could just as easily befall me.[47] Ethnography, from beginning to end, is often a lonely venture.

Looking back, however, I know my three audiences kept me sharp.

When I would favor one group, giving them just what they wanted to hear, the others would put up a fuss. These audiences did not just exist in my mind; they had a flesh-and-blood existence, as when I presented my work in front of groups of social scientists or when I returned to Arizona to learn what my crewmembers thought of the work. When I told an audience of sociologists about firefighters' love of Elk River, a love of place, they pushed me to conceptualize this love as a love of fate. And when my crewmembers read an earlier draft of this manuscript in which I had characterized them through limited terminology—with a vocabulary conditioned by the strictures of sociology—they rightly objected. As a result I rewrote a section in chapter 1 called "Women Firefighters," a relatively small section of the book that garnered a large proportion of their attention, and made my analysis more complex. In my experience, writing to multiple audiences, however trying, makes for more relevant *and* more rigorous sociology.

Taking It Back

The day after I received my first book contract, reassurance that this work would be published, I photocopied the entire manuscript and mailed it to each firefighter except Rex Thurman. (I thought it best to let my crewmembers read the manuscript before the boss did.) A month and a half later I flew back to Arizona, rented a car, and headed out on a weeklong trip to rendezvous with each crewmember and glean their thoughts, questions, and criticisms about the book. To ensure that the crew would be in Arizona (and not off in some other state fighting a blaze), I scheduled the trip during the off-season, early November; however, by this time the crew had scattered. I traveled all around the state: from the Utah-Arizona border to meet with Peter, who was guiding deer hunters through the Kaibab National Forest near Lee's Ferry, to the low desert of Tucson to shoot pool with Kris and Tank at a smoky dive called the Mint; from the ponderosa pine country of Show Low to eat chicken wings with Steve in a local sports bar, to the plateaus of Atwater to drink hot tea and eat fresh banana bread at Allen's dinner table. Thankfully, my rental car came with unlimited miles.

I suspected that only a handful of my crewmembers, the more literary types, would read the manuscript in full; but I was happily surprised to the contrary. Nearly every crewmember read the entire manuscript (endnotes included) and did so with care: Peter read it in one sitting, staying up till 4:00 in the morning and using a yellow highlighter; Diego read it twice and took notes; and Bryan called me the day he received the manuscript and pointed out a typo he had found in the opening pages. Of course, all the crewmembers paid special mind to how I represented them, taking issue with everything from their pseudonyms (When I met with Diego, he complained, jokingly, "You know, you gave me the most Mexican name known to mankind! Diego. *Goddamn!* You couldn't give me something else, man? That's as bad as Julio, man!") to what readers could potentially read into their words. But most also gave considerable attention to how *other* crewmembers were represented, to the main arguments of the book, to facts and minor details, to my prose and word choice, and even to grammatical structure and spelling. (For those few who did not read the book, including Thurman, I went over each part where they made an appearance, reading the passages aloud while they read over my shoulder.[48]) These conversations, all taped, lasted for hours. Kris took me out for cinnamon rolls at a hometown joint called Gus Balloons the morning after we played pool at the Mint. The coffee-wielding waitress asked us to leave after two hours. We relocated to a coffee shop near the University of Arizona campus and continued the conversation for another ninety minutes.

This book is better because of the attention and time my crewmembers generously devoted to an earlier draft. Many of the nuances and subtle-

ties of my arguments are the result of these insightful, challenging, and thoughtful conversations. Because Kris told me he agreed with my arguments regarding the incompetent dead but saw no alternative, I struggled to think of the implications of those arguments. Eventually I came to see how victim blaming upheld an organizational ethic of individualism, one that might help cause accidents. Peter urged me to rethink Goffman's term "the illusion of self-determinancy," which ultimately led me to change "illusion" to "illusio." When he and I sat at a picnic table at the foot of the sandy red Vermilion Cliffs, a few miles from his hunting camp, he pointed to a passage by Goffman that I had quoted and asked, with a tinge of offense in his voice, "Are you saying that we are 'full of blindness, half-truths, and illusions?'"[49]

I denied this and went on to clarify my point: "What I said, you know, is that I think firefighters, they don't linger on the bad part, the danger, that, uh, they don't have a lot of control over their time, incredibly long hours for not great wages, things like that. Would you say this is true?"

"Yeah," Peter answered. "I mean, they don't make that much money. The only way to make money is by the long hours and the overtime."

Peter had trouble not with the idea that I (through Goffman) was trying to present but with the language I had used. He, like so many of my crewmembers, helped me sharpen my language, checking my words against their reality. Often crewmembers would ask about certain phrases: *Do you*

really think he was "threatening his life"? Do you really think he "marooned" you with "no leadership"? These questions forced me to justify my word choices and therefore kept my descriptions honest and even-keeled. Sometimes prose gains a mind of its own. And sometimes the solace and silence of one's study encourages the taking of liberties, allowing "one's thoughts to roam in an ideal world where they encounter no resistance," to the extent that one begins to treat one's subjects as works of art "to be polished and sculpted."[50] The men at Elk River lent me their resistance by holding the words of this book up to the light of their lived experience.

Once each crewmember had finished reviewing the manuscript, I would ask if I could use his real name in the book. Most crewmembers told me they wouldn't mind in the least, but some said no.[51] Hence I left all the pseudonyms in place. I promised crewmembers confidentiality at the outset of the study because I suspected that would lead them to be less guarded. Steve's comments support my judgment: "If you told people this wasn't going to be confidential, I think it would have been different. I think there was a comfort level that, 'Hey, this is gonna be confidential. This is gonna be between us.'"

When I asked Rex Thurman if I could use his real name, he replied, "Just because I'm still a current employee, and my personal thoughts about the damn bird [the spotted owl] and shit like that, I'd appreciate it if you would not change it."

"Okay, I won't. But what about your picture being in there, though?"

". . . Yeah, use the picture. Don't use my name. . . . It's not in my best interest. I'm not gonna make you take anything out of there. Those are my true beliefs. But using my alias, that works for me. If they figure it out, so be it! 'Cause I was honest with you . . . and that's what you asked me, and that's want I wanted to do, to give you the true story and the realities of things in there. To still be employed there, it's not in my best interest to tie me with those [opinions] right now. Once I retire and you rewrite the book, you damn right put my name in there!"

All my crewmembers encouraged me to use their pictures, and after some critical thought, I have done so, reasoning that they could predict the repercussions of this decision better than I could.[52] However, it is crucial to add here that simply having people's approval to use images (or to reveal identities in other ways) does not absolve the ethnographer of considerable responsibility in pondering the implications of her actions. Ethnographers have to consider the consequences of their work even when their subjects do not. And, importantly, we have to think of short- *and* long-term consequences. Many crewmembers thought hard about the impact of this work, and they helped me realize certain consequences I had not anticipated. But I was still obliged to wonder, "How will this book affect their lives five, ten, twenty years from now?" When a crewmember's words or actions could have serious repercussions, I took it upon myself to disguise his identity so that even his own peers could not recognize him. For instance, no reader, not even my crewmembers, can identify the arsonist discussed in chapter 2. I crafted this story with extra care, and I discussed my presentation with the arsonist.

If ethnographers wish to safeguard their informants, then ensuring their anonymity is an effective way to do so. Successfully camouflaging individuals' identities—even (and sometimes especially) from their most intimate companions—can protect them from divorce, job termination, incarceration, or worse. Moreover, the promise of confidentiality lends credibility to the ethnographer; it allows and even encourages informants to disclose immoral and illegal behavior, the knowledge of which may provide depth, sophistication, and complexity to the analysis. In a time where political, military, and juridical leaders are criticizing—and even imprisoning[53]—journalists who refuse to reveal their sources, creating fear and doubt in the minds of informants with sensitive information, ethnographers must diligently protect those who confide in them. If the ethnographer's story can cause informants significant harm, then her loyalties, in nearly every case, must be to those who have invited her into the intimacies of their lives.

What the Firefighters Thought

Many crewmembers had very positive things to say about the book. For example, Kris told me, "I thought it was a good, a good way of showing how we approach risk. I thought that that was really well done because it's not a, it's not rushin' out there just trying to, to *fight* it just to fight it. I like that. You showed more depth than simply being macho." And I confess I was deeply rewarded when some crewmembers admitted to learning something about their lives from my study.

"I was reading it, and there're a lot of things I didn't realize until you pointed it out," Donald told me as we sat across from one another at a family-owned Chinese restaurant.

"Like what?" I asked.

"Like why we liked it so much, why it was so great. . . . There's just things out there that you would never get to do anywhere else. It was cool seeing it pointed out."

". . . What else?"

"Well, that they, they *desensitize* us. That's the best word you can use for it. . . . They say, 'It's dangerous, but you can be safe when you're doing it.' . . . You pointed out a lot of things that I haven't seen, and I thought that was cool."

Of course, these flattering comments (though both sets were accompanied by critical observations as well) were conditioned by specific social situations, contexts, and etiquette pressures that may have influenced crewmembers' responses. For one thing, there was our friendship. When I met Kris and Donald, we hugged and greeted each other warmly. It was good to see them, and I like to think they felt likewise. Out of courtesy and kindness, they might have kept some negative comments to themselves. There was also the fact that criticism can be harder to dish out than praise and platitudes. The giving and getting of harsh criticism is a practice peculiar to academics, and those without a scholarly disposition might find it awkward to voice disapproval. In addition, there was the communicative context to consider. That is, an ethnographer who asks, "So did you like it?" will mostly likely receive a much different response than the one who inquires, "What parts in the manuscript do you disagree with?"[54]

I attempted to ease these pressures by framing my conversations with crewmembers in ways that encouraged them to offer criticism. When I mailed them the manuscript, I included a cover letter stressing that the work was far from finished, that everything could be changed, and that their pointed suggestions, no matter how harsh, would help me greatly. And when I sat down with each crewmember, I began the conversation like this: "I want to emphasize that I'm not here to defend what I wrote. I'm here to learn from you. I'm here to see what you think about what I wrote, to get your feedback, criticisms, comments, anything."

I also began asking crewmembers what they had heard other crewmembers say about the work. I knew that many of them had talked to one another about it, and I discovered that asking about these conversations was an effective way to learn about the parts of the book that crewmembers took issue with. For instance, George told me, "This is, okay, this is one thing that I heard people talking about, like, not like everybody, but . . . it was about Elk River, and we, we ran around crazy. Or ran crazy. Or that we could just do whatever, and it was something in regards to that."

On another occasion, when I met Paul for breakfast at Denny's he told me, without prompting, "A lot of people are like, 'Ah, goddamn book,' and everything, but I think it's a good thing."

"Who said that?" I asked.

"Ah, you know, some people."

"Who?"

"Ummmm," Paul paused, considering if he should reveal the source. "Bryan."

"Okay, okay."

"You'll talk to him."

"Yeah, I'll talk to him."

"Yeah."

"What was he saying about it?"

"Ah, he was just having a hard time with it."

"Really?"

"Yeah, but . . . regardless of what people think about your book and everything, I think it's a good thing, and I think you did a good job. . . . Shit, it's the truth! . . . You told us exactly what you were going to do. . . . What I read and everything, it really looks good."

It was Bryan, then, not "a lot of people," who was complaining about the book. And when I asked Bryan about this, I learned that his criticisms were fairly minor and had to do with the specific ways he was depicted. And when, following George's tip, I began asking crewmembers if they thought I had depicted our crew as too unrestrained, one or two said yes and encouraged me to emphasize the ways they display discipline and hard work while on the job. Thus eavesdropping on crewmember-to-crewmember comments, tapping into these gossip channels, revealed specific points of concern or disagreement that one crewmember expressed to another but perhaps would not have said so forthrightly to me.

And should crewmembers have disagreed with me? One's answer will largely depend on one's position in the field of social science. Those who subscribe to a kind of psychoanalytic epistemology, who believe, with Bachelard, that "the first impression is not a fundamental truth," might be unnerved by analyses that do not differ from participants' accounts.[55] On the other hand, those who incline more toward phenomenology, who believe that if "ethnographic descriptions do not fit the texture of experience as lived by research subjects, then they may be useful only as projections of the researcher's imagination," might be skeptical of depictions that do not align succinctly with participants' ideas.[56]

In my experience, neither of these alternatives accurately reflects the indefinite and contradictory results one is confronted with on taking his findings back to the field. First off, it is one thing to "believe" in something you say during fleeting moments; it is quite another to say years later that you "believe" in those same words, frozen solid in concrete text. On reading their own words, many crewmembers experienced shock and discomfort. (After all, to say a four-letter word and to see it on paper are very different experiences.) As Steve said to me, "I'll tell you the truth, I didn't remember anything I said. . . . Everybody starts thinking, 'Man, what did I say? It's been so long. What did I say? I don't even know what I said.' And then a lot of people started reading this and said, 'Man, I don't even agree with myself!'" Ethnography—"vitality phrased"[57]—immobilizes words and actions performed at the speed of life. As such, asking people to assess their own interactions and conversations can produce regret ("I should have said . . ."), which can quickly lead to rationalization ("What I meant to say was . . .").

For example, some crewmembers rationalized their opinions toward other kinds of wildland firefighters by the mantra "everyone has a place." Steve explained, "There's a lot of people that talk crap about Hotshots, just how serious some people take it. . . . I just, you know, I used to get into all that too, you know, Hotshots do this and we do this, but it's not productive."

"But it goes on, right?"

"Yeah, it goes on! . . . But, I mean, everyone has their spot."

A person might have said something years ago that he would never say today. Nevertheless, the ethnographer is required to record what he witnessed at a specific time; hence he must guard against replacing complex and accurate depictions based on rigorous observation with idyllic ones based on retrospective reconstructions.

Crewmembers agreed with me on some points and disagreed with me on others, and some crewmembers disagreed among themselves on certain points. Rather than sort through all the details of these exchanges, most of which concerned points I considered rather minor, let me make one simple observation: the important question is not *if* they agree or disagree with you but *why* they do. When crewmembers' critiques were sound—when they pointed out how I had oversimplified a point, provided contradictory evidence that ran against an argument, or corrected a fact—I changed my analysis accordingly. But there were some occasions when I refused to alter my arguments not out of mulishness but because my observations and practices (and those of other crewmembers) were at odds with those of the critic. Of course, I did not expect crewmembers to agree with everything, especially insights that I labored to obtain through ongoing exercises of reflexivity long after I had left the field—insights, for instance, about the organizational common sense of the Forest Service or my more heterodox ideas regarding the impossibility of following the Ten and Eighteen. Thurman, for instance, told me, "I've been there and done it. And I know what has made me successful. And I know that it's not *not* believing in those Eighteen and Ten Standard Orders."

The native, no matter how wise, experienced, and respected, is not always right; nor is the ethnographer, no matter how inexperienced, always wrong.[58] And when these two categories adjoin in the body of a single being, the native ethnographer, the tension between inside and outside vantage points (assuming such things exist) dissolves, and all that is left is this tertium quid, this hybrid half scientist/half subject, who must make some tough decisions. In the end, I did the only thing left to do: I marshaled conclusions based on the best evidence at hand.

One more point about crewmembers' impressions. A handful of them thought the book told too many secrets. In writing about shooting off fireworks, underage drinking, and erotic jokes, I was airing our dirty laundry. Steve felt this way more than any other crewmember: "It's just like, I don't know. It's just like . . . it's kinda stuff that you don't go around telling people. . . . Some of this stuff out there, people will look at us . . . and think we're bad guys. . . . I completely understand you telling the way it was. I understand that. . . . But there's not a book out there about wildland firefighters that talks anything like *this*. . . . Certain people are gonna read this and think, 'Those guys *are nuts!*'" Steve did not contest the truthfulness of my account; what he contested was just how truthful that account ought to be. Bryan felt the same way, stating his case with the language of authority: "There's some stuff that took place out there that, you know, in my opinion, the public doesn't need to know about."

William Foote Whyte, after publishing *Street Corner Society*, was met with a similar reaction from some of the people he depicted. Several years after the book was published, one of the young Italian men Whyte wrote about told him, "The trouble is, Bill, you caught people with their hair down. It's a true picture, yes; but people feel it's a little too personal."[59] In the same way, I caught the men at Elk River with their hair down. I was there when they tucked in their shirts and stood up straight when Thurman and other supervisors inspected the station, and I was there when all the bosses had gone home and the isolated paradise of Elk River was left to the devices of its youthful and (at times) obstreperous firecrew. Such is the duty of the ethnographer. Unlike the fast-paced reporter who tends to capture people only at their very best or their very worst, the ethnographer must "study the whole."[60] In this book I have tried to avoid depicting firefighters in the soft glow of romanticism (a glow that seeps through a steadily growing genre that might be called "hero writing"), passing over complex and sometimes discomforting details; rather, I have attempted to represent firefighters' lives in their entirety, in both their flattering and embarrassing aspects. But throughout this study, I have always felt tugged in opposing directions by two competing commitments: a commitment to the whole and a commitment to my crewmembers.

Although a few crewmembers asked me to trim some embarrassing details, most wanted my descriptions left as they were, for they knew that sanitizing and euphemizing stories would erode the essence of Elk River. Most laughed at themselves, and indeed many were laughing at a different self—a more rambunctious, uncaged, and younger self. Things are different now. Peter is a father: he finally mustered up the guts to ask his girlfriend to marry him, and soon afterward they had a son. Nicholas married as well—the Hopi way—and had to stop firefighting to accept a janitorial job at a reservation high school, one that came with a steady income and benefits. J.J. quit the Forest Service to ride the rails for the Santa Fe Railroad. Bryan, though still with the Forest Service, is toying with the idea of becoming a professor of forestry at a junior college because, in his words, he doesn't want to "swing a tool for the rest of his life." Kris is considering getting a PhD in international relations from the London School of Economics. Tank was accepted (finally) into the University of Arizona's School of Architecture and is working diligently toward his degree. And George, Paul, and Donald were hired on as full-time workers for the Forest Service. Vince was not asked to return to work the following season.

For many of my crewmembers Elk River, in Donald's words, was "where you took your first step into real life." And since that time, many have taken several steps further. They have grown up, and to some extent many of the more uncouth scenes captured in the pages of this book reflect the "sins of their youth," as the psalmist calls them. As for their perceptions of risk, danger, and death—as well as their attractions to firefighting—they have not changed.

But why did my crewmembers care so much about preserving the essence of Elk River, even when it could cost them some embarrassment? The answer is simple: this is all that remains of the place. Elk River was shut down the year after my fieldwork was completed. The higher-ups in Jameson had been threatening to close the station for years, and in 2004 they finally did. Crew quarters are cleared out, boarded up, and overrun with weeds; the gates to the compound are secured by a heavy Master lock; and the stain and trim on the buildings (our hard work) is fading, peeling, and falling to the ground. "I went over there the other day. It's like a ghost town now," Nicholas told me with an elegiac voice. "And I felt, you know, *sad*. How come they *done* this, man? . . . I parked out to the side, and I was looking. *Damn*. I could see the engines parked there, you know, I was imagining it. You know, where people were and stuff like that. Like Thurman driving up and everybody scattering!" He laughed. "Then I slowly drove out of there. Looked back once, *damn*. . . . I looked back once and took off." Rumors compete as to what will be done with the place. Some crewmembers claim it will be used as a Boy Scout camp; others say Elk River will station inmate firefighters. And a few grind their teeth at another possibility: that the Forest Service will sell the station to Hutchinson, the millionaire, who would turn our solace from city dwellers into a solace for city dwellers. What is certain is that Elk River, as we knew it, is gone. It lives on only in the memory of those firefighters who slept in its quarters, cut its grass, washed its hose, stained its buildings, drove its engines, and, on its trails, took their first steps out into real life.

Glossary

Anchor point: Strategic location, preferably a natural barrier to fire, where a fireline can begin; chosen so handcrews are not flanked by fire.

Area of response (AOR): Forest district over which a firecrew is responsible.

Backburn: A fire purposely set in unburned fuel between the fireline and the active fire. Also called a burnout.

Black, the: Areas burned by wildfire. Sometimes designated as safety zones, as in "Should the fire jump the line, escape into the black."

Blowup: A sudden and dramatic increase in fire intensity, often accompanied by violent convection.

Bucket drop: Dumping of water or retardant from a bucket slung under on a helicopter.

Burnout: See Backburn.

Chain: Unit of linear measurement equal to sixty-six feet, usually measured in paces.

Chase truck: Pickup truck that follows a fire engine.

Combi: Short for "combination tool." A scraping tool used for digging line that joins a shovel's head with a narrow pick on a swiveling iron joint.

Control burn: See Prescribed burn.

Cramer fire: Wildfire in Idaho's Salmon-Challis National Forest; it claimed the lives of two firefighters in 2003.

Crown fire: Intense fire where flames burn through the tops of trees.

Deployment: Covering oneself with a fire shelter.

Direct line: Fireline dug directly in front of a moving wildfire. Also called a hot line.

Dispatcher: Person who receives smoke and fire reports and attempts to distribute resources and crews where needed.

Dog hair thicket: Overgrown and concentrated cluster of saplings.

Drip torch: Metal canister that drips an on-fire mixture of diesel fuel and gasoline onto vegetation. Used by firefighters during burnouts.

Duff: Partly decayed organic matter on the forest floor below the top layer of newly fallen vegetation.

Engine: Fire engine that can distribute water and foam.

Engine crews: Wildland firefighting crews who staff an engine.

Engine operator: Lower-level supervisor in charge of a fire engine and its crew.

Entrapment: A situation where firefighters are surrounded or overrun by fire and often are forced to deploy fire shelters.

Escape route: Designated path leading to a safety zone; a route that firefighters plan to take should a hazardous situation arise.

Fireline: Barrier of mineral soil constructed to impede and corral an advancing wildfire. Often called a handline if it is dug with hand tools.

Fire pack: Backpack worn by firefighters that stores equipment such as headlamps, MREs, fusees, flagging, and a fire shelter. Also called initial attack (IA) pack.

Fire shelter: Thin-layered aluminized tent designed to deflect radiant heat, into which firefighters escape during an entrapment.

Flagging: Bright plastic tape used to mark roads or signal hazards.

Fuel moisture: Amount of moisture in live and dead fuels, which allows firefighters to predict fire behavior.

Fusee: Flare used to ignite fuel during burnouts.

Green, the: Unburned vegetation.

Handline: See Fireline.

Head of fire: The side of the fire spreading at the fastest rate.

Heavies: Heavy fuels such as downed trees.

Helispot: A makeshift landing spot for helicopters.

Helitack: Wildland firefighting crew assigned to a helicopter.

Helitorch: Drip torch attached to a helicopter used to dispense large amounts of fire during prescribed burns or burnouts.

Hosepack: Backpack stuffed with a trunk line and a lateral hose and nozzle that can be quickly extracted.

Hotshots: Elite wildland firefighters deployed primarily in initial attack (IA) positions throughout North America.

Hotspot: Pocket of heat, usually concentrated in root systems, that has the potential to reignite a fire.

Incident commander (IC): Supervisor responsible for overseeing all operations during critical incidents.

Indirect line: Anticipatory fireline constructed a safe distance from an active fire.

Initial attack (IA): Suppressive actions that firefighters take on arriving at a wildfire.

Ladder fuels: Vegetation near the ground, such as low-hanging branches or tall shrubs, that allows fire to climb into the crowns of trees.

Lateral: Smaller hose, usually connected to a trunk line, that trails into the fire to emit water and foam.

LCES: Acronym for "lookouts, communication, escape routes, safety zones."

Light fuels: Fuels that have a fast rate of ignition and spread, such as plain grass and pine needles. Also called fine fuels.

Mann Gulch: Site of a wildfire in Montana's Helena National Forest; it killed a dozen smokejumpers in 1949.

Meals ready to eat (MRE): Packages of dehydrated food designed around meal themes.

Nomex: Brand name of flame-resistant fiber used to make fire pants and shirts.

Overhead: Top-level supervisors who direct firefighting operations.

Personal protective equipment (PPE): Firefighters' protective gear, including Vibram-soled boots, fire pants and shirts, leather gloves, hard hat, and fire shelter.

Plume-dominated fire: Powerful fire driven not by general wind currents but by currents created by the convection of the smoke column.

Prescribed burn: Wildfire purposely ignited to clear out overgrown forest areas or to reduce fuel. Also called a control burn.

Psi: Pounds per square inch, a unit used to measure water pressure.

PT: Physical training.

Pulaski: Furrowing tool with the head of an ax melded with an adze trenching blade. Usually the lead tool during line construction.

Reburn: Fire previously considered contained and controlled that reignites.

RH: Relative humidity.

Rodeo-Chediski fire: Fire that burned through northern Arizona in 2002, claiming over half a million acres and over four hundred homes. Also called the Rodeo-Chediski complex (meaning the joining of two fires).

Safety zone: Predesignated area, such as a large meadow or the black, selected for escape from fire.

Sawyer: Firefighter who uses a chain saw to fell trees and to trim limbs. Also called a faller or cutter.

SCBA: Acronym for "self-contained breathing apparatus," a structural firefighter's oxygen tank.

Sling psychrometer: A device used to obtain temperature and relative humidity readings. It consists of a pair of thermometers attached to a mount with a thin chain and is carried in a belt weather kit.

Slurry bomber: Large plane used to drop fire retardant (slurry) on wildfires. Also called an air tanker.

Smokejumper: Firefighter who reaches a wildfire by skydiving.

Snag: Dead tree that remains standing.

South Canyon fire: One of the deadliest American fires in recent years, ignited by lightning seven miles west of Glenwood Springs, Colorado; it killed fourteen firefighters on July 2, 1994. Also known as the Storm King fire.

Spot fire (spot): Fire beyond the perimeter of the main fire that is ignited by embers or debris tossed up by the main fire.

Structural firefighter: Firefighter located in a populated area charged with extinguishing building fires and responding to emergency calls.

Thirtymile fire: Fire that burned north of Winthrop, Washington; it killed four firefighters in 2001.

Torching: Complete engulfment of a tree or stand of trees, where the fire proceeds from the ground to the crown.

Trunk line: Large hose that encircles the periphery of fires, to which lateral lines are connected.

Yellow: Long-sleeved yellow fire shirt made out of flame-resistant material.

Notes

INTRODUCTION

1. I did not disguise names of firefighters or places not associated with Elk River. Rick Lupe, for example, is not a pseudonym. The promise of confidentiality was necessary for this research, for reasons I elaborate on in the appendix. However, this promise came with a price: it made it impossible for me to write about Nora, the only woman on the Elk River crew. I wrestled with this dilemma for months before coming to the conclusion that, rather than provide information about Nora that I thought was nonthreatening, information she might not see in the same light, all of Nora's interactions and conversations had to be excluded from the book. While reconsidering this decision near the end of this project, I talked with Nora about my decision. She agreed with—and was relieved greatly by—this decision. I have respected her wishes and have not written about her here.

2. National Wildfire Coordinating Group's Safety and Health Working Team, *Safety Gram for 2003* (Boise, ID: National Interagency Fire Center, 2003).

3. Further, because wildland firefighting agencies classify their workers by occupational series clusters ("forestry technicians"), not by job description ("firefighter"), it is impossible to calculate fatality rates. In chapter 6 I use data from the Bureau of Labor Statistics and the National Fire Protection Agency to estimate the fatality and injury rates of firefighters, comparing them with those of other dangerous professions.

For analyses of firefighting fatalities, see U.S. Department of Agriculture, *Wildland Firefighter Entrapments 1976 to 1999* (Missoula, MT: Forest Service Technology and Development Program, 2000); U.S. Department of Agriculture, *Wildland Fire Fatalities in the United States: 1990 to 1998* (Missoula, MT: Forest Service Technology and Development Program, 1999); National Fire Protection Association, *Special Analysis: U.S. Firefighter Fatalities as a Result of Wildland Fires, 1987–1996* (Quincy, MA: Fire Analysis and Research Division, 1998); and National Wildfire Coordinating Group, *Historical Wildland*

Firefighter Fatalities, 1910–1996 (Washington, DC: Department of the Interior and National Association of State Foresters, 1997).

4. Of course, many fire scientists and field engineers would disagree. See U.S. Department of Agriculture, *Surviving Fire Entrapments: Comparing Conditions Inside Vehicles and Fire Shelters* (Missoula, MT: United States Department of Agriculture Forest Service Technology and Development Program, 1997).

5. Drawing on the early works of Émile Durkheim and Marcel Mauss, but especially psychoanalytic theorists such as Gaston Bachelard, Bourdieu's sociology advocates that the analyst perform an epistemological break with all folk constructions and "spontaneous" knowledge in order to capture the true nature of social relations. See Pierre Bourdieu, Jean-Claude Chamboredon, and Jean-Claude Passeron in *The Craft of Sociology: Epistemological Preliminaries* (New York: Walter de Gruyter, 1991 [1968]).

6. Norman Maclean, *Young Men and Fire* (Chicago: University of Chicago Press, 1992); John Maclean, *Fire on the Mountain: The True Story of the South Canyon Fire* (New York: William Morrow, 1999).

7. For example, Karl E. Weick, "The Collapse of Sensemaking in Organizations: The Mann Gulch Disaster," *Administrative Science Quarterly* 38 (1993): 628–52; Diane Vaughan, "Targets for Firefighting Safety: Lessons from the Challenger Tragedy," *Wildfire* 6 (1997): 29–40; Jon Driessen, *Crew Cohesion, Wildland Fire Transition and Fatalities* (Missoula, MT: U.S. Department of Agriculture Forest Service Technology and Development Program, 2002); Jon Driessen, Linda Outka-Perkins, and Leslie Anderson, "Recommended Focus of Future Work on Entrapment Avoidance" (Missoula, MT: U.S. Department of Agriculture Forest Service Technology and Development Program, unpublished working document, 2002).

8. U.S. Department of Agriculture, *Wildland Firefighter Entrapments 1976 to 1999*.

9. Herbert Kaufman, *The Forest Ranger: A Study in Administrative Behavior* (Baltimore: Johns Hopkins Press, 1960), 237.

10. For sociological accounts, see Georg Simmel, "The Adventurer," in *Georg Simmel, 1858–1918,* ed. Kurt Wolff (Columbus: Ohio State University Press, 1959 [1911]), and Stephen Lyng, "Edgework: A Social-Psychological Analysis of Voluntary Risk-Taking," *American Journal of Sociology* 95 (1990): 851–86. For economic models, see Paul Slovic, *The Perception of Risk* (London: Earthscan, 2000), and Kip Viscusi and Wesley Magat, *Learning about Risk: Consumer and Worker Response to Hazard Information* (Cambridge, MA: Harvard University Press, 1987). For psychological theories, see Marvin Zuckerman, *Behavioral Expression and Biosocial Bases of Sensation Seeking* (Cambridge: Cambridge University Press, 1994), and Rüdiger Trimpop, *The Psychology of Risk Taking Behavior,* Advances in Psychology, vol. 107 (Amsterdam: North-Holland, 1994).

11. Erving Goffman, *Interaction Ritual: Essays on Face-to-Face Behavior* (Garden City, NY: Anchor Books, 1967), 185.

12. Ibid., 238; emphasis mine.

13. On noticing that I have described Goffman's essay as splitting the world into two "types of people," instead of, say, two types of structured situations, or interactional settings, someone is sure to quote me these words: "Not, then, men and their moments. Rather moments and their men." But Goffman also pointed out that "it is individual actors who contribute the ultimate materials" of the "syntactical relations" that constitute society. My purpose here is not to comment on Goffman's oeuvre but to home in on the essay at hand, "Where the Action Is," an essay that is concerned just as much (and, I would argue, even more) with the action seeker, in a Simmelian mode, as with situations of action. See Goffman, *Interaction Ritual,* 2–3.

14. Ibid., 268.

15. I should point out that Goffman was indeed talking about risk to one's health as well as risk to one's image. Although elsewhere Goffman quipped that life "may not be much of a gamble but interaction is," in the essay of interest here, he is very much interested in those times when life is a gamble, when facework and edgework are locked in a symbiotic relationship. Hence Goffman conflates impression management with the management of "risks" in the strictest sense of the term. The quotation above comes from Goffman's first book, *The Presentation of Self in Everyday Life* (Garden City, NY: Anchor Books, 1959), 243.

16. Pierre Bourdieu, *Masculine Domination* (Stanford, CA: Stanford University Press, 2001), 51.

17. Michael Kimmel, "Masculinity as Homophobia: Fear, Shame, and Silence in the Construction of Gender Identity," in *Theorizing Masculinities,* ed. Harry Broad and Michael Kaufman (Thousand Oaks, CA: Sage, 1994), 129.

18. Goffman, *Interaction Ritual,* 257.

19. By professional risk taking, I mean socially acceptable collective behavior that poses an immediate and serious threat to the health of individuals acting within the structure of a bureaucratic organization. In theory, the professional risk taker works to make her or his activity safer by employing knowledge gained through training and using specialized equipment.

20. The quotation is drawn from the opening page of Lord Morgan's book *The Anatomy of Courage* (Boston: Houghton Mifflin, 1967 [1945]). For more on the military trait of overconfidence and "positive illusions," see Dominic Johnson, *Overconfidence and War: The Havoc and Glory of Positive Illusions* (Cambridge, MA: Harvard University Press, 2004); Shelley Taylor and Peter Gollwitzer, "The Effects of Mindset on Positive Illusions," *Journal of Personality and Social Psychology* 69 (1995): 213–26; and William Goode, *The Celebration of Heroes: Prestige as a Social Control System* (Berkeley and Los Angeles: University of California Press, 1978).

21. See Robert Reiner's books, *The Blue-Coated Worker* (Cambridge: Cambridge University Press, 1978) and *The Politics of the Police* (Sussex: Wheatsheaf Books, 1985), as well as A. Daniel Yarmey, *Understanding Police and Police Work: Psychological Issues* (New York: New York University Press, 1990), and Peter Manning, *Police Work: The Social Organization of Policing* (Cambridge: MIT Press, 1977).

22. Carol Chetkovich, *Real Heat: Gender and Race in the Urban Fire Service* (New Brunswick, NJ: Rutgers University Press, 1997), 18. Also see Dennis Smith, *Report from Engine Co. 82* (New York: Saturday Review Press, 1972); Michael Perry, *Population 485: Meeting Your Neighbors One Siren at a Time* (New York: HarperCollins, 2003); and Louise Wagenknecht, "Pride and Glory of Firefighting Is Hard to Resist," in *Wildfire: A Reader,* ed. Alianor True (Washington, DC: Island Press, 1996), 196–99.

23. See Jack Haas's articles, "Learning Real Feelings: A Study of High Steel Ironworkers' Reactions to Fear and Danger," *Sociology of Work and Occupations* 4 (1977): 147–70, and "Binging: Emotional Control among High Steel Ironworkers," *American Behavioral Scientist* 16 (1972): 27–34.

24. Alvin Gouldner, *Patterns of Industrial Bureaucracy: A Case Study of Modern Factory Administration* (New York: Macmillan, 1954); John Fitzpatrick, "Adapting to Danger: A Participant Observation Study of an Underground Mine," *Sociology of Work and Occupations* 7 (1980): 131–58.

25. Tom Dwyer, *Life and Death at Work: Workplace Accidents as a Case of Socially Produced Error* (New York: Plenum, 1991); Wilfrid Denis, "Causes of Health and Safety Hazards in Canadian Agriculture," *International Journal of Health Services* 18 (1988): 419–36; Kirsten

Paap, "Masculinity under Construction: Gender, Class, and Race in the Construction Industry" (Madison: University of Wisconsin–Madison, PhD diss., 1999).

26. This percentage is based on data procured from the Office of Personnel Management's document "Demographic Profile of the Federal Workforce Publication" from 2004. This percentage breakdown by gender is not completely accurate owing to the way the U.S. Forest Service categorizes its workers. Firefighters may be classified under three occupational series clusters, grouped by numbers: 401 (general management, supervisors), 460 (professional forestry workers, those with a college degree in forestry), and 462 (forestry technicians). Forestry technicians make up the bulk of the wildland firefighting force; however, employees working in the timber and wildlife sectors of the Forest Service are also grouped in this category. Within this occupational category, there were a total of 17,166 workers in 2004, of whom 13,728 were men, approximately 80 percent. (An equitable ratio is observed in the professional forestry workers [series 460]: 2,467 men out of 3,187 total workers, approximately 77 percent.) This is the best estimate the data will permit me to make, but since there most likely are variations across gender in terms of occupational duties and placement within this category, this number is imprecise. When I compare my estimate with the one advanced by Women in the Fire Service, a nonprofit organization committed to collecting data on women firefighters—namely, that less than 3 percent of structural firefighting positions are staffed by women—I am inclined to believe my estimate is inflated.

27. Though see Dorothy Nelkin and Michael Brown, *Workers at Risk: Voices from the Workplace* (Chicago: University of Chicago Press, 1984).

28. Thus many social psychologists, following Goffman, have overlooked processes of organizational socialization, explaining risky behavior by relying on notions of masculine performativity carried out in interactional contexts. And though many sociologists of high-risk organizations have paid attention to such processes, they have been more concerned with how organizations succeed or fail than with how they socialize workers to risk.

There are some important exceptions to this rule, including Bridget Hutter's book on railroad workers in the United Kingdom, *Regulation and Risk: Occupational Health and Safety on the Railways* (New York: Oxford University Press, 2001), and Diane Vaughan's book on the organizational culture of NASA, *The "Challenger" Launch Decision: Risky Technology, Culture, and Deviance at NASA* (Chicago: University of Chicago Press, 1996). In chapter 4 I begin considering the literature on high-risk organizations.

29. Mary Douglas, *Risk Acceptability according to the Social Sciences* (London: Routledge and Kegan Paul, 1986), 83.

30. Here I am not conflating "risk" as dangerous activity with "risk" as uncertainty (where risk becomes analogous to an error term); rather, I am referring to theorists who apply rational-choice models to explain, for instance, how individuals react to natural disasters, as Slovic does in *The Perception of Risk,* or why individuals assault others, as Robert Hoffmann does in "Mixed Strategies in the Mugging Game," *Rationality and Society* 13 (2001): 205–12.

31. For example, Stephen Lyng, ed., *Edgework: The Sociology of Risk-Taking* (New York: Routledge, 2004); Jennifer Lois, *Heroic Efforts: The Emotional Culture of Search and Rescue Volunteers* (New York: New York University Press, 2003).

32. Goffman, *Interaction Ritual,* 238.

33. Douglas, *Risk Acceptability.*

34. Pierre Bourdieu and Loïc Wacquant, *An Invitation to Reflexive Sociology* (Chicago: University of Chicago Press, 1992), 123. To Bourdieu, the foundational reason behind this error is the conflicting temporal existences of the scholar and her subject. The scholar

exists in a state of leisure (*skole*). She has the luxury to reason about others, to freeze time, and to assume people have the leisure to reason. On the other hand, the actor is in constant motion. She does not have the time to think about each action, to ascribe it meaning, and to place it in an equation. In *The Logic of Practice* (Stanford, CA: Stanford University Press, 1990 [1980]), Bourdieu claims that these different temporal outlooks produce "the antinomy between the time of science and the time of action, which tends to destroy practice by imposing on it the intemporal time of science" (81).

35. See Loïc Wacquant's entry "Habitus" in Jens Beckert and Milan Zafirovski, eds., *International Encyclopedia of Economic Sociology* (London: Routledge, 2005), 315–19.

36. Pierre Bourdieu, *Pascalian Meditations* (Stanford, CA: Stanford University Press, 2000), 164–67.

37. Ibid., 169.

CHAPTER ONE: COUNTRY MASCULINITY

1. Several books on firefighters detail a process of sons' following in their fathers' footsteps. See Steve Delsohn, *The Fire Inside: Firefighters Talk about Their Lives* (New York: HarperCollins, 1996), and Douglas Gantenbein, *A Season of Fire: Four Months on the Firelines in the American West* (New York: Jeremy Tarcher and Penguin, 2003).

2. This did not seem to affect how well George and Steve fit in at Elk River. In fact, although George's and Steve's fathers had more education than many other crewmembers' parents, their families did not differ substantially along other lines, including income and lifestyles. This begs the question: Should George and Steve be identified as "middle class," and should their coworkers be identified as "working class"? I answer in the negative. Throughout this book, I conceptualize class as something that cannot be defined strictly by one's relation to the market, job title, or income; in my view, influenced by Max Weber's and Pierre Bourdieu's writings, class relations must be conceptualized as different styles of life. In *Distinction: A Social Critique of the Judgment of Taste* (Cambridge, MA: Harvard University Press, 1984 [1979]), Bourdieu argues that class distinctions cannot be reduced to measures of earning or types of occupations, for they have an embodied (habitual) existence manifest in tacit consumption patterns, culinary preferences, musical predilections, bodily movements, fashion sense, architectural tastes, and so forth. As Rogers Brubaker observes, paraphrasing Bourdieu, "Class divisions are defined not by differing relations to the means of production, but by differing conditions of existence, differing systems of dispositions produced by differential conditioning, and differing endowments of power or capital." In this light, all of my crewmembers can be thought of as coming from similar class backgrounds. See Rogers Brubaker, "Rethinking Classical Theory: The Sociological Vision of Pierre Bourdieu," *Theory and Society* 14 (1985): 761. Also see Erik Olin Wright, ed., *Approaches to Class Analysis* (New York: Cambridge University Press, 2005), and Elliot Weininger, "Class and Causation in Bourdieu," *Current Perspectives in Social Theory* 21 (2002): 49–114.

3. For a thorough explication of the important role personal contacts play in connecting individuals with jobs, see Mark Granovetter's classic study *Getting a Job: A Study of Contacts and Careers,* 2nd ed. (Chicago: University of Chicago Press, 1995 [1974]). This book focuses on professional, technical, and managerial occupations. For studies that demonstrate how blue-collar workers rely on personal contacts when locating jobs, see Peter Marsden and Karen Campbell, "Recruitment and Selection Processes: The Organization Side of Job Searches," in *Social Mobility and Social Structure,* ed. Ronald Breiger (New York: Cambridge University Press, 1990), 59–79, and Harold Sheppard and A. Harvey Belitsky, *The Job*

Hunt: Job-Seeking Behavior of Unemployed Workers in a Local Economy (Baltimore: Johns Hopkins Press, 1966).

4. Mark Tebeau, *Eating Smoke: Fire in Urban America, 1800–1950* (Baltimore: Johns Hopkins University Press, 2003); Terry Golway, *So Others Might Live: A History of New York's Bravest, The FDNY from 1700 to the Present* (New York: Basic Books, 2002).

5. With respect to age, gender, and class characteristics, the Elk River Firecrew is fairly representative of other wildland firefighting crews, in particular, and other workforces staffing high-risk organizations, in general. See U.S. Office of Personnel Management, *Demographic Profile of the Federal Workforce Publication* (Washington, DC: Office of Personnel Management, 2004); Bureau of Labor Statistics, *Household Data Survey* (Washington, DC: Bureau of Labor Statistics, 2005).

6. Of course, there are many young men who grow up in rural working-class America and do not become wildland firefighters. Many of my crewmembers' peers who lived down the block now earn a paycheck repairing cars, stocking shelves, patrolling prison yards, or operating warehouse forklifts. How do my crewmembers differ from their peers? I did not interview crewmembers' counterparts who work in other professions, and accordingly I cannot address this question with any empirical certainty. However, I can identify three characteristics most of my crewmembers possess that may set them apart from their peers. Besides sharing a country-masculine upbringing, most crewmembers had fathers who were actively invested in cultivating within them "country competence," a phrase I explore later in this chapter; they had interpersonal connections to the Forest Service; and they developed an infatuation with fire early in life. (More than one crewmember set his backyard on fire as a child, a point I take up in chapter 2.) Again, to provide these characteristics some causal significance, I would have to widen my sample, interview my crewmembers' counterparts in other professions, and determine if my crewmembers possess certain characteristic that set them apart. That is, to speak technically, I would have to develop a research model that avoids selecting on the dependent variable. But the purpose of this chapter is not to determine the important forces that cause some working-class rural men and not others to join firecrews; rather, it aims to describe some key features many of my crewmembers share that help explain why they *gravitate* toward the universe of wildland firefighting and, more important for the overarching aims of this book, to show how crewmembers' childhood and adolescent experiences helped them *acclimate* to the demands of wildland firefighting as well as to the organizational common sense of the Forest Service. In other words, the question pursued in this chapter is not so much Why do they come while others do not? as Where do they come from, and what do they bring with them?

7. Maclean, *Young Men and Fire,* 26.

8. Many claim that the distinction between rural and urban lifestyles is more often in individuals' minds than in the actual patterns of social life. On this idea and on what might be called "the culture of the country" or "rural identity," see Michael Bell's books, *Childerley: Nature and Morality in a Country Village* (Chicago: University of Chicago Press, 1995), and *Farming for Us All: Practical Agriculture and the Cultivation of Sustainability* (University Park: Pennsylvania State University Press, 2004).

9. Those going to college, like Kris and Tank, view their approaching careers with contradictory feelings of excitement and dread. They are eager to begin, but they are not looking forward to leaving the Forest Service to work indoors. Perhaps this is why Tank undertook a major that blends analytical and creative skills with manual labor—architecture—and why Kris remains dissatisfied with his choice of history as a field of study.

10. See Michèle Lamont, *The Dignity of Working Men: Morality and the Boundaries of Race, Class, and Immigration* (Cambridge, MA: Russell Sage Foundation and Harvard University

Press, 2000); David Collinson, *Managing the Shopfloor: Subjectivity, Masculinity, and Workplace Culture* (New York: Walter de Gruyter, 1992); and Paul Willis's classic, *Learning to Labour: How Working Class Kids Get Working Class Jobs* (Farnborough, UK: Saxon House, 1977).

11. Claude Lévi-Strauss, *The Savage Mind* (Chicago: University of Chicago Press, 1966).

12. Most social theorists who investigate the role cultural binaries play in shaping social life take their inspiration from Émile Durkheim's work on classification, especially *The Elementary Forms of the Religious Life* (New York: Free Press, (1995 [1912]) and (with his nephew, Marcel Mauss) *Primitive Classification* (Chicago: University of Chicago Press, 1963 [1903]). Claude Lévi-Strauss's best explication of binary systems of differentiation, "practico-theoretical logics," he called them, is found in *The Savage Mind.* Bourdieu, a great admirer and grinding critic of Lévi-Strauss, maintained a keen interest in the reproduction and function of cultural binaries throughout his oeuvre. His most careful and ethnographically informed treatment of this subject is found in *The Logic of Practice,* especially 143–283. Finally, Jeffrey Alexander has done much to advance our understanding of how symbolic sets might operate in American politics: see Jeffrey Alexander and Philip Smith, "The Discourse of American Civil Society: A New Proposal for Cultural Studies," *Theory and Society* 22 (1993): 151–207, as well as Alexander, "Citizen and Enemy as Symbolic Classification: On the Polarizing Discourse of Civil Society," in *Cultivating Differences: Symbolic Boundaries and the Making of Inequality,* ed. Michèle Lamont and Marcel Fournier (Chicago: University of Chicago Press, 1992), 289–308. These theorists have very different renderings of the nature and function of symbolic binaries, and within the sociology of culture there are ongoing rancorous debates around precisely this issue. But the purpose of this book is not to get lost in these debates; rather, my aim is to the marshal the conceptual power of sociology to understand what makes firefighters tick or, more specifically, what makes them risk. The symbolic binary pitting country people against city people is of central importance to this task.

13. It turns out Clarence is right: rural America is indeed where the military finds its soldiers. According to a recent study, a significantly disproportionate number of soldiers who died in the Iraq War came from rural communities; see Robert Cushing and Bill Bishop, "The Rural War," *New York Times,* July 20, 2005. And for an analysis of how military recruitment strategies in the United Kingdom tap into visions of "protecting the countryside" and the culture of the country, see Rachel Woodward, "Warrior Heroes and Little Green Men: Soldiers, Military Training, and the Construction of Rural Masculinities," *Rural Sociology* 65 (2000): 640–58.

14. Although they self-identify as "country boys," some of my crewmembers make sure to distance themselves from "really backwoods folk." Consider Diego's comments: "I'm not a city boy, you know, people that lived in the city their whole life. They don't know anything out of the city. Like, certain people, not out here. Out here, everybody out here knows the outdoors shit, but I'm not completely a country boy where I live out in the backyard, drinking and making moonshine and shit. I don't know, I would describe myself not in the middle, but closer to a country boy than a city boy." "Country folk" have long been depicted as stupid in the mainstream media, and my crewmembers reasonably are hesitant to identify with such parochial and backward caricatures. For discussions of the creation of the category "white trash" in America and of stereotypes targeting poor rural people, see Matt Wray and Annalee Newitz, eds., *White Trash: Race and Class in America* (New York: Routledge, 1996).

15. At least this is what Frédéric Moreau believed when he was forced to choose between a stable and safe life in the country with his mother and a chancy life of dreams and art in the city (Paris, to be exact) with his "grand amour," Marie Arnoux. See Gustave Flaubert, *A Sentimental Education* (New York: Oxford University Press, 1989 [1869]), 101.

16. After all, didn't Alvin Gouldner, in the introductory pages of *The Coming Crisis of Western Sociology* (New York: Basic Books, 1970), a classic in the field, warn radical social thinkers not to succumb to "one of the most vulgar currents of American culture: to its *small-town,* Babbitt-like anti-intellectualism and know-nothingism" (4–5; emphasis mine)?

17. In the appendix I discuss the importance of reflexivity as well as how my dual identity (half sociologist/half firefighter) affected my fieldwork.

18. Cf. Lamont, *Dignity of Working Men.*

19. See Max Weber, "Class, Status, Party," in *From Max Weber: Essays in Sociology,* ed. H. H. Gerth and C. Wright Mills (New York: Oxford University Press), 180–95.

20. Although many of my crewmembers share consumption patterns, assumptions about the world, and lifestyle choices, there is also a large amount of variation within the crew. J.J., for example, prefers hip-hop to country music; Diego would rather play "Final Fantasy" video games or chess after work than go fishing; Scott does not drink beer at all; Tank does not go hunting. However, these intercrew variations do not refute the notion that my crewmembers are bound together by a country-masculine lifestyle; rather, they suggest that country masculinity, like all variants of masculinity, takes on an ideal-typical existence that is more than the sum of its parts (an existence sui generis, as Durkheim would say). It entails requirements, styles, and principles that no self-described country boy fully embodies. For more on this point, see Robert Connell, *Gender and Power* (Stanford, CA: Stanford University Press, 1987).

21. One might wonder why crewmembers did not associate inner-city crime with racial groups. Three potential answers spring to mind. First, and most simply, perhaps they did not even think of such an association. Second, they may have viewed racial stereotyping as a taboo subject at Elk River because it is such a racially diverse space. Third, they may have been uncomfortable admitting prejudice to me in particular, since I had developed a reputation at Elk River as one who does not take racist, sexist, or homophobic comments lightly (more on this in the appendix).

22. See Judy Addelston and Michael Stirratt, "The Last Bastion of Masculinity: Gender Politics at the Citadel," in *Masculinities in Organizations,* ed. Cliff Cheng (Thousand Oaks, CA: Sage, 1996), 54–76; Anastasia Prokos and Irene Padavic, "'There Oughtta Be a Law Against Bitches': Masculinity Lessons in Police Academy Training," *Gender, Work, and Organization* 9 (2002): 439–59; and Janice Yoder and Patricia Aniakudo, "'Outsider Within' the Firehouse: Subordination and Difference in the Social Interactions of African American Women Firefighters," *Gender and Society* 11 (1997): 324–41.

23. Classic studies on women entering male professions include Cynthia Cockburn's books, *Brothers: Male Dominance and Technological Change* (London: Pluto Press, 1983) and *Machinery of Dominance: Women, Men, and Technical Know-How* (London: Pluto Press, 1985), as well as Elizabeth Moss Kanter's vivid ethnography *Men and Women of the Corporation* (New York: Basic Books, 1977). More recently, Cynthia Fuchs Epstein has written on the creation and reproduction of gendered boundaries in the workplace; see her article "Workplace Boundaries: Conceptions and Creations," *Social Research* 56 (1989): 571–90, and her chapter "Tinkerbells and Pinups: The Construction and Reconstruction of Gender Boundaries at Work," in Lamont and Fournier, *Cultivating Differences,* 232–56.

24. Aileen Ballantyne, "Council Clash on Baptism of Fire Women: Reinstatement of London Fireman Leads to Political Row," *Manchester Guardian,* February 1, 1985.

25. Women in the Fire Service, *Sexual Harassment: Women Firefighters' Experiences* (Madison, WI: Women in the Fire Service, 1996). For a study of the patriarchal nature of military culture, see Carol Burke, *Camp All-American, Hanoi Jane, and the High-and-Tight: Gender, Folklore, and Changing Military Culture* (Boston: Beacon, 2004).

26. Kris believed that if Elk River were not so isolated, then its crew's comments would not be so gauche: "If more women were present, I think the environment would be different. Looking at Jameson [a crew stationed within the town of Jameson, not in an isolated area of the forest], who always had more women on the crew, well, judging from just the little work that I've done with them, it's a different environment. It's not the sexist jokes. It's not the references. It's not always the same game over and over and over. So, I think a lot of it has to do with situation." For investigations and reflections on the effects that extremely isolated environments have on human (especially male) behavior, see Jeffrey Johnson, James Boster, and Lawrence Palinkas, "Social Roles and the Evolution of Networks in Isolated and Extreme Environments," *Journal of Mathematical Sociology* 27 (2003): 89–121, and Lawrence Palinkas, E. K. Eric Gunderson, Albert Holland, Christopher Miller, and Jeffrey Johnson, "Predictors of Behavior and Performance in Extreme Environments: The Antarctic Space Analogue Program," *Aviation, Space, and Environmental Medicine* 71 (2000): 619–25.

27. The Maltese cross has been adopted by urban fire departments in the United States and Australia. The symbol has its roots in the Crusades, when the Knights of St. John first encountered fire as a weapon of warfare at the hands of the Saracens, who hurled glass containers of naphtha (a highly flammable liquid) and flaming torches on the knights from high city walls. The Knights of St. John, or so the legend goes, accordingly became the world's first firefighters. For their efforts to best the Saracens, those knights who were not burned alive in the siege were awarded a medal of honor by other crusaders, one that became known as the Maltese Cross (named after the island of Malta, in the Mediterranean Sea, where the Knights of St. John lived). For present-day firefighters the cross stands for honor and protection and marks one's induction into a sacrificial brotherhood.

28. Bourdieu, *Logic of Practice*, 73.

29. See Richard Sennett and Jonathon Cobb, *The Hidden Injuries of Class* (New York: Vintage, 1972); David Halle, *America's Working Man: Work, Home, and Politics among Blue-Collar Property Owners* (Chicago: University of Chicago Press, 1984); Lillian Rubin, *Families on the Faultline: America's Working Class Speaks about the Family, the Economy, Race, and Ethnicity* (New York: HarperCollins, 1994); Lamont, *Dignity of Working Men*.

30. I borrow this second conceptual pairing from Charles Tilly's *The Vendée* (Cambridge, MA: Harvard University Press, 1964), 50.

31. Some may claim this is not because Vince had a distinctly different upbringing than his crewmembers but because he simply is incompetent. "In every organization," the critic might say, "there is somebody who just does not get it, who cannot perform as well as his colleagues." But this criticism calls for a less rigorous socioanalysis; it suggests we stop with the observation of incompetence and not trouble ourselves with explaining it. I believe it is much more than an unhappy coincidence that Vince both is not as adept at the formal and informal practices of firefighting as his crewmembers, *even after seven years of experience,* and is the product of a different (noncountry) upbringing. I believe the latter fact helps to explain the former.

32. Cf. Paul Rabinow, *Reflections on Fieldwork in Morocco* (Berkeley and Los Angeles: University of California Press, 1977), especially his notion of "a doubling of consciousness."

33. Neither did I. My father, a preacher, was never good with his hands, and I never enrolled in high school vocational courses such as auto shop or woodworking. I was tracked in accelerated academic classes. However, I did play high school sports (football and basketball). In addition, I grew up hiking, camping, and fishing with the Boy Scouts, and I acquired an appreciation for hunting as an adolescent. Although Vince and I shared an

ignorance of automobiles, I entered Elk River with more country-masculine capital than he did, and I was more at home in homosocial male environments.

34. Douglas Harper, *Working Knowledge: Skill and Community in a Small Shop* (Chicago: University of Chicago Press, 1987).

CHAPTER TWO: THE SANCTUARY OF THE FOREST

1. See Lewis Coser, *Greedy Institutions: Patterns of Undivided Commitment* (New York: Free Press, 1974). Not all U.S. Forest Service compounds are as isolated as Elk River; many are in small towns. For example, Elk River's sister firecrew, the Jameson squad, is in Jameson, an unincorporated town of roughly 3,800. (Recall that Jameson is a pseudonym.) Further, most of the time wildland firefighters are not "on call" twenty-four hours a day as are structural firefighters. In my four years at Elk River, on only one occasion was the crew summoned to a fire in the Wannokee Forest after having closed the station and retired to crew quarters; we had been released at 5:00 and a helicopter pilot spotted the fire less than thirty minutes later. However, I have witnessed several occasions when crewmembers were summoned to an off-district assignment during the night or even on their day off. On these occasions the engine crew was "made available"; that is, it voluntarily went on call for a short time by registering through a national dispatch center. At Elk River, this occurred only after monsoon rains fell on the Wannokee Forest and drowned the fire season.

Although Elk River is a very isolated encampment, it should not be thought of as a "total institution," a term that has been used hundreds of times since Erving Goffman first coined it in *Asylums: Essays on the Social Situation of Mental Patients and Other Inmates* (Garden City, NY: Anchor Books, 1961). At crew quarters, crewmembers are bound by very few rules; they do not come under serious supervision, and generally they are not responsible for responding to smoke calls once the workday ends. When a lookout spots a smoke near the end of the workday but neither helicopter pilots nor firefighters in engines can locate the fire, the standard protocol is to let the fire burn and smolder through the night and to meet at the station early the following morning in hopes that the lookout can spot the smoke column again. And as long as crewmembers show up on time and ready to work the next morning, they can do whatever they wish, including leaving the compound. The universe of wildland firefighting is demanding and greedy, but it is not totalizing in Goffman's sense of the term.

2. For example, Herbert Gans, *The Urban Villagers: Group and Class in the Life of Italian-Americans* (New York: Free Press, 1962), 29.

3. To fully comprehend the lives of risk takers, we must examine them in their completeness. We must concentrate not only on moments of furious action but also on periods of lackluster inaction. And we must situate high-energy scenes within the broader temporality of professional risk takers' lives, which follow a low-energy rhythm most of the time.

4. Although many of my crewmembers are certainly proud to bear the title "firefighter"—especially those who work in low-status jobs during the off-season—and are quick to use the "firefighter pickup line" to court women, they quickly discover that wildland firefighters are not allotted the same prestige, respect, or sex appeal as structural firefighters. (I explore this theme in detail in chapter 4.) While it is true that some relish the opportunity to introduce themselves as firefighters, status, like money and adventure, is not the primary reason most crewmembers return to Elk River season after season.

5. Just as Mauss finds that some Eskimo societies have two vastly different existences that correspond to the climate patterns of summer and winter—where summer is a time of festivities, energy, and social activity and winter a time of lethargy, hibernation, and

boredom—wildland firefighters organize themselves around a similarly polarized way of life. See Marcel Mauss, *Essai sur les variations saisonnières des sociétés Eskimos: Étude de morphologie sociale* (Paris: Presses Universitaires de France, 1950).

6. Gaston Bachelard, author of *The Psychoanalysis of Fire* (Boston: Beacon Press, 1964 [1938]), would agree: "What I recognize to be living—living in the immediate sense—is what I recognize as being hot. Heat is the proof *par excellence* of substantial richness and permanence: it alone gives an immediate meaning to vital intensity, to intensity of being. In comparison with the intensity of fire, how slack, inert, static and aimless seem the other intensities that we perceive. They are not embodiments of growth. They do not fulfil their promise. They do not become active in a flame and a light which symbolize transcendence" (111). Naming fire "the ultra-living element," this philosopher-psychoanalyst saw in the flames a tension between good and evil. To Bachelard fire was also hermaphroditic: the woman was in the smoke, the man in the flames. Bachelard built on Freud, who conceptualized human control over fire as an "extraordinary and unexampled achievement." Freud argued (now infamously) that when the first man managed to squelch his sexual instinct over the erotic excitement that fire brought forth, that is, when he resisted urinating on it, he became a master of civilization. See Sigmund Freud, *Civilization and Its Discontents* (New York: Norton, 1961 [1930]).

7. Tim O'Brien, *The Things They Carried* (New York: Broadway Books, 1990), 80–81.

8. Larry Hendricks, "Wildfires Blamed on Forest Firefighter," *Arizona Daily Sun,* November 11, 2005; Wyatt Buchanan, "Firefighter Accused of Setting Three Wildfires Blazes in Summer Were on Los Padres National Forest Lands Where He Lived," *San Francisco Chronicle,* November 25, 2004; U.S. Fire Administration, *Firefighter Arson: Special Report,* USFA TR-144 (Emmitsburg, MD: U.S. Fire Administration and FEMA, 2003); Timothy Huff, *Fire-Setting Fire Fighters: Arsonists in the Fire Department—Identification and Prevention* (Quantico, VA: Federal Bureau of Investigation, 1994); Ken Cabe, "Firefighter Arson: Local Alarm," *Fire Management Notes* 56 (1996): 7–9.

9. In 2005 Bryan actually did get such a job: he is currently a burn boss who oversees prescribed burning operations.

10. Comments like this support the theory of risk taking exemplified by Georg Simmel's writings on adventure, a theory (mentioned briefly in the introduction) that has to do with self-actualization. According to this line of thought, whose modern incarnation is found in Steven Lyng's theory of "edgework," risk taking is a purposeful rejection of the confinements of modernity: people caged by the boredom and routine of postindustrial "normal life" search for risky avenues to release their spontaneous and creative urges. For these theories, thrill lust is the only explanation as to why individuals seek out high-risk occupations when safer ways of earning a living are available; however, as I will soon demonstrate, such accounts do not adequately capture the motivations driving the firefighters at Elk River.

Moreover, since such accounts understand risk as a form of escapism from the lackluster workday, it is doubtful they can *ever* adequately explain why people take up dangerous *occupations*. Anticipating this criticism, Lyng suggests that professional risk takers are motivated by a dialectic of spontaneity and constraint to opt out of monotonous factory work altogether. However, this thesis is unsatisfactory for at least two reasons. First, since most people join high-risk organizations at a young age, they have not experienced the economic alienation needed to produce the reactive spontaneity leading to edgework. Second, arenas of professional risk taking can themselves be alienating and boring; in fact, most of the professional risk takers' days are filled with insipid tasks such as paperwork and waiting. See Simmel, "Adventurer," and Lyng, "Edgework."

11. If they aren't madmen, one might reason, perhaps they are saints. Perhaps firefighters are heroic and idealistic beings full of virtue, who willingly (almost sacrificially) charge toward gigantic walls of flame. Journalists often frame firefighters as moral heroes of the modern day. For instance, in *Season of Fire,* Douglas Gantenbein expounds, "There's also a strong moral element to firefighting, a chance to do good. Young people are naturally idealistic" (44). See also Jerry Laughlin, *Last Alarm: True Stories of Fire Fighters* (Batterymarch Park, MA: National Fire Protection Association, 1986). And some social scientists have explained high-risk activities by invoking altruistic motivations. For example, when writing about search and rescue volunteers in *Heroic Efforts,* Jennifer Lois states, without the slightest sign of caution, that "like professional ambulance workers, police officers, military personnel, and fire fighters, Peak's rescuers risked their lives to serve others" (14). Lois goes on to explain that her book is a study of "true heroes." Yet most wildland firefighters rarely encounter situations that call for moral fortitude and altruistic sacrifice. They very rarely have a chance to save lives (and if they do, it is usually the lives of fellow firefighters). Sometimes wildland firefighters save vacation cabins, summer homes, and even permanent dwellings, and they might even experience the extraordinary chance to protect entire communities from fiery devastation. But they rarely save homes, villages, or people. Wildland firefighters usually rescue trees, shrubs, stumps, and grass—not exactly victims that arouse young people's sense of duty. In fact, many wildland firefighters believe forest vegetation would prosper if they simply let forest fires burn themselves out. That is, many think that more (not less) fire would lead to both healthier forests and less dangerous wildfires. On this point see Stephen Pyne, *Smokechasing* (Tucson: University of Arizona Press, 2003), and Samuel Sheridan, "My Turn: We Must Fight Fire with Fire—Literally," *Newsweek,* September 29, 2003.

12. Those who suggest that the men at Elk River fight fire primarily because they lust after life on the edge, who claim, as Lyng does, that "what draws people to 'extreme' sports, dangerous occupations, and other edgework activities is the intensely seductive character of the experience itself," greatly misunderstand these firefighters. They depict them in a simplified and distorted light by inflating the *least important* motivation behind firefighters' choices and passions. The quotation above is drawn from Stephen Lyng, "Edgework and the Risk-Taking Experience," in Lyng, *Edgework,* 5.

13. Pyne, *Smokechasing,* 181.

14. GS rates change each year and vary across regional zones. They are set by the U.S. Department of Personnel Management.

15. For those going to college, wildland firefighting, while lucrative, might hinder professional development. For example, although Tank will most likely make more money in a summer than most of his counterparts at the University of Arizona's School of Architecture, he will not be establishing professional connections or cultivating drafting skills like those who spend their summer interning at an architectural firm.

16. On hearing this argument, one might claim that just because higher-paying alternative jobs exist in theory, my crewmembers may not have access to these jobs or even know about them. One might furthermore state that if crewmembers live in areas with high unemployment, alternatives jobs could be few and far between. I would point out that this is accurate only in areas with exceptionally high unemployment and poor economic resources, such as many Native American reservations. In all other areas, wildland firefighting, along with structural firefighting, does not function like a large-scale employer. Although firefighters' preferences are undoubtedly shaped by economic and social forces, most are not forced onto the fireline by market pressures. Moreover, as I already suggested, the profession is especially difficult to penetrate without interpersonal network ties. Struc-

tural firefighting, especially, is known for being a working-class profession that is very competitive. In *Real Heat,* Carol Chetkovich notes that in Oakland, some fire departments often receive over a thousand applications for only two or three positions. Wildland firefighting is not quite that competitive, but, judging from several conversations I have had with U.S. Forest Service supervisors, an open position on a firecrew regularly receives a great many applications.

17. In this way, Tank resembled the seaman whom Goffman briefly mentioned in *The Presentation of Self in Everyday Life:* After a lengthy stay at sea, surrounded only by other male sailors, he returns home and, during supper, unconsciously asks his mother to "pass the fucking butter" (14–15).

18. It is worth pointing out that this gendered geography, which classifies the country as wild, uncivilized, and masculine and the city as delicate, civilized, and feminine, is a theme that runs throughout American folklore and literature. Both Walt Whitman, who often sees himself in nature (see, for example, "Live Oak, with Moss"), and Whitman's "dear Friend and Master" Ralph Waldo Emerson portray the country in their works as a wild man's land and the city as the site par excellence of femininity. Additionally, some strains of ecofeminism, found in works such as Carol Travis's book *The Mismeasure of Women* (New York: Simon and Schuster, 1992), reproduce this gendered schematic, though slightly in the opposite direction, by advancing the claim that women are peaceful and connected with Mother Earth while men are destructive and disconnected from nature. And I would be remiss not to mention Robert Bly's infamous "book about men," *Iron John* (Reading, MA: Addison-Wesley, 1990), in which his wildman protagonist must escape the burdens of modern civilization.

19. It is notable that neither J.J. nor Donald curbed his behavior when girlfriends visited them at crew quarters. In fact they seemed to act more rowdy. They shot fireworks toward the clouds and at each other; they yelled and laughed loudly; they chased each other and wrestled. Accordingly, it seems that the primary reason for crewmembers' great self-discipline at Dave's Sports Bar was not the presence of girlfriends per se but civilization itself.

20. Goffman, *Presentation of Self in Everyday Life,* 56.

21. Max Weber, *The Protestant Ethic and the "Spirit" of Capitalism* (New York: Penguin, 2002 [1905]).

22. "Breakfast in the morning" refers to crewmembers' returning to their rooms after PT to shower, change into work clothes, and bring something to eat to the conference room for the morning briefing (most popularly, microwave burritos). Bringing food, Allen thought, was largely responsible for recurrent tardiness. "Welfare" is the odd name attached to a small pantry at Elk River out of which crewmembers could "buy" a Snickers bar or an ice-cream sandwich by noting the amount on a card with their name and paying for it sometime before the season ended.

23. These events may lead one to wonder how closely wildland firefighters are supervised during the workday. During fires and other emergency situations, firefighters are closely supervised, usually by multiple overseers. But most of these firefighters' work hours, as I pointed out earlier, consist of downtime, during which they are often left unsupervised. For example, when Allen, Steve, and Peter are behind on paperwork, they often tell the crew to sharpen tools, make hosepacks, or cut the grass and weeds around the compound—tasks carried out with little supervision. (However, the assigned tasks always get done; although they enjoy a good time, my crewmembers also pride themselves on being hard workers.) Other times, as when the crew goes patrolling, crewmembers are always under a superior's eyes. But these eyes usually are those of an engine operator—Allen,

Peter, or Steve—all of whom are fairly easy-going. This is not to say that these engine operators let their crewmembers do anything they want; however, these operators usually do not object to their goofing off a bit, so long as their work gets done and nobody gets hurt. And it goes without saying that my crewmembers act very different when they come under the stern gaze of Rex Thurman and other high-ranking Forest Service supervisors.

24. See, for example, Mitchell Duneier, *Sidewalk* (New York: Farrar, Straus and Giroux, 1999), and Philippe Bourgois, *In Search of Respect: Selling Crack in El Barrio* (Cambridge: Cambridge University Press, 1995).

25. Goffman, *Interaction Ritual,* 43.

26. C. Wright Mills, "Situated Actions and Vocabularies of Motive," *American Sociological Review* 5 (1940): 904–13.

27. And in doing so, they resemble the hundreds of Appalachian miners of the forties, fifties, and sixties who, after migrating to metropolises (Chicago in particular) and securing good-paying, stable factory jobs, eventually migrated back to the mountains of eastern Kentucky to work for meager wages in dilapidated coals mines, in order to return to the land and culture that had birthed them, land and culture they recognized and loved. On the Appalachian migration (and reverse migration), see Allen Batteau, ed., *Appalachia and America: Autonomy and Regional Dependence* (Lexington: University of Kentucky Press, 1983); Kathryn Borman and Phillip Obermiller, *From Mountain to Metropolis: Appalachian Migrants in American Cities* (Westport, CT: Bergen and Garvey, 1994); and Jack Kirby, "The Southern Exodus, 1910–1960: A Primer for Historians," *Journal of Southern History* 49 (1983): 585–600.

28. Although I already advanced this clarifying point in the notes to chapter 1, it seems worthwhile to offer it once more: This chapter is not about the presence of certain motivations that drove my crewmembers to the U.S. Forest Service and the lack of certain motivations that drove similarly situated individuals to other professions; rather, it is about the passions and persuasions—the *libido*—driving those already committed to the profession of firefighting. If I took up the former focus, I would most likely glean a much more superficial understanding of firefighters' motivations. On the relation between questions of human motivation and causal arguments, see John Levi Martin's article, "What Is Field Theory?" *American Journal of Sociology* 109 (2003): 1–49.

29. The phrase "permanent back region" is taken from Goffman's *Presentation of Self in Everyday Life,* 124–26. And on the notion of freedom and happiness being produced, not constrained, by moral regulation, one need look no further than the writings of Émile Durkheim, especially *Socialism and Saint-Simon* (Yellow Springs, OH: Antioch Press, 1958) and *Moral Education: A Study in the Theory and Application of the Sociology of Education* (New York: Free Press, 1961 [1925]).

CHAPTER THREE: A JOKE BETWEEN BROTHERS

1. Tebeau, *Eating Smoke.*

2. Thomas Von Essen, *Strong of Heart: Life and Death in the Fire Department of New York* (New York: Regan Books, 2002); Tony Hendra, *Brotherhood* (New York: American Express, 2001).

3. Mary Douglas, "The Social Control of Cognition: Some Factors in Joke Perception," *Man* 3 (1968): 361–76.

4. These include James Evans, *World's Best (or Worst) Firefighter Jokes* (New York: Evans, 1994); Jeff Hibbard, *The Little Red Book of Firehouse Pranks* (Frazier Park, CA: Jeff Hibbard, 1997); Michael Dahl and Brian Jensen, *Three-Alarm Jokes: A Book of Firefighter Jokes* (Mankato, MN: Picture Window Books, 2004).

5. Alfred Radcliffe-Brown, "On Joking Relationships," in *The Social Anthropology of Radcliffe-Brown,* ed. Adam Kuper (London: Routledge and Kegan Paul, 1977 [1940]), 174–88; Christopher Wilson, *Jokes: Form, Content, Use and Function* (New York: Academic Press, 1979); Goffman, *Interaction Ritual.*

6. Goffman, *Interaction Ritual,* 25.

7. One senior ethnographer, looking out for my best interests, advised me to take a second look at this story because he feared it would lead some readers to perceive me as overly macho, even chauvinistic. "But this happened," I told him. "I'm not proud of it. But this *is* what happened." He told me to show caution and run the story by feminist sociologists. I followed his advice, but in the end I decided to keep the story. I did so not to present myself as some heroic defender of romance. (I hope readers agree with me that my reaction was precipitate and juvenile.) I did so, rather, because, as a firefighter, belonging to the clan I hoped to understand, I had to be willing to subject myself to the same level of scrutiny, of exposure, that I had asked of my crewmembers.

8. In Kris's words: "I talk shit to Diego about hooking up with his sister, but it's not like I am *seriously* trying to hurt Diego or trying to hook up with his sister just to spite him or anything. It's just a way to get him to respond, and he'll go at it with something else."

9. Douglas, "Social Control of Cognition"; Radcliffe-Brown, "On Joking Relationships."

10. William Labov, *Language in the Inner City: Studies in the Black English Vernacular* (Philadelphia: University of Pennsylvania Press, 1972); David Pakin, "The Creativity of Abuse," *Man* 15 (1980): 45–64; Elisa Everts, "Identifying a Particular Family Humor Style: A Sociolinguistic Discourse Analysis," *Humor* 16 (2003): 369–412.

11. Durkheim, *Elementary Forms of the Religious Life,* 317. In *Gender and Power,* Connell observes that in some peer groups made up of boys from working-class families, intimacy is marked by semiplayful punching. Boys hit each other "playfully, but hard": "No one who is not a friend is admitted to this intimacy" (85).

12. For example, John Reisman, "Intimacy in Same-Sex Friendships," *Sex Roles* 23 (1990): 65–82; H. Wright, "Men's Friendships, Women's Friendships, and the Alleged Inferiority of the Latter," *Sex Roles* 8 (1982): 1–20. Although, importantly, male and female friendships share more similarities than differences: see Michael Monsour, "Meanings of Intimacy in Cross- and Same-Sex Friendships," *Journal of Social and Personal Relationships* 9 (1992): 277–95.

13. I have been speaking in terms of hierarchy. So, naturally many might expect me to sketch a power schematic for the entire crew, placing this crewmember beside or below that one. But this practice can be problematic, primarily because hierarchies are in constant motion. Hierarchies rearrange themselves as those at the bottom climb and those at the top tumble—or, more fleetingly, as those at the bottom challenge and those on top slip. Moreover, although it is easy to assign people to the zenith and to the nadir (points occupied in this case by Thurman and Vince), it is difficult to fill in the middle. And, I may further ask, by what criteria should I order people? Formal titles will not do, since some subordinates tend to be more respected than their supervisors. I could use some measure of "status," but then I would be met with situations where formal titles trump informal influence and vice versa. This would force me not only to employ a rather arbitrary distinction between formal and informal statuses but also to design dozens of schematics that correspond to dozens of situations. These sticky quandaries expose the "misplaced concreteness" of the diagrams in many ethnographic monographs, diagrams that, no matter how carefully prepared, seem to freeze people in locked positions and to present a false depiction of static organization. To me what is most interesting about hierarchies

is not their pencil-sketched structure but what happens when a general ordering of positions is challenged.

14. Michel Foucault, *Discipline and Punish: The Birth of the Prison* (New York: Vintage Books, 1977), 12.

15. Cf. Douglas, "Social Control of Cognition."

16. Sonya Rose, *Limited Livelihoods: Gender and Class in Nineteenth Century England* (Berkeley and Los Angeles: University of California Press, 1992); Lamont, *Dignity of Working Men*.

17. Cf. Michel Foucault, "The Eye of Power," in *Power/Knowledge: Selected Interviews and Other Writings 1972–1977*, ed. Colin Gordon (New York: Pantheon, 1980), 146–65.

18. Goffman, *Interaction Ritual*, 13.

CHAPTER FOUR: REAL FIREFIGHTERS DRIVE GREEN ENGINES

1. Johan Goudsblom, *Fire and Civilization* (London: Penguin, 1994).

2. James Coleman, *Power and the Structure of Society* (New York: Norton, 1974); Charles Perrow, *Normal Accidents: Living with High-Risk Technologies*, 2d ed. (Princeton, NJ: Princeton University Press, 1999). Works that have left a significant mark on the study of high-risk organizations include Karl Weick's many articles, including "Organizational Culture as a Source of High Reliability," *California Management Review* 29 (1987): 112–27; "Mental Models of High Reliability Systems," *Industrial Crisis Quarterly* 3 (1989): 127–42; "The Vulnerable System: An Analysis of the Tenerife Air Disaster," *Journal of Management* 16 (1990): 571–93; and of particular interest to this book, his "Collapse of Sensemaking in Organizations." Also useful are Diane Vaughan's rigorous study of the role organizational culture plays in system breakdowns; the work of James Short Jr., including his American Sociological Association presidential address, "The Social Fabric at Risk: Toward the Sociological Transformation of Risk Analysis," *American Sociological Review* 49 (1984): 711–25; Karlene Roberts's research on military organizations and hazardous technologies explored in articles such as "Managing High Reliability Organizations," *California Management Review* 32 (1990): 101–13, and Karlene Roberts, Suzanne Stout, and Jennifer Halpern, "Decision Dynamics in Two High Reliability Military Organizations," *Management Science* 40 (1994): 614–24; and Lee Clarke's books, *Mission Improbable: Using Fantasy Documents to Tame Disaster* (Chicago: University of Chicago Press, 1999) and, most recently, *Worst Cases: Terror and Catastrophe in the Popular Imagination* (Chicago: University of Chicago Press, 2005). For overviews of the field, see Dianne Vaughan, "The Dark Side of Organizations: Mistake, Misconduct, and Disaster," *Annual Review of Sociology* 25 (1999): 271–305, and Lee Clarke and James Short Jr., "Social Organization and Risk: Some Current Controversies," *Annual Review of Sociology* 19 (1993): 372–99.

3. For exceptions, see Hutter's *Regulation and Risk* and Vaughan's *Challenger Launch Decision*.

4. I advance the term "organizational common sense" instead of simply using the often-employed "organizational culture" primarily for two reasons. First, the concept of organizational culture has grown inflated and elusive since it was born through studies of organizations' "informal" practices in the fifties—e.g., Elliot Jacque's *The Changing Culture of the Factory* (London: Tavistock, 1951) and Melville Dalton's *Men Who Manage: Fusions of Feelings and Theory in Administration* (New York: Wiley, 1959)—and nurtured by researchers in the eighties looking to lock down the term: e.g., William Ouchi, "Markets, Bureaucracies, and Clans," *Administrative Science Quarterly* 25 (1980): 129–41, and William Ouchi and Alan Wilkins, "Organizational Culture," *Annual Review of Sociology* 11 (1985): 457–83.

Entire books have been dedicated to defining "organizational culture," and it has come to mean anything from workplace joking patterns, the rituals of coffee breaks, institutional atmosphere, and dress codes to communication styles and task ranking. (For a discussion of the history and recent usage of the term organizational culture, see John Weeks, *Unpopular Culture: The Ritual of Complaint in a British Bank* [Chicago: University of Chicago Press, 2004].) As the term has grown in popularity, inside and outside academia, it has become vague, all-encompassing, and unspecific, and nowadays no one seems to know exactly what it means. Conversely, organizational common sense carries a very specific meaning. It connotes the presence of a paradigm, in Thomas Kuhn's sense, so widely accepted by an organizational community that it remains unspoken, allowing the organization to function smoothly. In this sense, unlike the notion of organizational culture, which often reinforces a false and crude analytic separation between "formal" and "informal" practices, organizational common sense eschews any such separation and instead forces us to seek out the unarticulated assumptions beneath an organization's articulated doctrines, regulations, injunctions, and procedures.

The second reason the term organizational common sense is preferable to organizational culture is that the latter term most often implies a widely known and easily articulated mode of behavior, a set of clearly stated norms and values that newcomers either "buy into or leave." Although several theorists have offered *definitions* of organizational culture that emphasize tacitly shared commonplaces—for a review, see Joanne Martin, *Organizational Culture: Mapping the Terrain* (Thousand Oaks, CA: Sage, 2002), 57–58—in practice many researchers grasp organizational culture by relying solely on actors' articulated modes of expression, their "vocabularies of motive," to employ C. Wright Mills's valuable phrase. This way of proceeding is legitimate but superficial. I want to increase the magnification by focusing on a more deeply recognized, albeit rarely specified, "stock of self-evidences," as Bourdieu calls them in *Pascalian Meditations* (98). I refer to this collection of commonplaces as organizational common sense.

5. Some may find my reasoning a bit circular here, but organizational conduct, much like scientific conduct (as Kuhn showed), is rather circular. (As Karl Weick notes in *The Social Psychology of Organizing*, 2nd ed. [Reading, MA: Addison-Wesley, 1979], "People in organizations repeatedly impose that which they later claim imposes on them" [152].) We can reread Thomas Kuhn's groundbreaking book *The Structure of Scientific Revolutions* (Chicago: University of Chicago Press, 1962) as one of the most famous studies of organizational common sense. Kuhn found that scientific knowledge is cumulative only to the extent that it is built on fundamental paradigmatic axioms—the common sense of the scientific field—which are destroyed from time to time during "scientific revolutions." Claiming that organizational behavior is reproductive and circular does not mean it is airtight and impenetrable to change. Revolutions do come; in the world of wildland firefighting, we can regard the Mann Gulch fire as a sort of revolutionary moment. However, most organizational behavior is "normal": stubbornly intractable and tautological. See, as an illustration, Weeks's *Unpopular Culture*, an ethnography that demonstrates how a British bank, despite undergoing radical structural and managerial changes over the course of many years, has experienced very little change in its "organizational culture."

6. In Bourdieu's parlance, a classification struggle is a battle that takes place in a delineated field over certain symbolic prizes—especially the ability to name, to assign meaning and membership, and to claim authority. What is ultimately at stake in these struggles is the right to control classificatory schemes, language, representations, and principles of vision and division. Classification struggles, then, are "struggles over the monopoly of power to make people see and believe, to get them to know and recognize, to impose the legitimate

definition of the divisions of the social world and, thereby, to *make and unmake groups.*" Pierre Bourdieu, *Language and Symbolic Power* (Cambridge, MA: Harvard University Press, 1991), 221.

7. Mary Douglas, *How Institutions Think* (Syracuse, NY: Syracuse University Press, 1986), 92.

8. Traditionally, organizational scholars have focused on how organizations control their workers—through rewards and punishments (e.g., Amitai Etzioni, *Modern Organizations* [Englewood Cliffs, NJ: Prentice-Hall, 1964]), hierarchical structures (e.g., William Ouchi, "The Transmission of Control through Organizational Hierarchy," *Academy of Management Journal* 21 [1978]: 173–92), or other methods ("ideology," contractual relationships, etc.)—without paying much attention to the question of trust. But if we ask, How does an organization win over its members? before we ask, How does an organization control its members? then we are forced to hold in abeyance hasty (and often misguided) assumptions about why workers are attracted to a certain organization and come to identify with it. To control its members effectively and without coercive methods that only exacerbate resistance and rebellion, it must imbue them with a high degree of trust and respect. As such, before we can fully understand how an organization controls its workers, we must understand how it socializes individuals into workers. This is why the question of trust, dealt with in this chapter, must precede the question of control, dealt with in the chapters that follow.

9. The photograph displayed here comes directly from the website of AZFIRE (http://www.azfire.org) and is used with the organization's permission. A representative from AZFIRE named Dave, who asked me not to disclose his last name because "some of the nut cases are into violence," explained to me (by e-mail) why he helped found AZFIRE: "I am just an ordinary city person who happens to have gotten madder than hell at the actions of the enviros. The billboard of course has as its purpose the constant reminder to those driving through Jameson . . . that the destruction they are seeing could have been avoided were it not for the actions of these idiots . . . the enviros who have opposed all sensible forest policy." It is interesting to note, for reasons that will soon become apparent, that Dave is not a bona fide country boy but a city dweller with a vacation cabin near Jameson. This example goes to show that, although there is a correspondence between the antipathy between city and country and that between "environmentalist" and "antienvironmentalist" (to employ crude, yet in vivo, categories), this correspondence is not perfect. Being from the country certainly does not mean one will automatically (deterministically) hold political views in opposition to those advanced by several environmental groups, or vice versa.

10. For example, although the Sierra Club strongly supports prescribed burning, it believes the U.S. Forest Service favors the needs of the timber industry over the needs of rural communities threatened by wildfire. Further, the Sierra Club argues that the Forest Service should not focus on the complete suppression of wildfire; its main concern should be protecting forested communities.

11. Delving deeper into the complicated and nuanced political struggle over how best to manage America's wilderness and natural resources is, of course, a task far beyond the scope of this book. Other books, such as Stephen Pyne's *America's Fires: Management on Wildlands and Forests* (Durham, NC: Forest History Society, 1997) and Henry Wright's *Fire Ecology: United States and Southern Canada* (New York: Wiley, 1982), take up this task. In this section what I mean by "environmentalists" is "those damn environmentalists." My purpose here is not to recreate the actual political stances and strategies of various environmental organizations—in fact, many self-described environmentalists hold beliefs about forest management

similar to those of my crewmembers—but to capture my crewmembers' opinions on organizations and people they label environmental, threatening to the interests of Forest Service firefighters, and wrong. Plainly, the only definition of "environmentalist" that matters here is the one my crewmembers advance.

12. See Stephen Pyne, *The Year of the Fires: The Story of the Great Fires of 1910* (New York: Penguin, 2001).

13. Evidence for this is found not only in the fact that all my crewmembers agree about thinning and burning overgrowth, but also in the countless articles, books, and editorials by wildland firefighters across the United States advocating such practices. These include Sheridan, "My Turn," and Pyne, *Smokechasing*.

14. Vince was deeply troubled by his run-in with the snake. He was unusually quiet the rest of the day, and he didn't eat during the lunch break. You should always avoid snakes, he told me, since they bring bad luck.

15. Nicholas would later explain to me, "For us [Hopis] . . . seeing an owl, especially at night, is like seeing an evil omen. You usually don't see them in the day, unless you're in the trees or something, but seeing them at night is really bad. . . . It means that something really terrible will happen."

16. Georg Simmel, "Sociability: An Example of Pure, or Formal, Sociology," in *The Sociology of Georg Simmel,* ed. Kurt Wolff (New York: Free Press, 1964 [1907]), 40–57.

17. Cf. Goode, *Celebration of Heroes.*

18. Of course, if a group of structural firefighters posed the same question, this firefighter might be tempted to offer a very different answer; it is reasonable to assume that his answer is structured in part by the situation. If so, it would only go to show that firefighters with dual identities (as both wildland and structural firefighters) must navigate the divide between firefighters with extra care.

19. Bourdieu, then, goes too far in *The Logic of Practice* when he claims, "Knowing the fundamental principle of division . . . one can recreate—and therefore fully understand—all the practices and ritual symbols on the basis of two operational schemes" (223). The country boy cannot rely on the fundamental principle of division (city/country) to help him make sense of the classification struggle taking place between different breeds of wildland firefighters; instead, he must creatively adapt by forming new oppositional schemes molded in accordance with intraorganizational antagonistic relations. When discussing how the habitus adjusts to new situations, Bourdieu tends to focus almost exclusively on instances when it reproduces itself with seamless efficiency; when a primary habitus "misfires" because it is not prepared for a specific social situation; or when it is painfully colonized by imposing alien social, political, and economic structures. What is missing in his oeuvre is an analysis of what happens when the correspondence between an older form of socialization and a new one is neither 100 percent nor zero, when the habitus neither rises magnificently to the new situation nor fails miserably. In such instances the habitus is forced to adapt to new situations for which it is unprepared through inventive forms of creative action.

20. This idea, of course, comes from Alexis de Tocqueville, *Democracy in America* (New York: Perennial Classics, 2000 [1835]), 538.

21. Southwest Indian Firefighter (SWIFF) crews are another brand of wildland firefighting squad. Most are sponsored by the Bureau of Indian Affairs and are not standing crews but are organized as the need arises. SWIFF crews can take on many forms, acting like Hotshots sometimes and like engine crewmembers on other occasions. Because they are amorphous and temporary, I have decided not to analyze SWIFF crews as a separate type of

wildland firefighting unit. However, it is worth pointing out that because these crews are mobilized based on need, other kinds of wildland firefighters tend to look down on them as being poorly trained.

22. Terry Brenner, "Pulaski: The Man, the Tool," *American Forests* 90 (1984): 36–38.

23. After he spent two seasons on a Hotshot crew, Kris told me that the Shots "absolutely hate combis," the tool most engine crewmembers claim is the most versatile and important. Shots see combis as ineffective and annoying (because one must constantly tighten the joint that allows the shovel head to pivot) and prefer more durable scraping tools, such as "rhinos," hoes with enlarged and curved heads, or "vipers," hoes with triangular heads. In these different preferences we find one of many acts of distinction that separate one variety of wildland firefighter from another.

24. See Nicholas Evans, *The Smoke Jumper* (New York: Dell, 2001), and Murray Taylor, *Jumping Fire: A Smokejumper's Memoir of Fighting Wildfire* (New York: Harcourt, 2000).

25. Gantenbein, *Season of Fire,* 141.

26. There is another reason for the animosity Hotshots and engine crewmembers exhibit toward helitack crews: Because that group can reach a fire more quickly than can engines or Hotshots and because many fires are small and can be efficiently handled by helitack crews, many times the dispatcher finds it unnecessary to send engine crews and Hotshots to the fire after the chopper arrives. Thus helitack crews are often blamed for "stealing fires" and the hazard pay that comes with them.

27. Because the U.S. Forest Service is the most prominent organizational host of wildland firefighters, and the subject of this book, I have concentrated only on this organization; however, firefighters work under many other institutional auspices, such as the Bureau of Land Management, the U.S. Park Service, private contractors, the Department of Corrections (inmate firefighters), and the Bureau of Indian Affairs. Firefighters employed by the Forest Service enter into a classification struggle with these groups as well in defining the most authentic type of wildland firefighter, and to fully elucidate these symbolic relationships, I would have to analyze the entire field of wildland firefighting organizations, not simply a subfield of wildland firefighting made up only of Forest Service firefighters— a task beyond the scope of this book.

28. After 2003, several of my crewmembers accepted positions on other kinds of wildland firefighting crews and have adjusted their opinions to correspond to their positions within the field of wildland firefighters. For example, whereas Kris joined the Hotshots in 2004, Tank became a member of a helitack crew; and the two best friends often bicker about the superiority of their newfound specialties.

CHAPTER FIVE: LEARNING AND BURNING

1. John Krebs, "Original Ten Standard Orders," in "Think While You Fight Fire: 2002 Fireline Safety Refresher Training, Student Workbook" (Boise, ID: Bureau of Land Management, 2002), 7.

2. Although we linked each of the Eighteen Situations to violations of the Fire Orders, the official training booklet did so with only seven Situations: "The 18 Situations That [Shout] Watch Out can be divided into two categories as follows: Eleven of the 18 are purely situations that are of the utmost importance to be alert to and be ready to deal with, like noticing the wind changing or the air getting hotter and drier. Others we might at least influence, like removing the fuel between you and the fire. We must do something to cope with them, and backing off may be one of the options. The other seven situations are categorically *violations* of the 10 Orders. Yes, we need to watch out, but more importantly,

we need to either simply start following the order, or quit fighting the fire. It is always unacceptable to remain in one of these seven situations. For example, Situation 1 (Fire not scouted and sized up) is a direct violation of Standard Order 2 (Know what your fire is doing at all times.). . . . We can change these situations by obeying the pertinent Fire Orders. In fact, here they are: Situation 1 is a violation of Order 2. Situations 3 and 17 are both violations of Order 4. Situations 5, 6, and 7 are all in violation of Order 8. Situation 12 is a violation of both Orders 2 and 5."

3. This may be region-specific, for wildland firefighters stationed in other parts of the country have informed me that their training consisted of several practical exercises, including igniting and extinguishing "practice fires." I participated in only one practice fire, during which crewmembers battled an imaginary blaze in a canyon—and this was an auxiliary exercise, not a drill specific to our official training. In a similar vein, recruits do continue to receive informal training even after their official training ends. This informal training takes place in everyday interactions with experienced crewmembers, who introduce the new recruits to the tools and techniques of firefighting—but these interactions, like the practice fire, are not part of the official curriculum.

4. My crewmembers also did not think much of Krebs's suggestion to rearrange the Orders. To them it was not the order of the Orders that mattered but the ability to carry out the Ten and Eighteen on the fireline. As Thurman put it to the crew during a morning briefing: "They figured we would save lives by changing the Orders. We haven't. We continue to kill people. . . . We're still killin' folks. The bottom line is, they're not adhering to [the Orders]."

5. On March 18, 2004, Leonard Gregg was sentenced to ten years in prison and was ordered to pay restitution in the whopping amount of $27,882,502 for damages caused by the Rodeo fire. Valinda Jo Elliott was not charged with any crime, since the courts reasoned that she did not act with criminal intent. Some members of the White Mountain Apache Tribe saw the discrepancy between Gregg's receiving the maximum sentence and Elliott's going without reprimand as a blatant act of institutionalized racism. But individuals on the Apache reservation were not the only ones who felt that Elliott should be punished: citizens of the smaller communities devastated by the Rodeo-Chediski fire, especially those who lost their homes, also wanted Elliott to pay. Jeremy Stocklen, the law-enforcement officer for Wannokee, told me he attended a town hall meeting in one of these smaller communities, held in the high school gymnasium. When a U.S. attorney named Paul Charlton announced that Elliott would not be charged with any crimes, a middle-aged man seated toward the rear of the audience, high in the bleachers, shouted "No!" Then, he stood up angrily, hoisted a large piece of charred wood above his head, and heaved it onto the gymnasium floor below, splitting the wooden floorboards. "That's all I have left," the man shouted. "That's all I have left! And she gets nothing? But that's all I have left!" The man was escorted out of the gymnasium by the police and was later charged (ironically) with damaging city property.

6. The Rodeo-Chediski fire occurred during the season before my ethnographic study took place. In the appendix I explain how I reconstructed this event (with the help of several crewmembers), as well as my reasons for relying on this fire.

7. See Don Zimmerman, "The Practicalities of Rule Use," in *Understanding Everyday Life: Toward the Reconstruction of Sociological Knowledge,* ed. Jack Douglas (London: Routledge and Kegan Paul, 1971), 221–38.

8. One could argue, fairly enough, that we did not need lookouts because the task did not qualify as "potentially dangerous." Indeed, this was the argument Peter put to me after reading an earlier version of this manuscript (more on this in the appendix):

"I don't know if you can violate that if it's not a potentially hazardous situation. Right? If it wasn't a potentially hazardous situation, I mean, you know, I don't know if you can violate that . . . ."

"But what is a potentially hazardous situation on a wildfire?" I asked.

"I mean, if you got snags or something, you always have somebody looking out. I mean, it doesn't have to be somebody up on a hill looking down. You can have it that everybody, you know, everybody's kind of a lookout. On these little dinky fires, you know, everybody's kinda a lookout out when you're digging line around a campfire or something. But the ones that we got that are bigger, that are goin' and blowin' a little bit, you've got your airplanes and things like that looking out for you."

Peter believes that potentially hazardous situations are easily identifiable, and I agree with him to a large extent, since there are many situations (e.g., digging line downhill, snags, spot fires) that are immediately identifiable as hazardous. Yet since threats of harm saturate nearly every activity of wildland firefighting, distinguishing "potentially dangerous" scenarios from those that lack danger is, in my eyes, anything but a clear and attainable task.

9. At least one other analyst has made the same observation. See Ted Putnam, *The Ten Standard Firefighting Orders: Can Anyone Follow Them?* (Missoula, MT: Mindful Solutions, 2002).

10. Of course, an Order or a Situation can be violated to varying degrees. Firefighting is not arbitrary, and the Ten and Eighteen are certainly not unhelpful or useless. But even the most careful firefighter will never fully live up to these mandates. During my last season at Elk River, I dug line on about twenty fires, and on each of them at least one Order or Situation was bypassed—they had to be.

11. This phrase is taken from Peter Manning's essay, "Talking and Becoming: A View of Organizational Socialization," in Douglas, *Understanding Everyday Life,* 239–56.

12. Harold Garfinkel enjoyed showing how rules can never adequately explain behavior; regularly, he did so by invoking the metaphor of a game. Rules, no matter how elaborate, cannot capture every stipulation and contingency of their application; and, more to the point, the rules of a game do not capture the actual practices involved in playing the game. Just because we know that the bishop can move only diagonally does not mean that we also know the various strategies the chess player employs when using the bishop to checkmate her opponent. See Harold Garfinkel, "A Conception of, and Experiments with, 'Trust' as a Condition of Stable Concerted Actions," in *Motivation and Social Interaction,* ed. O. J. Harvey (New York: Ronald Press, 1963), 187–238. For an overview of Garfinkel's reflections on rule following, see Harold Garfinkel, *Studies in Ethnomethodology* (Englewood Cliffs, NJ: Prentice-Hall, 1967), especially 104–15, 186–207, and 262–83, as well as Harold Garfinkel, *Ethnomethodology's Program: Working out Durkheim's Aphorism* (Lanham, MD: Rowman and Littlefield, 2002), 197–218. And for a clear secondary reading, see John Heritage, *Garfinkel and Ethnomethodology* (Cambridge: Polity Press, 1984), 120–29. Bourdieu links the tendency of social scientists (namely, anthropologists) to explain everyday action through rules to the legalistic tradition; see Pierre Bourdieu, "Marriage Strategies as Strategies of Social Reproduction," in *Family and Society: Selections from the Annales Économies, Sociétés, Civilisations,* ed. Robert Forster and Orest Ranum (Baltimore: Johns Hopkins University Press, 1977), 117–44.

13. According to Peter Manning, rules governing police behavior do not clarify types of engagement but confuse them. Although police officers do not "understand" the multiplicity of regulations crafted to guide their behavior, they "fear" them because they are not sure how to avoid being accused of violating these regulations. See Manning, *Police Work,* 161–79.

14. This is what Wittgenstein meant when he observed that "'obeying a rule' is a practice." See Ludwig Wittgenstein, *Philosophical Investigations* (Oxford: Blackwell, 2001 [1953]), pt. 1, par. 202.

15. Bourdieu, "Marriage Strategies as Strategies of Social Reproduction," 141.

16. Charles Taylor sums up this problem concisely: "What on paper is a set of dictated exchanges under certainty is lived on the ground in suspense and uncertainty. This is partly because of the asymmetrical time of action, but also because of what is involved in actually acting a rule. A rule doesn't apply itself; it has to be applied and this may involve difficult, finely tuned judgments. . . . Just being able to formulate rules won't be enough. The person of real practical wisdom is marked out less by the ability to formulate rules than by knowing how to act in each particular situation." Charles Taylor, "To Follow a Rule . . . ," in *Bourdieu: Critical Perspectives,* ed. Craig Calhoun, Edward LiPuma, and Moishe Postone (Chicago: University of Chicago Press, 1993), 45–60. See also Mustafa Emirbayer's and Ann Mische's discussion of "practical evaluation" in "What Is Agency?" *American Journal of Sociology* 103 (1998): 962–1023.

17. Bourdieu, "Marriage Strategies as Strategies of Social Reproduction," 127.

18. See Loïc Wacquant, "Pugs at Work: Body Capital and Bodily Labour among Professional Boxers," *Body and Society* 1 (1995): 65–93.

19. The notion that firefighting competence can be fully attributed to firefighting experience is not untrue but is incomplete. We might say, following Goffman, that this notion, held by most of my crewmembers, reflects a "rhetoric of training." This rhetoric (produced by the Forest Service) assumes that each crewmember is, to quote Goffman, "someone who has been reconstituted by the learning experience and is now set apart from other men." When discussing the rhetoric of training, an element to be found in all organizations, Goffman suggests that most of the training an organization demands of its workers is unnecessary because most organizational tasks can be effectively accomplished with little formal instruction. Contrary to Goffman's (rather brash) suggestion, I argue that the reason formal organizational training might seem excessive is not that workers do not need extensive training, but that they have already been trained. Thus, instead of assuming that one can accomplish an organizational task with far less training than the organization offers because the task is "easy," we should investigate workers' histories to discover if they enter the organization "already trained" for specific tasks. On the "rhetoric of training," see Goffman, *Presentation of Self in Everyday Life,* 46–47.

20. Bourdieu, *Logic of Practice,* 59.

21. This idea is akin to Merton's notion of "anticipatory socialization"; see Robert Merton, *Social Theory and Social Structure* (Glencoe, IL: Free Press, 1957), 265.

22. Foucault, *Discipline and Punish,* 135.

CHAPTER SIX: TAKING THE "WILD" OUT OF WILDFIRE

1. Dorothy Smith, *The Everyday World as Problematic: A Feminist Sociology* (Boston: Northeastern University Press, 1987), 140.

2. Although a handful of Orders and Situations deal with collective behavior (namely, leadership and maintaining communication), the Ten and Eighteen are marshaled to promote an individualist, not a collectivist, organizational ethic. I elaborate on this later.

3. Krebs, "Original Ten Standard Orders," 7.

4. This last terminological pairing comes from the work of Donald Roy. See his "Work Satisfaction and Social Reward in Quota Achievement," *American Sociological Review* 18 (1953): 507–14, and "Efficiency and 'The Fix': Informal Intergroup Relations in a Piece-

work Machine Shop," *American Journal of Sociology* 60 (1954): 255–66. One can also find the division between organizational perspectives and workers' perspectives in the work of Howard Becker, *Boys in White* (Chicago: University of Chicago Press, 1961), and in Goffman, *Presentation of Self in Everyday Life* and *Asylums*.

5. Although, as I demonstrate in chapter 8, seasonal firefighters sometimes criticized the Ten and Eighteen whereas permanent supervisors were reluctant to do so, every member of the Forest Service with whom I came in contact valued these mandates. On closer inspection, this finding is not as surprising as it first appears. Analysts have established how isomorphism within organizations seeking to maximize legitimacy is supported by a widely shared language, mode of thinking, and ritualized practices. Moreover, the degree to which lower-placed members accept an organization's common sense might closely resemble that of higher-placed members, since the former are subjected to intense socialization while the latter have long accepted the unspoken assumptions of their host organization. And as Robert Merton once observed, organizational elites may owe their high-ranking placement to the very fact that they accepted the vision and values of the organization when they held subordinate positions. See John Van Maanen, "Breaking In: Socialization to Work," in *Handbook of Work, Organization, and Society,* ed. Robert Dubin (Chicago: Rand McNally, 1976), 67–130; John Van Maanen and Edgar Schein, "Toward a Theory of Organizational Socialization," *Research in Organizational Behavior* 1 (1979): 209–64; Merton, *Social Theory and Social Structure;* Meyer and Rowan, "Institutionalized Organizations."

6. Although one might think Bryan is putting on a show for Thurman, providing exactly what the boss wants to hear, when I compare these remarks with Bryan's observations recorded earlier, I am left with the impression that he believes deeply in his responses. (Bryan later confirmed this.) In fact, throughout my fieldwork I witnessed little difference between crewmembers' public responses to death and their private rationalizations during conversations and interviews. Triangulating methods (comparing observations with interview transcripts) leads me to conclude that their outward reactions reflect not managed performances concealing deeper feelings but sincere beliefs.

Furthermore, Thurman is doing two things here. Not only is he reminding his crewmembers that they are responsible for their own actions, he is also criticizing the Forest Service for not holding supervisors responsible for their incompetence. I will return to these points in chapter 8.

7. Mills, "Situated Actions and Vocabularies of Motive." For a thorough exploration of how situated actors use vocabularies of motive retrospectively to order their actions, see D. L. Wieder's forgotten classic, *Language and Social Reality* (The Hague: Mouton, 1974); and for an analysis of how rules are employed in a risky profession, see Manning, *Police Work.*

8. Bourdieu, *Pascalian Meditations,* 51.

9. Moments like this, when firefighters show caution and are encouraged to push forward regardless, are fairly rare. While it may be true that George decided to cut the coal-covered log because he felt that Allen had threatened his masculinity (another plausible explanation is that George needed to be reassured by a supervisor that he could handle the task), supervisors rarely use masculine honor as leverage to urge crewmembers into dangerous situations. Other researchers, however, have found that workers often agree to carry out dangerous tasks after their supervisors "attack their masculinity." See, for example, Paap, "Masculinity under Construction."

10. Goode, *Celebration of Heroes,* 184.

11. Firefighting is a dangerous occupation, though there is reason to believe that some industrial occupations have higher fatality and injury rates. Using data from the Bureau of

Labor Statistics (BLS), the table below compares the fatality and injury rates of firefighting in 2005 with the ten most dangerous industrial jobs, as well as with those of police officers and security guards. Workers in fishing and fishing-related occupations die on the job at a higher rate than any other workers, and drivers/sales workers and truck drivers (followed by structural metal workers) have the highest injury rates. According to these data, firefighting (a category that includes both structural and wildland firefighting) appears "less perilous" than other dangerous occupations. However, since BLS data are limited to wage and salary workers in the private sector, they exclude volunteer and state workers—who make up the bulk of the firefighting workforce—thereby underestimating the dangers of firefighting. The National Fire Protection Agency (NFPA) collects data on firefighter fatalities and injuries, including those of volunteers and state employees. According to these data (which do not capture every firefighting fatality or injury, owing to a lack of synchronization between agencies), 87 firefighters died in 2005 (down from 104 in 2004), at a rate of 7.65 firefighters per 100,000, and over 80,100 were injured that same year (up from 76,515 in 2004), at a rate if 70.5 firefighters per 10,000. Of the 87 that died, only 15 were wildland firefighters or workers performing activities related to wildland firefighting. (The data do not permit this distinction to be made with injuries. Further, it is impossible to calculate fatality rates of wildland firefighters with NFPA data, since the organization does not keep a record of seasonal workers.)

Select Occupations with High Fatality and Injury Rates, 2005

Occupation	Fatalities	Fatality Rate[1]	Injuries	Injury Rate[2]	N
Fishing and fishing-related workers	48	118.4	130	34.2	38,000
Logging workers	80	92.9	1,370	161.2	85,000
Aircraft pilots and flight engineers	81	66.9	880	72.7	121,000
Structural iron and steel workers	35	55.6	1,830	290.5	63,000
Refuse and recycling collectors	32	43.8	1,880	257.5	73,000
Farmers and ranchers	341	41.1	140	1.7	827,000
Electric power line installers and repairers	36	32.7	2,450	222.7	110,000
Drivers/sales workers and truck drivers	993	29.1	109,190	320.3	3,409,000
Miscellaneous agricultural workers	176	23.2	12,320	176.5	698,000
Construction laborers	339	22.7	39,270	263.4	1,491,000
Police officers	123	18.2	190	2.8	677,000
Firefighters	28	11.5	130	5.3	243,000
Security guards	60	7.2	9,240	113.5	814,000

Source: Bureau of Labor Statistics, 2005
[1] Per 100,000 workers
[2] Per 10,000 workers

In absolute terms, then, firefighting does not appear to injure or kill as many workers as the most hazardous occupations, especially those strained by taxing production pressures that force workers to take unnecessary risks. However, in relative terms firefighting is very dangerous. That is, firefighting is much more likely to kill or injure its workers than are other jobs to which my crewmembers have access: firefighters are twice as likely to die on the job as painters and automobile mechanics, six times more likely to die than janitors and cashiers, and fourteen times more likely to die than those working in food preparation and serving occupations. Compared to many other working-class jobs, the relative risk of firefighting is quite high. U.S. Department of Labor, Bureau of Labor Statistics, *Census of Fatal Occupational Injuries* (Washington, DC: U.S. Department of Labor, 2005); National Fire Protection Agency, *Firefighter Fatalities in the United States—2005* (Quincy, MA: National Fire Protection Agency, 2006); National Fire Protection Agency, *U.S. Firefighting Injuries—2005* (Quincy, MA: National Fire Protection Agency, 2006).

12. When I asked crewmembers the average number of firefighters who die each year, responses ranged from zero to over one hundred. Only a handful offered an accurate estimate. (This wide variation does not correspond to differing perceptions of risk; rather, it shows that most firefighters do not seriously consider the hazards of their occupation.) Since most crewmembers are unaware of the "actual" dangers of firefighting—since they do not possess the "given characteristics of a situation" around which "rational behavior" is based, as James March and Herbert Simon would say—they do not craft their perceptions around "reasonable" estimates of being injured or killed. Accordingly, the Forest Service still faces the problem of motivating them to participate in relatively hazardous work. See James March and Herbert Simon, *Organizations* (New York: Wiley, 1958), 150.

13. For example, James Short Jr., "Defining, Explaining, and Managing Risks," in *Organizations, Uncertainties, and Risk,* ed. James Short Jr. and Lee Clarke (Boulder, CO: Westview Press, 1992), 3–23; Christopher Hook and David Jones, eds., *Accident and Design: Contemporary Debates in Risk Management* (London: University College London Press, 1996); and Vincent Henry, *Death Work: Police, Trauma, and the Psychology of Survival* (New York: Oxford University Press, 2004), especially 32–34. For a discussion of another phrase that divides objective hazards from perceptive risks, "the social amplification of risk," see Roger Kasperson et al., "The Social Amplification of Risk: A Conceptual Framework," *Risk Analysis* 8 (1988): 177–87.

14. Goffman, *Interaction Ritual,* 184.

15. It is notable that Goffman reserves the idea of an illusion only for professional risk takers. To Goffman, there is no illusion in the thinking of the leisurely risk taker (the gambler, the bullfighter, the "player"); their risk is somehow the outcome of clear, conscious calculation.

16. On the notion of "illusio," see Pierre Bourdieu, "The Peculiar History of Scientific Reason," *Sociological Forum* 6 (1991): 3–26, and Bourdieu and Wacquant, *Invitation to Reflexive Sociology,* 98–100.

17. Bourdieu, *Pascalian Meditations,* 232–33.

18. Cf. John Meacham, "Wisdom and the Context of Knowledge," in *Contributions in Human Development,* vol. 8, *On the Development of Developmental Psychology,* ed. Deanna Kuhn and John Meacham (Basel: Karger, 1983), 187, and Weick, "Collapse of Sensemaking in Organizations."

19. Some scholars who have researched women employed in traditionally male-dominated occupations have suggested that women workers not only adapt to the masculine practices of their male counterparts but tend to do so in an exaggerated fashion, acting "too masculine." See, for example, Orna Sasson-Levy's work on women in the Israeli

Army: "Constructing Identities at the Margins: Masculinities and Citizenship in the Israeli Army," *Sociological Quarterly* 43 (2002): 357–83, and "Feminism and Military Gender Practices: Israeli Women Soldiers in 'Masculine' Roles," *Sociological Inquiry* 73 (2003): 440–65.

20. We can now see the fine line women firefighters must walk to earn the respect of their male coworkers. If they act "too feminine," they can be made into objects of sexual fantasy, as I discussed in chapter 1, but if they act "too masculine," they can be considered loose cannons who overexert themselves. For a description of women's experiences on an Australian wildfire crew, see Helen Cox, "Women in Bushfire Territory," in *The Gendered Terrain of Disaster: Through Women's Eyes,* ed. Elaine Enarson and Betty Hearn Morrow (Westport, CT: Praeger, 1998), 133–42. For accounts of women's experiences working in the urban fire sector, see Yoder and Aniakudo, "'Outsider Within' the Firehouse," and Chetkovich, *Real Heat.* For studies of the experiences of female police officers, see John Brewer, "Hercules, Hippolyte and the Amazons—or Policewomen in the RUC," *British Journal of Sociology* 42 (1991): 231–47; Bonnie McElhinny, "An Economy of Affect: Objectivity, Masculinity and the Gendering of Police Work," in *Dislocating Masculinity: Comparative Ethnographies,* ed. Andrea Cornwall and Nancy Lindisfarne (London: Routledge, 1994), 159–71; and Prokos and Padavic, "'There Oughtta Be a Law Against Bitches.'" And for analyses of women in the military and the masculine nature of military culture, see Cynthia Enloe, *Does Khaki Become You?* (New York: HarperCollins, 1988); Kayla Williams, *Love My Rifle More Than You: Young and Female in the U.S. Army* (New York: Norton, 2005); and Burke, *Camp All-American, Hanoi Jane, and the High-and-Tight.*

CHAPTER SEVEN: THE BEAVER CREEK FIRE

1. Cf. Erving Goffman's discussion of "make-work" in *Presentation of Self in Everyday Life,* 109–11.

2. In various memoirs firefighters—like other professional risk takers—confess to longing for disaster. For example, in *Population 485,* volunteer firefighter Michael Perry writes, "There are times, when the black dog has me backed deep in the cave, that I hope—this is ignoble—that the pager will go off" (161). Professional risk takers are thus caught in a precarious psychological position. They do not want others to suffer, but it is through others' suffering that their life gains purpose and fulfillment. They do not want to wish for the wildfire, the murder, the bombing, the heart attack, or the house fire, but in order to wish for a life of meaning and excitement—or more specifically a life without banality—they must. Firefighters *do* long for adventure, as the theories of Simmel and Lyng predict; but as I pointed out in chapter 2, these theories do not tell the whole story—at least in the case of Elk River. For adventurers, there are stronger intoxicants than adventure itself.

3. Allen later explained that during this time he was walking the fire's perimeter and planning with another supervisor from Jameson. The reason we didn't hear his voice over the radio, he told me, was that he was communicating with air tankers and helicopters on another channel.

CHAPTER EIGHT: THE INCOMPETENT DEAD

1. Thanks to the work of organizational scholars, we know much about how sensemaking leads to organizational breakdown (e.g., Weick's studies); but we know little about how organizational breakdown leads to sensemaking. We have devoted vast amounts of energy attempting to understand why organizations fail, but in doing so we have neglected how organizations systematically react to failure. (For an exception, see Fiona Haines, "The

Show Must Go On: The Response to Fatalities in Multiple Employer Workplaces," *Social Problems* 40 [1993]: 547–63.) Yet this question is equally important because it allows us to understand how organizations maintain legitimacy when things fall apart; how in times of crisis they not only avoid scrutiny from the community but also sustain obedience from workers.

2. This requires simultaneously exploring how other wildland firefighting organizations, such as the Bureau of Indian Affairs and the Bureau of Land Management, manage death, since fatalities are handled through interagency collaborations.

3. Jim Paxton, "Firefighter Warrior Led Crew That Saved Pinetop, Show Low," *Arizona Republic,* June 21, 2003.

4. Of course, some external eulogies are more elaborate than others: Lupe's, for instance, was somewhat atypical in this respect since he had become widely known for his efforts fighting the Rodeo-Chediski fire. Nevertheless, it seems that all fallen firefighters, no matter their status, are honored with similar public tributes: flattering newspaper accounts, letters of sympathy from politicians, and organizationally sponsored funeral ceremonies at the local and national levels (e.g., annual memorial ceremonies at the National Fire Academy).

5. It is also the sort of symbolic ritual most social scientists have paid attention to. See Michael Sledge, *Soldier Dead: How we Recover, Identify, Bury, and Honor Our Military* (New York: Columbia University Press, 2005); Harvey Rachlin, "Police Officer Deaths: Funerals," *Law and Order* 42 (1994): 137–43; and Henry, *Death Work.*

6. Douglas, *How Institutions Think,* 112. See also John Meyer and Brian Rowan, "Institutionalized Organizations: Formal Structures as Myth and Ceremony," *American Journal of Sociology* 83 (1977): 340–63; Paul DiMaggio and Walter Powell, "The Iron Cage Revisited: Institutional Isomorphism and Collective Rationality in Organizational Fields," *American Sociological Review* 48 (1983): 147–60; and Frank Dobbin, *Forging Industrial Policy: The United States, Britain, and France in the Railway Age* (New York: Cambridge University Press, 1997).

7. On the concept of organizational legitimacy, see Roy Suddaby and Royston Greenwood, "Rhetorical Strategies of Legitimacy," *Administrative Science Quarterly* 50 (2005): 35–67, and Mark Suchman, "Managing Legitimacy: Strategies and Institutional Approaches," *Academy of Management Review* 20 (1995): 571–610.

8. Cf. Tom Wolfe, *The Right Stuff* (New York: Farrar, Strauss, and Giroux, 1979), and Henry, *Death Work.*

9. Bureau of Indian Affairs, *Sawtooth Mountain Prescribed Burnover Fatality Factual Report* (Fort Apache Agency, AZ: Bureau of Indian Affairs, 2003), 12.

10. This is why Bourdieu, Chamboredon, and Passeron argue, in *The Craft of Sociology,* "The sociologist's struggle with spontaneous sociology is never fully won, and he must conduct unending polemics against the blinding self-evidences which all too easily provide the illusion of immediate knowledge and its insuperable wealth" (13). To Bourdieu, the sociologist must always reflect on how his positioning in various fields, especially the field of scientific production, influences his approach to research; and I might add that the organizational sociologist, especially one who is firmly embedded in the organizational structures he wishes to comprehend, must develop a habit of turning his critical analysis inward, scrutinizing how his thinking has been influenced by the institution he has joined and wishes to explore. For a deep elaboration on reflexivity as Bourdieu sees it, see Pierre Bourdieu, *Science of Science and Reflexivity* (Chicago: University of Chicago Press, 2004), 88–94. Clifford Geertz writes about the "diary disease" that haunts the anthropologist's languid reflexive practices in an insightful book titled *Works and Lives: The Anthropologist as Author* (Stanford, CA: Stanford University Press, 1988).

11. Nuvamsa wrote: "Since your approval of the Sawtooth requires a change, we will return to the proposal to complete the blacklining in the fall. We will change the maximum temperature to 70 degrees and change the minimum fuel moisture to six percent. . . . This prescription will have less impact on brush and ladder fuels and will make follow-up treatments more difficult. These ladder fuels are one of the major fuel problems on the reservation. We need to projects [sic] that help us resolve this problem. Brush is only perpetuated if prescriptions are not warm enough."

12. On May 12 Paul DeClay Jr., a tribal forest manager, sent a memorandum to the BIA forest manager, the BIA superintendent, the fire management officer, and the White Mountain Apache Tribe chairman requesting cancellation of the second phase of the Sawtooth burn operation. The letter reads: "Due to the recent news of a prescribed fire in New Mexico escaping control lines, I do not feel comfortable with your proposed prescribed burn in the Sawtooth Mountain area today. For the record, I am recommending and requesting the cancellation of the Sawtooth Prescribed Burn." DeClay's warning was not heeded.

13. The lesson we might learn from this is that high-risk organizations might avoid accidents if they resist underestimating risk and instead overestimate threats; that is, they should attempt to imagine "worst case scenarios," regardless of their rarity, and plan accordingly. See Lee Clarke's *Worst Cases* and *Mission Improbable*.

14. This relative humidity reading may even have been too high. (Belt weather kits do not offer the most accurate measurements.) An automated weather station nearby recorded a relative humidity of 8 percent at 2:11 p.m.

15. Tom Beddow, a pilot, flew over the Sawtooth burn at approximately 2:40 p.m., precisely the time of the entrapment. He was interviewed by the investigative team and reported seeing "severe crowning with 100 foot flame lengths and the smoke column was going straight up about one thousand feet." We know for certain that the flames were at least sixty feet tall because of the complete torching of the pines.

16. The report also claims that "it was unclear on May 14 who was to serve as a lookout." But this claim is simply wrong. It *was* very clear who was to serve as lookout: Harry Lupe. And Rick Lupe knew this, which is the reason he requested weather readings from Harry.

17. Weick, "Collapse of Sensemaking in Organizations," and Driessen, "Crew Cohesion, Wildland Fire Transition and Fatalities."

18. The manuals most frequently cited in fatality reports as guiding documents are U.S. Department of Agriculture, *Accident Investigation Guide, 2003 Edition* (Missoula, MT: U.S. Department of Agriculture Forest Service Technology and Development Program, 2003); U.S. Department of Agriculture, *Investigating Wildland Fire Entrapments* (Missoula, MT: U.S. Department of Agriculture Forest Service Technology and Development Program, 1995); U.S. Department of the Interior, *Departmental Manual 485* (Washington, DC: Office of Managing Risk and Public Safety, 1999), chap. 7, "Incident/Accident Reporting/Serious Accident Investigation"; Bureau of Land Management, *Serious Accident Investigation Chief Investigator's Manual* (Washington, DC: U.S. Department of the Interior and Bureau of Land Management, 2003).

19. U.S. Department of Agriculture, *Accident Investigation Guide,* 38; see also Bureau of Land Management, *Serious Accident Investigation Chief Investigator's Manual,* 42–45.

20. U.S. Department of Agriculture, *Investigating Wildland Fire Entrapments,* 15.

21. U.S. Department of Agriculture, *Accident Investigation Guide,* 16.

22. Bureau of Land Management, *Serious Accident Investigation Chief Investigator's Manual,* 46–54. See also the formidable list in U.S. Department of Agriculture, *Accident Investigation Guide,* 19–23.

23. Bureau of Land Management, *Serious Accident Investigation Chief Investigator's Manual,* 70; emphasis mine.

24. U.S. Department of Agriculture, *South Canyon Fire Investigation* (Missoula, MT: U.S. Department of Agriculture Forest Service Technology and Development Program, 1994); Rocky Mountain Research Center, *Fire Behavior Associated with the 1994 South Canyon Fire on Storm King Mountain, Colorado* (Ogden, UT: Rocky Mountain Research Center, 1998).

25. U.S. Department of Agriculture, *Thirtymile Fire Investigation Report* (Winthrop, WA: U.S. Forest Service, 2001).

26. U.S. Department of Agriculture, *Accident Investigation Factual Report: Cramer Fire Fatalities, North Fork Ranger District, Salmon-Challis National Forest, Region 4* (Missoula, MT: U.S. Department of Agriculture Forest Service Technology and Development Program, 2003).

27. I chose to emphasize these reports for three specific reasons. First, most wildland firefighters are aware of the tragedies these reports examine. Second, these three fires are regularly used as "teaching tools" for firefighters, as examples of how not to act on the fireline—that is, as fires in which firefighters are thought to have made fatal mistakes. And third, these three fatality reports are exemplary: long, meticulously documented, and thorough, they are reports that other investigative teams have tried to replicate. For a further comparison of these three fires, see Jim Payne, *Fatality Fires: Analysis of Causal Factors* (Missoula, MT: U.S. Department of Agriculture Forest Service, 2003).

28. U.S. Department of the Interior and Bureau of Land Management, *Sadler Fire Entrapment Investigation* (Washington, DC: U.S. Department of the Interior, 1999), 27.

29. The investigative report of the Romeo fire, which occurred on the Los Padres National Forest in 1971, exonerates the four firefighters who were burned over, criticizes the Forest Service for contracting out bulldozer operations to unqualified personnel, and locates the causes of the fatalities solely in managerial mistakes and equipment malfunctions. The report on the Bell Valley fire of 1973 argues that the incident commander of the fire placed a young firefighter in a dangerous situation and failed to foresee the impending threat. While the fatality report on Arizona's Dude fire of 1990 that killed six firefighters finds that the dead firefighters violated several of the Ten and Eighteen, it also finds that managerial, equipment, and environmental causes contributed to the burnover; in fact, the report seems to identify managerial and environmental factors as the primary causes of the accident. And all four types of causes are identified as leading up to the fatal engine entrapment that occurred during Wyoming's Kates Basin fire of 2000, though extreme environmental forces are given primacy. See Los Padres National Forest, *Romeo Fire Investigation Report* ([Goleta, CA]: Los Padres National Forest, Region Five, 1971); "Report of Investigation Fatality: Steve Mark Arrollado, Firefighter" (report conducted by Joseph Springer, assistant deputy state forester, Robert Paulus, division training officer, and Pressley Kent, law enforcement coordinator, 1973); U.S. Forest Service, *Accident Investigation Report: Dude Fire Incident, Multiple Firefighting Fatality* ([Phoenix, AZ]: Tonto National Forest, Southwestern Region, 1990); U.S. Department of the Interior and Bureau of Indian Affairs, *Kates Basin Fatality Report* (Fort Washakie, WY: BIA Wind River Agency, 2000).

30. U.S. Department of Agriculture, *Investigating Wildland Fire Entrapments,* 6.

31. U.S. Department of Agriculture, *Wildland Fire Fatalities in the United States: 1990 to 1998,* 8, 11–12.

32. Thus the Forest Service focuses on victims' shortcomings in widely circulated material (such as training brochures) even as it admits in esoteric fatality reports that other factors (managerial, equipment, environmental) are to blame as well. This finding is somewhat different from those of others who have claimed that organizations, at all levels, respond

to mistakes or accidents by denying responsibility and (often) by blaming the victim. Cf. Charles Bosk, *Forgive and Remember: Managing Medical Failure* (Chicago: University of Chicago Press, 1979); Leo Tasca, "The Social Construction of Human Error" (PhD diss., State University of New York, Stony Brook, 1989); Marilynn Rosenthal, Linda Mulcahy, and Sally Llyod-Bostock, *Medical Mishaps: Pieces of the Puzzle* (Buckingham, UK: Open University Press, 1999); Haines, "Show Must Go On."

33. We can now see that organizational elites, such as high-ranking officers and fire investigators, possess the illusio of self-determinacy. And although permanent supervisors are less likely to criticize the Ten and Eighteen than are seasonal firefighters (as I discuss later on), all the people I spoke with, no matter their position in the organization, believe to varying degrees in the importance of these mandates.

34. U.S. Department of Agriculture, *Findings from the Wildland Firefighters Human Factors Workshop: Improving Wildland Firefighter Performance under Stressful, Risky Conditions; Toward Better Decisions on the Fireline and More Resilient Organizations* (Missoula, MT: U.S. Department of Agriculture Forest Service Technology and Development Program, 2000), 9.

35. Sociologists have levied that same protest against high-risk organizations. See Diane Vaughan's articles, "The Trickle-Down Effect: Policy Decisions, Risky Work, and the *Challenger* Tragedy," *California Management Review* 39 (1997): 355–77, and "Targets for Firefighting Safety."

36. Supervisors never criticized the Ten and Eighteen in this manner. In fact, the elites I observed and interviewed—and my data capture the opinions of actors positioned on four different levels of the organizational hierarchy: firefighters, low-level supervisors (such as Peter and Allen), midlevel supervisors (such as Thurman), and high-level supervisors (such as MacCloud and Crasser)—seemed to believe in the importance of these rules just as much as (perhaps more than) seasonal firefighters.

37. The ethnographer's poking and prodding often stir up doubt and uncertainty in individuals who usually have never asked themselves such questions or who arrived at answers long ago. As Paul Rabinow observes in *Reflections on Fieldwork in Morocco*, "Whenever an anthropologist enters a culture, he trains people to objectify their life-world for him. . . . The anthropologist creates a doubling of consciousness" (119). If firefighters' articulations are less than clear and consistent, it is because questions that pick apart the common sense of their host organization cannot help but bring to mind certain tacit ways of knowing that they have long since uncritically internalized and forgotten.

38. Pierre Bourdieu, *Practical Reason: On the Theory of Action* (Stanford, CA: Stanford University Press, 1998), 40.

39. The quotation is from Henry, *Death Work*, 35. But see also Sledge, *Soldier Dead;* Rachlin, "Police Officer Deaths"; Carol Fullerton et al., "Psychological Responses of Rescue Workers: Fire Fighters and Trauma," *American Journal of Orthopsychiatry* 112 (1993): 371–78; Beverley Raphael et al., "Who Helps the Helpers? The Effects of Disaster on the Rescue Workers," *Omega* 14 (1983): 9–20; and Manning, *Police Work.*

40. See W. Richard Scott and John Meyer, *Institutional Environments and Organizations: Structural Complexity and Individualism* (Thousand Oaks, CA: Sage, 1994); Meyer and Rowan, "Institutionalized Organizations."

41. March and Simon, *Organizations,* 152.

42. There is evidence that other high-risk organizations behave differently, prizing solidarity, not individualism. This further demonstrates that firefighters' responses to death reflect a learned behavior crafted by organizational socialization informed by (yet not reducible to) broader cultural patterns. Cf. Morris Janowitz, ed., *The New Military: Changing Patterns of Organization* (New York: Russell Sage Foundation, 1964); John Van Maanen,

"Pledging the Police: A Study of Selected Aspects of Recruitment Socialization in a Large Urban Police Department" (PhD diss., University of California, Irvine, 1972).

43. While it is true that some fatality reports have suggested ways the policies of the Forest Service should change, more often than not they conclude by ritualistically demanding that firefighters pay the Ten and Eighteen more respect.

44. Maclean, *Young Men and Fire,* 7.

45. Because being a competent firefighter is intrinsically bound up with the symbolic reproduction of country masculinity, the incompetent dead fail both at firefighting and at manliness. Just as some women blame rape victims for not performing up to the standards of femininity ("her skirt was too short, she was asking for it") or blame single mothers as if they had acted alone in creating their babies, my crewmembers blame victims of fire for (quite literally) not living up to certain standards of masculinity. For studies of gendered processes of blame, see Esther Madriz, *Nothing Bad Happens to Good Girls: Fear of Crime in Women's Lives* (Berkeley: University of California Press, 1997); Helen Benedict, *Virgin or Vamp: How the Press Covers Sex Crimes* (New York: Oxford University Press, 1992); and Jacques Donzelot, *The Policing of Families* (New York: Pantheon, 1979).

CONCLUSION

1. Or, in the case of the self-actualization theories of Simmel and Lyng, they risk to feel alive, to test and stretch and temper themselves. Their risk taking is a purposeful rejection of the confinements of modernity; it is a "no, never" to the humdrum, iron-cage bureaucracy that is today's professional life. This idea, like Goffman's theory of character building, is limited and was not supported by the firefighters at Elk River.

2. Bourdieu, *Pascalian Mediations,* 149.

3. Goffman, *Interaction Ritual,* 267.

4. Others have demonstrated how businessmen, intellectuals, engineers, and other professionals make risky decisions in their respective lines of work; this study, by contrast, has not focused on how firefighters make risky decisions but on how they are socialized to place their bodies in harrowing situations, to "work and live with risks," as James Short would put it. In so doing, it has generated findings in many respects different from those of other ethnographies of high-risk organizations. To take but one example, Vaughan discovered that a "normalization of deviance" pervaded NASA's work group culture: engineers identified risks, classified many as "acceptable," and pushed on, not as amoral calculators but as agents operating under the shared assumption that technical deviations were standard operating procedure. I found that, when socializing workers to danger, the Forest Service does not separate acceptable risks from unacceptable ones but underplays the hazards of firefighting altogether; to my crewmembers and their supervisors, no risks are "acceptable." Moreover, even though the Ten and Eighteen are unreachable (unlike the "impractical" yet not impossible specifications from which NASA engineers deviated), the Forest Service (unlike NASA) does not provide firefighters with "rules to circumvent other rules." Rather, it functions under two untenable assumptions: that these rules should never be breached and that fatalities primarily are the result of such breaches. And, of course, Vaughan, concerned with other important lines of inquiry, did not explain how NASA might have encouraged the astronauts to accept such a risky mission. But such questions of compliance were of central importance to this study. Traditionally, sociologists interested in worker compliance have focused on the shopfloor. Although Burawoy said little about how factory workers are socialized to danger, he had much to say about how they collude with the company in the accumulation of profit. Finding that a culture of "making out" saturated shopfloor interac-

tions, he argued that workers partake in a game to escape the drudgery of the labor process and in so doing acquiesce to the rules and relations of capitalist production. Likewise, I found that firefighters consent to the organizational common sense of the Forest Service; however, their consent is not secured through a game but through an intentional and persistent pedagogical process. See Zur Shapira, *Risk Taking: A Managerial Perspective* (New York: Russell Sage Foundation, 1995); Gideon Sjoberg, "Intellectual Risk Taking, Organizations, and Academic Freedom and Tenure," in *Edgework: The Sociology of Risk-Taking,* ed. Stephen Lyng (New York: Routledge, 2004), 247–72; Michael Burawoy, *Manufacturing Consent: Changes in the Labor Process under Monopoly Capitalism* (Chicago: University of Chicago Press, 1982); Short, "The Social Fabric at Risk"; Vaughan, *Challenger Launch Decision*.

5. On the concept of expertise, see Hubert Dreyfus and Stuart Dreyfus, *Mind over Machine: The Power of Human Intuition and Expertise in the Era of the Computer* (New York: Free Press, 1986).

6. Émile Durkheim, *The Evolution of Educational Thought: Lectures on the Formation and Development of Secondary Education in France* (London: Routledge and Kegan Paul, 1977 [1938]), 11.

7. It is also distinct from historically informed ethnographies—e.g., Clifford Geertz's *The Social History of an Indonesian Town* (Cambridge: MIT Press, 1965) and Renato Rosaldo's *Ilongot Headhunting, 1883–1974: A Study in History and Society* (Stanford, CA: Stanford University Press, 1979)—which place ethnographic data in a historical context but do not necessary advance a historically minded ethnographic methodology.

8. Other ethnographers have used the concept of habitus in their ethnographic pursuits. See Pierre Bourdieu, *The Algerians* (Boston: Beacon, 1962 [1958]); Annette Lareau, "Invisible Inequality: Social Class and Childrearing in Black and White Families," *American Sociological Review* 67 (2002): 747–76; and Loïc Wacquant, *Body and Soul: Notebooks of an Apprentice Boxer* (New York: Oxford University Press, 2004).

9. Durkheim, *Evolution of Educational Thought,* 12.

10. On the notion of historicizing the habitus, see Pierre Bourdieu, "Making the Economic Habitus: Algerian Workers Revisited," *Ethnography* 1 (2000): 17–41.

11. Michael Burawoy, "The Extended Case Method," in *Ethnography Unbound: Power and Resistance in the Modern Metropolis,* ed. Michael Burawoy et al. (Berkeley and Los Angeles: University of California Press, 1991), 279.

12. Bourdieu, *Pascalian Meditations,* 51.

13. A word of caution: When trying to avoid scholastic ethnocentrism, ethnographers can easily slip too far in the opposite direction and overstress "the native point of view." Wacquant advances three reasons why this hunt for the native point of view is fruitless: first, the native point of view itself might be a chimera, for in reality what is usually found is "a range of discrepant, competing, or warring viewpoints"; second, "natives" might not have a "view" at all, since individuals approach their worlds through prereflexive stances of "ontological complicity"; and third, in the vein of ethnomethodology, if a native point of view does exist, it is questionable that one can discursively recreate it. Moving away from scholastic ethnocentrism does not mean moving toward an ethnography of the native point of view; rather, it means moving toward a social science that indefatigably and ardently seeks to reconstruct the practical nature of human behavior. See Loïc Wacquant, "The Pugilistic Point of View: How Boxers Think and Feel about Their Trade," *Theory and Society* 24 (1995): 489–535.

14. E.g., Anthony King, "Thinking with Bourdieu against Bourdieu: A 'Practical' Critique of the Habitus," *Sociological Theory* 18 (2000): 417–33; Alex van den Berg, "Is Social Theory Too Grand for Social Mechanisms?" in *Social Mechanisms: An Analytical Approach to*

Social Theory, ed. Peter Hedström and Richard Swedberg (Cambridge: Cambridge University Press, 1998), 204–37.

15. Bourdieu, *Logic of Practice,* 11.

16. Gary Alan Fine, ed., *A Second Chicago School? The Development of a Postwar American Sociology* (Chicago: University of Chicago Press, 1995).

17. David Matza, *Becoming Deviant* (Englewood Cliffs, NJ: Prentice Hall, 1969); Matza coined the term "loyalty to the phenomenon."

18. "In any case," writes Katz, "before thrashing about in arguments over whether we must or must not bring causal arguments to ethnography, we should first appreciate how subtly and usefully we are already doing it." See Jack Katz, "From How to Why: On Luminous Description and Causal Inference in Ethnography (Part I)," *Ethnography* 2 (2001): 449, as well as the adjoining essay, "From How to Why: On Luminous Description and Causal Inference in Ethnography (Part II)," *Ethnography* 3 (2002): 63–90.

19. Karl Marx, "Thesis on Feuerbach," in *The Marx-Engels Reader,* 2d ed., ed. Robert Tucker (New York: Norton, 1978 [1845]), 145.

20. E.g., Mary Douglas and Aaron Wildavsky, *Risk and Culture: An Essay on the Selection of Technical and Environmental Dangers* (Berkeley and Los Angeles: University of California Press, 1982), and Peter Moore, *The Business of Risk* (Cambridge: Cambridge University Press, 1983).

21. Wolfe, *Right Stuff,* 27–28. Whereas Wolfe captures the illusio of self-determinacy at work in the minds of fighter pilots but does not identify its genesis or how it might be created and reproduced by the common sense of the Navy, I have demonstrated that the illusio, in the case of wildland firefighters, has an organizational existence.

22. E.g., Denis, "Causes of Health and Safety Hazards in Canadian Agriculture," and Dwyer, *Life and Death at Work.*

23. If safety precautions decelerate organizational activity, then organizations facing production pressures might have a pronounced interest in socializing workers to prize organizational output over their own well-being. Cf. Nelkin and Brown, *Workers at Risk;* Vaughan, *Challenger Launch Decision.*

24. When doing so, they should attempt to go beyond the limitations of this study. While investigating how organizations socialize workers to danger, this study relied on the case of the U.S. Forest Service, concentrating specifically on the Elk River Firecrew. Future studies might generate findings that extend, deepen, or challenge those reported here by employing longitudinal methods that trace how processes of organizational socialization unfold over time or by constructing a comparative inquiry into different locations within a single organization (e.g., multiple firecrews) or different high-risk organizations. Cf. John Van Maanen, "Police Socialization: A Longitudinal Examination of Job Attitudes in an Urban Police Department," *Administrative Science Quarterly* 20 (1975): 207–28.

Besides allotting its workers significant discretion in the face of danger, the Forest Service also differs from many high-risk organizations in that it is more or less insulated from production pressures. Researchers should continue to investigate how such pressures condition workers' risk perceptions, how workers' decisions are structured by such pressures, and how strained organizations sometimes forfeit safety for profit. Cf. W. G. Carson, *The Other Price of Britain's Oil: Safety and Control in the North Sea* (New Brunswick: Rutgers University Press, 1982); Carol Heimer, "Social Structure, Psychology, and the Estimation of Risk," *Annual Review of Sociology* 14 (1988): 491–519.

Furthermore, analysts who travel farther up the organizational hierarchy than I have done here, who investigate how individuals positioned at the highest echelons of the organization craft procedural rules, react to failure, and internalize, challenge, or reject the common sense of their organization, would help to reveal how elite actors participate in the process of making workers deployable. And my findings would have been enriched had I interviewed firefighters who experienced firsthand the death of a fellow crewmember. If group cohesion is positively correlated with the severity of group initiation, as social psychologists have long argued, then we might expect workers whose colleague is killed to respond differently than those who learn of a stranger's death. See Elliot Aronson and Judson Mills, "The Effect of Severity of Initiation on Liking for a Group," *Journal of Abnormal and Social Psychology* 59 (1959): 177–81.

Finally, the Elk River Firecrew is homogeneous in many respects (e.g., gender, class background). Future studies of high-risk organizations that investigate more heterogeneous settings—settings that include a number of women and workers plucked from different social positions—might discover more heterogeneous responses to organizational socialization than I did, just as they might conclude, with Burawoy, that organizations have the power to render similar a panoply of divergent dispositions. (We should bear in mind, however, that compared to similar occupations, my sample is fairly representative. As I demonstrated earlier, most posts in high-risk organizations are staffed by men from working-class backgrounds.) Cf. Bridget Hutter, "'Ways of Seeing': Understandings of Risk in Organizational Settings," in *Organizational Encounters with Risk,* ed. Bridget Hutter and Michael Power (Cambridge: Cambridge University Press, 2005), 67–91; Nelkin and Brown, *Workers at Risk.*

25. Kaufman, *Forest Ranger,* xi. And for a classic study of factory workers' compliance, see Michael Burawoy, *Manufacturing Consent.*

26. Perrow, *Normal Accidents.*

27. See the thick interagency document titled "Wildland Firefighter Safety Awareness Study" put together by the United States Forest Service, the National Park Service, the United States Department of the Interior, the United States Fish and Wildlife Service, and the Bureau of Indian Affairs.

28. James Reason, *Human Error* (New York: Cambridge University Press, 1990); James Reason and Klara Mycielska, *Absent-Minded? The Psychology of Metal Lapses and Everyday Errors* (Englewood Cliffs, NJ: Prentice-Hall, 1982).

29. Michelle Ryerson and Chuck Whitlock, "Use of Human Factors Analysis for Wildland Fire Accident Investigations," paper presented at the Eighth Annual Wildland Fire Safety Summit, Missoula, Montana, April 2005. And for James Reason's "Swiss cheese model," see his *Managing the Risks of Organizational Accidents* (Burlington, VT: Ashgate, 1997). A truncated version of the model can be found in his "Human Error: Models and Management," *Western Journal of Medicine* 172 (2000): 393–96.

30. Ryerson and Whitlock, "Use of Human Factors Analysis for Wildland Fire Accident Investigations."

31. The quotations are drawn respectively from Clarke and Short, "Social Organization and Risk," 387, and from Perrow, *Normal Accidents,* 4. For a critical analysis of human error studies, see Charles Perrow, "The Organizational Context of Human Factors Engineering," *Administrative Science Quarterly* 28 (1983): 521–41.

32. E.g., Vaughan, "Targets for Firefighter Safety"; Clarke and Short, "Social Organization and Risk"; Leo Tasca, "The Social Construction of Human Error" (PhD diss., Stony Brook: State University of New York–Stony Brook, 1989).

33. Driessen, "Crew Cohesion, Wildland Fire Transition, and Fatalities," 5; Weick, "Collapse of Sensemaking in Organizations," 650; and Rocky Mountain Research Center, "Fire Behavior Associated with the 1994 South Canyon Fire on Storm King Mountain, Colorado."

34. Many have found that firefighters who have experienced burnovers or entrapments ignored supervisors' commands. But if firefighters are taught to direct their faith inward, if they are taught not to trust anyone but themselves (though rarely in so many words), then why should we be surprised when they fail to listen to leaders during moments of crisis? Perhaps, then, firecrews become trapped not because they are disobedient but because they are too obedient, not because they are deviant but because they operate with the individualizing illusio of self-determinancy propagated by the Forest Service. Perhaps, also, if firefighters faced with a lethal and foreign scenario on the fireline experience a "cosmology episode," as some have argued, in which their world no longer makes sense to them, in which they suddenly think to themselves, "I have never experienced anything like this before," then the source of this sudden strangeness, this violent loss of meaning, is to be found not in the blazing and blistering of the fire itself (or in the foreign topography or strange weather, for that matter), but in the paralyzing scenario in which the firefighter abruptly is forced to shift his trust from himself to his leader. In the same vein, if the firefighters at Mann Gulch and South Canyon refused to drop their tools to hasten their escape from the gigantic walls of flame that would soon overrun them, perhaps it was not because their fire tools were "meaningful artifacts" that were somehow central to their "firefighting identity," as has been suggested, but because someone *told* them to drop their tools and they refused to place their trust in someone else's hands. Cf. Weick, "Collapse of Sensemaking in Organizations," and Karl Weick, "Drop Your Tools: An Allegory for Organizational Studies," *Administrative Science Quarterly* 41 (1996): 301–13.

35. Diane Vaughan has advanced the same claim in "Targets for Firefighter Safety."

36. On the importance of role-playing in high-risk organizations, see Clarke, *Worst Cases* and *Mission Improbable*.

37. See also Vaughan, "Targets for Firefighter Safety."

38. See Meyer and Rowan, "Institutionalized Organizations."

39. Besides, when we select on the outcome without incorporating negative cases into our sample—that is, when we look for important factors that led to burnovers on fatal fires without examining whether those factors are present on nonfatal fires—we have no chance of forming accurate causal claims.

40. However, we must also ponder the *negative consequences* that may result from an organizational culture of collectivism.

APPENDIX: BETWEEN NATIVE AND ALIEN

1. For example, Emiko Ohnuki-Tierney, "'Native' Anthropologists," *American Ethnologist* 11 (1984): 584–86; Anthony Jackson, ed., *Anthropology at Home* (London: Tavistock, 1987); Mariza Peirano, "When Anthropology Is at Home: The Different Context of a Single Discipline," *Annual Review of Anthropology* 27 (1998): 105–28.

2. Mary Louise Pratt, "Fieldwork in Common Places," in *Writing Culture: The Poetics and Politics of Ethnography,* ed. James Clifford and George Marcus (Berkeley and Los Angeles: University of California Press, 1986), 27–50. Thomas Holt, *The Problem of Race in the Twenty-first Century* (Cambridge, MA: Harvard University Press, 2000), 17.

3. Charles McCabe, *Fearless Spectator* (San Francisco: Chronicle Books, 1984).

4. Edward Hall, *The Silent Language* (Garden City, NY: Anchor Books, 1973 [1959]).

5. The crew, in fact, knew of my intentions even before I set foot at Elk River in 2003, since months before the season got under way I had asked Thurman for permission to carry out this study. He in turn put the question to other crewmembers. Thus all of the interac-

tions included from that season took place with crewmembers' full recognition of my research agenda. Scenes from previous seasons are discussed later on.

6. Although, as Duneier points out in *Sidewalk,* the ethnographer can never fully know how much he is trusted.

7. See also Loïc Wacquant, "Carnal Connections: On Embodiment, Apprenticeship, and Membership," *Qualitative Sociology* 28 (2005): 445–74.

8. Moreover, some crewmembers doubted the possibility of publication (though I told them this was my ultimate goal) and believed that in the end my data would simply end up, as one of them put it, "tucked away in a file somewhere." This probably led them to behave much less guardedly than had I been some accomplished writer whose work was guaranteed to be published.

9. I say this not to construct some ridiculous representation of the enlightened and educated ethnographer among the philistine firefighters—many of my crewmembers held egalitarian and sophisticated views on issues of gender and sexuality (among other things)—but to indicate one way my reputation may have silenced crewmembers on some occasions. It is notable, however, that it did not stop some crewmembers from making sexual jokes in my presence dozens of times.

10. See Jennifer Platt, "On Interviewing One's Peers," *British Journal of Sociology* 32 (1981): 75–91.

11. The phrase is Bourdieu's. See Pierre Bourdieu, *Homo Academicus* (Stanford, CA: Stanford University Press, 1988), xi.

12. Many ethnographers, thinking, in spite of their trade, within "a variable paradigm," to evoke Andrew Abbott's phrase, seem to define insider and outsider status based on a handful of markers deemed crucial to social identity and positioning—namely, the dominant conceptual triumvirate of race, class, and gender. White ethnographers who study poor nonwhite groups, for instance, often announce that racial barriers are impossible to traverse. Consider Liebow's reflections, as but one comment plucked from dozens: "In my opinion, this brute fact of color . . . irrevocably and absolutely regulated me to the status of outsider." I do not doubt the accuracy of this statement, especially since it came from a white man studying jobless black men in the late 1960s, but I wonder why ethnographers often downplay other "brute facts" of division like education, something that undoubtedly separated Gans from the bar-frequenting young Italian adults of *The Urban Villagers,* since he could not seem to abandon his genteel academic language for the foul-mouthed tongue of the beer-drinking denizens. I wonder, further, if such taxonomic thinking would not lead us to the wrongheaded conclusion that, say, all black men who studied other black men would be "insiders." It would be naive to assume that the author of *The Philadelphia Negro,* W. E. B. Du Bois, who was never seen wearing anything other than a three-piece suit, was an insider ethnographer when interviewing black Philadelphians living in some of the city's harshest slum districts. And I wonder, finally, as Wacquant has wondered, if informants can even be considered insiders to one another, since each person in a bounded group will diverge from others on multiple levels. We should therefore show caution when deploying this insider/outsider antinomy. I would be reluctant to call myself an insider had I not participated in the life of Elk River long before this study was designed. See Elliot Liebow, *Tally's Corner: A Study of Negro Streetcorner Men* (Boston: Little, Brown, 1967), 248; Gans, *Urban Villagers,* 341; W. E. B. Du Bois, *The Philadelphia Negro: A Social Study* (Philadelphia: University of Pennsylvania Press, 1996 [1899]); Wacquant, "Carnal Connections," 450 n. 8; and, for a skeptical comment on "native anthropology," see Adam Kuper, "Culture, Identity and the Project of a Cosmopolitan Anthropology," *Man* 29 (1994): 537–54.

13. Erving Goffman, "On Fieldwork," *Journal of Contemporary Ethnography* 18 (1989): 129.

14. To take but one example: While in Morocco, Rabinow was forced to reconceptualize his cultural categories only after his Arabic language teacher, whom he had considered a friend (a sentiment apparently not shared by the teacher), tried to swindle him with a lie. See *Reflections on Fieldwork in Morocco,* 29.

15. This captivating, if clunky, phrase belongs to Bronislaw Malinowski. See *Argonauts of the Western Pacific* (Long Grove, IL: Waveland Press, 1984 [1922]), 18.

16. Goffman, "On Fieldwork," 127.

17. Ibid., 128.

18. Edward Evans-Prichard fell under a similar spell when studying witchcraft (though, notably, he counted this to his advantage). In *Witchcraft, Oracles, and Magic among the Azande* (Oxford: Clarendon Press, 1976 [1937]), he writes, "If one must act as though one believed, one ends in believing, or half-believing as one acts" (244).

19. Hugh Mehan and Houston Wood, *The Reality of Ethnomethodology* (New York: Wiley, 1975). Also see Melvin Pollner and Robert Emerson, "Ethnomethodology and Ethnography," in *Handbook of Ethnography,* ed. Paul Atkinson, Amanda Coffey, Sara Delamont, John Lofland, and Lyn Lofland (London: Sage, 2001), 118–35.

20. Evans-Prichard, *Witchcraft, Oracles, and Magic,* 243.

21. Hortense Powdermaker, *Stranger and Friend: The Way of an Anthropologist* (New York: Norton, 1966).

22. Nancy Scheper-Hughes, "The Primacy of the Ethical: Propositions for a Militant Anthropology," *Current Anthropology* 36 (1995): 416.

23. Cf. Gaston Bachelard, *Formation of the Scientific Mind: A Contribution to a Psychoanalysis of Objective Knowledge* (Manchester, Eng.: Climamen, 2002 [1938]).

24. George Orwell, "In Front of Your Nose," *London Tribune,* March 22, 1946.

25. Reflexivity should not be confused with self-disclosure. While self-disclosure implies captious confessions, rueful purges that can transform *scientia populus* into *scientia apologia,* carried out through *individual acts* of contrition, reflexivity means "objectifying the subject of objectification" by historicizing and critically analyzing one's thinking in ways that elucidate how it is a product of an academic discipline and the scholarly universe of which it is a part as well as of the multiple positions one occupies in matrixes of social, cultural, economic, and political relations. Such reflexivity is carried out through *collective acts* of criticism. See Bourdieu, *Pascalian Mediations,* 49–92; Bourdieu, *Science of Science and Reflexivity,* 88–94; and Bourdieu and Wacquant, *Invitation to Reflexive Sociology,* 36–46.

26. Claude Lévi-Strauss, *Tristes Tropiques* (New York: Washington Square Press, 1973 [1955]), esp. 47, 438.

27. Roy D'Andrade, "Moral Models in Anthropology," *Current Anthropology* 36 (1995): 399–408.

28. Pierre Bourdieu, "Participant Objectification," *Journal of the Royal Anthropology Institute* 9 (2003): 281–94; Pierre Bourdieu, *Le bal des célibataires: La crise de la société paysanne en Béarn* (Paris: Seuil, 2002); Bourdieu, *Homo Academicus;* Loïc Wacquant, "Following Pierre Bourdieu into the Field," *Ethnography* 5 (2004): 387–414.

29. See Duneier, *Sidewalk,* 339.

30. This is not a question of Truth versus untruth but one of different modes of presentation. All ethnographers need to think about how social patterns and performances are influenced by their presence, their questions, and their gadgets. See Peter Metcalf, *They Lie, We Lie: Getting on with Anthropology* (London: Routledge, 2002).

31. Wacquant, *Body and Soul,* viii. Also see Mehan and Wood's discussion of "becoming the phenomenon" in *Reality of Ethnomethodology.*

32. Lyng, "Edgework," 862 n. 8.

33. Wacquant, *Body and Soul,* xi.

34. I borrow this phrase from Paul Willis (personal communication).

35. These include dropping things off Paquesi Perch and playing on the swing at Jack's Canyon (both briefly mentioned in chapter 2); the heated interaction between Bryan and me, so memorable in both our minds that we had little trouble reconstructing it; the famous story of Thurman's calling George a "little bitch," a story alive and well in the collective memory of the firefighters at Elk River; the time George rescued the rattlesnake Marcos Constañco had caught; and the time Nicholas suggested killing baby barn owls (all four events are recorded in chapters 3 and 4). The final instance of this type of data is the stress debriefing that followed the Rodeo-Chediski fire (described in chapter 6).

36. As I mentioned above, interviews were taped. In controlled settings, such as those that typically occurred at the end of the workday, crewmembers seemed to exhibit little caution in the presence of a tape recorder.

37. For a discussion of the importance of timing during ethnographic inquiries, among other important points relevant to fieldwork, see Maria Cristina González, "The Four Seasons of Ethnography: A Creation-Centered Ontology for Ethnography," *International Journal of Intercultural Relations* 24 (2000): 623–50.

38. And here we notice yet another benefit of embedded ethnography: that it enriches in-depth interviews. Ethnographic observations shape interview questions. Furthermore, while in the field, ethnographers can build up trust, which will affect how people respond to interview questions.

39. Zora Neal Hurston, *Dust Tracks on the Road* (New York: Harper Perennial, 1996 [1942]), 143.

40. See Alfred Schutz, "Common-Sense and Scientific Interpretation of Human Affairs," in *The Collected Papers,* vol. 1, *The Problem of Social Reality,* ed. Maurice Natanson (The Hague: Martinus Nijhoff, 1962), 3–47.

41. For critical evaluations of such an approach, see Dennison Nash and Ronald Wintrob, "The Emergence of Self-Consciousness in Ethnography," *Current Anthropology* 13 (1972): 527–42, and Robert Emerson and Melvin Pollner, "Difference and Dialogue: Members' Readings of Ethnographic Text," *Social Problems* 3 (1992): 79–98.

42. Diane Vaughan, "NASA Revisited: Theory, Analogy, and Public Sociology," *American Journal of Sociology* 112 (2006): 353–93; Howard Becker, Herbert Gans, Katherine Newman, and Diane Vaughan, "On the Value of Ethnography: Sociology and Public Policy, A Dialogue," *Annals of the American Academy of Political and Social Science* 595 (2004): 246–76; Scheper-Hughes, "Primacy of the Ethical."

43. Everett Hughes, "Sociologists and the Public," in *The Sociological Eye: Selected Papers on Work, Self, and the Study of Society,* ed. Everett Hughes (Chicago: Aldine-Atherton, 1971), 455–63.

44. Cf. Val Colic-Peisker, "Doing Ethnography in 'One's Own Ethnic Community': The Experience of an Awkward Insider," in *Anthropologists in the Field: Cases in Participant Observation,* ed. Lynne Hume and Jane Mulcock (New York: Columbia University Press, 2004), 82–94.

45. Lila Abu-Lughod, "Writing against Culture," in *Recapturing Anthropology: Working in the Present,* ed. Richard Fox (Santa Fe, NM: School of American Research Press), 137–62.

46. Joan Didion, *Slouching towards Bethlehem* (New York: Farrar, Straus, and Giroux, 1968), xiv.

47. William Foote Whyte, *Street Corner Society: The Social Structure of an Italian Slum,* 4th ed. (Chicago: University of Chicago Press, 1993 [1943]), 342–54.

48. Once I had incorporated my crewmembers' suggestions, I mailed the revised manuscript to Thurman.

49. Goffman, *Interaction Ritual,* 43.

50. Durkheim, *Evolution of Educational Thought,* 280.

51. Most of the crewmembers who preferred pseudonyms did not give a concrete reason for their preference other than "paranoia." Consider my conversation with Bryan:

> "I wanted to think about maybe even using your real names. . . . But what do you think about that?" I asked.
>
> "I kinda like the pseudonyms. Yeah, I kinda like that," he replied.
>
> "What do you like about them?"
>
> "Just 'cause I've worked for Steve [who gave a similar response] too long. I'm paranoid. Paranoia."
>
> "Really? Do you see anything in here that you wouldn't want someone to associate with you?"
>
> "Uhhh [long pause], not necessarily. But that's only saying it from reading it one time."

52. My decision to include crewmembers' pictures brings up a question: To whom is this material confidential? There is nothing stopping those in the Forest Service who have access to past employment records from looking up my name and discovering the real location of Elk River, and those with close ties to Elk River most likely will be able to recognize the characters in this book (pictured or not) from their quirks and descriptions. I was not willing to write under a pen name, nor was I willing to grossly distort the unique qualities of crewmembers until they were unrecognizable even to themselves. So a select group of insiders who put in the effort would probably be able to discover some of the real names behind the pseudonyms. (I suppose it is this way for most ethnographies.) My crewmembers were well aware of this, which is the reason I took pains to talk in depth with each of them about his role in the book. This text, then, is *confidential to outsiders,* individuals (including Forest Service personnel) who are not connected to Elk River but whom crewmembers could encounter in other spheres of their lives, in the present and in the future. In this context, therefore, using pseudonyms does at least three things: it masks crewmembers' identities from most readers; it allows crewmembers to deny associations offered by the select group of insiders who might be able to crack the code; and it removes the possibility of having a permanent record, of having one's real name forever connected to some action or utterance.

53. This was the case for *New York Times* reporter Judith Miller, who was jailed for contempt of court after refusing the reveal the identity of a source who had leaked the name of an undercover CIA agent.

54. See Robert Emerson and Melvin Pollner, "On the Uses of Members' Responses to Researchers' Accounts," *Human Organization* 47 (1988): 189–98; Michael Bloor, "Techniques of Validation in Qualitative Research: A Critical Commentary," in *Contemporary Field Research: Perspectives and Formulations,* 2nd ed., ed. Robert Emerson (Prospect Heights, IL: Waveland Press, 2001), 383–96.

55. Bachelard, *Psychoanalysis of Fire,* 1. Sociologists tend to focus on the differing worldviews of the scientist and the nonscientist, believing, with Schutz, that the two have fun-

damentally dissimilar ways of understanding the world. Anthropologists, by contrast, tend to concentrate on the differing worldviews of the native and nonnative, accepting, with Lévi-Strauss, that no matter how long one lives in the plateau of the western Mato Grosso, one cannot escape fleeting recollections of the French countryside or Chopin's études. See Schutz, "Common-Sense and Scientific Interpretation"; and Lévi-Strauss, *Tristes Tropiques,* 429.

56. This quotation is pulled from Jack Katz's "Ethnography's Warrants," *Sociological Methods and Research* 25 (1997): 391, an article that precisely underscores this issue yet does not seem to advocate for one position over the other.

57. Geertz, *Works and Lives,* 143.

58. Rabinow, *Reflections on Fieldwork in Morocco,* 46.

59. Whyte, *Street Corner Society,* 352.

60. The phrase is borrowed from the thoughtful introduction to Halle, *America's Working Man,* xii.

Acknowledgments

This book was not my idea. It was Mustafa Emirbayer's. *On the Fireline* began as my master's thesis. Mustafa was my adviser, and early on in the project he suggested I turn the thesis into a book. At first I resisted, but he kept encouraging me and in the end won me over. His dedication to this project was beyond generous. He read the manuscript in full several times with extreme care, offering helpful feedback on everything from my arguments to my prose. When I received my first contract, I presented Mustafa with a box of red pens to replace all the ink he had spilled on earlier drafts of this work. Without Mustafa's support and guidance the book would not have been conceived, let alone completed.

Working with the editors of the Fieldwork Encounters and Discoveries Series has brought high challenges and higher rewards. I am particularly indebted to Robert Emerson and Mitchell Duneier for their stimulating and sophisticated insights. Paul Willis offered a bounty of creative comments. And Philippe Bourgois, Michael Burawoy, Gary Alan Fine, Bridget Hutter, Jack Katz, Bowen Paulle, and Loïc Wacquant tendered encouraging words along with pointed criticisms, from all of which this book has benefited enormously.

While studying in the Sociology Department at the University of Wisconsin–Madison, I have profited from critical engagements with many scholars. In various ways Michael Bell,

Jane Collins, Myra Marx Ferree, Robert Freeland, Joan Fujimura, Chad Goldberg, Philip Gorski, Mara Loveman, Cameron Macdonald, John Levi Martin, Douglas Maynard, Alfonso Morales, Pamela Oliver, Jane Piliavin, and Erik Olin Wright all helped make this book a better one. I owe Ruth López Turley a very special debt; she has helped me more than she knows. On the eighth floor, I thank Patrick Brenzel, Sandy Ramer, and especially Michelle Bright, who over and over again—and always with a smile—dropped everything to help me out.

I am obliged, also, to dozens of smart, passionate, and supportive graduate students who fill the halls of the Sewell Building. Peter Brinson has always been an insightful reviewer and, more important, a great friend who, it seems, is guilty of making me a better person. Black Hawk Hancock kept me up until 4:00 in the morning with talk of ethnographic excursions. Shamus Khan read the entire manuscript when it was still in its infancy and demanded more. And besides offering incredibly intelligent criticism, Lisa Wade assigned this book, in manuscript form, in her Introduction to Sociology course at Occidental College. I thank all her students, who, through their questions and papers, taught me a great deal.

In addition, I have been fortunate enough to study beside the likes of Megan Andrew, Jay Burlingham, Hae Yeon Choo, Wendy Christensen, Matthew Dimick, Cynthia Golembeski, Hanna Grol-Prokopczyk, Abby Kinchy, Amy Lang, Kate McCoy, Pablo Mitnik, Matthew Nichter, Rebekah Ravenscroft-Scott, Martin Santos, Adam Slez, Teddy Weathersbee, and Eva Williams (honorary member of the Sociology Department). Each, in her or his way, sharpened my thinking.

It was in Kirin Narayan's course on ethnographic writing that I learned to shake awake sleeping verbs. I thank Kirin and all the anthropology students in that class for offering thoughtful comments on various pieces of this book. Kate Hiester, who I know will one day write a beautiful book, was my biggest help.

Sarah "Amira" De la Garza at Arizona State University's Hugh Downs School of Human Communication is responsible for introducing me to the poetics and ethics of ethnography. Thank you, Dr. De la Garza, for all you taught me about this craft and about myself. At the Hugh Downs School, I also thank Dan Brouwer and Belle Edson. And I hope Mr. Howell, my high school English teacher—who, through his famous extra credit luncheons, taught me to construct a sentence—will accept this belated note of gratitude.

For their committed and challenging suggestions, I thank the participants in the Politics, Culture, and Society, Sociology of Gender, and Social Psychology and Microsociology seminars at the University of Wisconsin–Madison, those in the Putting Pierre Bourdieu to Work II Conference at the University of California–Berkeley, and those in attendance at the Chicago Ethnography Conference at the University of Chicago. In part this work benefited from funding by the Department of Sociology at the University of Wisconsin–Madison, the Institute for Research on Poverty, and the Phi Kappa Phi National Honor Society.

For sharing with me their unpublished research, I thank Jon Driessen and Linda Outka-Perkins; for his kind advice, I thank Tim Sullivan; and for their detailed feedback that has proved very helpful, I thank the anonymous reviewers at other presses.

At the University of Chicago Press, I had the privilege of working with Doug Mitchell, the Roy Haynes of academic publishing. Thank you, Doug, for believing in this book and its author. I owe Tim McGovern a heartfelt word of appreciation for making sure this manuscript ended up near the top of the pile. Alice Bennett, who took a break from her retirement to edit this book, is a miracle worker.

All the firefighters I met throughout the course of my fieldwork made this book possible. I am especially grateful to my friends at Elk River. Thank you all—for investing wholeheartedly in this study, for sacrificing so much of your time not only to field my questions but also to thoughtfully scrutinize the finished product, and for allowing yourselves to be vulnerable in front of me even though you seemed to know that, to quote the great Lithuanian-Polish poet Czesław Miłosz, "Once a writer is born into a family, that family is doomed."

Thank you Evelyn, Sean, Daniel, and Brett Lupe. And thank you Wendell Peacock.

My dear friends Paul and Chrissy Greer not only read the manuscript and offered warm words of reassurance but also opened their home when I returned to Arizona to discuss the manuscript with my crewmembers. James John McKinney, to whom I am indebted for so many things, listened to my stories with keen interest and persistence. Donald Tibbs, an old teacher turned confidant, is the reason I study sociology.

Tessa Joy, my wife, exhibited angelic patience throughout. She invested in my arguments and my words, casting a keen literary eye over hundreds of sentences with which I interrupted her days. On top of taking her first steps into a challenging new career, she labored to give me sanctuary to write; more, she bore with my obsessiveness, my long hours, and, when the words would not come, my crankiness. It is humbling when it sinks in: all this would have been impossible without you. In all moments: gratitude and love.

My sister-hero, Michelle, while living in Swaziland, managed somehow to read the entire manuscript. I am grateful for her heartfelt and honest thoughts, the least of which are about this book. Maegan, my youngest sister, reminds me, more than anyone else, of the important things in life. My parents, Nick and Shavon Desmond, imbued me from childhood with a spirit of learning and tricked me into thinking I could do anything I set my mind to. Thank you for reading this manuscript. Thank you for teaching me the hard lessons. And thank you for loving me unrelentingly. To the both of you this book is dedicated.

Index

340n4; Forest Service management of, 228–36, 247–51, 263, 267; processing, 244–51; Ten and Eighteen shape understanding of, 177–78; wildland firefighter reaction to, 3–5, 257–64, 267–68, 336n6

Declay, Paul, Jr., 341n12

denial, 194

deployment, 2, 146, 153–54, 279, 309

Didion, Joan, 296

digging line, 1, 134–35, 138–39, 162–63, 215–17; complexities of, 167–68

DiMaggio, Paul, 340n6

direct line, 133, 310

"dirt monkeys," 139

dispatcher, 207, 310

dispositional theory of action, 13, 266

Dobbin, Frank, 340n6

dog hair thicket, 123, 310

Douglas, Mary, 10, 118, 233, 326n3, 327n9, 346n20

downtime as primetime, 56, 80–82

Dreyfus, Herbert, 345n5

Driessen, Jon, 277, 314n7, 341n17

drip torch, 12, 236, 310

DuBois, W. E. B., 349n12

Dude fire of 1990, 220; fatality report, 342n29

duff, 209, 210, 310

Duneier, Mitchell, 326n24, 349n6, 350n29

Durkheim, Émile, 88, 100, 268, 269, 314n5, 319n12, 326n29, 352n50

Dwyer, Tom, 315n25, 346n22

ecofeminism, 325n18

edgework, theory of, 323n10, 324n12

Eighteen Situations That Shout "Watch Out!", 1, 145, 146–51, 279–80, 332n2. *See also* Ten and Eighteen

Elk River Firecrew (pseud.), 1, 3, 21–30; homogeneity of background, 346n24; racial diversity, 320n21. *See also* wildland firefighter habitus; wildland firefighters

Elk River Fire Station (pseud.), 64–69, 306–7; as country-masculine sanctuary, 85–86; crew quarters, 67–68, 84–88; isolation, 322n1; "welfare," 325n22

Elliott, Valina Jo, 155, 333n5

embedded ethnography, 2, 284, 288, 293–94, 351n38

Emerson, Ralph Waldo, 325n18

Emerson, Robert, 350n19, 351n41, 352n54

Emirbayer, Mustafa, 335n16

Endangered Species Act, 121

engine, 65, 310

engine crews, 133, 138, 139–40, 310; animosity toward helitack crews, 332n26

engine operator, 310

Enloe, Cynthia, 339n20

entrapment, 2, 5, 146, 278–79, 310, 348n34

environmentalists: argue for less involved approach to forest management, 121; vs. Forest Service, 118, 119–25, 330n11

epistemological break, 4, 286–91, 340n10

Epstein, Cynthia Fuchs, 320n23

escape route, 149, 158, 166, 181, 310

ethnocentrism, scholastic, 11–12, 269–70, 290, 345n13

ethnographer: consideration of consequences of work, 300; indigenous, 283, 284–87, 289; insider, 290–91, 296–97, 349n12; optimal vantage point, 289–90; safeguarding of informants, 301; sociological, 283

ethnography: and confidentiality, 300–301, 352n52; diagrams created from, 327n13; embedded, 2, 284, 288, 293–94, 351n38; "the encounter," 283–84; etymology of, 283; of the habitus, 268–72; member checking, 297–307; objectivity, 291; recording and representation, 291–96; retrospective, 294–95

Etzioni, Amitai, 330n8

Evans, Nicholas: *The Smoke Jumper,* 137, 289

Evans-Prichard, Edward, 290, 350n18

exaggerating deviance, 247–50, 257–64

"experience qualification," 169, 193

external eulogy, 229–31, 232–33, 340n4

"face," 111

fatality and injury rates: occupations with high, 2005, 337n11; wildland firefighters, 2, 191, 313n3